PC Magazine® Windows® XP Solutions

Second Edition

Neil Randall

Wiley Publishing, Inc.

PC Magazine® Windows® XP Solutions, 2nd Edition

Published by
Wiley Publishing, Inc.
10475 Crosspoint Boulevard
Indianapolis, IN 46256
www.wiley.com

Copyright © 2006 by Wiley Publishing, Inc., Indianapolis, Indiana

Published simultaneously in Canada

ISBN-13: 978-0-471-74752-9
ISBN-10: 0-471-74752-1

Manufactured in the United States of America

10 9 8 7 6 5 4 3 2 1

2B/RZ/RQ/QV/IN

For general information on our other products and services or to obtain technical support, please contact our Customer Care Department within the U.S. at (800) 762-2974, outside the U.S. at (317) 572-3993 or fax (317) 572-4002.

Wiley also publishes its books in a variety of electronic formats. Some content that appears in print may not be available in electronic books.

Library of Congress Cataloging-in-Publication Data:

Randall, Neil.
  PC Magazine Windows XP solutions / Neil Randall. — 2nd ed.
    p. cm.
  Includes index.
  ISBN-13: 978-0-471-74752-9 (pbk.)
  ISBN-10: 0-471-74752-1 (pbk.)
  1. Microsoft Windows (Computer file) 2. Operating systems (Computers) I. Title.
  QA76.76.O63R362 2005
  005.4'46--dc22
                                                    2005023677

Credits

EXECUTIVE EDITOR
Chris Webb

SENIOR DEVELOPMENT EDITOR
Jodi Jensen

TECHNICAL EDITOR
Mark Justice Hinton

PRODUCTION EDITOR
Felicia Robinson

COPY EDITOR
Foxxe Editorial Services

EDITORIAL MANAGER
Mary Beth Wakefield

PRODUCTION MANAGER
Tim Tate

BOOK DESIGNER
Kathie Rickard

VICE PRESIDENT & EXECUTIVE GROUP PUBLISHER
Richard Swadley

VICE PRESIDENT AND EXECUTIVE PUBLISHER
Joseph B. Wikert

PROJECT COORDINATOR
Ryan Steffen

GRAPHICS AND PRODUCTION SPECIALISTS
Denny Hager
Jennifer Heleine
Amanda Spagnuolo
Ron Terry

QUALITY CONTROL TECHNICIANS
Leeann Harney
Jessica Kramer
Carl William Pierce
Charles Spencer

PROOFREADING AND INDEXING
TECHBOOKS Production Services

About the Author

Neil Randall has been writing about computers for twenty years, beginning with the Commodore and moving through every type of PC and every operating system available since then. He has published hundreds of articles, columns, and reviews in numerous magazines during that time, and he is currently a Contributing Editor for *PC Magazine*. He has published eight books on computer topics, including the effective use of Internet technologies and resources, publishing Web sites, and the history of the Internet. He is a professor at the University of Waterloo in Canada, where he teaches multimedia applications, interface analysis and design, and digital design.

For Heather, whose endurance can only inspire.

Contents at a Glance

Contents

Acknowledgments

Thanks again to Microsoft, obviously the *sine qua non* for this book, and to Chris Webb for getting it through the hoops. And thanks to Jodi Jensen, who has shown more patience with me than I would have.

And thanks once again to Catherine and Michelle, who have managed to grow up to become truly fine young women despite a father who has spent enough time in his basement to make Gollum seem like a sun worshipper.

Introduction

Welcome to the Second Edition of *PC Magazine Windows XP Solutions*. This time around, in response to your suggestions, I've beefed up the coverage of security and data backup, and I've covered Windows XP Service Pack 2 (SP2) in detail. I had finished writing the first edition just as SP2 was starting to undergo beta testing, but between then and now it has become a mainstay of Windows XP.

As a frequent contributor to *PC Magazine* over the past eight years, particularly in the "Solutions" section, I've had the pleasure of writing about Microsoft's operating systems—covering features, usability, technology, and hints and tips. Windows XP has fascinated me from the minute I downloaded and installed the first beta version back in late 2000. This book covers the issues I've been asked about most often, as well as a number of topics I've long wanted to explore on my own.

Released over two years ago, Windows XP has worked — and sold — so well that only now does Microsoft seem eager to release the next Windows version. Codenamed Longhorn, this version will be in limited beta testing by the time this book is released and is scheduled to be available to the public at some point in late 2006 (which means that you shouldn't count on seeing it until mid-2007 or so). Assuming a 2007 date, this means that Windows XP will have reigned as the company's primary desktop environment for five years by that point, and certainly longer while consumers start to upgrade. Five-plus years in the computer world is a long, long time.

The question, even after Longhorn releases, will be whether or not people flock to it. After all, Windows XP works very well, and Microsoft's continual updating of Windows XP means that it has not grown particularly long in the tooth. Furthermore, as this book emphasizes throughout, you can customize every major element of Windows XP to suit your needs precisely. Unlike previous versions of Windows, this one never gives you the sense that you're stuck with something no matter how much it annoys you or hinders you over the course of daily use. If you don't like something, just change it — then change it again as often as you like.

This book helps you do just that. It also helps you work with the programs included in Windows XP, build a Windows XP network, add hardware and software to your Windows XP environment, make Windows XP the center of your Internet activity, and fix the major Windows XP problems. The book takes as its basis the countless hours I've spent with this important operating system: installing, reinstalling, configuring, networking, and just generally playing with Windows.

Over the course of two decades writing about computers, operating systems have fascinated me most. And, to be honest, I've never met one I didn't like. Okay, the Commodore 64 OS had its downside, and the Atari ST locked up too often, and MS-DOS 3.3 was one of the worst things to look at in computing history. I spent months with each of them, however, figuring out how to make them work the way I thought they should have worked in the first place. I loved my three Amigas, I tried hard to make my first Macintosh crash, I took my chances with those extremely geeky early versions of Linux, and I gave the underappreciated BeOS a very real chance. This fascination continued throughout the various incarnations of Windows, beginning with Windows 2.0 back in 1987 and proceeding up the Microsoft food chain to Windows 3.0, 3.1, 3.11, NT 3.5, NT 3.51, 95, 98, 98 Second Edition, 2000, Millennium Edition, and finally, XP. With each release, I saw Windows getting better in different ways. But to me, four releases stand out as landmarks: Windows 3.0, the first version that actually worked; Windows 95, with its significant revamping of the interface; Windows 2000, the first usable network workstation from Microsoft; and Windows XP, the culmination of the lot.

What you get in Windows XP is an operating system both mature and novel. Certainly Microsoft's most stable operating system to date, it combines this stability with a growing degree of security (the constant updates have helped in this regard) and draws on the years of development of such technologies as file systems, networking, and hardware recognition. You can fairly easily restrict who accesses which files and folders in Windows XP, you can quickly connect your Windows XP machine to a network, and you can plug hardware into it without wondering if it will ever work. On top of all of this, Microsoft has placed a multilayer interface with enough new features to satisfy those who love new ways of doing things, yet maintained a firm entrenchment in Windows interfaces of the past.

Who Should Read This Book?

I've written this book for Windows users who want to get more out of their Windows XP installations and for current Windows XP users looking to move beyond the basics and into more advanced topics. The idea is to present answers to questions I've been asked over the years about this operating system, along with solutions to issues you'll almost certainly encounter as you use Windows XP for an increasing range of purposes. When I've had to choose (to keep the book to a reasonable size), I've opted for important but lesser-known topics or variations on standard topics.

With this focus, this book is ideally suited to home users who want additional Windows XP expertise, to small business users who want to explore how to expand the capabilities of their Windows XP systems, and to anyone who finds himself or herself on the receiving end of questions about how to make Windows XP work the way its users want.

What You Need to Use This Book

For the most part, the solutions offered in this book will work on Windows XP Home Edition, Windows XP Media Center Edition, and Windows XP Professional. Some things, however, work only with the more advanced Windows XP Professional. So if you want to use these solutions, you have no choice, unfortunately, but to upgrade. Fortunately, Windows XP Home Edition upgrades easily to Windows XP Professional, so you needn't be concerned with losing anything other than an hour's time or so, but there's no question that Windows XP Professional costs more.

Some of the features covered in this book that apply only to Windows XP Professional include:

- Standard File Sharing (Chapter 25)

- Group Policy configuration (Chapter 27)

- The Encrypting File System (Chapter 6)

- Remote Desktop (Chapter 10)

- Remote Assistance (Chapter 10)

- Web Server and FTP Server (Chapter 30)

Windows XP Professional offers other unique features as well, including the capability of downloading multilingual interface add-ons, the capability to connect to network domains, and the capability to take advantage of PCs with more than one processor. These features do not appear in this book, but they demonstrate the very real sense that Microsoft has designed Windows XP Professional to be the more capable of the two operating systems. For many users, however, the Home Edition works perfectly well, and given its lower price, it might well be the right choice for you.

Conventions Used in This Book

To help you get the most from the text and keep track of what's happening, I've used a number of conventions throughout the book:

- When a new term is introduced, it is shown in *italics*.

- Characters you are asked to type appears in **bold**.

- Keyboard shortcuts are shown like this: Ctrl+A. Sometimes, I show a shortcut that looks like this: Winlogo+E. This shortcut uses the Windows Logo key—the key with the Windows "flag" image that is generally in the lower-left corner of your keyboard between the Ctrl and Alt keys. Pressing and holding down the Winlogo key while you press the E key is a quick way to open a My Computer screen. Sometimes, you also need to type something after pressing the Winlogo key combination. For example, this command sequence

  Winlogo+R, **regedit**

  tells you to press and hold the Winlogo key while pressing the R key (which opens the Run dialog box) and then type **regedit** and press Enter. This is a pretty fast way to open the Registry Editor (see Chapter 16 for more on this topic).

Icons Used in This Book

Following is a brief description of the icons used to highlight certain types of material in this book.

Tip

Each Tip gives you additional information that adds to the topic under discussion. The information typically springs from something in the immediately preceding paragraph and provides a succinct suggestion that you might want to follow while working through the chapter. In effect, a Tip says, "You should try this as well."

Note

A Note is just that: a note. Usually a note provides information related to the topic under discussion but not essential to it for the purposes of working through that topic. A Note says, essentially, "Here's an interesting point about the topic."

Caution

Each Caution in this book alerts you to something worth paying attention to — for example, something that can cause you problems while working with the current topic. A Caution says, "Before going any further, make sure that you consider this point."

How This Book Is Organized

This book offers a wide range of solutions. The sheer complexity of Windows XP means that learning it completely requires months of working with it, but the 80-20 rule applies here very well: you can learn 80 percent of the features that give you the most bang for your buck in roughly 20 percent of the time it would take to learn every single feature this operating system contains. This book gives you that 80 percent along with a taste of the other 20 percent. It assumes that you already know the basics of working with Windows — using the mouse, dragging and dropping icons, opening programs, and copying files, for example — and that you're ready to take the next steps toward mastery.

At the end of each of the eight parts in the book, you'll find a short write-up of utility software you can purchase or download to help you with that part's tasks and needs. Of course, I can't guarantee that any of the products listed will actually be available by the time you read this book or that any of the listed prices will be accurate (which is why I haven't listed very many). But as I was writing the utility sections I made every attempt to point you in the direction of reliable, available software.

Part I: Securing Windows XP

Once upon a time, buying and using a computer meant getting excited about all the fascinating software you could acquire and use. That's still the case, but the buzz surrounding computers today is much more about security, intrusion, infection, and theft—a far darker lexis that requires far different attention. Part I focuses on four major security solutions for Windows XP: downloading and installing Service Pack 2, working with firewalls, installing and configuring antivirus software, and using antispyware software. Service Pack 2 fits into this mix precisely because its focus is on security. As a result, you could consider the first part of this book something of an equivalent to locking the doors before sitting down to enjoy your favorite book or TV show, but that's computing life these days.

Part II: Avoiding Disaster

No matter how careful you are with your system, eventually something will go wrong. Part II outlines the numerous methods that come with Windows XP for preventing problems in the first place, with a chapter devoted to what you can do when they occur. Here, you learn about configuring Windows Update, backing up your files and folders, and working with the Encrypting File System. Part II also provides solutions for a malfunctioning Windows, showing you what to do when Windows won't boot properly, how to restore your system to a previously functional state with System Restore, and how to close misbehaving programs.

Part III: Taming the Internet

Windows XP practically demands that you connect it to the Internet, offering an impressive variety of programs to help you make use of that constantly growing communication and information source. Part III shows you how to configure the Internet Explorer Web browser to function precisely as you need and how to use some of the lesser-known features of the Outlook Express email program. Here, you also learn about the two remote-control programs built into Windows XP: Remote Desktop and Remote Assistance. I demonstrate how to take advantage of both to work with PCs in other locations.

Part IV: Letting Windows' Hair Down: The Creative and Entertaining Side of Windows XP

Of course, using Windows XP isn't all about changing the interface and making problems go away. It's also about having a good, productive, and creative time. Part IV shows you three primary means of doing so. Without buying a single extra program, you can use Windows XP to transfer and edit photos from your digital camera, make videos complete with fancy transitions, and capture music for your portable audio player. If you haven't yet used Movie Maker 2 or Windows Media Player 10, both part of Windows XP, you might be surprised at what they'll let you accomplish in a short period of time.

Part V: Changing the Interface

For the past several years, Sun Microsystems has based much of its image on the motto *The network is the computer.* Especially today, with millions of computers connected to the Internet and many of these connected to local, regional, or national company networks as well, the motto has a substantial ring of truth. For those of us who use our computers for work, play, and everything in between, a different motto might well hold sway. My personal belief is that the *interface* is the computer because the interface gives us the tools we need to make things happen. If you think about it, you see only the interface, not the computer itself (unless you have the technical training necessary to understand what's going on under the hood). We see screens filled with text and graphics, not the zeros and ones that lie behind them; we see program icons rather than executable files; we see windows layered on top of one another, not the screen redraw that occurs when we click one of those windows to make it active.

Because the interface lies at the core of the Windows XP experience, Part V of this book focuses squarely on how to use it and, just as importantly, how to tailor it to your needs. You have an enormous amount of choice over how Windows looks and feels, with customizations available in a wide range of locations. Change any and all of it to help you work more effectively and enjoyably.

Part VI: Installing and Removing Hardware and Software

Of course, even with all the features built into Windows XP, it remains in one sense only the foundation on which to build a complete computing experience. Part VI examines the ins and outs of installing software and hardware, making sure it works right, and, when necessary, getting rid of it. The chapters in this part provide solutions for adding hardware devices to your system, including opening up your computer case to do so and finding new drivers for your hardware and new updates for your software. Also available here are details on hard disk maintenance, one of the most effective ways to keep your PC in good working order.

Part VII: Who Owns What? Working with Users, Permissions, and Policies

Anyone coming to Windows XP Professional from the much less technologically advanced worlds of Windows 95/98/ME can quickly get lost in the intricacies of user accounts, access permissions, and figuring out how to move data, when necessary, from one Windows XP installation to another. Part VII covers all these issues, showing you where to find important user data such as email files and Internet favorites settings, as well as how to make your folders private so that nobody else can get into them. The complexities of the Group Policy settings also find their way into this section, illustrating yet another method of customizing the interface the way you want it, but this time in a more technical fashion.

Part VIII: Networking Your Home or Business

Windows XP is built for the Internet, but it's also built for connection to a local network for the purpose of sharing resources. Part VIII covers the various types of networks available and demonstrates how to connect to them. It also shows how to share an Internet connection between two or more computers by using a cable or DSL router and how to set up a wireless network using the built-in support offered by Windows XP. In addition, here you can learn the fundamentals of setting up a Web server and a file transfer server with Internet Information Explorer.

Part IX: Appendixes

The appendixes cover two crucial elements in working with Windows XP: installing and reinstalling the operating system itself. They discuss the different types of installation, issues surrounding dual-boot installation with other operating systems, and how to perform a painless reinstallation without losing your important data.

Part I

Securing Windows XP

Chapter 1

Windows XP Service Pack 2

Why place this chapter first? Quite simply, if you're running Windows XP, you should also be running Service Pack 2 (SP2). The purpose of SP2 is to render Windows XP more secure, less vulnerable to attacks from the Internet, and more easily integrated with existing third-party security software. SP2 was introduced to the world just after the first edition of this book was completed, and for that reason it represents the single most important change to XP in the intervening months. Even if you never bothered to install Service Pack 1 — for whatever reasons — you owe it to yourself to get SP2 on your system as quickly as possible.

This chapter covers the features of SP2, along with details about downloading (or ordering it on CD) and installing it. Consider this the first step in making your Windows XP machine and the data it stores safer and more stable, a process continued in the chapters that follow.

Getting and Installing Service Pack 2

By far, the easiest way to acquire Service Pack 2 is to through Windows Update. As covered in Chapter 5 (for all Windows Update functions, not just the service packs), you can use Internet Explorer to head for the Windows Update site (www.windowsupdate.com), or you can set Windows to update itself automatically. If you choose the latter method, depending on your settings Windows will do one of the following:

- Inform you that Service Pack 2 is available and let you download and install it

- Inform you that it has downloaded Service Pack 2 and let you install it

- Download and install it without your intervention

In the first two instances, you must use the resulting dialog boxes to tell Windows to put the service pack in place. See the section "The Installation Itself" a little later for details.

There are two other ways to acquire SP2:

- **Order the free CD:** From the Microsoft site, navigate to the Windows XP area, follow the link to Service Pack 2, and look for the link to order it on CD. As of this writing, the URL is www.microsoft.com/windowsxp/downloads; of course, this URL can change at any time. The CD is free to all (not just those in the United States), so this is worth having whether or not you plan on installing Service Pack 2 that way.

- **Download the SP2 File:** Numerous download sites have SP2 available as a single, large file. One example is www.download.com, where you'll find it as a 266MB download.

Tip

There's a particularly strong reason to install a service pack from CD rather than from Windows Update. If your computer is already compromised — that is, it has already contracted viruses, spyware, and so on — any subsequent download can be affected, including items from Windows Update. For this reason, if you want to use the protection features of SP2, you're much better off ordering the CD and installing from it, simply because the CD won't be compromised. That said, for a completely clean PC, the best idea of all is to reinstall Windows XP from scratch and apply SP2 from the CD after doing so. For instructions on reinstalling Windows XP, see Appendix B. And hey, there is lots in this book to keep you busy while you wait for the CD to arrive.

Before the Installation

Most software you install on your system takes little if any preplanning. Download the file or insert the CD, step through the installation process, and away you go. Usually, you don't even have to shut down any programs before starting, although it's never a bad idea to do so (and a warning box almost always tells you to do so).

Any time you modify your operating system (OS), however, you should always do so with as clean a system running as possible — and with everything you need backed up, just in case disaster strikes. It's not absolutely necessary (many SP2 installations have been done without this planning), but it's recommended anyway.

Following is a list of suggestions for ensuring the greatest possible likelihood that SP2 will install without problems.

1. **Give yourself some time to do the installation properly:** Plan on spending an evening doing the installation, ideally longer. It might take less. While the actual installation is in progress, don't plan to do anything on the PC.

2. **Perform a backup of the files you can't live without:** This includes programs whose installation CDs you no longer possess, and those whose CD or registration keys you couldn't find if your life depended on it. See Chapters 4 and 26 for more on data backup.

3. **Perform a full virus check on your system:** Be sure to set your antivirus software to include all files, including system files and program files. Include all your hard drives. Depending on how much data you have stored on your drives, this process could take several hours. See Chapter 2 for sites to visit to conduct online antivirus checks.

4. **Perform a full spyware check on your system:** Delete all spyware files and programs located. If you know you have programs that include spyware, delete them from your system thoroughly. See Chapter 3 for sites to visit that offer free online spyware scans.

5. **Get rid of as many programs you can from the Startup folder, and prevent as many programs as possible from automatically loading when Windows starts:** These programs won't likely do any harm to the installation, but your SP2-enhanced Windows will start more quickly without them; besides, you've been wanting to get rid of those time-wasters for a while anyway, right?

6. **Ensure that you have adequate space:** Check that you have at least 2GB of space available on your primary Windows XP hard drive.

7. **If you are installing to a notebook PC, plug in the power cord:** Do not run it on battery power. If the batteries fail during installation, you can cause significant damage to Windows itself (although SP2 is good at recovery).

8. **Using the disk utility of your choice (Microsoft's CHKDSK is fine), check your hard drives for errors:** Let the utility correct the errors, and proceed from there. See Chapter 22 for more on working with hard drives.

9. **Go to Windows Update, before installing SP2, to get your PC up to date with the latest files:** This is particularly true of noncritical updates. However, if Windows Update lists SP2 as an available download, this means that its scan of your PC has indicated that you may install it without difficulty. Before doing so, however, go to step 10.

10. **Download and install the latest device drivers for as many hardware devices as you need:** You can get these from the support areas of the manufacturers' Web sites. Examples include drivers for hard drives (particularly SATA drives and RAID systems), video cards, sound cards, external drives, printers, and more. Again, these aren't actually necessary, but doing this will ensure that SP2 installs on top of a fully up-to-date system.

11. **If your PC has more than one account, log off all users from your PC, and log in as an administrator:** Better yet, reboot the PC to clear out all users and log in as an Administrator. If you do not have an Administrator account, let someone with such an account perform the SP2 installation. If your PC has one account only, it's almost certainly an Administrator account anyway. However, see Chapter 24 for more on establishing and determining user accounts.

The Installation Itself

Ideally, your SP2 installation will require no thought, no intervention, and no actual work. Start it up and away it goes, with your next act being simply to log in as a user and go back to whatever you were doing before the installation. In fact, in most installations, this is precisely what happens. Here is the process.

1. Start the installation by doing one of these things:

    a. Downloading from Windows Update

b. Inserting your SP2 CD

c. Double-clicking your downloaded SP2 installation file

2. Confirm that you want to update the system. If you're not sure, if there's something you want to update in Windows before you do so, or if you just don't want to take the time right now, this is a good place to cancel the process.

3. If you are installing from Windows Update, Windows XP now downloads the files necessary to perform the installation. You may continue working during this process; Windows lets you know when the download is complete and installation is ready to commence. If you are installing from the CD or the full downloaded file, you don't get this respite — installation begins immediately.

4. Once in progress, the installation of SP2 acts much like installation of any other software — except that it takes longer. In fact, it can take as long as an hour (although it usually takes less).

What SP2 Brings to the Table

When Microsoft says that something is necessary, you're probably tempted to just download it, install it, and be done with it. Usually, it turns out to be a good idea; no matter what the nay-sayers might suggest, Microsoft does actually want its products to run properly and not be the subject of continuing claims about lack of security, stability, or sense. In the case of service packs for Microsoft's operating systems, however, installation is always a good idea. In every case, these service packs offer improvements to the OS itself. These improvements range from bug fixes, to new versions of programs, to fundamental changes in security.

That said, you will also always hear horror stories. No matter how many people successfully install a service pack, you will hear only from the people who, for whatever reason, had a bad time of it. And there's no question that some PCs accept Windows service packs much less readily than others do. The problem is that it's hard to figure out why. Possibly it's an incompatible piece of hardware; possibly it's an old driver or two that simply refuse to get along. Possibly the PC is already loaded with viruses or other malicious software and simply doesn't install anything without incident. And possibly, it's simply a combination of hardware and software elements that just don't work together with the upgrades that the service pack installs.

There is, however, one thing that can safely be said for *any* Windows service pack installation: If the version of Windows XP already installed on your system doesn't work well, installing a service pack probably won't help. In fact, it might make it worse. Don't install a service pack expecting it to heal your PC, the way installing an antivirus program or a disk repair utility can help. Those programs are designed to take an ailing system and make it healthier. Windows service packs are designed to make the operating system more effective. But service packs are not healers.

Still, there are numerous reasons to install any Windows service pack, but especially Windows XP Service Pack 2. The following sections explain some of the major reasons. The assumption here is that you do not already have Service Pack 1 on your system. For those who do, the text includes notes about what is different in Service Pack 2.

Note

You do not have to install Service Pack 1 before installing Service Pack 2. SP2 contains all the features and fixes of SP1, adding many of its own.

Improved Security

Analysts and critics of Windows XP have continually focused on security issues. As with previous versions of Windows — especially since the popularization of the Internet — XP has been suscepti- ble to hackers, crackers, intruders, and thieves, and this susceptibility has made IT-savvy businesses and users wary of running Windows (including the XP version) on their main production PCs. Service Pack was designed from the outset primarily as an improvement on XP's security, and to that end, it incorporates numerous important security features.

Primary among these security features is the Windows Firewall. To be sure, SP2 doesn't actually represent the first appearance of the Firewall; it appeared, in fact, with the original Windows XP. However, SP2 improves the capabilities of the Firewall along with its default performance. Later in this chapter you look at how to configure the firewall; for now, it's important to note that the firewall is turned on by default in SP2, and that — more important — it has been added to the startup and shutdown processes of Window XP to minimize intrusions from the Internet in the time between the loading of the networking subsystem and the appearance of the desktop. Previously, that time offered a window of opportunity for hackers to break into system and establish control of the network.

The most visible sign of the concern for added security is the Windows Security Center, covered (like the Firewall) in its own section later in this chapter. The purpose of the Security Center is to provide a central interface from which you can see at a glance whether or not Automatic Updates, the Firewall, your browser settings, and your antivirus software are in place, and from which you can configure the features of these security tools. The Security Center loads automatically when you install SP2, encouraging you to take advantage of its controls in order to secure your PC against all possible threats (or at least the ones that it can manage).

Improved Web and Email Functions

For many of us, most of the day is spent on the Web or in email. As a result, email and the Web are the two primary targets for outside intruders. Not all intrusions are malicious, but at the very least, all are inconvenient and are often flat-out annoying. SP2 helps you recover some of the time and energy you've been wasting until now dealing with these annoyances by providing additional fea- tures in Windows' two major built-in Internet programs: Internet Explorer (IE) and Outlook Express (OE). Here is a list of the most significant features added to these two programs:

- **Protection from downloads (IE):** One of the classic methods of compromising your PC is for Web pages to initiate procedures to store files on your hard drive. SP2 provides Internet Explorer with an Information Bar, which appears immediately below the Address Bar and informs you each time IE recognizes a potentially harmful download. These downloads typically come from ActiveX controls, but they can include other recognized problem files as well, such as .exe files (program executables). Whenever the Information Bar appears, you can hover the mouse pointer over it to discover what is being called to your attention and to take action. Two menu items appear: Download File and What's the Risk? Choose the first to override the Information Bar and download the file in question; choose the second to go to the Microsoft site where an explanation page explains what the danger is. In the case of a download, IE causes a Security Warning window to appear, letting you Run or Save the file; in the case of ActiveX controls, it lets you configure IE to accept or reject all such files from specific sources or to ask you every time one appears.

- **Protection from downloads (OE):** Microsoft email products (the full Outlook program in particular) have suffered terribly from their susceptibility to viruses and other malicious code sent as attachments and as images within messages. With SP2, Outlook Express is far more watchful for such code, blocking suspicious attachments and, by default, not displaying graphics in a message opened in a separate window or in the Preview pane. As with IE's Information Bar, you can view the messages by clicking the block notification and instructing OE to download them, but some attachments are simply blocked from download completely. If that happens, and you know the code is valid, you can reply to the sender to have that person reattach and resend them. If you're not certain, be glad that the attachment has been blocked.

- **Control of IE add-ons:** Numerous programs add capabilities to IE to allow you to work with files germane to those programs from within your browser. Typical examples include virus checkers, download utilities, and the unending stream of toolbars available from Google, Yahoo!, MSN, and practically everywhere else. SP2 adds a Manage Add-ons window to IE, accessible via IE's Tools menu. Figure 1-1 shows this utility, in whose viewing pane is displayed all the add-ons currently loaded in IE. Another view, available by clicking the drop-down menu in the Show field, allows you to see what add-ons IE has used, not just those currently loaded. You can click the name of each add-on and choose to Enable or Disable it. If it is an ActiveX object, you can click the Update ActiveX button to have IE go to the manufacturer's site and download the latest version. The most important element here is the capability to disable add-ons because they often result in the worst slowdowns you'll experience when using IE.

- **Protection from the resizing of IE windows:** Few things are more annoying than having your browser window resized simply because you went to a specific Web site and loaded a specific page. Resizing is caused by scripts deliberately encoded to cause the browser window to enlarge (they could shrink it as well, but they never do), a method unscrupulous Web authors use to ensure that you see the pages they want you to see (by hitting you over the eyeballs with them). SP2 gives IE the code needed to stop these scripts from running, thereby eliminating the resizing problem. If you want larger windows, you can resize them yourself.

- **Blocking of popups:** Unwanted resizing of browser windows might be among the most annoying events when Web browsing, but having new windows pop up on their own is infuriating beyond belief. Popups are designed to focus your attention and force you to notice something (usually an ad or a survey) you wouldn't otherwise pay attention to. Popups are intrusive, disruptive, counterproductive, and just plain rude. Numerous toolbars (Google, Yahoo!, MSN) prevent popups from appearing; but with SP2, Internet Explorer can block them as well. And as with all pop-up blockers, you can choose to have the popup appear if you want. After IE has informed you that it has blocked a popup, hold down the Ctrl key while clicking the link, and it will appear as a separate window.

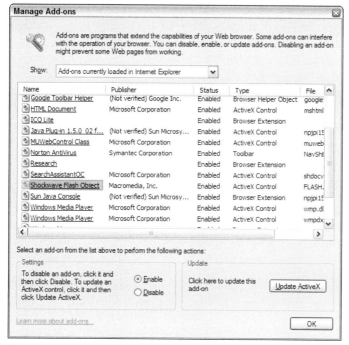

Figure 1-1: Internet Explorer's Manage Add-ons dialog box.

Other Enhancements

The original Windows XP was the first Microsoft OS that offered built-in support for wireless networks, but *Wi-Fi* (Wireless Fidelity, formally known as the IEEE 801.11 networking standard) was relatively new at the time and the support was limited. Service Pack 1 improved the capability of XP machines to connect to wireless LANs, but SP2 makes it easier still. SP2 allows Windows to recognize Wi-Fi broadcasts more reliably, enabling instant connections to public wireless networks in locations such as airports, schools, libraries, coffee shops, and other hotspots. Simply turn on your notebook and wait for XP to offer a choice of connections.

Also in the networking vein, SP2 improves the interplay between XP's networking and the Bluetooth standard. (Bluetooth is the specification for wireless personal area networks.) Whereas it was often previously necessary to spend considerable amounts of time configuring XP in order to have the connection actually work, with SP2 the connections are more frequently immediate. They're not as reliable as Wi-Fi connections, and in fact are often compared to the Wi-Fi capabilities of XP as of Service Pack 1. But if you own Bluetooth equipment, anything's better than what it was like before, so this will come as a particularly pleasant improvement. Whether or not Bluetooth continues to evolve and capture market share remains to be seen, but Bluetooth devices — ranging from keyboards to network adapters and print servers — are certainly appealing for a wide range of reasons. SP2 makes them that much more appealing.

Only one other major enhancement ships with SP2: a new version of Windows Media Player. WMP 10 is covered in detail in Chapter 14, so here I'll simply say that it works more capably with

DVD movies and that it offers numerous music (and other media) download purchases from directly within the program. In addition, facing obvious competition from the iPod, particularly the iPod's ease of building playlists, WMP 10 gives you better tools for organizing your music files.

Using the Windows Security Center

The Windows XP Security Center, which installs with SP2, is an easily accessible, easily comprehended dialog box designed to help you keep your XP installation more secure. It appears automatically after the SP2 installation, providing you with only a few choices, but these choices are crucial for security enhancement.

Figure 1-2 shows the Security Center in action. You can open the Security Center from the Control Panel (click Start, choose Control Panel, and double-click the Security Center icon), and you'll want to do so to configure it to your needs. Notice that Figure 1-2 shows only one possible view of the Security Center; what it actually looks like depends entirely on how you have your own PC configured. For example, if you have none of the displayed component categories installed, you will see buttons allowing you to configure it to include those components once you do install them.

The Security Center has five separate areas, four of which offer configuration options. The following sections provide a rundown of the four configurable areas, along with what to do with them to make your computer more secure.

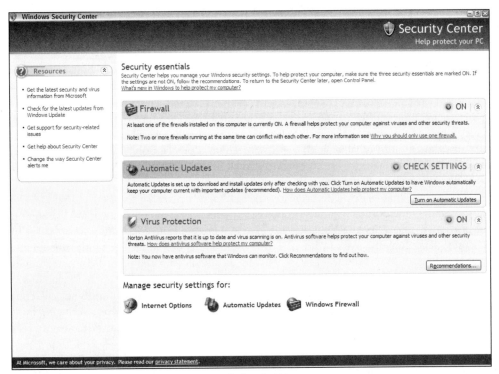

Figure 1-2: Windows XP Security Center installed with SP2.

Resources

The bar on the far left of the Security Center houses the Resources area. At first glance, this area seems nothing more than a set of links to information screens, but in fact, it's more valuable than that. Each of the five links offers its own useful security details:

- **Get the latest security and virus information from Microsoft:** This link leads to the Security home page on the Microsoft site (www.microsoft.com/security/default.mspx). That page, shown in Figure 1-3, provides a wealth of detail surrounding security updates, viruses and other malicious software, and how to configure your PC for the highest possible security. Clicking the link More Security Updates on this page, for example, leads to a list of security bulletins and downloads. Farther down the page (not shown in the figure), the Trustworthy Computing section provides a list of best practices and technology information.

- **Check for the latest updates from Windows Updates:** Clicking this link leads to the Windows Update site (covered in detail in Chapter 5). It's useful to have the link on the Security Center, especially as you get more and more used to checking the Security Center for possible issues surrounding your PC.

Figure 1-3: Microsoft's Security site.

Get support for security-related issues: This link leads directly to the Microsoft Support home page for security issues, a compendium of information about intrusions, viruses, and protection mechanisms. Included here are recent announcements about dealing with security problems, including information about such matters as how to determine if a security warning, received via email or the Web, is genuine.

Caution

When you receive an email message about security or about the need to log in to an account in order to confirm anything at all, **DO NOT COMPLY** unless you are *absolutely* certain the message is legitimate. To determine legitimacy, visit the Web site of the organization or company that apparently sent the information to you, and browse their site for information surrounding fraudulent messages. The general rule of thumb is that sites such as banks, eBay, and any other site that can get their hands on your money will *never* issue such messages. Sending fraudulent messages in order to gain access to your accounts is known as *phishing* and is one of the most dangerous security problems facing computer users today.

 Get help about Security Center: Clicking here loads the Windows Help system for the Security Center applet. It's a pretty useless Help page.

 Change the way Security Center alerts me: This link opens the dialog box shown in Figure 1-4. Checking each of the options (Firewall, Automatic Updates, and Virus Protection) tells Windows to inform you when your computer might be at risk because of the way you have Security Center configured. Although less useful than the warnings provided by some third-person security utilities, this is certainly a step in the right direction for Windows itself. Notice that the pictured dialog box has the Virus Protection button unchecked; you might choose to do this if your antivirus software already has its own alert system.

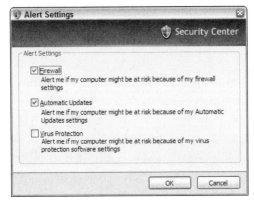

Figure 1-4: The dialog box for configuring Security Center alerts.

Firewall

The Firewall area of the Security Center gives you a button for turning Firewall monitoring on or off, as well as a link to a Help screen explaining why you should use only one firewall on your system. The answer to the second point is that different firewalls work differently, to the degree that they might very well prove incompatible with one another. That said, many users have two or even three firewall packages running on their PCs: the Windows Firewall, a third-party firewall (such as ZoneAlarm), and the firewall built into their network routers.

However, if you install a product such as Norton Firewall, the installation strongly recommends that you let the product disable the Windows Firewall automatically. Users attempting to work with both firewalls simultaneously have reported slowdowns and lockups.

The most important Security Center link to the Firewall is in the Manage Security Settings area at the bottom of the screen. Clicking this link yields the Windows Firewall configuration dialog box with its three tabs: General, Exceptions, and Advanced. From here, you control the workings of the Windows Firewall; even if you change nothing, exploring its various screens lets you see what firewalls actually do.

The General tab offers only three choices: On (recommended), Off (not recommended), and Don't allow exceptions. By default, except on Domain installations of SP2, only the first choice is selected. If you install a third-party firewall product that does not automatically disable the Windows Firewall, check the Off radio button and click OK to disable it manually in favor of the newly installed product.

The check box labeled Don't Allow Exceptions tells Windows to ignore any settings under the Exceptions tab, which you come to next. Essentially, checking this box tells Windows to inform you of any and all incoming data from the Internet, no matter what. This setting means that you will have to override every single program with a connection from the Internet, even those such as email and Web browsing that you do all the time. Check it only if you have the time to do such extensive monitoring.

The heart of the Firewall lies in the Exceptions tab. As Figure 1-5 shows, this tab displays a list of some of the programs and services currently installed on your PC (see the following bulleted list for adding others), along with a check mark denoting which ones you are allowing to bypass your firewall. To force Windows to block a program from bypassing the firewall, uncheck its box and click OK. To prevent Windows from even notifying you of such occurrences, uncheck the box at the bottom of the dialog labeled Display a Notification When Windows Firewall Blocks a Program. With this box checked, you have the option of overriding the Firewall each time a block occurs; with this box unchecked, Windows Firewall blocks programs without your intervention (which essentially means that you won't be able to use those programs if their design is to download data).

At the bottom of the dialog box are these four buttons:

- **Add Program:** This button opens the Add Program dialog box, which consists of a list of everything installed on your PC, letting you manually select (or browse for) the programs you want to control via the Firewall. This option is important for adding programs that Windows has not initially determined to perform data downloads but that you know do engage in such activity.

- **Add Port:** This button allows you to declare that data using a specific port, which uses either the TCP or the UDP protocol, will bypass the firewall automatically. The primary use for this option lies with online games that require specific ports to work properly. When you open a port for any purpose, however, you should always return to the Windows Firewall dialog box after using it in order to close it again. Intruders are always looking for open ports — to leave them open invites disaster.

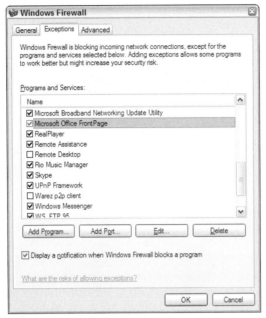

Figure 1-5: Allowing exceptions to Windows Firewall blocking.

Edit: This button shows you the folder path for the program you've selected in the list and lets you change the scope of the exclusion. Figure 1-6 shows the dialog box that appears when you click the Change Scope button (this button is also available when you click the Add Port button). The options are for any computer on the network to allow this program through the firewall, for only those in this computer's subnet (with all PCs outside that subnet blocking the program), or for a customized list of PCs (listed by IP address) that will allow that program to bypass the firewall. If you have only one member of your family or your office who needs to unblock data from a specific program, use this feature to unblock that person's PC address.

Figure 1-6: The Change Scope dialog box.

▪ **Delete:** This button gives you the option of deleting a program from the Programs and Services list. Doing so prevents it from being monitored entirely, so before deleting it, consider simply checking it and, therefore, allowing it access as an exception.

The Advanced tab of the Windows Firewall dialog box (see Figure 1-7) offers still more options. In the Network Connection Settings area, you can specify which of the connections shown in your Network Connections folder will use the Windows Firewall. Be aware, however, that unchecking an option renders that connection open to unprotected intrusion. It is possible to allow one or more connections to use the Windows Firewall while other connections use a third-party firewall. There's little (if any) reason to ever do that, though.

Figure 1-7: The Windows Firewall Advanced tab options.

You can specify the firewalled components of each connection by clicking the Settings button. This opens the Advanced Settings dialog box, with one list of selectable items under the Services tab and another under the ICMP (Internet Control Message Protocol) tab. Each item you choose for inclusion will be available through that specific network connection to anyone who uses that connection. For example, you can specify whether users on that network connection are able to access FTP or Web servers or Windows features such as Remote Desktop.

If you want to study the workings of the Windows Firewall, click the Settings button in the Security Logging area. The resulting Log Settings dialog box lets you specify if you want to log successful connections or dropped data packets, along with where on your system to store the log file created by this option. You can also specify the maximum size of the file, 4MB by default, but as small or as large as you want. With the logging feature turned on, you can open the file at any time (using any text editor, such as Notepad) to see what the firewall has been doing. The information is highly technical and is primarily useful for troubleshooting purposes. But if you're determined to understand firewalls (and especially the differences among firewalls), the details can be fascinating.

Automatic Updates, Virus Protection, and Manage Security Settings

The Automatic Updates and Virus Protection Settings areas work similarly. Both provide information about what the specific feature does, and both offer a button that lets you turn the feature on. Automatic updates are covered in detail in Chapter 5, and antivirus protection is covered in Chapter 2.

Windows XP does not have any built-in antivirus protection (although rumors persist that it will be added before too long). What the Security Center does, however, is work in conjunction with third-party antivirus packages (from McAfee, Symantec, and so on) to monitor your system continually for attempted viral intrusion. Clicking the Recommendations button (refer back to Figure 1-2) yields a dialog box with only one choice: whether to monitor your antivirus software yourself (the default) or allow Windows XP to do so for you. Check the box if you regularly check your antivirus settings. If you see no Recommendations button, it means that Security Center already knows that the antivirus software is installed and that you want Windows to monitor it.

At the bottom of the Security Center are three links under the heading Manage Security Settings for: Internet Options, Automatic Updates, and Windows Firewall. All three simply open the dialog boxes necessary for configuring these options. Internet Options are discussed in Chapter 9, and Automatic Updates are covered in Chapter 5. The Firewall settings are detailed in the section immediately following this one.

All three dialog boxes are available from the Control Panel; having them in the Security Center is merely a matter of convenience.

Summary

Windows XP Service Pack 2 provides a level of security that no desktop version of Windows has managed to achieve in the past. The Windows Firewall alone is worth the price of admission; however, the Security Center points to a solid future of drawing together the myriad threads of security options that have been available to Windows users for a long time but that have always worked disparately and often at odds with one another. Third-party security solutions remain not only valid but also frequently preferred. But even out of the box—except for the crucial omission of antivirus software—SP2 can render any PC much less vulnerable than before. Simply put, do not let anyone in your office or your household run Windows XP without it.

Chapter 2

Protecting XP against Viruses

I f you buy a new computer these days, it's likely to ship with an antivirus package. This fact, more than anything else, should convince you of how widespread viruses have become and how much the computer industry has come to accept their inevitability. Quite simply, viruses are a fact of computing life.

If your computer did not come with an antivirus package, you should install one before you do anything else. These things aren't luxuries; you need them. Very few viruses actually do significant harm to your PC, but it takes only one such infection to make your life thoroughly miserable. Furthermore, even those viruses that don't destroy data or programs can slow down your PC or cause it to behave unpredictably. Even worse, however, is the fact that the entire purpose of a computer virus is to spread. If you don't protect your PC, you will almost certainly start sending viruses to other people. Safe computing isn't just about you.

The other reason to install an antivirus package is that, increasingly, these packages deal with more than just viruses. Other forms of malicious software, including spyware (covered in Chapter 3), can also affect your system and even your privacy. You don't want this stuff glued to your hard drives or floating around in memory, but most of us have at least a small amount of it. Some PCs, especially those that have no protective software tools, are inundated with it.

Tip

Just say no. That's the best guideline I can possibly give you. If you get a message on your computer asking if you want something downloaded and/or installed, click the No or Cancel button. There are reasons to allow downloads — updated virus definition files, automatic updates from Microsoft, new Acrobat Reader versions from Adobe, for example — but before pressing the Yes/OK/Install button, be *absolutely* certain you know what you're letting yourself in for. The primary cause of intrusion problems on personal computers, especially Windows machines, is user ignorance; perhaps that's a tough word to use, but unfortunately it fits. People simply don't realize that anything you don't specifically ask for, no matter how nicely the request might be phrased, is designed to do something you probably don't want it to do. Just say no, and you'll be much better off.

This chapter deals with viruses and virus protection programs. Chapter 3 deals with spyware. Between the two of them, and especially when used in conjunction with a firewall program (see Chapter 1), you have a decent chance of protecting your computer from the majority of intrusions you're likely to experience in your daily computer use.

Understanding Viruses, Worms, and Trojans

There are thousands of viruses out there, and many different categories of viruses, but generally they all fit a single basic definition. A virus is a computer program intentionally designed to associate itself with another computer program in a way that when the original program is run, the virus program is run as well; the virus replicates by attaching itself to other programs. The virus "associates" itself with the original program by attaching itself to that program or even by replacing it, and the replication is sometimes in the form of a modified version of the virus program.

Notice the *intentionally designed* part of the definition. Viruses aren't just accidents. Programmers with significant skills author and develop them, and then find ways to get them onto the computers of the unsuspecting. The stronger antivirus programs get, the harder the virus authors work to get around them. For many virus authors, the whole thing is simply a challenge; for others, the point is having a good time making computing life uncertain or even miserable.

Viruses have quite correctly gained a reputation for harmfulness, but in reality many are not harmful. Yes, some damage files or perform other forms of destructiveness, but many are simply minor annoyances or, from the user's perspective, nothing at all. To be considered a virus, a program need only replicate itself; anything else it does is extra. Of course, the whole point behind viruses is that they run without the user's awareness, but that's not strictly necessary. You could knowingly create a self-replicating program, attach it to another program, and run it on your own machine so that it spreads, and it's still a virus. But that's not the way it usually happens.

Even relatively pain-free viruses aren't completely harmless, of course. They consume memory and CPU resources, thereby affecting the speed and efficiency of your machine. Furthermore, the antivirus programs that sniff them out and eliminate them also consume memory and CPU resources; many users, in fact, claim they slow the computer down noticeably and are more intrusive than the viruses themselves. In other words, viruses affect your computing life even when they're not actually doing anything.

Virus Types

The preceding explanation of viruses is actually more specific than the way we tend to use the term *virus*. In fact, it is often called a *program virus* or a *file virus* in order for commentators to differentiate it from other types of viruses. These viruses, which also go by the names *file infectors* and *parasitic viruses*, are those viruses that attach themselves to an executable file (that is, programs), and are the most common and the most discussed. The virus typically waits in memory for the user to run other programs, using such an event as a trigger to infect that program as well. Thus, they replicate simply through active use of the computer. There are different types of file infectors, but the concept is similar in all of them.

Other virus types (although not all are technically viruses) include *boot sector viruses*, *macro viruses*, *email viruses*, *worms*, *Trojan horses*, and droppers. All these programs are part of a category of program known as *malware*, or malicious logic software. What they all have in common is that they act without the user's knowledge, committing some kind of act inside the computer that they are intentionally designed to do.

Boot sector viruses or infectors reside in specific areas of the PC's hard disk, those that are read by the computer at boot time. True boot sector viruses infect only DOS's boot sector, while a subtype called MBR viruses infect the master boot record. Both of these areas of the hard disk are read during the boot process, during which the virus is loaded into memory. Viruses can infect the boot sectors or floppy disks, but typically a virus-free, write-protected boot floppy has always been a safe way to start the system virus-free. The problem, of course, is guaranteeing that the floppy itself is uninfected, a task that antivirus programs attempt to do.

Macro viruses work much the same way as program viruses, which makes sense, because macros are simply small programs. These viruses make use of the fact that many programs ship with programming languages built in. The languages are designed to help users automate tasks through the creation of small programs called *macros*. The programs in Microsoft Office, for instance, ship with such a built-in language, and in fact provide many of their own built-in macros. A macro virus is simply a macro for one of these programs. This type of virus became known through its infection of Microsoft Word. When a document containing the virus macro is opened in the target application, the virus runs and does its damage. In addition, it is often programmed to copy itself into other documents so that continual use of the program results in continual spread of the virus. Viruses for Microsoft Office programs are so common that, by default, when you open a Microsoft Office program, the capability to run macros is disabled. You have to tell Office to turn that feature on.

Email viruses have become a major source of malware distribution in the past few years. They function (mostly) by automatically mailing themselves to everyone in the user's contact list. Microsoft Outlook has been the primary target for email viruses because of Outlook's popularity.

A *worm* is a program that replicates itself but doesn't infect other programs. It copies itself to and from floppy disks, or across network connections, and sometimes it uses the network to run. One type of worm, the host worm, uses the network only to copy itself onto other machines, while another type, the network worm, spreads parts of itself across networks and relies on network connections to run its various parts. Worms can also exist on a non-networked computer, in which case they copy themselves to various locations on your hard drives.

The *Trojan horse* name comes from the Greek myth, best recounted in *The Odyssey*, in which the Greek army gave a wooden horse as a gift to the Trojans and then hid inside the horse as it was taken into Troy. They jumped out and captured the city, ending the long siege. The idea in computers is the same. A Trojan horse is a program that is hidden inside a seemingly harmless program and launches when that program is run. It is designed to perform actions that the user doesn't want performed. Trojan horses do not replicate themselves.

Droppers are programs designed to avoid antivirus detection, usually by encryption that prevents antivirus software from noticing them. The typical function of droppers is to transport and install viruses. They wait on the system for a specific event, at which point they launch themselves and infect the system with the contained virus.

Related to these programs is the concept of the *bomb*. Bombs are usually built into malware as a means of activating it. Bombs are programmed to activate when a specific event occurs. Bombs based on time events activate at a specific time, typically using the system clock. For example, a bomb could be programmed to erase all .doc files from your hard drive on New Year's Eve. Other bombs use logic to activate: an example might be to wait for the twentieth instance of a program launch and at that time erase the program's template files. In fact, looked at this way, bombs are just malicious scripts or scheduling programs.

Viruses can be thought of as special instances involving one or more of these malware programs. They can be spread through droppers (although they need not be), and they use the worm idea to replicate themselves. While viruses are not technically Trojan horses, they act like them in two ways: first, they do things the user doesn't want done; second, by attaching themselves to existing programs, they effectively turn the original program into a Trojan horse (they hide inside it, launch when it launches, and commit unwanted acts).

Viruses Keep Getting Smarter

The macro virus concept works because the programming language provides access to memory and hard disks. So, in fact, do other recent technologies, including ActiveX controls and Java applets. True, these are designed to protect the hard disk from the program (Java better than ActiveX), but the fact is that these programs can install themselves on your computer simply because you visit a Web site. Obviously, as we become increasingly networked, and as we expect such conveniences as operating system upgrades over the Internet, we put ourselves at greater risk from viruses and other malware. Although many people have never had a virus attack, the chance of a destructive one increases constantly. So it makes sense to guard against it. Like it or not, that almost certainly means getting a good antivirus program, of which several — including some free ones — are available. Go to any good download site and try one out. Make sure, however, that you can frequently update it because new viruses continue to appear.

Virus authors are nothing if not innovative, and they have constantly come up with new ways of thwarting antivirus software. *Stealth viruses*, for example, are viruses that mislead the antivirus software into thinking that nothing is wrong. Essentially, a stealth virus retains information about the files it has infected and then waits in memory and intercepts antivirus programs that are looking for altered files. It gives the antivirus program the old information rather than the new. *Polymorphic viruses* alter themselves when they replicate, so that antivirus software that looks for specific patterns won't find all instances of the virus; those that survive can continue replicating.

Several other types of smart viruses are appearing regularly, as the game of cat and mouse between virus authors and antivirus software producers continues. Recent efforts, for example, have concentrated on other genres of communication software, particularly in instant messaging programs such as AOL Messenger and MSN Messenger/Windows Messenger. The idea is to have instant messages that provide cleverly worded links ("lol you'll like this" is one example) that unsuspecting IMers will click. 2005's Kelvir worm is perhaps the most nefarious of these; it attempts to spread itself to IM contacts, and to each machine it downloads additional software.

Also increasing are the methods by which viruses and Trojans — along with spyware in particular (spyware is covered in Chapter 3) — can hide themselves from detection. The best example of these, called *rootkits*, demonstrates the degree to which it has become necessary to have help in monitoring your system. A rootkit is a collection of software tools that intruders install on computers after they've gained user access (usually by other intrusion means). The rootkit collects usernames and passwords, creates "backdoors" into which other malware can be installed, and contains mechanisms by which it can hide itself from intrusion. Persistent rootkits store themselves in the registry or in the file system and launch whenever Windows loads. Kernel-mode rootkits function at the core of the operating system and are virtually undetectable because they intercept the operating system's basic processes. Detecting rootkits has become a major goal for antivirus and anti-spyware software, although standalone tools such as Sysinternals' *rootkitrevealer* (www.sysinternals.com) focus exclusively on such detection.

How a Virus Works

Viruses work in different ways, but here's the basic process.

First, the virus appears on your system. It enters your system, usually as part of an already infected program file (.com or .exe), and in the past almost exclusively through the distribution of infected floppies (the famous *boot sector viruses*). Today, viruses are frequently downloaded from a network as part of a larger download, such as part of the setup files for a trial program, as a macro for a specific program, or as an attachment on an email message.

Note that the email message *itself* is not usually a virus, but with JavaScript as a component of HTML-based messages they can be. A virus is a *program* and must be run to become active. A virus delivered as an email attachment, therefore, does nothing until you run it. You run this kind of virus by launching the email attachment, usually by double-clicking it. One way to help protect yourself from this kind of virus is simply never to open attachments that are compressed files (such as .zips), executable files (.exe or .com), or data files for programs, such as office suites, that provide macro writing features. A graphics file or a sound file is safe, for example, because it is none of these; then again, it's possible to intentionally misname files in an attempt to get users to open them and, in doing so, create malware problems.

A virus starts its life on your PC, therefore, as a Trojan horse–like program. It is hidden within another program or file and launches with that file. In an infected executable file, the virus has essentially modified the original program to point to the virus code and launch that code along with its own code. Typically, it jumps to the virus code, executes it, and then jumps back to the original code. At this point, the virus is active, and your system is infected.

Once active, the virus either does its work immediately — these are called *direct-action* viruses — or sits in the background as a memory-resident program using the *terminate and stay resident* (TSR) procedure allowed by the operating system. Most are of this second type are called *resident* viruses. Given the vast range of activities allowed by TSR programs, everything from launching programs to backing up files and watching for keyboard or mouse activity (plus much more), a resident virus can be programmed to do pretty much anything the operating system can do. Using a bomb, it can wait for events to trigger it and then go to work on your system. One of the things it can do is scan your disk or (more significantly) your networked disks for other running (or executable) programs and copy itself to those programs to infect them as well.

Using Antivirus Programs

Antivirus programs are utilities that track, inform you about, quarantine, clean, or delete files that contain known or suspected viruses. Notice the last part of this sentence: *known or suspected viruses*. By far the more important of these two adjectives is *known*; antivirus software can function effectively only if it knows precisely what it is looking for. The *suspected* part refers to the capability of this sophisticated software to recognize patterns in virus construction: If it detects a pattern within a file it has scanned that comes close to matching the various virus patterns contained in its database, it will let you know and offer to quarantine that file for you.

So, what does your antivirus program *know*? Very simply, any virus code that it has been programmed to look for. When your antivirus utility conducts a scan of your files, it examines the code of any files you specify to see if those files contain code that matches one or more virus *definitions* the utility contains. The virus definition file, therefore, determines the effectiveness of your antivirus utility; it cannot detect viruses that are not contained in the definition file. Because of this, your antivirus utility is next to useless unless you keep it continually updated.

Fortunately, all antivirus utilities contain a means of updating the definition files. Either you download the files from the manufacturer's Web site manually, or you configure the utility to connect to the Web site every so often (your choice) to check for updated definition files — along with updates to the program itself — and download and install them. If you have a broadband Internet connection, you might as well configure your utility to check daily.

Tip

If you are responsible for other peoples' computers — those of family members or fellow office workers, for instance — check them occasionally to determine that (a) the antivirus utility is running, and (b) the definition files have been updated. One of the most common mistakes PC users make is to shut off the automatic update feature of these utilities but think they are protected because the antivirus program is indeed running. All the utility can do in that situation is ensure that the PC remains uninfected by old viruses; it can do nothing to guard against newcomers.

For the purposes of this chapter, I have decided to focus on one antivirus package, Symantec's Norton AntiVirus (which I abbreviate as NAV). This is not in any way meant to denigrate the other popular antivirus packages out there: McAfee VirusScan, Trend Micro PC-cillin Internet Security, Kapersky Antivirus, or any others. In fact, in comparative reviews, Norton AntiVirus has not typically proven better than the others in any significant way. Its choice for this book is primarily the package's popularity and the fact that it serves just fine as an example of what antivirus software accomplishes.

Scanning from the Web

It's not actually necessary to purchase an antivirus package if all you want to do is check your PC's current virus situation. Increasingly, antivirus vendors are offering scanning of your PC directly from their Web sites, a process that tends to take a bit longer than local scanning but which has four major benefits:

■ You can successfully scan a PC that does not have the latest virus definition files installed locally.

■ You are always assured of the most up-to-date virus scan possible.

■ You can scan PCs on which, for whatever reason, you cannot install antivirus software.

■ You can get a second opinion to see if the results are different from those of your installed antivirus program.

The next two figures show the Web pages for two of the more popular Web-based antivirus scans. Figure 2-1 is the User Agreement page for McAfee FreeScan, accessible from the McAfee home page (www.mcafee.com).

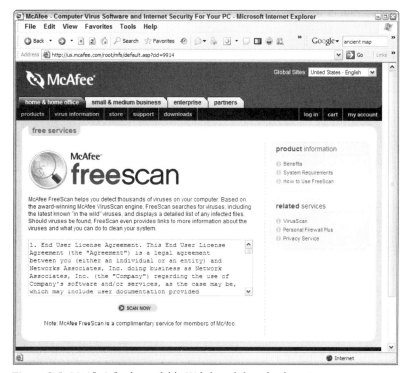

Figure 2-1: McAfee's freely available Web-based download service.

Figure 2-2 shows the starting page for Trend Micro's Housecall, the online free virus scan corresponding to their PC-cillin product (www.trendmicro.com).

In both cases, you need to agree to a download of an ActiveX control to have the virus-scanning software start, and this is indeed one of two apparent strikes against this method of virus checking. Since some of the fear surrounding malware is precisely the vulnerability of your PC to software placed on your hard drives from outside, it seems counterintuitive from a security standpoint to allow an ActiveX control to install itself on your PC and then allow that control to scan all the files on your system. To be sure, there's no way a reputable company would do anything so stupid as to cause damage or steal data in this way, but that won't stop everyone from being concerned.

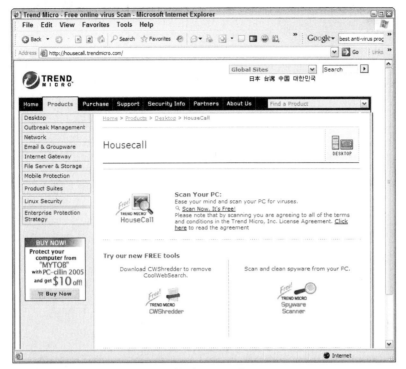

Figure 2-2: A similar service available from Trend Micro.

The other issue is much more functional. Web-based scans tell you what's on your system right now, but they do nothing to prevent additional viruses from infecting your PC from that point on. A locally installed antivirus program continually checks your PC's memory, the files you download from the Internet, and much more. In other words, an installed package acts as a preventative, while a Web-based scan acts only to determine what's already wrong.

That said, however, these free scan sites can save you time and again, so don't hesitate to use them. And, while you're at it, say thanks that they're available at all.

Getting Started with Norton AntiVirus

You have several choices when it comes to acquiring Norton AntiVirus. The first is to purchase it as a standalone package, either from your local computer store or through the Symantec online store at www.symantecstore.com. Figure 2-3 shows the page from this store for the most recent (as of this writing) version of the product. As the figure shows, you can buy the package and have it shipped to you, you can buy only a downloadable version, or you can buy both. You can also purchase a backup CD of the product — not a bad idea, actually, as long as you have the extra 10 bucks.

Figure 2-3: Buying your antivirus product online.

Symantec has made the software available in several other packages as well. It forms one of the core elements of Norton Internet Security (including the AntiSpyware Edition), as well as Norton SystemWorks, a product that has been available from the company for several years. SystemWorks incorporates the antivirus package with utilities for hard disk security and repair, disk clean-up, system monitoring, and much more. These products made their start—and indeed the company's start—as Norton Utilities. When you consider the difference in price between the antivirus package on its own ($49.95) and the full utility package ($69.95), it probably makes sense to get the whole shebang.

The first step, of course, is to install the software. This is actually simpler with Windows XP than with Windows 9.x versions, as long as you're using the recommended NTFS file system. For the FAT32 file system—the file system used on Windows 95, 98, and ME—NAV installs a Rescue feature that enables you to create emergency disks that are usable if your XP installation fails to start. With Windows XP (or Windows 2000) and the NTFS file system, however, this feature not only doesn't work, it isn't even installed. So, it becomes even more crucial to keep your system backed up, using a backup program or ghosting program.

Once installed, NAV automatically launches its LiveUpdate feature. This features works very much like any automatic update feature, informing you that updates are available from the company's download site and giving you the opportunity to perform the update at that moment or waiting until later. Immediately upon installation, you should perform the update without even thinking about it. If you don't, you'll be out of date before you start.

LiveUpdate is shown in Figure 2-4. In this figure, the utility is accessing the Symantec site to determine if any of the Norton SystemWorks programs or data files (such as virus definition files) on your PC need updating. If you own NAV on its own, the Products and Components window will show far fewer programs, of course, but the principle remains the same. LiveUpdate tells you what's available for download and lets you download and install them with one click. You should launch LiveUpdate manually on a periodic basis, but by default it monitors Symantec's site and informs you automatically of any updates it finds.

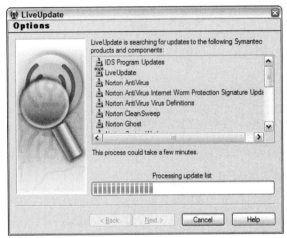

Figure 2-4: LiveUpdate in the process of downloading component and data file information.

The Norton AntiVirus Control Panel

For manual scans, configuring the software and checking out all available options launch the NAV control panel. Figure 2-5 shows the control panel with the NAV button on the left side selected; in a standalone NAV product, this will be the only button available. In this figure, all options are selected, as the check mark beside each one indicates. The date to the right of three of the features states when that function was last performed or, in the case of Renewal Date, when the subscription runs out. Each year, you must renew NAV, most recently at a cost of $19.95, in order to continue having access to the latest virus definition files.

In addition to the status display shown in Figure 2-5, this front page of the control panel gives you two other options. The most important is the Scan for Viruses button, from which you can perform manual scans of your system. As Figure 2-6 shows, this screen lets you choose how extensive you want the scan to be. You can scan the entire computer (a task of a few hours on a typical system these days) or scan only the floppy drives, only the removable drives (such as CDs), only one or more of the hard drives, only specified folders, or, to help you isolate virus-inhabiting files, only specific files on your system. Clicking any of the last three options yields a related dialog box that lets you select precisely what you wish to do; clicking any of the first three launches the scan immediately.

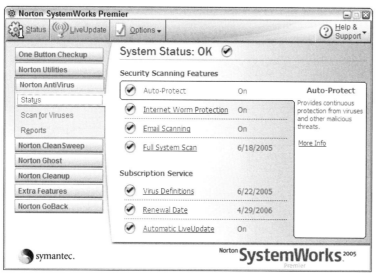

Figure 2-5: The Status display of NAV's control panel.

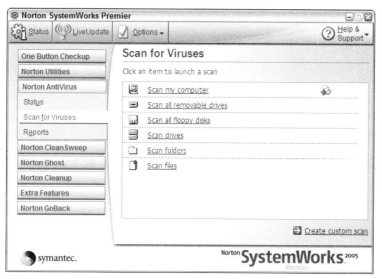

Figure 2-6: Options for manual scanning.

The third choice on the control panel is to read the numerous reports that NAV compiles as it goes about its business. Figure 2-7 shows the report screen, with the threat alerts highlighted. This example shows the capacity of NAV to locate spyware (covered in Chapter 3) rather than viruses per se, but that's only because this particular PC had not experienced a virus threat during the range of dates covered in the report (or NAV didn't catch them). Note that from this dialog box you can't actually do anything about the items caught during scanning; this is simply a report, but a highly informative one nevertheless.

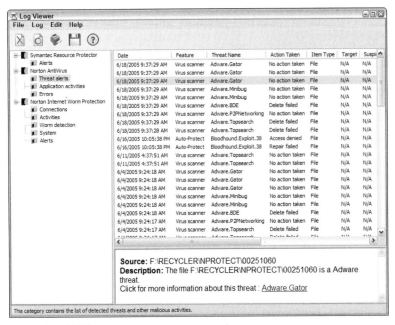

Figure 2-7: NAV's report screen.

Tip

Norton AntiVirus helps you keep your system up to snuff even further by adding to the Windows interface. In My Computer, for example, you can right-click a file or folder and choose Scan with Norton AntiVirus, to have the program perform an immediate scan of only that component. The package also adds a toolbar to Internet Explorer.

Configuring Antivirus Software

As you might expect, Norton AntiVirus, like all antivirus products, is highly configurable. Upon installation, all the most important features are turned on, but you can opt to disable specific features or enable even more features to give yourself the best mix of convenience and protection.

Why do I say convenience? Because antivirus software by its very nature is intrusive. It has to examine everything being downloaded to your system, it has to update its malware definition files, and it has to launch itself at specified times in order to conduct scans of your hard drives. If you also have it set to examine all files you upload, including email messages, all this scanning can cause the system to slow down appreciably, at times to the extent that you swear something is not working. This is especially true of operations it performs in the background; it's not uncommon to be waiting for a Web page to appear, or a large graphics file to open, only to discover that the antivirus program has been hogging system resources performing one of its numerous functions. For this reason, NAV (again, like all such packages) lets you turn some of those functions off if you wish, or schedule them at the most convenient times possible.

Figure 2-8 shows the NAV Options dialog box. When using your antivirus package, take some time to explore the various possible configurable elements; sometimes they're not immediately apparent. In NAV, for example, the entire left side of the Options screen consists of numerous configurable elements. Figure 2-8 shows only one such grouping — the Auto-Protect options — and not even all the ones available in this group. Clicking the Auto-Protect menu item on the left yields additional subcomponents, each of which you may configure as you see fit.

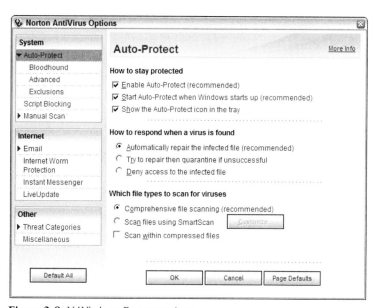

Figure 2-8: NAV's Auto-Protect options.

The following list highlights some of the more interesting options and what they do:

- **Auto-Protect:** The Auto-Protect feature allows NAV to monitor your system continuously, detecting malware as it appears on your PC. With a slow processor, this feature can take a significant toll on your PC's performance. That's really the only reason you should even consider toggling the feature off. If you do have it on, it's also a good idea to have it load with Windows so that it can begin its monitoring immediately. The middle of the screen lets you choose whether you want NAV to automatically attempt to repair files in which it detects malware, attempt to repair them but quarantine them if it cannot, or deny access to the file. If you know a user does not understand the dangers associated with viruses, the denial option might be your best bet to ensure that no file with improper code detected gets used on the system.

- **Script Blocking:** This feature allows NAV to stop software scripts from being run on your PC, thereby helping you avoid viruses that enter your system as part of the script. This feature does not attempt to detect the virus; instead, it presents you with a dialog box letting you choose whether or not you want the script to run (unless you choose the option to have it simply block the script without telling you). As with everything else related to security, if you don't know what it is, don't allow it to happen.

- **Manual Scan:** When you suspect something bad might have made it to your PC, or if you simply want extra peace of mind, periodically perform a manual scan. The options here are similar to any scan except that you can include or exclude your PC's boot records and/or master boot records. These are low-level areas of the primary hard drive; if infected with a virus, they launch that virus every time you boot up your PC.

- **Email**. Given the preponderance of email-related viruses and other malware, you should definitely consider leaving all email scanning features toggled on (their default). The two major choices are to scan incoming messages and/or outgoing messages. If you choose the latter, every time you send an email from one of the supporting programs (such as Outlook Express), you see a small notification box giving you the progress of the virus scan for that message (or those messages if you send more than one at a time). This option is important less for your own system than for those of your recipients; so out of sheer courtesy, be sure to leave it toggled on. However, it does slow down the sending process somewhat, especially on slow systems or systems with slow Internet connections. The only other option in the Email section is to monitor for worms, an obvious choice to include.

- **Internet Worm Protection**. Apart from worm blocking in email, NAV gives you the option of monitoring your system for worms at all times, preventing access in numerous ways. For the most part, you need not concern yourself with configuring this feature; the default settings handle the vast majority of cases, and NAV will learn your preferences as you use your programs. Using this dialog box, however, you can configure the feature precisely as you wish, setting the options for individual programs, incoming and outgoing connections, and how to deal with Trojans. Figure 2-9 shows the Trojan configuration dialog box, which simply lists the Trojans NAV knows about and lets you block them or allow them. Because NAV identifies Trojans by specific rules programmed into it, it sometimes misidentifies files as containing Trojans when in fact they do not. If you know this to be the case, toggle that particular Trojan identification off.

- **Instant Messenger:** Because Instant Messaging software has become increasingly vulnerable to malware, antivirus programs now protect IM as well as email. You have the option in NAV of adding virus protection to the three most popular IM programs: AOL Messenger, Yahoo Messenger, and MSN Messenger (there is no option to include others, such as ICQ). You also have the option of automatically informing the sender when you receive a message containing a virus.

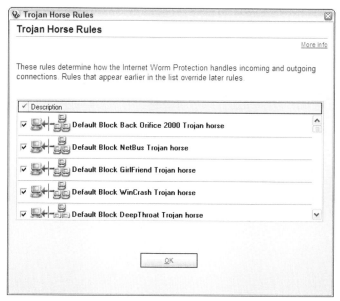

Figure 2-9: A list of Trojans whose rules are programmed into NAV's database.

■ **Threat Categories:** You don't have to allow NAV to scan your system for all possible threats. The Threat Detection Categories dialog box (which you open by clicking the Threat Categories item in the left pane) lets you uncheck those you don't want it to detect, presumably because you have other programs on your PC that do so. For example, if you have a third-party spyware package running (Chapter 3 covers spyware), you might want to uncheck the spyware and adware boxes, letting the dedicated package do its work without conflict with NAV.

Summary

Your antivirus program is the best friend you have on your computer. Ideally, you wouldn't need it, of course, because nobody would stoop so low as to write viruses in the first place, or they would be caught and jailed for it. But people do write them, many of them in fact, and there's absolutely no reason you should be the one to suffer for it. Any major antivirus utility package will do, so if you don't have one already, find one that suits your price range and your needs and install it. You can't possibly be sorry about it.

Chapter 3

Dealing with Spyware and Adware

Spyware and adware make up a category of software, called *malware*, that takes advantage of two facts of life with a computer in the early twenty-first century: Almost everybody is on the Internet, and almost nobody pays attention to what they put on their PCs. In general, Spyware refers to programs that, without the user's knowledge, collect information from the PC and transmit it to one or more servers over the Internet. Adware takes a different approach by sitting in memory and occasionally displaying banners on programs that have been scripted to perform this function. Together, these two categories of software have caused a great many users a great many problems over the past couple years — to the degree that one of the collective nicknames for this software is *scumware*. The programs are difficult to spot and, in some cases, quite difficult to remove from the PC.

This chapter briefly examines spyware and adware and demonstrates how to monitor and remove it using dedicated utilities. It also shows the complexity, in one particular case, involved in removing spyware/adware manually.

What Are Spyware and Adware?

One of the biggest questions concerning spyware and adware lies with definitions. Until you can state precisely what something is, it's impossible not only to deal with it in all cases but also to legislate against it — although two bills, HR 29 and HR 744, are wending their way through the U.S. legislative processes as of this writing (a Google search on the two bills will reveal the text). Indeed, the computer industry itself can't make up its mind about how to define it, a problem for even those companies who wish to comply with both legislative decisions and consumer satisfaction.

What's the problem? First of all, the word "spyware" itself is confusing.. Although the term now refers to a fairly broad range of software (as I discuss later), originally, it meant software that, unknown to the user, acquired personal information and sent it to whomever it was programmed to. In other words, it was spying on you. This could include programs that collected keystrokes or a wide variety of other information, the primary element being the user's lack of awareness of what was going on. In some cases, such as those involving programs included with other packages (see the section on removing KaZaA, below), the user was even unaware that the program was being (or had been) installed. But in most cases, users installed the software without even bothering to check; that's how this category of programs became so widespread.

Two questions (at least) come to the fore here. First, if a user installs the software despite a warning stating that it will operate in the background and help "customize" the computing experience, does that make it all okay? Second, what happens with other forms of data-monitoring software placed unknowingly on the user's hard drive, a category into which cookies fall? The answer to the first question should be easy, in the sense that we're all responsible for our own lack of vigilance. But are the explanations that appear with the installation enough to guide users realistically? Given the tendency of a great many people to click OK no matter what they see, obviously there are issues here. Is user ignorance something software vendors should be allowed to take advantage of? The questions increase in complexity, of course, when examined in the corporate and institutional domains.

The second question is the subject of continual debate among software companies of all kinds, not just those who produce anti-spyware and anti-adware products. One big question surrounds cookies. These little bits of code are placed on your hard drive by, in fact, many Web sites, and you allow them simply by configuring your Web browser to do so — or, more specifically, by not preventing it from doing so. When you visit a site, the Web server software looks for cookies appropriate to that domain, then "remembers" your settings, or your username, or what's in your shopping cart, and so on. So, in a sense, cookies track who you are and where you've been. Does that make them spyware?

According to numerous anti-spyware programs, yes. But according to other sources, no. Microsoft's Anti-Spyware program (covered below) does not scan for cookies by default (you can do so manually) because to deactivate and destroy cookies renders the browsing experience slower and in some ways less enjoyable. An argument also exists that cookies can be used to eliminate popups that first-time visitors receive; the cookie identifies you as someone who has already seen that ad or filled out that survey and does not bother you again. Eliminating the cookie would result in greater annoyance, not less. A counterargument suggests that it's easy for today's monitoring software to distinguish between cookies that gather information in order to track user behavior and those that do not. But the point is that there's no consensus yet about whether even the behavior-tracking cookies are properly categorized as spyware.

In addition to this confusion, several companies have taken exception to having their products labeled spyware or adware in the first place. The argument here is that if consumers choose to activate the products, knowing full well what they do, they shouldn't have a negative label attached to them — which, unquestionably, the words "spyware" and "adware" have become. Other companies have deliberately incorporated adware into their offerings, arguing that they provide useful information to customers without performing objectionable actions such as monitoring keystrokes or Web navigation patterns. Furthermore, numerous software products send information to the vendor without anyone complaining, or at least not with the same complaints as with malware. Windows XP itself offers to send data whenever a program (or the operating itself) crashes, which means it has already gathered this information against such an occurrence. This would hardly be classed as spyware, but it's certainly similar to that negatively considered category.

When all is said and done, however, you're not likely to encounter anyone who actually *wants* spyware on their systems. This chapter details how you can control it and, ultimately, get rid of it.

Working with Spyware/Adware Programs

As the spyware and adware epidemic has grown, so has the number of software packages designed to deal with it. In this section, I examine two types of programs: those that handle spyware and adware exclusively, and those with spyware/adware monitoring and deleting capabilities built into a larger package of utilities.

Dedicated versus Bundled Anti-Spyware Programs

If you're serious about controlling spyware and adware, you should consider installing a program designed specifically to identify, monitor, and delete it. That way, you have a utility that does only one job, and you can be sure that, as long as the vendor supports the program to industry standards, it will be constantly current and always able to deal with the latest threats. Bundled utilities typically upgrade several of the included programs at once, which means that if the spyware portion needs updating, but another utility in the package will be ready within a day or two, it makes sense to hold back the entire bundle to ensure a more efficient download and installation for the user. The problem with this approach, of course, is that you might miss a crucial detection during that delay.

The three programs examined briefly here belong to different categories. The first is shareware — that continuingly valuable category that produces many of the most useful utilities out there. The second is from Microsoft itself, designed as an add-on to Windows XP. The third is a component within a larger group of utilities. Obviously, it makes sense to give the Microsoft item a try, because it's intended to run with XP, but because you can try all three for absolutely no cost, why not take them all for a spin?

Tip

To get the best results out of anti-spyware packages, have only one running at a time. This is especially true if your goal is to compare one program against the other, because otherwise you can't really pick out their individual strengths and weaknesses.

SPYBOT SEARCH & DESTROY

Originally released in 2002, Spybot Search & Destroy (better known as SS&D, of course) has gained the reputation as one of the best standalone spyware detectors, monitors, and removers in the business. SS&D is available free, although the Web site (www.safer-networking.org) quite reasonably asks for a donation to defray the numerous costs (to say nothing of the time spent) encountered by the developers. Unlike another equally highly regarded utility, LavaSoft's Ad-Aware, SS&D is not available as a purchased package (although Ad-Aware also has a free version); you download the latest version (1.4 as of this writing), install it, and when you discover it works, go to the site and contribute to someone who helps keep your system safe.

Installation is simple and fast (although you should create a Restore Point with System Restore before doing so, in case you want to reverse the process). Upon installation, you're immediately presented with a dialog box labeled "Legal Stuff," which tells you that if you remove advertisement robots (adware) with SS&D, you might not be able to run the host programs they came with. Just say OK, and continue the installation. This is precisely what you *want* the program to do. You then get a small utility offering to make a backup of your Windows registry, another good idea at this time.

Once this is done, a rather mysterious button appears in the installation wizard called "Immunize this System." The explanation is no less mysterious: "Now that you are up-to-date, it is recommended that you apply some basic Immunization. Just click the button to do this." Go ahead and press the button, because SS&D simply wants to configure itself to block some known malware from functioning on your system. Version 1.4 blocks over 6000 such products with its simple immunization.

As with all such products, the next step is to let SS&D perform its magic. On the main screen, click the Check for Problems button and sit back and watch. With its default settings, SS&D uses its built-in database of known threats to search your system and block the worst offenders as you work, and to delete any it has found. You can click the Settings button to change this configuration so that SS&D does even more than what its initial setup handles. For example, as Figure 3-1 shows, it lets you select which cookies you wish to retain on your system if you configure the program to routinely erase your usage tracks. Using the Tools menu, you can have SS&D stop programs from loading when Windows boots, another useful service.

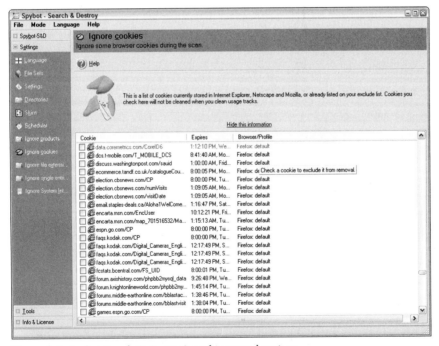

Figure 3-1: Spybot Search & Destroy's cookie control settings.

Essentially, though, SS&D simply sits in the background and guards your PC against the latest spyware programs. When it locates them, it displays them in a color-coded format, with red representing the most important threats and green representing the usage tracks. It then lets you choose which threats to delete and it provides information on how to work with the usage tracks, including ignoring specific ones and/or dealing only with those from specific products. It then does whatever is necessary to get rid of the threats, including changing the registry settings that the programs have already changed. It works, and that's all you really care about.

MICROSOFT ANTISPYWARE BETA

As of this writing, Microsoft AntiSpyware is still in beta version 1.0. But like SS&D, it works. In fact, the two packages seem to work together very well (unexpectedly so) to provide a two-pronged protection against spyware and adware. Figure 3-2 shows the program loaded and ready for a system scan. Options are few in this program, because its purpose is simple: it checks your system for known spyware and adware threats, reporting on whatever threats it locates and either allowing you to take action or quarantining or removing the threats automatically depending on how you've established the configuration.

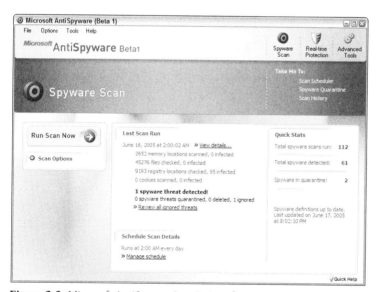

Figure 3-2: Microsoft AntiSpyware's main interface screen.

Figure 3-2 also shows the results of a scan for spyware, after clicking the Scan Now button on the main interface screen. The Quick Stats area shows the number of scans that have been run on the current system, as well as the number of spyware files detected and the number currently held in quarantine. This should be useful information, of course, but its cumulative nature makes it less so. In this particular example, for instance, the number of files detected includes 3–4 files detected numerous times. The more important information occurs in the Last Scan Run section; in this case, the program has noted 95 infected registry entries. Sounds bad, until you see that there's only one actual spyware threat (at least, according to this utility). To deal with these results, click the View details link, which yields the dialog box shown in Figure 3-3.

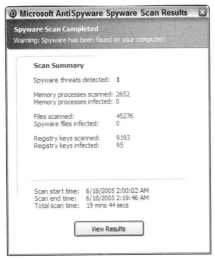

Figure 3-3: The results of a spyware scan.

This information is precisely the same as the details on the main interface screen following a scan, except that you can click the View Results button in order to do something about the detected threats. Figure 3-4 shows the result of clicking this button, the Spyware Scan Results screen. Each threat offers a drop-down menu that allows you — as the figure shows — to Ignore, Quarantine, Remove, or Always Ignore the detected threat. On the right-hand side of the dialog box is an explanation of the selected threat, along with a useful paragraph of advice. Here, the threat is low, and ignoring it won't hurt anything. Mind you, that's merely the opinion of the people who created the database of possible threats, so feel free to take it on yourself to ignore or delete as you wish.

By default, Microsoft AntiSpyware scans your system every day at 2:00 a.m. On the Schedule screen, you can change the schedule to whatever time of the day you wish, and the frequency to daily, weekly, or monthly. Be sure to schedule the scan for a time of day you will not be using the PC. While not as resource-intensive as an antivirus scan, the AntiSpyware scan unquestionably slows your system, to the degree that you'll find it difficult (and frustrating) to carry on normal activities while it is in progress.

One of the better elements of the AntiSpyware utility is the ability to control the tracks your PC use leaves behind. Figure 3-5 shows the Tracks Erase screen, accessible from the Advanced Tools button. Each of these programs or activities leaves a trail of what you did, and the idea here is to erase those trails so that nobody knows where you've been, what forms you've filled out, what you've put in the form fields, and so on.

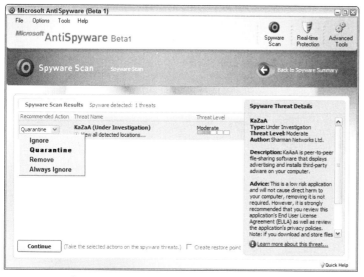

Figure 3-4: Taking action against a spyware threat.

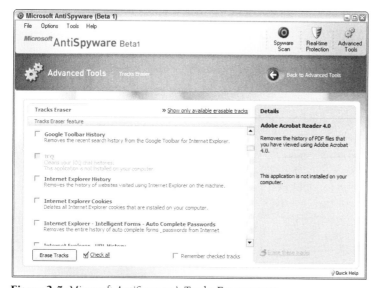

Figure 3-5: Microsoft AntiSpyware's Tracks Eraser screen.

Some of the more useful tracks to erase from this dialog box include the following:

▓ **Google Toolbar History:** If you use the Google toolbar to perform your searches, your search strings are saved in the toolbar. You can erase them manually, but AntiSpyware can do this for you. The Google Toolbar (strangely enough) does not provide an auto-erase function.

- **ICQ:** By default, the ICQ chat program saves transactions of your chat sessions. Rarely do you need these, and often you don't even want them.

- **Internet Explorer History:** If you don't want another user of your system knowing where you've been surfing, check this option to erase the history.

- **Internet Explorer Intelligent Forms:** IE's automatic forms completion feature is an obvious time-saver, but it's an equally obvious information risk. Checking this option gets rid of all saved form information, highly useful for privacy purposes.

- **Kazaa:** If you use Kazaa as your P2P program, you might want to get rid of your search history automatically. This option lets you do so.

- **Recent Documents:** This option is available here for several programs, including Windows XP itself. Checking the option clears out the information on the last files accessed for those programs.

- **Temporary Files:** For both IE and Windows itself, you can automatically clear out any temporary files the system has saved.

Once you've made your selections, click the Erase Tracks button. If you want AntiSpyware to retain your selections, check the Remember Checked Tracks box at bottom right.

Incidentally, some of these tracks can be adjusted elsewhere within Windows XP: the Taskbar Options dialog box and TweakUI, to cite just two examples. See Chapter 16 for information on configuring the Taskbar, and Chapter 18 for details on TweakUI.

YAHOO! TOOLBAR

Numerous toolbars are available for download, at no cost, from the Internet. Google, MSN, and Yahoo! are among the most popular. All of them have their useful features, and all of them clog up the nice, neat elegance of your browser toolbar. Yahoo! has recently added a utility called Anti-Spy to its toolbar, and to be sure, it's highly useful. Not as useful as a standalone product, but an excellent supplement to your main anti-spyware program.

After installing the Yahoo! toolbar, check the Anti-Spy button located third from the left after the Search Web button (the Anti-Spy button looks like a crosshairs). Choose Run Anti-Spy; the software immediately checks for updates and then presents the main interface screen. From here you can check the options to have it scan for cookies or to have it scan immediately upon launching it (or both), or you can just click Begin Scan to see what it locates on your system.

The progress area on the Scan Results screen (see Figure 3-6) tells you what the program is currently looking at—the registry, common file locations, or system memory. When finished (it takes only a minute or two even on a large system), it presents you with a list of threats found, along with the option to Remove or Allow each threat. To learn more about a threat, select it and double-click the View Details command.

If you choose to Remove a threat, Anti-Spy informs you that doing so might cause some programs to malfunction and that you might be breaking a licensing agreement. If you're uncertain whether or not to delete the threat, use System Restore to create a Restore Point on your system before performing the removal.

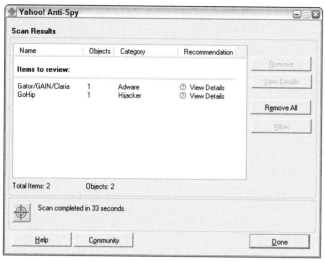

Figure 3-6: The results of a scan using Yahoo! toolbar's Anti-Spy.

Getting Rid of Old KaZaA the Manual Way

One of the earliest and most often cited culprits in spyware installation was KaZaA (hereafter just Kazaa without the bizarre capitalization). Newer versions of the software (starting in 2004) have become much clearer about what gets installed, so this section deals with older Kazaa installations. These are still happily running on thousands (if not millions) of hard drives out there, quite possibly yours. Because it takes a great deal of effort to eliminate all traces of old Kazaa from your PC, a separate section seemed necessary to help those who need to do so.

Kazaa was once the unquestioned leader in peer-to-peer file-sharing software. Despite frequent warnings from the computer and mainstream press, the program got more and more popular daily. The original Napster held the number one spot until the music industry got together to destroy it with lawsuits, but the Kazaa Media Desktop had at this point avoided any such problems (although not suggestions about threats) because it did not itself provide the network from which downloads took place (it used the Open Source and noncentralized Gnutella network as its basis).

Despite the software's popularity (or perhaps because of it), many of Kazaa's users have had problems galore. Uninstalling early Kazaa can cause enormous problems because getting rid of Kazaa itself does not usually get rid of everything that installed along with Kazaa. The Kazaa installation procedure asks if you want to install a variety of additional software, and, even though you can say no to these requests, very few people do. Installing software has become so routine and so relatively safe that users tend to assume that clicking the OK buttons during the process won't do any harm. Most of the time, they're right. With Kazaa, they're not.

What Kazaa Installs

Here's the problem. Kazaa installs not only itself but, unless you watch carefully during installation, additional programs as well. Specifically, a full installation of Kazaa also installs SaveNow, which is designed to provide "contextually relevant offers" (as quoted from the Kazaa Setup Wizard) and, in the next screen of the Setup Wizard, a set of "Promotional Software." SaveNow, combined with the promotional software, includes the following software that Kazaa tries to install:

- **SaveNow:** Downloads promotional Web sites to your computer to help you search for products.

- **New.net:** Allows creation of Web sites with unofficial domain names — in practice, it simply becomes annoying.

- **Delfin Media Viewer:** Shows movie trailers, portions of MP3 songs, games, and so on without your requesting them.

- **MediaLoads:** Delivers content to your desktop while you eat, sleep, or go out on dates.

- **b3d Projector:** Displays ads on the Kazaa program itself.

Note

Most of the problems with Kazaa that I've been called upon to fix have been for the program bundle examined here. Different versions of Kazaa have installed different programs, but as of this writing, the current version (2.6) has cut the additions considerably. The discussion here applies most directly to the equally widely distributed earlier versions, although differences exist in many of them.

Simply put, you should allow *none* of these programs — not a single one — on your PC. If you have not yet installed Kazaa, do so *only* without these programs. With the exception of New.net, a bothersome add-on, all of these programs perform some form of adware or spyware functions. Not only that, but Kazaa also includes technology from Cydoor, which inserts itself into your registry, can be uninstalled only with extreme difficulty, and sends you customized ads based on a unique code with which it tracks you. Together, these programs turn your PC into a machine that spits out information about you regularly and sucks in files you couldn't possibly want. And, unlike those pesky telephone solicitors who call you at dinner time every night, you can't just hang up.

How to Get Rid of Kazaa and All Its Buddies

Uninstalling Kazaa itself is easy. Open the Add/Remove Programs utility in Control Panel, locate Kazaa Media Desktop, and click the Change/Remove button. A few clicks later, you've deleted it. But, you haven't deleted the rest of the programs Kazaa installed. They continue doing what they're doing and, very largely, without you knowing it. To uninstall Kazaa fully, including all its associated programs, perform the following steps:

1. Use System Restore to create a restore point for your system. If, after all the activity in this list, your PC has trouble operating, enter System Restore again (you can do so in Safe Mode), and restore the PC to the newly saved time.

2. Unload Kazaa from memory. Closing the program the normal way doesn't accomplish this goal because Kazaa minimizes itself to the icon tray and continues to run. Find the program in the icon tray, right-click it, and choose Exit. To ensure that you have unloaded it, press Ctrl+Alt+Delete to open the Task Manager, find Kazaa in the list, and shut it down.

3. Open the Add/Remove Programs utility in Control Panel, locate Kazaa Media Desktop, click the Change/Remove button, and follow the wizard to uninstall it. With Kazaa itself gone, it's time to work on the other programs.

Tip

For best results when removing any program, reboot Windows after every uninstallation. Doing so sets the Registry to its most up-to-date state and prevents any possible conflicts. In most cases, the reboot isn't strictly necessary, but, when removing problem software, such as the programs listed here, the reboot provides an extra degree of reassurance.

4. Open Task Manager, see if SaveNow appears in the list, and end it. Reopen Add/Remove Programs, and uninstall SaveNow.

5. Repeat this process for MediaLoads, New.net, and b3d Projector.

6. Open My Computer or Windows Explorer. From the Tools menu, choose Folder Options. Click the View menu, scroll down the Advanced Settings list, and click the Show Hidden Files and Folders radio button.

7. Still in My Computer or Windows Explorer, locate the following folders and files:

   ■ C:\Documents and Settings*your_username*\Start Menu\kazaa\: Delete the entire folder and then repeat for *every* user's folder in Documents and Settings. If the Default User and All Users folders contain this folder, delete them as well.

   ■ C:\Documents and Settings*your_username*\Desktop\: Delete any item with "Kazaa" or "My Shared Folder" in the name.

   ■ C:\Windows\System32\: Delete the following files: cd_clint.dll, cd_gif.dll, cd_swf.dll, and cd_load.exe. Also look in C:\Windows\System if the files are not in Windows\System32. Deleting these files removes the Cydoor technology installed with Kazaa.

   ■ C:\Windows\BDE: Delete the entire folder.

   ■ C:\Program Files\BDE: Delete the entire folder.

- bdedownload.dll, bdedata2.dll, bdefdi.dll, bdeinsta2.dll, and bdeinstall.exe: Delete all these files — you might have to search for them, but you will find most in C:\Windows\System32.

8. To guarantee that all possible traces of these programs are gone, you need to edit the registry. Again, do not do so unless you know exactly what you are doing, and, even then, not until you have backed up the registry (but, without doing this, the programs or at least their DLL files can reappear). This can take a considerable amount of time, and you are unlikely to track down every single entry. For example, the following list shows the entries created by b3d Projector:

   - HKEY_LOCAL_MACHINE\Software\Brilliant Digital Entertainment

   - HKEY_CLASSES_ROOT\TypeLib\{82FC7881-AACC-11D2-B9C6.0000E842E40A}

   - HKEY_CLASSES_ROOT\b3d_auto_file

   - HKEY_CLASSES_ROOT\ BDEPLAYER.BDEPlayerCtrl.1

   - HKEY_CLASSES_ROOT\ CLSID\{51958169-D5E3-11D1-AA42-0000E842E40A}

   - HKEY_CLASSES_ROOT\Interface\{51958168-D5E3-11D1-AA42-0000E842E40A}

   - HKEY_CLASSES_ROOT\b3dini_auto_file

   - HKEY_CLASSES_ROOT\CLSID\{67925165-C4B6.11D2-B9C6.0000E84F59A6}

   - HKEY_CLASSES_ROOT\Interface\{51958167-D5E3-11D1-AA42-0000E842E40A}

   - HKEY_CLASSES_ROOT\Interface\{67925164-C4B6.11D2-B9C6.0000E84F59A6}

   - HKEY_CLASSES_ROOT\s3d_auto_file

   - HKEY_CLASSES_ROOT\ BDESmartInstaller.BDESmartInstaller

   - HKEY_CLASSES_ROOT\BDESmartInstaller.BDESmartInstaller.1

   - HKEY_CLASSES_ROOT\.b3dini

   - HKEY_CLASSES_ROOT\BDEPLAYER.BDEPlayerCtrl

   Other keys in HKEY_CLASSES, HKEY_CURRENT_USER\Software, and HKEY_LOCAL_ MACHINE\Software contain elements of the installation for the other programs. Search through as many as you can, but you'll soon be able to tell by the behavior (or, we hope, lack of behavior) of your PC if any elements remain.

9. Reboot your computer.

10. Open the System Configuration utility (click the Start button, choose Run, type **msconfig**, and press Enter), and click the Startup tab. Scroll through the list to see if any likely items remain from this group of programs. If so, uncheck the entry, and click OK until Windows restarts.

Congratulations. You've uninstalled the highly problematic Kazaa Media Desktop! It takes time, but it's worth it. Your machine is your own again.

Summary

Spyware is a major concern. At its worst, it sends information, without your knowledge, to Web sites and databases you might not wish to be a part of. Even at its most harmless, however, it can seriously slow your system and use up significant amounts of memory. Along with viruses, spyware represents one of the most serious problems with computing today, and you owe it to yourself to do everything you can to avoid it and, if necessary, get rid of it. You have a lot to lose.

Part I

Utilities

Numerous utilities are available for controlling viruses, spyware, and Internet intruders. You have to purchase many of them, but some function partially in their shareware versions, and a few are entirely free. Most offer the substantial benefit of a try-before-you-buy program, so you can determine the effectiveness of the product, your need for it, and how well you like working with it.

Our suggestion is to download and try as many of these as you can to see the differences among them and to learn how each can help you. While this guideline holds true for all utility categories discussed in this book, it is especially true for this group, which focuses on keeping your system safe. But along with the suggestion to try a number of them we must caution you that, used in conjunction with one another, these utilities can cause problems, especially when it comes to antivirus programs. You'll do best to have only one utility running at a time, although you can comfortably run more than one firewall.

Antivirus Utilities

Norton AntiVirus (www.symantec.com), covered in Chapter 2, is the granddaddy of antivirus programs and an extremely popular one even to this day. However, numerous others are available, many of which have made their mark because PC manufacturers have installed them on their products before selling them to consumers. One of the most widely used is McAfee's VirusScan (www.mcafee.com), in version 9 as of this writing, which like Norton AntiVirus is available via subscription. For roughly $40 per year for either program, you get a package of well-regarded software that does its job as well as any. Depending on which reviews you read, either McAfee or Norton works more efficiently on a typical home user's PCs, and both work comparably in small business environments. There's really very little difference between them.

Also like Norton AntiVirus, McAfee VirusScan also comes bundled in software suites. McAfee's Internet Security Suite combines the company's VirusScan, Personal Firewall, SpamKiller, and Privacy Service products, for less than double the price of VirusScan alone. Personal Firewall runs in conjunction with the Windows Firewall or can replace it on your system if you prefer to run only one. Privacy Service offers parental controls over incoming downloads and provides warnings whenever intrusions occur that might endanger your personal data, including data related to identity theft (it attempts to detect phishing attempts, for instance). VirusScan Professional, another bundle, includes VirusScan along with the company's anti-spyware and anti-spam utilities. Many of these programs are also bundled in the McAfee RedZone Suite, and these products offer access to the online scanning version of the anti-malware programs.

Also in the anti-malware business is Central Command (www.centralcommand.com), which offers a wide variety of utilities not only for Windows users but for numerous Linux and Unix systems as well. Vexira Antivirus is the utility that concerns us here. The key differentiating point for Central Command's products, as the company's name suggests, is that they're controllable over a network, and in that way they are clearly designed for business use. In fact, Central Command offers its Antivirus product for Windows Server networks as well as for Linux and Unix networks, and with all its products IT managers (or whoever serves that function in smaller companies) can keep all the workstations, and possibly servers, malware-free and guard the entire network.

Trend Micro's PC-cillin Internet Security (www.trendmicro.com) is a single product merging features similar to the suites mentioned previously. Well known for years as the antivirus program included with various newly purchased PCs, PC-cillin continues as a popular and critically successful antivirus program. The Internet Security package adds to this utility by including anti-spyware, anti-phishing, and such niceties as Wi-Fi intrusion detection (to help you determine whether someone is tapping into your Wi-Fi network), spam filtering, and a personal firewall. As with other vendors, Trend Micro offers a fully functioning 30-day evaluation copy from its Web site. It also offers a free online virus scan, as does Panda Software (pandasoftware.com/activescan).

Alwil Software (.avast.com) provides easily the most compelling argument for insisting that everyone you know install antivirus software. Its product, Avast Antivirus, is free, and is easy to use and well proven. You may not use Avast on a business system, however; for that, you'll need to purchase the Professional edition. The company also offers a PDA version of the utility because PDAs have increasingly become the targets of virus writers.

BitDefender (www.bitdefender.com) also offers a free version of its desktop antivirus product, BitDefender Client Standard. The free version, BitDefender Free Edition, offers a full range of antivirus capabilities, including scheduled scanning and automatic virus definition updates, and tosses in a very nice skins feature, allowing you to customize the interface in a variety of different ways.

Anti-Spyware Utilities

Despite the fact that nobody seems to know exactly what spyware is, anti-spyware packages have become increasingly numerous over the past 18 months. Many offer free versions, so your best bet is to select two or three, try them, and then try a few more, until you get one or two you especially like.

Tip

Because some spyware installations are (in effect) spyware of a sort themselves, albeit harmless, you should install anti-spyware programs only after using System Restore to set a restore point. This will allow you to turn back your system to the time of the restore point if you notice anything unusual (such as slowdowns) occurring in your daily work.

Spybot Search & Destroy (www.safer-networking.org) is one of the better-known spyware utilities, which is why I featured it in Chapter 3. But it's far from the only free utility out there for controlling spyware and adware. Among the others, also included in Chapter 3, are Microsoft's Anti-Spyware, and various "lite" versions of packages, the most famous of which is Ad-Aware SE (www.lavasoft.com). Other programs, such as Computer Associates' Pest Patrol (www.ca.com) offer a downloadable trial version, which scans your system but does not fully remove the offenders; for full functionality, you must purchase it (in other words, like trial versions of pretty much every other kind of software).

Several sites offer free malware scanning. Computer Associates is one of these; the scan is available at http://store.ca.com/v2.0-img/operations/safer/site/ab/promo53025.htm. Another is Ewido Networks (www.ewido.net/en/), which promotes its commercially available ewido Security Suite by providing an especially strong online scanner (which picked up details missed by the free Yahoo! toolbar scanner in my case). Another is PC Tools Software's Spyware Doctor (www.pctools.com/spyware-doctor). However, these services aren't really online scanners; instead, you download a program to your PC, install it, and perform the scan that way. This is nowhere near as convenient as the free antiviral scans available online, although to be fair those services also require a program download and installation — but as an ActiveX script, its installation is easier.

Spyware utilities are readily available for purchase. In addition to those already mentioned here, you can obtain the BPS Spyware Adware Remover from BulletSoft (www.bulletproofsoft.com), a package that includes firewall, phishing, and Trojan/worm protection and an especially useful utility package in the aforementioned Spyware Doctor from PC Tools. Spyware Doctor includes a pop-up blocker, a keylogger blocker, phishing and adware protection, and so on. Indeed, most of these packages guard against — and remove — numerous spyware-type threats.

Firewall Utilities

You have a good range of excellent choices when it comes to firewall protection. In addition to Symantec, McAfee, and Trend Micro, all mentioned previously, which include firewall protection as part of their security suites or as standalone products (in the case of Symantec and McAfee), and of course Microsoft, which has a firewall that ships as part of SP1 and SP2, numerous other vendors have developed strong firewall products.

Note

All firewall products state that they should be used exclusively, without other firewall software loaded. In fact, Norton Internet Security, upon installation, is quite insistent that you disable Windows Firewall, going so far as offering to disable it for you. The principle is that multiple firewalls can conflict with one another, leaving your system either more vulnerable than with one product, or possibly so protected that it becomes almost nonfunctional. In practice, you'll do best with a dual-firewall setup: one that comes with your broadband or wireless router and one that comes with a software package. But you can certainly have more than one software firewall running if you wish; just be prepared to deal with numerous messages, warnings, and configuration information screens as you perform your daily online activities.

Perhaps the best known of the standalone firewall utilities is ZoneAlarm (www.zonealarm.com), which offers its firewall product as a free product as well as a purchasable product, ZoneAlarm Pro, with additional features (including email security). In addition, you can get ZoneAlarm as part of the ZoneAlarm Security Suite, which includes antivirus, anti-phishing, and anti-spam software, and as part of a wireless security suite as well. ZoneAlarm is highly customizable, warns you continually of threats and intrusions (unless you configure it for silent protection), and works very well in conjunction with the firewall capabilities of most popular broadband and wireless routers.

Other firewall products operate similarly to those already mentioned. Kerio Personal Firewall (www.kerio.com) makes your desktop invisible to outside intruders, blocks pop-up windows and banner ads, and detects a wealth of hacker intrusions. Kerio specializes in enterprise-level products, and its desktop firewall products take advantage of that specialization. Tiny Software (www.tiny software.com) recently acquired by industry giant Computer Associates, offers Tiny Firewall, which watches all network activity, establishes intrusion protection as you work, and offers a tool called Track 'n' Reverse, which lets you see any changes to your files or your registry and reverse them so that your system is as it was before. Think of this as a kind of System Restore at the microlevel, and you have the idea.

Another full-featured product is Sygate Personal Firewall (www.sygate.com), available as a free download for the Standard version or by purchase for the Pro version. Sygate's product offers an especially usable interface and an out-of-the-box configuration that makes it easy for even beginners to get a firewall established. By all means, try out the Sygate and ZoneAlarm freebies before making a firewall choice.

Testing Your Setup

How do you know you're actually safe? To test your firewall, visit Gibson Research Corporation (www.grc.com) and follow the links to ShieldsUp! This site runs numerous free, fast online tests of common vulnerabilities. Another free online tester can be found at www.pcflank.com. Testing your browser's vulnerabilities is the job of the free Browser Security Test (http://bcheck.scanit.be/bcheck). GFi will send a free series of email messages to you with attachments intended to expose holes in your email software (gfi.com/emailsecuritytest).

Microsoft has a free, heavy-duty Baseline Security Analyzer (microsoft.com/MBSA) available for download. It is intended to "detect common security misconfigurations and missing security updates on your computer systems."

Part II

Avoiding Disaster

Chapter 4

Backing Up
Your Data

I t's the great truism of computing: Back up your data. Everybody knows it, yet many ignore it. Computers work so smoothly most of the time, especially the part about saving files to the hard disk, that days, weeks, even months go by before people start getting antsy about having all those files sitting on their drives without a backup anywhere in recent memory. Partly this is the fault of the hard drive manufacturers because they keep making their products more reliable, but mostly the fault lies in the emergence of PC as a widespread, commonly used appliance. Except in business settings, where backups tend to occur far more regularly, computers today are partly about convenience and entertainment, and convenience and entertainment just don't go well with the forethought that regular backups demand.

Then again, maybe the computer manufacturers and operating system designers deserve some of the blame. If backing up files has such great importance, why is it avoidable at all? Why don't computers come with built-in backup systems that kick in automatically? The answer, of course, is that such things cost money, and computer makers constantly strive to keep prices as low as possible. Except in business, once again, people tend to see data backup as optional or as something that affects everyone else but not them, so they don't want to pay the extra money for the backup equipment. So, without a federal law — possibly an international one — forced backups won't likely happen. Too bad, really.

As the owner of a Windows XP system, you have several backup techniques at your disposal, but some require the purchase of additional software and, in some cases, additional hardware as well. This book's premise lies in the ability to perform important day-to-day functions from within Windows XP itself, so it covers these other options in the "Utilities" section at the end of Part Two. The more serious your backup needs, the more you should consider third-party solutions, but you can work very well with only the techniques available with the operating system. This chapter outlines each of those techniques and shows how you can use them to develop a usable and effective backup strategy.

Backup Basics

There's nothing magic about backups. Backing up data means, at the very least, making a copy of that data. In others words, if you have a copy of a file, you have a backup of that file. Knowing this, however, leads to the three primary questions about backups:

- Where do I put the copy?

- How do I make the copy?

- What do I do if I need to recover the copy?

The methods outlined here answer these questions in various ways. No matter which method you use, the principle of data backups never changes. Having only the original copy of a file is the same as having only the original copy of your most important legal documents or photograph collection. To prevent the disaster or disappointment of losing this copy, you make a copy of the item and store it in a location where (a) you'll be able to find it, and (b) it will be safe from problems affecting the original.

The answer to point (b) matters a great deal. If you store your backup files on the same hard drive partition as the original, you lose both if, for any reason, you reformat or otherwise lose access to the partition. You're quite a bit better off storing them on separate partitions of the same hard drive because most actions affecting one partition have no effect on the other, but you still lose them both if the hard drive fails. To gain any sense of real security, you should save your backups to a separate storage device, such as a tape drive, a CD-RW drive, or a DVD burner, or a separate hard drive. You can even store backup files on floppy disks, amazingly still the default for Microsoft's own Backup Utility (covered later in this chapter), but unless you have only really small files to back up, floppies work only as an emergency backup device.

A Guide to Backup Media

Each storage medium offers advantages and disadvantages, as the following sections demonstrate.

Floppy Disks

Floppy disks are used primarily for backup of small files, such as text files and simple word processing files.

ADVANTAGES

They are inexpensive and readily available, including all those you've collected over the years and no longer need.

DISADVANTAGES

Each floppy stores only 1.4MB of data, so a typical MP3 song would require three or four of them. Your data files alone, unless you write exclusively text files, likely require dozens of floppies for a backup. Furthermore, because you must stay at your PC to swap floppies in and out of the drive during backup, long backups tend to be extremely tedious.

RECOMMENDATION

Not worth bothering with except for backing up only a few small files.

Compact Discs

Compact discs (CD-Rs and CD-RWs) are typically used for regular backups of fairly large files and folders, including multimedia files such as graphics and music.

ADVANTAGES

Almost all new PCs ship with CD-RW drives, and if you don't have one, you can get a new one for $100 or less. Discs are also inexpensive. CD backup software is plentiful, and each CD holds roughly 650MB of data. In addition, once you've completed your backup, you can easily copy the CDs to store in another location entirely.

DISADVANTAGES

650MB sounds like a lot until you start backing up hard drives of 60GB or larger, in which case, you will easily need 80 to 100 of them. Furthermore, CD media tends to deteriorate in quality, so you shouldn't rely on only CDs as your backup method. Also, not all CD drives read all CDs correctly.

RECOMMENDATION

Good choice for backup, especially for PCs with an existing CD player but a fairly small hard drive. Even better if you don't intend to add another hard drive any time soon.

Digital Video Discs

Digital video discs (DVDs) are typically used for regular backup of fairly large files and folders, including multimedia files such as graphics and music.

ADVANTAGES

DVDs store much more than CDs, 4.7GB compared with 650MB for CDs. You can create decently sized limited backups, particularly of important data files and program downloads you need in case of reinstallation. Software that comes with DVD burners usually includes backup utilities, and DVD media prices are dropping along with the burners themselves. As with CDs, you can make copies of DVD backups, providing an easy method of getting a second backup.

DISADVANTAGES

Competing standards (that great computer industry oxymoron) provide the major problem with considering DVDs as your primary backup technology. DVD+RW, DVD-RW, DVD-RAM: choose wrong, and you might have a bunch of unusable backups only a year from now. DVD-RAM probably works best for backup purposes, but not all DVD burners even support DVD-RAM. Price is a current issue, but it is becoming less important with each passing month. Finally, even though DVDs can hold 4.7GB of data, a full backup of a new 120GB hard drive requires a couple dozen.

RECOMMENDATION

Very good choice, better than CDs given the storage capacity. However, DVD burners are roughly twice as expensive as CD burners, and DVD media are about twice as expensive as CDs. Furthermore, only the most recent backup software recognizes DVDs as backup media.

Separate Hard Drives

Separate hard drives are usually used for regular backup of partial or entire hard drives.

ADVANTAGES

With the price of hard drives dropping (at least in cost per gigabyte), and with the speed and ease of backup to a hard drive, if you can afford this method, you should adopt it immediately. You can install an internal drive for this purpose and, in doing so, give yourself the greatest backup speed of all. For not a great deal more money, however, you can buy a large FireWire or USB 2.0 external drive and experience not a great deal of speed difference (USB 1.0 or 1.1 is another matter entirely from a speed standpoint). You can perform regular backups that are easily located when you need to restore them, and in the case of an external drive, you can take the entire backup to another computer as well. Finally, hard drives offer much greater storage capacity than any other method demonstrated here, so you can back up entire hard drives in one easy step without the need to monitor the process.

DISADVANTAGES

Internal hard disks can be difficult to install. Other than that, the only disadvantage to this method is that fact that, when you need more hard drive space for your system, the temptation arises to use the backup drive, and in the process you could possibly wipe out the backups.

RECOMMENDATION

This is your best choice for extensive backups, bar none. Hard drives are less expensive than they've ever been, with a 120GB drive typically selling for $100–$130 or so. Put two of these in your system, and you can back up your entire system nightly if you wish, using any of today's backup packages. Give yourself an extra drive for your daily work, and you can back up the main components of your system to the third drive. And so on. Internal drives are less expensive than external drives, but the latter are also dropping in price regularly. For example, at the time of this writing, online stores are selling Maxtor 80GB external drives for $99. At this price, a small business could maintain one internal drive worth of data and two external drives, each with the same backup data, for a truly secure system. That same small business, on a network, could back up the primary data from all PCs to one large hard drive, rendering the cost even lower.

USB Thumb Drives

Also called Pen drives and Flash drives, these USB drives are compact and easy to carry, and they work extremely well for limited backups.

ADVANTAGES

USB thumb drives are extremely small, they weigh next to nothing, and they offer a surprisingly large amount of storage (1GB and higher). In most cases, Windows XP recognizes them as soon as you plug them into your USB port, and you can use them as you would any other folder on your PC. Many public computers (at universities, for example) have USB ports available for this function, so it's easy to take your documents with you, plug the thumb drive into another PC, and keep working.

DISADVANTAGES

They store too little data to function as a major backup solution. They work best only as a place to store backups of important documents, a valuable function to be sure but not the only one you'll want to consider.

RECOMMENDATION

Whatever backup system you decide upon, include this as an added component. They're great when working on PCs other than your own, so that you can save to the thumb drive instead of the PC's own hard drive, and they have become the predominant technology for transporting a limited number of files from place to place. At $50 or so for a 256MB drive and $80 for 512MB, you really can't go wrong.

Tape Drives

Tape drives are typically used for full regular backup of partial or entire hard drives.

ADVANTAGES

Tape drive support is built into all backup software, because backup software over the years has assumed this method. Tapes are reliable and longlasting, and methods have been well developed over the years. Furthermore, because tape is used *solely* for backup purposes, you won't be tempted, as you might with a secondary hard drive, to use the tape for other purposes.

DISADVANTAGES

A good tape drive costs between $200–$300, and you might have to install a controller card as well. Furthermore, you don't usually find them in the standard computer stores. Media (tapes) can be relatively expensive as well. You must install the tape drive and configure it to get it working. Retrieving data can be slow because of the frequent need to switch tapes.

RECOMMENDATION

If you have a tape drive already in place, keep it. If not, you're better off with an extra internal or external hard drive. Tape drives and media were once the primary backup technology for businesses, but they have become increasingly costly (compared to other technologies) and even difficult to find.

Network Drives

Network drives provide a wide range of backup functions.

ADVANTAGES

Backing up to a network drive means placing your data in the safest place possible: on another computer entirely. If you control the network completely, this method works much like the secondary hard drive option. You can schedule regular backups easily, and you can protect them from other users using network security options. This method is faster than all other methods except secondary hard drives, as long as the network is fast.

DISADVANTAGES

If you use both computers, your backups take up space on the network drive. Furthermore, if you don't have full access rights on the network computer, your ability to restore backed-up data depends on the person who does. Also, if the network experiences a slowdown, so will your backup.

RECOMMENDATION

For business purposes, network backups are highly recommended. With them, you can restore your network's data quickly and easily, and you have full control over it. For home purposes, network backup is less useful because it's usually easier simply to back up each machine locally, but they can provide a strong option for controlled backup.

Third-Party Backup Options

Because of the importance of data backup, numerous companies produce specialized backup software. Backup utilities offers advanced features in the following areas in order to differentiate it from the Windows Backup utility and from software included with CD and DVD burners:

- Support for all current media types, including all DVD formats, Zip disks, Pen storage, and so on

- Highly specific backup selections, combinations of files and folders in any location

- On-the-fly compression of files, to provide reduced file sizes in the backup

- Automatic comparisons of data after the backup, taking a number of forms

- Support for multi-CD or multi-DVD backups, with a single backup spanning as many discs as necessary

- Detailed backup schedulers

- Detailed methods of including or excluding file types

- Backup from remote computers

In addition, some backup utilities now include the technology known as *ghost imaging*, or just plain *ghosting*. A ghost image captures the entire hard drive, backing it up to the point where you can restore your entire system from it. This technique represents an important difference from data backup in that the image can include partitioning information and other files, such as the Master Boot Record (MBR) that backup utilities do not. If you're serious about backups, you should combine a backup utility with a ghosting utility; this combination offers as close a guarantee as possible that you will be able to restore lost data.

Copying Files Manually and Automatically

Nothing substitutes for the ease and reliability of copying files manually. If you have a separate folder for your most important data files, for example, simply copy the entire folder to a separate hard drive, a CD-RW or DVD, or a network drive. If you want to save a bit of disk space, send the folder to a compressed folder first and then copy the zipped folder to the backup location.

To copy files for backup purposes, use Windows Explorer by clicking Start, right-clicking on My Computer, and choosing Explore. In the double-pane interface, locate or create the folder you wish to copy the files *to* in the left-hand column; then, in the main window, click the files or folders you wish to copy. Right-click on the items (you can multiple-select and do this), and drag them to the backup folder, choosing Copy from the context menu. After Windows has finished copying, click on the backup folder to ensure that all the files are there.

Tip

If you copy an entire folder, you can perform a quick validity check by right-clicking on each folder in Windows Explorer and choosing Properties. The Properties dialog box displays not only the size of the folder in megabytes or gigabytes (5.24GB in this example) but also the number of files and subfolders the folder contains (1,537 files and 22 folders in this example). If the Properties dialog box of both the original and the backup folders display the same numbers, in all likelihood your backup has worked. To be even more certain, however, spend a few minutes exploring both folders to check for the same filenames, the number of file types, and any other comparative feature you want to check. If one or more files or subfolders are of particular importance, check these diligently, to the extent of opening several backup files to be sure.

Using the Backup Utility

Although Microsoft doesn't draw much attention to it, Windows XP contains a perfectly useful backup utility. Although sporting as unimaginative a name as the Windows team could possibly have dreamed of—it's called Backup Utility—this program provides enough features that you won't likely need to consider third-party backup utilities until you know your specific needs and can shop for one accordingly. If you own Windows XP Professional Edition, you can find Backup Utility by clicking the Start button and looking in the All Programs → Accessories → System Tools folder.

Windows XP Home Edition owners have the Backup Utility, but it might not be installed. If it is not, you can install it manually from the XP installation CD. Put the CD in your CD drive, open Windows Explorer, and install the utility from the ValueAdd folder.

Like all such programs, Backup Utility contains two major functions: backing up data and restoring it. The wizard opens by having you choose between the two functions and takes you through the process of your choice. You can switch from Wizard mode to Advanced mode by clicking the "Advanced Mode" hyperlink on the wizard's opening screen, and you can switch back again by choosing the Switch to Wizard Mode option in the Tools menu of the Advanced Mode interface. Here we'll work with the Wizard.

In the first step of the Backup Wizard, you select what you want to back up (see Figure 4-1). The My Documents and Settings option automatically chooses your My Documents folder as well as your

Favorites, Cookies, and Desktop folders. Assuming that you have saved all your data in My Documents, this selection backs up everything you have created on the PC and, therefore, functions well for a periodic backup. If your data files reside elsewhere, however, and your email data almost certainly will (not even Microsoft's own email programs store their data in these folders), you will want to customize the backup further. The second choice on the screen, the Everyone's Documents and Settings option, simply extends the selection to include the same data from all user accounts.

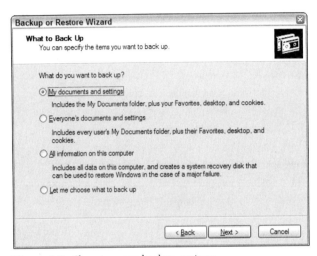

Figure 4-1: Choosing your backup options.

The last two choices show the two extremes of your backup options. If you choose the All Information on This Computer option, you instruct Backup to copy everything on your PC to your backup device. If you have backup media with sufficient space available, you should perform such a backup once, after which you can add to it. If you have a computer with even one large hard drive, let alone the increasing likelihood today of multiple hard drives, choosing this option takes a great deal of time and, more importantly, a great deal of media. If you plan to back up to your CD-RW drive, prepare for a long, drawn-out, and CD-consuming session. Practically speaking, backing up your entire system works only when you have a second hard drive or a good tape system to work with.

By comparison, the fourth choice, the Let Me Choose What to Back Up option, offers the greatest flexibility. Choosing it and clicking Next reveals the Items to Back Up window (see Figure 4-2), with a folder tree of the PC on the left and the items inside the selected folders on the right. Open the folders on the left, choose the items you wish to copy, and click Next to move to the Backup Type, Destination, and Name screen. Here, you choose your backup media by clicking the Browse button and navigating to the device where you want to store the backup. You can also label the backup, an especially good idea if you intend to keep more than one type of backup. The Backup program automatically time-stamps and date-stamps the backup file, so you don't need to include the date here (otherwise an obvious choice), but labeling your backup is still a good idea.

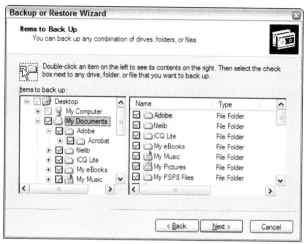

Figure 4-2: Selecting the items to copy.

One extremely useful set of options appears unfortunately almost buried beneath the Advanced button. Clicking this button reveals a drop-down menu consisting of five backup types:

- **Normal:** Copies the selected files into the backup file, marking them as backed up. This is the standard form of backup, but not necessarily the best for your purposes.

- **Copy:** Copies the files only, without marking them as backed up.

- **Incremental:** This extremely useful option backs up the selected files only if you have created or modified them since you last backed them up. In other words, this option saves time and disk space by examining the current files in the backup and copying only the files in those same folders that were not there last time or that bear a later date and time. If you perform regular backups, this is probably your best choice.

- **Differential:** The same as Incremental, but it does not mark them as backed up.

- **Daily:** Not a bad habit to get into, this type backs up any files that were created or modified today, and only if they reside in the folders chosen for this backup. If you store your word processing files in My Documents, for example, and you have already backed up My Documents, running the Daily backup each day (as its name clearly wants you to do) backs up any new and changed files in My Documents.

The next screen of the wizard gives you three more backup choices. With the Verify Data After Backup option, you instruct the program to compare the data in the original folders with the data in the backup file to guarantee the accuracy of the backup. Obviously, this is an excellent choice to make, but the comparison can increase the length of the backup session by double or more. Also available on this screen is the Use Hardware Compression, If Available option in which Backup will interact with your hardware to compress the files to save space (if your hardware does not support compression, the option is grayed out). The third choice, the Disable Volume Shadow Copy option, prevents Backup from copying files if you are currently working with them (for example, a spreadsheet open on your desktop). Check this option only if you intend to copy the files manually later.

Clicking Next opens the Backup Options dialog box, as shown in Figure 4-3. Here you make a choice if you already have a backup on your selected backup drive and if Backup finds identical file names. You can opt to append the new backup to the existing files or to replace the existing files with the new ones. The safer bet is Append, but Replace consumes less disk space.

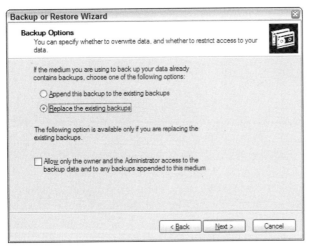

Figure 4-3: The Append or Replace option.

Finally, you decide when to run the backup: now or at a later scheduled time. Clicking the Later option reveals a scheduler; here you can click the Set Schedule button and make a number of selections. In addition to the date and time, you can click the Show Multiple Schedules box and set a number of scheduled backups. If you click the Settings button, you can give additional commands to the backup program (actually to the Windows Task Scheduler), instructing it (see Figure 4-4) to stop if the task runs longer than a specified number of hours, allowing it to start only if the computer has been idle for a specified number of minutes, and preventing the backup from starting when the computer is running on batteries.

Once you have even a single backup saved, you can access its contents by using the Backup Utility to restore it. You can do so using the Restore Wizard or the full program. Open the full program by starting the wizard normally and clicking the Advanced Mode link in the middle of the Welcome screen. This action yields the Welcome screen of the full program, and clicking the Restore and Manage Media tab gives you access to the restore process. You can restore the entire backup, but more typically you need only specific folders or even just certain files. Use the two panes to choose precisely the items you want.

Next, choose where you want to place the restored files. By default, Backup restores them to their original location, but by clicking the drop-down menu below the leftmost pane, you can choose to restore the selected file or folder to an alternate location, or, if you wish, you can restore all selections

to a single folder instead (making them easy to keep track of). In the Options dialog box (Tools →
Options), you can choose what to do if, during Restore, the Backup Utility finds a file with an identical name in the restoration folder. By default, Backup does not replace that file, but you can instruct
it to do so, or to do so only if the restored file is newer than the file already there.

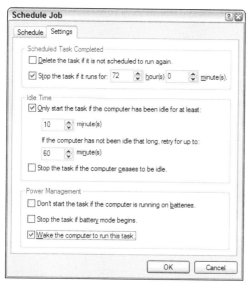

Figure 4-4: The Settings dialog in Backup.

Using the Recycle Bin as a Backup Assistant

The Recycle Bin takes its name, of course, from the recycle bins that you use (well, *should* use) every
day of your life. It stores your unwanted documents, memos, folders, and other items until you
decide to empty it. Your PC's Recycle Bin on your computer, however, is much more sophisticated
than the real-world bins: It acts as a safety net for your deleted items. Each time you decide to delete
an item from your computer, the item is placed in the Recycle Bin and remains there until you
choose to delete it permanently. If you mistakenly delete your résumé, for example, or an earlier version of a report you suddenly discover you need again, you can easily restore them to their original
location as long as you haven't emptied the bin.

The Recycle Bin as Backup?

How is the Recycle Bin a backup medium? It's not, of course, at least not in the sense that you would
normally consider one. When you consider, however, that the purpose of backup media is to let you
restore files after the originals no longer exist, the Recycle Bin offers some fascinating possibilities. It

functions, after all, like a rudimentary backup system, providing a guarantee against loss. By adjusting its characteristics, you can give yourself another way to help you reclaim missing data.

You do so by controlling the size of your recycle bin and the schedule for emptying it. Because items in the Recycle Bin use up disk space, Windows allows you to configure the size of each Recycle Bin (Windows assigns one to each hard drive), thereby limiting the amount of disk space that deleted items can take up. To change the storage capacity of the Recycle Bin, right-click on the Recycle Bin icon on your desktop and choose Properties. Move the slider to increase or decrease the amount of disk space that you want to set aside for deleted items. You can also use different Recycle Bin settings for different drives by clicking Configure drives independently, or you can opt for a single size for all drives by clicking Use one setting for all drives.

The first stage in using the Recycle Bin as a backup tool consists of resizing all the hard drives to make them larger than you would normally want them. While you use extra disk space as a result of enlarging them, you increase the chances that the Recycle Bin will be able to store all your deleted files. The size of your Recycle Bin matters for two reasons. First, as a hard drive begins to fill up, Windows automatically reclaims space for that drive from the Recycle Bin by deleting files from it, starting from the oldest and moving forward. Second, if a deleted item is larger than the capacity of the Recycle Bin, that item will be permanently deleted without being saved. To allow the Recycle Bin to back up your files, you must ensure that it can accommodate a significant amount of data. For example, if you want the Recycle Bin to keep your Movie Maker files available for restoration once you've deleted those, you'll need an especially large bin.

Using the Recycle Bin

When you no longer need a specific file or folder because the contents are outdated or you have already backed the information up to disk, you can move that item to the Recycle Bin. To delete an item, right-click on the item and choose Delete, or select the item and press the Delete key, or drag the item to the Recycle Bin icon on the desktop (or in Windows Explorer).

Each time you send an item to the Recycle Bin, Windows displays a confirmation message. You can prevent these confirmation messages from opening by right-clicking the Recycle Bin icon on the desktop, choosing Properties, and clearing the check box labeled Display Delete Confirmation Dialog.

Now here's where the backup possibilities kick in. Because the Recycle Bin is nothing more than a folder — albeit a folder with specialized characteristics — you can restore items that you have placed in it (by dragging or by deleting). When you restore an item from the Recycle Bin, you instruct the computer to return the item to the location from which you initially deleted it. For example, if you deleted a folder called Training from the Company Procedures subfolder of your My Documents folder, when you restore that folder, Windows places it back where it came from.

To restore a deleted item, navigate to the Recycle Bin, right-click the file that you want to restore, and then choose Restore.

Tip

To restore several deleted items at the same time, hold down the Ctrl key on your keyboard and then click each item that you want to restore. When you have finished selecting all the items, choose File → Restore in the Recycle Bin. If you restore a file originally located in a folder that you have since deleted, Windows will recreate that folder in its original location, and restore the file to that folder.

When the Recycle Bin is full, you can empty it by double-clicking on the Recycle Bin icon on your desktop and choosing File → Empty Recycle Bin. But if you wish to use the Recycle Bin as a backup device, you obviously don't want to do this. In fact, when using the Recycle Bin as a backup device you'll need to monitor it frequently to make sure that you're not losing files you might need later. Keep watch on how full the Bin is because if you try to send a file to it that is larger than the space available, Windows will complain and force you to resize the Bin or delete the file. It's all too easy to hit the Delete option and lose the file for good.

Caution

You can permanently delete an item without sending it to the Recycle Bin. If you hold the Shift key down while deleting an item — by right-clicking on the item and choosing Delete or by holding the Shift key as you drag it to the Recycle Bin — you bypass the Recycle Bin entirely and delete the item in a way that retrieving it, if at all possible, requires the use of specialized command-line tools. For obvious reasons, you should avoid this method of deleting files if you plan to use the Recycle Bin as a secondary backup tool. However, if you want to ensure that other users do not find your deleted files, by all means permanently delete them.

Summary

Backing up matters. In fact, it matters as much as anything in your computing life. Use the Backup Utility in Windows XP regularly, and, just as important, make manual backups of important folders and files at least once a week. Never let yourself get caught in a situation where you have no backup copies of important files you're currently working on because that's just inviting disaster. Your data is just too important.

Chapter 5

Windows Update: Letting Microsoft Protect Windows XP for You

You can do a great deal of work to protect Windows XP on your own, but Microsoft has a vested interest in helping you along. Contrary to the image sometimes presented by disgruntled users as well as the computer press, Microsoft really does want its software to work well. (Not well enough to prevent you from buying the next version, of course, but then, no software company can afford that much excellence.) Like other companies, but on a huge scale and with more watchful eyes on it, Microsoft continually offers updates to Windows XP, correcting bugs and plugging security holes. Usually, they work. When they don't, the company posts a further update.

To update, patch, and add to Windows XP, turn to Windows Update. This chapter examines three essential elements of Windows Update: automatic updates, security patches, and service packs.

Using Windows Update

Windows Update acts as the central resource for software updates to the Windows XP operating system. You can still download some of this software and install it manually by visiting the Microsoft downloads site at www.microsoft.com/downloads, but even if you download everything you can find on this site related to Windows XP, you still won't have the most up-to-date version of the operating system. Windows Update contains not only additional downloads, but also updates and patches stored nowhere else. Furthermore, Windows Update performs all necessary actions automatically. It scans your Windows installation to collect information about the version numbers and dates of Windows files and components and then, after you accept its suggestions, starts the download process on your computer and completes the task by installing these items automatically.

To access Windows Update, open Internet Explorer (yes, you must use IE version 5 or higher to access Windows Update) and go to www.windowsupdate.com. Alternatively, you can choose Windows Update from IE's Tools menu. Figure 5-1 shows the result, the front page of the Windows Update site, with its choice of Express or Custom updates.

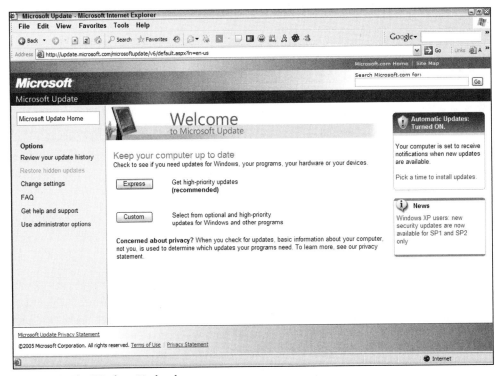

Figure 5-1: The Windows Update home page opens.

Exploring Privacy Issues

Before choosing an update link, click the Windows Update Privacy Statement link at the bottom of the screen, and read Microsoft's statement of what information Windows Update collects during the updating process. After the reassurance that None of this configuration can be used to identify you, the privacy statement lists the details about what is collected, including the following:

- **Operating system version number:** The version number of Windows XP itself, indicating to Windows Update whether, for example, a service pack download should be made available.

- **Internet Explorer version number:** The version number of Internet Explorer, used to determine if specific Internet Explorer downloads or service packs need to be included on the list of available updates.

- **Version numbers of software for which Windows Update provides updates:** The version numbers for Windows Messenger, Backup Utility, and numerous other programs covered by Windows Update.

- **Plug and Play ID numbers of hardware devices:** Identification for hardware devices connected to your PC, allowing Windows Update to determine which hardware drivers to include as part of the available updates listing.

- **Region and language setting:** Your geographical location, used by Windows Update to determine which language options and alternatives to list.

- **Product ID and Product Key:** Information about Windows XP itself, to determine if you have a legal copy. If you do not, Microsoft retains the information for possible future action.

According to the privacy statement, Windows Update does not collect names, addresses, email addresses, or any similar personal information. The process, though, generates a Globally Unique Identifier (GUID) and stores it on your hard drive (much like a cookie) to track whether the downloads and installations succeed. Microsoft compiles much of this information to generate overall statistics, and the privacy statement continually reassures you that it gathers no information whatsoever that points to you. Of course, you can choose whether to believe these reassurances.

Note

Many people take exception to the way Windows Update scans their hard drives, not wanting any outside agent collecting information from their PCs. This is thoroughly understandable; In many ways, Windows Update provides another example of Internet intrusion. You have two things to consider if you think this way. First, Microsoft's market position makes it particularly susceptible to analysis and examination by government, the press, and the public. If it does anything weird, questionable, or otherwise untoward with a tool as ubiquitous and powerful as Windows Update, the company will likely get hammered from many directions. You can probably feel as assured as you can about anything that Microsoft has no plans to abuse Windows Update by scanning your hard drive and stealing information from you (the company already knows how to get your money, after all). Second, Microsoft typically makes its most important updates — those related to security — available by conventional download as well as through Windows Update, so to keep your Windows XP installation safe (if not completely up-to-date), you don't need Windows Update at all.

To have Windows Update do what it deems necessary — scanning your system to see what requires updating and implementing that analysis automatically — click the Express button. To choose for yourself which elements to update, click the Custom button.

Scanning for Updates

If you are accessing Windows Update for the first time, you'll need to install some software from Microsoft to have the site scan your PC. Figure 5-2 shows the page you'll be shown when you arrive at the site, complete with a button for installation of the software.

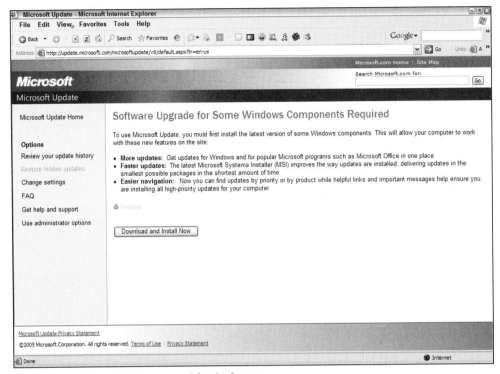

Figure 5-2: Windows Update accessed for the first time.

To begin the update process, click either the Express or the Custom button. After a minute or more, Windows completes the scan and presents its results in a statement that Windows has — or has not — located updates for your system. The Express update locates only critical updates and recommended updates, while the Custom option (see Figure 5-3) displays, in the pane on the left, the number of available updates under the categories discussed in the bulleted list below. For both types of Update, if Windows has determined that updates are available, you can click the Review and Install Updates link to see precisely what the service has located. As you add items to the update list (using the Custom feature), the numbers to the right of the Review and Install Updates link increase to reflect the number of items, the cumulative size of the files, and the time it will take to download them.

The first statement you see tells you what, if any, critical updates are available, and the second states whether other, noncritical updates are available. The left side of the main screen, as also shown in Figure 5-3, contains three choices under the Pick Updates to Install link.

The three choices are:

■ **High Priority:** By far the most important examine category, these downloads update Windows to guard against significant possibilities of crashes and other malfunctions and to provide greater security for your PC. Many critical update downloads consist of patches designed to correct security flaws discovered because of system break-ins by intruders, while others plug security holes that Microsoft has discovered through testing. Service packs, which are High Priority items) are discussed in the "Understanding Service Packs" section later in this chapter.

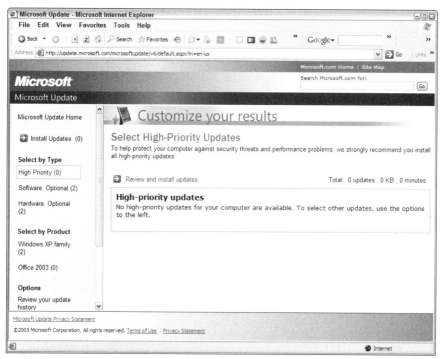

Figure 5-3: Windows Update after the Custom scan.

    ■   **Software, Optional:** This is a catchall name for any number of noncritical updates, rang-
ing from new features to changes to programs included with the Windows installation. The
five updates referenced shown in Figure 5-2 covered issues ranging from USB availability
and wireless network security to the Advanced Network Pack—a collection of files providing compatibility with Internet Protocol version 6—and a package supporting the new
HighMAT format for creating CDs. None of these can be construed as critical to the operation of your PC, so they get lumped together under a separate category. You can install as
many or as few of these updates as you want.

    ■   **Hardware, Optional:** Hardware drivers for devices attached to your system, including
video cards, sound cards, removable drives, modems and network cards, printers and
scanners, and so on. These are Windows signed drivers, meaning that they have passed
Microsoft's approval tests. You can install as many or as few of these as you want.

Selecting Updates

Click any of the links to begin the process of selecting updates from that category. To choose the
Windows Update items to install, scroll through the list and click the Add button for the updates you
want. Windows Update displays the number of updates you've chosen at the top of the main window, beside the Review and Install Updates link, and also on the left with the identically named link.

You can click either link to see what you've selected and to remove any items from your selections, as shown in Figure 5-4.

Note

Windows Update automatically selects all critical updates for inclusion in your download and installation. You can remove these if you want, but you have very little reason to do so. Critical updates are important.

When you're satisfied with your choices for download and installation, click the Review and Install Updates link, and then click Install Now. Windows presents you with the End User License Agreement and lists the updates to which it applies. Clicking Accept begins the final process (if you don't accept the agreement, Windows Update closes). A dialog box displays the download and install progress for you. Typically, the Install portion takes longer than the download — in fact, a great deal longer than the download if you have broadband Internet access. However long it takes, the process often slows other programs in Windows while it is taking place, so the best approach to completing a Windows Update with numerous selections is to start the downloads and go make yourself a snack.

After installation, Windows might instruct you to reboot your computer. As always, you can ignore it if you want, but something on your system might not work right as a result. Remember that, especially in the case of critical updates, you've just altered Windows XP itself.

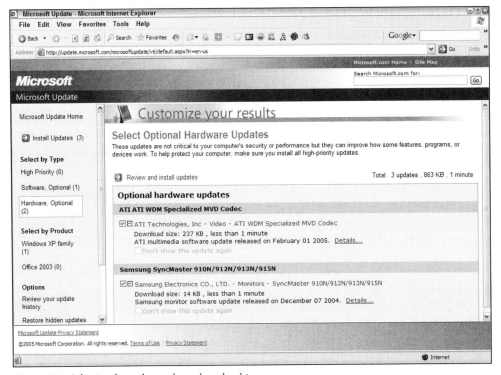

Figure 5-4: Selecting from the ready to download items.

Setting Up Automatic Updates

In an ideal world, computers would update themselves and not bother you about it. You'd wake up in the morning to a refreshed and revamped system, and everything would work just a little better than it did the night before. Of course, you'd have to trust whoever did the updating, and you'd have to know that the updates would always work to your benefit, but if you could get past those obstacles, automatic updates would represent a kind of technological paradise.

Windows Update provides an automated service, and while not exactly nirvana, it works well, particularly because of the importance of critical updates. You can set up Windows XP to download and install updates without any intervention on your part. The automatic update system covers only Windows itself, not third-party programs or other utilities, and it functions more or less as you'd hope an automatic update feature would.

To set your configuration, open the System Properties dialog box from the Control Panel (double-click either System or Automatic Updates) or by right-clicking My Computer and choosing Properties). Select the Automatic Updates tab (see Figure 5-5).

Figure 5-5: Set up your automatic updates.

To have your PC help you (or not) with automatic updates, check one of the following options:

- **Automatic (recommended):** Windows handles its own updating. At the time you schedule, using the drop-down menus to specify frequency and time of day, Windows connects to Windows Update, downloads any available updates, and installs them. Only High Priority updates are acquired in this fashion; to get optional updates, you still need to visit the Windows Update site.

- **Download but let me choose:** Windows downloads the updates and then asks if you want to install them.

- **Notify:** Windows checks the Windows Update site for available items and informs you if it finds any. A dialog box appears identifying the updates and asking if you want to download and install them; you can postpone the process until later if you wish.

- **Turn off Automatic Updates:** Shuts down the Automatic Update feature. You should consider this one only if you have the self-discipline to remember to visit Windows Update frequently to update your PC manually. Lots of people don't (me, for instance).

Choosing Automatic provides two benefits. First, it does everything for you. Second, it does not interfere with your work; as long as you are not actually working at the computer during the scheduled update time, you do not experience slowdowns or the sudden appearance of dialog boxes. The disadvantage, of course, is that you don't control the process. Of all the options, this one demands that you trust Microsoft most.

Understanding Security Patches

Windows is the most frequently attacked operating system in the world. Why? Theories proliferate, but most pundits agree on two major reasons: Windows has too many security holes, and attackers tend to dislike Microsoft. Whatever the reasons, Microsoft is forced to issue security patches for Windows with alarming frequency, making them available on the Windows Update site as well as through download pages and third-party sites. Quite simply, Microsoft wants the patches out there, readily available in many Internet locations, so that Windows users can download them, install them, and, in doing so, ward off the intruders.

Note

You can use Windows Update to download and install security patches and service packs automatically. If you dislike using Windows Update or want to keep manual track of the additions to Windows XP.

Your first stop is the Microsoft site itself (www.microsoft.com). Whenever the company releases an important patch for Windows, it informs visitors to Web site, either on the home page or on the Windows front page (www.microsoft.com/windows). If you see a new patch highlighted on one of these pages, click the link to its download page.

Numerous other sources also provide information about the latest security patches. For example, the *PC Magazine* Web site (www.pcmag.com) updates its news stories, and it places news about important Windows patches at the top of the list. Other computer news sites such as Newslinx (www.newslinx.com) and eWeek (www.eweek.com) also provide these details, and you can subscribe to them (free) to get the headlines delivered to your inbox. All major newspapers feature patch stories as well, so subscribe to your favorite (again, the free online version) and read about security downloads as information about them becomes available. (In the process, you can learn a great many other things about the world as well—always a nice extra.)

Installing a security patch in this manner differs from installing it using Windows Update. Once you've reached the download site, click the download link to begin the process. When the File Download dialog box appears, you have two choices: Open or Save. For the greatest ease, click the Open button. When the download finishes, the file launches automatically and prepares the installation. If you feel at all unsure about security, save the file to your hard drive, and then locate the file and double-click it to launch it.

Understanding Service Packs

Microsoft occasionally makes available a full suite of upgrades that are collectively known as a *service pack*. Service packs collect all updates released since either the previous service pack or the release of the product itself. In the case of Windows XP, Service Pack 1 (SP1) included a huge array of fixes as well as a few new features, including built-in support for the USB 2.0 hardware specification. Since SP1, Service Pack 1a appeared, addressing a few issues only, and Service Pack 2 (see Figure 5-6) is now available to add an array of security enhancements that Windows users have been demanding. For more information about SP2, go to www.microsoft.com/windowsxp/sp2.

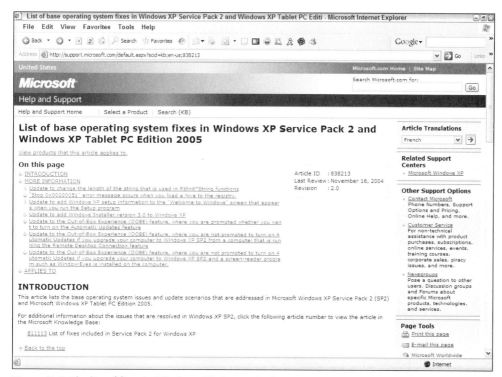

Figure 5-6: The list of fixes in Windows XP Service Pack 2.

If you don't want to engage Windows Update too often, one sensible strategy is to use Windows Update for Windows XP critical updates only and then wait for the rest of the updates until the next service pack is released. As with security patches, you can find notices about Windows service packs on the Microsoft site and all the computer news sites, as well as, frequently enough, the major newspapers.

Whatever update strategy you choose, when a service pack becomes available, you can install it in two ways. Microsoft makes its service packs available on Windows Update with a one-click download and installation, certainly the most convenient method. If you prefer, either because you don't like using Windows Update or because Windows Update does not work well on your system, you can install the service pack as follows:

1. In Internet Explorer, go to www.microsoft.com/downloads. In the section called Search for a Download, type **service pack 2 for IT professionals** in the Keywords field and click Go. On the resulting page, click the link to Windows XP Service Pack 2 for IT Professionals. The page for this version of the Service Pack appears (see Figure 5-7).

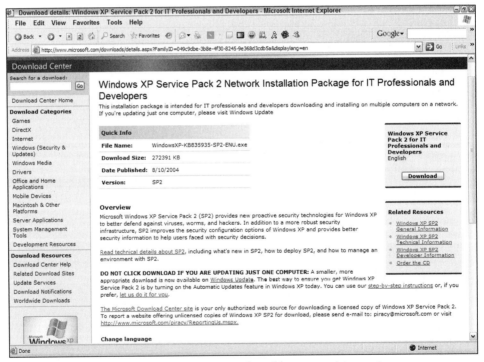

Figure 5-7: The service pack download page provides information and instructions.

2. Click Download.

3. Save the file to a location of your choice on your hard drive.

4. With the download complete, locate the file and double-click it. The service pack installation begins.

Microsoft Office Update

Although it is not part of Windows XP, many people associate Microsoft Office (now Microsoft Office System) with Windows anyway. They have a very good reason for doing so: Office or one of its components (most often Microsoft Word) frequently ships with new systems. As it turns out, they have yet another reason for associating the two, because Office has an update site very much like that of Windows XP. Unlike Windows Update, however, Office Update does not offer an option to download and update new files automatically. You need to do so manually.

To update your Office software, open Internet Explorer and go to http://office.microsoft.com. Click the Downloads link on the left, and look on the page for the Check for Updates link (usually at the top right). Like Windows Update, Office Update then scans your system for Office software. Office Update lists the available updates in a column on the right side of the browser window, beginning with any Office service packs. These service packs are entirely unrelated to Windows service packs; Office service packs contains fixes and patches only for programs in the Office suite of software.

Make your selections, and then click Start Installation. Internet Explorer downloads the software and runs the update program, applying the components to your Office applications.

One important note here, though: By the time this book is published, Office updates will be included in Windows Update. There will no longer be a need to look elsewhere for updates to your popular Microsoft software. However, accessing Office Update directly will still work.

Tip

If you connect to the Internet through a dial-up modem, downloading the service packs can take hours. If you prefer, you can order the service pack on CD by clicking the link at the bottom of the Service Pack page.

Summary

With your operating systems, you want continual support, and support comes frequently in the form of fixes, patches, and add-ons. Windows Update provides the easiest method for keeping your Windows XP installation current, but if you prefer, you can perform certain elements of the update manually. This is especially true of security patches and service packs, which are downloadable from the Microsoft Web site and elsewhere. (Third-party software contains its own similar update processes, some of it Web-based, some of it merely the application contacting the download site, and you owe it to yourself to keep it as current as possible as well.) While software has always undergone updates and revisions, the fast and easy Internet connections of today mean that no software is ever truly finished or completely up to date. In the case of Windows, given its susceptibility to ever more inventive forms of intrusion and hacking, Microsoft's recognition that it's never completely finished is surely a good thing.

Chapter 6

Recovering from Windows XP Problems

Y ou might get through month after month of Windows XP use without experiencing any difficulties. Don't bet your house on it, but it could happen. More likely, however, you will
encounter problems with your Windows XP installation once, twice, and perhaps more times during
the course of a few months' activity, and you might very well need to categorize some of these problems as serious. This chapter features a wide range of reasonably simple techniques for dealing with
problems as they occur. Reasonably, that is, because any time your computer malfunctions, no matter what kind of computer it is or which operating system it runs, your life takes a turn for the distinctly *uneasy*. Windows XP experiences fewer problems than earlier versions of Windows, but you'll
still likely experience your share, so these problem-solving techniques can come in handy.

Is Windows Really More Breakable Than Other OSs?

Does Windows really malfunction more than other operating systems? Certainly, listening to Apple
Macintosh owners or Linux users, you would assume the innate fragility and/or unreliability of
Microsoft's operating systems.

Mac owners have a good point: The Mac breaks down very little, freezes rarely, and generally causes
almost no problems. What they neglect to mention, however, is the reason for this. Although it's
possible that Microsoft hires programmers inferior to Apple's, it's unlikely. So, the reason has to lie
elsewhere, and indeed two major ones come to mind. First, early Windows versions were built on the
MS-DOS operating system, which was never intended for the complexities that Windows demanded of
it. With Windows XP, however, MS-DOS is gone, for all intents and purposes; so, what else might cause
the problems? The answer, predominantly, is the attempt Microsoft has made to provide compatibility
with the many thousands of products released over the years for the PC market. Most Windows
problems at the desktop level result from hardware device conflicts, but the reality of the PC market is
that third-party hardware products will always be with us. By comparison, very few companies
produce hardware for the Macintosh, and Apple maintains a tight control over those that do. Even so,
the Apple community today is experiencing problems with third-party software for its newest operating
systems, so the compatibility argument seems even more appropriate.

Continued

Is Windows Really More Breakable Than Other OSs? *(Continued)*

Linux is also more stable than earlier Windows versions, at least at the server level — or so the reports indicate (although arguments against this notion definitely exist). On the desktop, today's Linux distributions probably show roughly an equal stability with Windows XP, perhaps a little better than equal. However, what it gains in stability it loses in ease of use, particularly when it comes to installing software and updating programs (and the operating system itself). Linux has come a long way, but it still remains harder to use than Windows. And yes, it crashes and, in fact, it will do so as you install programs from a variety of vendors and programmers.

Without question, however, Windows XP is the most stable Windows to date — far more stable than Windows 95, 98, or Me — and offers far more software and hardware compatibility than Windows 2000. And that's the important point.

This chapter covers a variety of methods for recovering from problems with your Windows XP installation, beginning with the precaution of using System Restore to take a snapshot of your system in running order.

Using System Restore to Avoid Headaches

If you take only one idea away from this book to apply to your Windows XP experiences, take this: System Restore can save your sanity. Before installing anything on your computer, hardware and software alike, load System Restore and set a restore point in case anything goes wrong. If your computer starts acting strangely afterward, you can open System Restore again and restore your machine to that point. In fact, train yourself to set a restore point once a week or so, even when your PC works perfectly because Windows deletes your restore points after 90 days by default. In other words, if you look up one day and your PC works, capture the moment.

Note

System Restore also deletes restore points when you disable it on your main drive or when you reinstall the operating system. It also deletes restore points selectively as your hard drive fills up, deleting the oldest points and leaving the most recent intact as long as possible.

System Restore is so important, in fact, that Microsoft has configured it to set restore points automatically. The utility functions in the background, monitoring your system and waiting for an event to trigger it. Automatic triggers include the following:

- Every 24 hours (configurable)
- Whenever you install a software program
- Whenever you install a hardware device with an unsigned driver

▨ Whenever Automatic Update installs software

    ▨ Whenever you use the Windows Backup Utility to recover data

This list seems reasonably exhaustive, but a number of events can occur that make adding your own restore points a very good idea. For example, if you install a new program, Windows XP automatically creates a restore point at the moment you begin the installation. If you later restore your PC to that moment, that program's files and registry settings will disappear. Any data files you have created remain in place, so that causes no concern. But if you've performed other installations in the meantime, particularly of nonprogram software, such as media files or other add-ons, to get rid of them using System Restore you might have to back up all the way to the moment before installing that important application. More important, setting your own restore points lets you restore your system to precisely the point you want, helping you avoid any unwanted deletions.

To set a restore point, follow these steps:

1. Choose Start → All Programs → Accessories, select the System Tools folder, and click System Restore.

2. On the Welcome to System Restore screen (shown in Figure 6-1), choose the Create a Restore Point option and click Next.

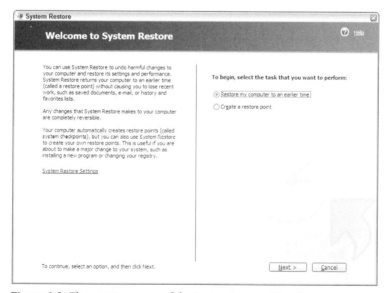

Figure 6-1: The opening screen of the System Restore Wizard.

3. On the next screen, type in a descriptive name for the restore point. If you are setting a restore point to install the program Quicken, for example, you might name it **Before installing Quicken**. The instructions on the screen tell you that System Restore will add the current date and time to the restore point, so you don't need to include that information in the description.

4. Click Create to set the restore point. Windows responds with a screen confirming the new restore point and showing you the time, date, and description. Click Close to exit System Restore.

Restoring to an Earlier Time

Whenever you find Windows performing strangely, particularly if you've recently installed new hardware or software, you can turn back the clock to one of your restore points. Open the System Restore utility, and on the Welcome screen click the Restore My Computer To An Earlier Time option. Clicking Next takes you to the Select a Restore Point screen, as shown in Figure 6-2. By default, System Restore highlights the most recent restore point you've set on the current day, and you can click any date and read the description to see which point you want to use. In fact, Figure 6-2 shows two possible points, the most recent taking place before the installation of the audio software and the other an automatically set restore point (roughly three hours before) that Windows calls a *System Checkpoint*.

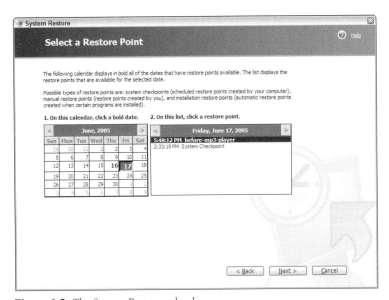

Figure 6-2: The System Restore calendar.

Tip

To determine whether you should use a specific restore point, click on that point and then on each high-lighted calendar date after that time. If you see an installation of either hardware or software on a date (or even just a time) later than the selected restore point, you will lose that installation. In the case of hardware, keep in mind that after the system restoration Windows will try to install the drivers automatically. As long as you have them available, you can quickly reinstall them. If Windows Update has installed software, however (System Restore notes this activity in the description), you will need to return to Windows Update and reinstall the program.

After choosing the restore point you want, click Next. Figure 6-3 shows the resulting screen, with a warning to close any open programs and save data. It also informs you that it will shut down Windows and restart with the settings of the time shown in the restore point description. Specifically, it restores the registry and all necessary system files to their earlier state. Performing these replacements rolls back any changes made by the new installations, an extremely important point — especially if the changes were intentionally harmful, as with some viruses, worms, and spyware.

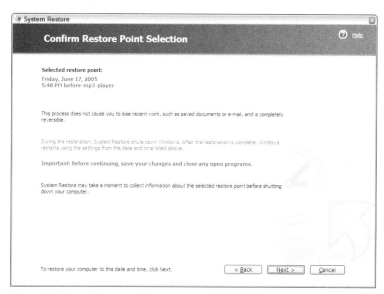

Figure 6-3: Last chance to change your mind about restoring your system.

Tip

If you have trouble loading Windows XP, you can still use System Restore. Following the instructions in the "Safe Mode and Other Startup Menu Options" section later in this chapter, boot your computer into Safe Mode. When the interface appears, Windows informs you that you are about to enter Safe Mode and asks if you wish to launch System Restore to restore Windows to an earlier point instead. If you go past this point, you can load System Restore from the System Tools menu as well.

Configuring System Restore

You can configure System Restore to work more to your liking. You should consider doing this if you want to give System Restore more or less hard disk space and if you want to change the default settings for creating automatic restore points and for deleting saved points. By default, System Restore reserves 12% of each hard drive for its restore points, it sets an automatic restore point (that is, a system check-point) every 24 hours, and it starts deleting restore points after 90 days. You might decide that you would rather keep your restore points for 6 months (180 days) instead of 90 days, and you need to give System Restore more disk space to do so. If you want to keep the disk space as it is, you can achieve the same goal by increasing the interval between automatic restores to 48 hours instead of 24.

You can configure the amount of reserved disk space via the System Properties dialog box. Open System Properties from the Control Panel or by right-clicking the My Computer icon and choosing Properties. Click the System Restore tab to begin your configuration, and the dialog box shown in Figure 6-4 appears.

Tip

To open the System Properties dialog box from the keyboard, press Winlogo+Break.

Figure 6-4: Configuring the System Restore utility.

By default, System Restore monitors all hard drives, using a specific amount of disk space on those drives to do its work. If you'd prefer not to use the utility at all, check the box at the top of the dialog box to turn off System Restore for all drives. Alternatively, you can disable System Restore on each drive individually by highlighting that drive, clicking the Settings button, and checking the Turn Off System Restore on This Drive option (see Figure 6-5). When you do this, Windows excludes that drive from the entire process so that you cannot back that drive up to an earlier point. Programs installed to that drive, however, will still be affected by a restoration if you installed them after the date on the restore point. Windows resets the registry to that date, and the restored registry will no longer include information about the application in question.

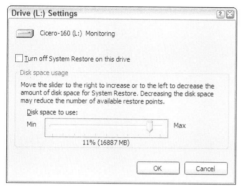

Figure 6-5: Changing the disk space allotment for restore points.

Figure 6-5 shows not only the disabling option but also the slider for changing the amount of disk space used for restore points on that drive. Move the slider left to decrease the reserved space and to the right to increase it. For System Restore to work most effectively, and especially if you install software or hardware (or both) regularly, set all drives to their maximum disk space allotment and let the utility back up everything it possibly can.

Changing the default intervals for automatic creation and deletion of restore points is considerably more involved, primarily because it demands that you edit the registry in all its intimidating glory. If that weren't enough, you also have to do the multiplication necessary to convert days into seconds.

Caution

Because editing the registry can cause your system to malfunction, you should always back it up before you make any changes. To back up the registry, open the Registry Editor by clicking Start → Run and typing **regedit** in the Run box. In the Registry Editor dialog box, choose File → Export. Check the All button under the Export Range heading at the bottom of the dialog box in order to back up the entire registry. If you have a FAT or FAT32 file system, save the registry file on that drive so that you guarantee access to it if you need to restore it. Restoring the registry is a matter of loading Windows XP into Safe Mode (see the next section), opening the Registry Editor, choosing File → Import, and locating and opening the registry file. Then simply reboot, and Windows should work the way it did before.

The following steps let you change the intervals for both automatic creation and deletion of restore points:

1. Click Start and choose Run. Type **regedit** in the Open field and press Enter to launch the Registry Editor.

2. Expand the folder called HKEY_LOCAL_MACHINE by clicking its plus sign (+).

3. Expand the Software folder in the same way, and then scroll down to the Microsoft folder and expand it as well.

4. Scroll to the Windows NT folder and expand it, and then click the CurrentVersion folder.

5. Scroll to the System Restore folder and click it. Figure 6-6 shows the result, a list of keys in the right-hand pane.

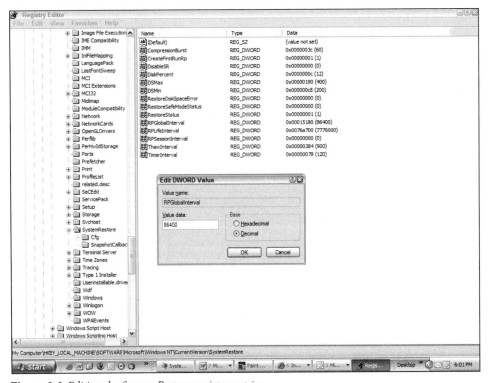

Figure 6-6: Editing the System Restore registry entries.

6. To change the timing of the automatic restore point setting, right-click the RPGlobalInterval key and choose Modify.

7. In the resulting Edit DWORD Value dialog box, click the Decimal radio button, revealing the value as 86400. This is the number of seconds that pass between each automatic

restore point: 86,400 seconds equals 24 hours. You can change this value to anything you like, but bear in mind that the time calculated is based only on when the PC is powered on and Windows XP is running. For example, if you want to increase the amount of time to 48 hours, type **172800** in the box and click OK. The Edit DWORD Value dialog box closes, and the Data column in the Registry Editor reflects the change.

8. To change the amount of time that expires before Windows automatically deletes a restore point, follow the procedure in step 7, but this time, modify the RPLifeInterval key instead. The default value, 7776000 seconds, equals 90 days. To double this value so that restore points hang around for six months, type the value **15552000**.

9. Reboot to set these values. Note that you do not have to save the Registry Editor itself. As soon as you make the changes, the registry changes.

With System Restore functioning precisely the way you want, you're ready to take your system back in time if negative things start happening. Now you can concentrate on installing your hardware.

Safe Mode and Other Startup Menu Options

The vast majority of the time when you launch Windows XP, you get to the Welcome screen after a few minutes of loading time. Sometimes, however, you don't get there at all, and other times you want to stop the OS to try to repair something before it enters full boot mode. For this reason, Windows XP offers a Startup menu, an unadorned screen with white text on a black background, no mouse support, and a series of options designed to let you troubleshoot the OS.

Accessing the Startup Menu

You can access the Startup screen in three different ways: by forcing it to appear, launching it from a dual-boot menu, or configuring it to appear via the System Configuration utility.

On a system containing a single installation of Windows (that is, most PCs), you must normally time a key press to force the Startup screen to appear. Specifically, hold the F8 key down as your computer boots. Before pressing the key at all, however, you should wait until after the PC has run through its BIOS check and is about to load Windows itself (yes, it takes timing). If you don't wait, you could fill up the keyboard buffer, causing the computer to beep; if this happens, release F8, wait for a couple of seconds, and try again. Furthermore, don't get frustrated if you miss the opportunity and Windows starts to load normally. Mistiming has happened to everyone who's tried this method.

On a dual-boot system (a PC containing at least two Windows installations), accessing the Startup menu takes much less precision. Wait for the boot menu to appear, use the arrow keys to move the highlight to the OS you want to launch, and press F8. A list of startup options follows. Select the Startup mode you want and press Enter, after which you are returned to the first screen. Press Enter again to launch the selected OS in the selected Startup mode. The only timing issue here is pressing F8 before the default operating system launches automatically, typically after a 30-second wait.

If you have Windows XP loaded and functioning, you can use the System Configuration utility to command Windows to restart in one of the Startup modes. To do so, open the utility by clicking Start, selecting Run, typing **msconfig** in the Open box, and pressing Enter. When the System Configuration

Utility dialog box opens, click the BOOT.INI tab to access the Boot Options interface (see Figure 6-7). Here you can force Windows to load in the following different ways, each of which is explained later in this chapter:

- **/SAFEBOOT:** This option boots Windows XP into Safe Mode, with one of the following options:

  - **MINIMAL:** Standard Safe Mode (the default option). It is available on the Startup menu as Safe Mode.

  - **NETWORK:** Safe Mode with networking enabled. It is available on the Startup menu as Safe Mode with Networking.

  - **DSREPAIR:** On systems with the Active Directory enabled, booting with this option lets you make repairs to the Active Directory. It is available from the Startup menu as Directory Service Restore Mode.

  - **MINIMAL (ALTERNATESHELL):** This rather fancy name simply boots Windows into Safe Mode with a command-line prompt only, with no graphical interface. It is available on the Startup menu as Safe Mode with Command Prompt.

- **/NOGUIBOOT:** Windows does not display the Windows XP splash screen during the boot process. This is useful if you really loathe the Windows logo. It is unavailable on the Startup menu.

- **/BOOTLOG:** Windows logs every activity during the boot process, creating a file you can examine for loading errors. It is available on the Startup menu as Enable Boot Logging.

- **/BASEVIDEO:** Boots Windows with the default VGA driver, giving you an unattractive screen to look at; however, by avoiding your video driver, this method is helpful in sorting out problems with your graphics card. It is available on the Startup menu as Enable VGA Mode.

- **/SOS:** Windows displays the name of each driver as it loads, helping you determine which drivers might be causing problems. /SOS slows boot time considerably because it also checks your hard disk's file system as Windows loads. It is available from the Startup menu as Debugging Mode.

In the System Configuration utility, click the option you want and then the Close button. Reboot your PC, and Windows boots as instructed.

Note

When you've finished troubleshooting Windows, return to the System Configuration utility and uncheck your choices. Until you do so, Windows will continue to load in the specified boot mode.

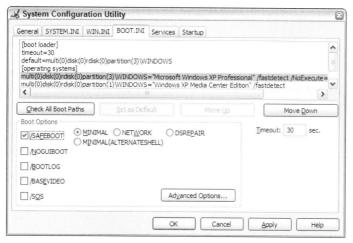

Figure 6-7: The BOOT.INI tab on the System Configuration utility.

Windows provides another way to access Safe Mode, but not a way that you choose. When Windows attempts to load but fails (even if you manually restart in the middle of a boot-up), a truncated version of the Startup menu appears automatically on the next boot attempt.

Safe Mode

The most common reason for accessing the Startup menu is to launch Windows in Safe Mode. Safe Mode is exactly what its name indicates—a safe means of starting your Windows XP system. In this context, the word *safe* means, more than anything else, certain. You won't get your full system up and running, but what you do get will work. From Safe Mode, you can troubleshoot your system, adjust your configuration, uninstall programs, and, as long as you select the Safe Mode with Networking Option, access online help over the Internet.

Note

Sometimes your system will not even let you boot into Safe Mode. If this condition persists, often your only choice is a reinstallation of Windows XP (see Appendix B). Before resorting to such an undertaking, however, turn your computer off for a couple of hours and try booting again. If it still doesn't work, and if you have a boot floppy—even from an earlier Windows version—boot with it and then reboot to try Windows XP once more. There's no real technical reason why such techniques work, but sometimes they do. Maybe even operating systems need a rest.

Safe Mode works by launching Windows with only the files, settings, and drivers necessary for it to operate. Specifically, it loads the basic Windows files along with standard drivers for keyboard, mouse, monitor, and devices such as your hard drives. It dispenses with third-party drivers and inessential drivers you might have installed after initially setting up the OS, and it also bypasses many of the settings stored in the Windows registry. In other words, it loads a minimal version of Windows, one that can function on all standard PCs, largely independent of the hardware and software installed in a particular PC.

The effectiveness of Safe Mode lies in the fact that most of the problems affecting the Windows boot process result from the hardware and software specific to that PC, not from the standard, unadorned Windows environment. If you've installed a new video driver, for example, and you no longer get an image on your monitors, entering Safe Mode tells Windows to bypass the newly installed video drivers and revert to the good old SVGA drivers, which are unquestionably boring but nearly always functional. With Safe Mode running, you can uninstall those drivers and then install an earlier version of them on restart.

Of course, Safe Mode has a built-in strike against it: If you need it, that means you're having problems. As a result, you see it only when you've already tried everything you could think of to fix your system and failed. Because you typically turn to it only in emergency situations, you might consider working with it regularly just to maintain familiarity with it. Enter Safe Mode periodically, navigate your way around (especially to the Windows configuration utilities and dialog boxes), and then shut down and boot normally. That way, when disaster strikes you'll be ready.

Safe Mode with Networking

To use Safe Mode most effectively, choose the Safe Mode with Networking option. Doing so loads Windows with the same minimal configuration as standard Safe Mode, except that it loads your networking hardware and software. This gives you access to, among other things, the networking protocol (TCP/IP) that connects you to the Internet. This mode is especially useful for downloading updated drivers to help you get your system working properly, but it can also be a godsend if Windows refuses to load normally but you desperately need to check your Internet email or to log on to your company network. If networking problems led you to Safe Mode in the first place, though, choosing Safe Mode with Networking obviously stops being a good idea.

Safe Mode with Command Prompt

If you know how to use MS-DOS commands (if you need to ask, you don't), Windows provides a startup mode you'll find useful for certain purposes. Choosing Command Prompt Only from the Startup menu loads Windows without the graphical user interface (GUI) — or, you might say, without Windows itself. You end up with a minimal system, far fewer drivers and registry instructions than usual (and thus far fewer potential system conflicts), and a command prompt staring you straight in the face and waiting for you to type something. You still need to log on — use an Administrator account for this purpose (see Chapter 24 for details on creating accounts) — but once there, you can copy files, restore system files, and much more. The problem is that you'll have no help system to guide you.

Enable Boot Logging

The Windows XP boot logging option instructs Windows to create a text file that keeps track of the drivers and system services that load with the OS. If Windows fails to load, you can enter Safe Mode and examine this file to determine where the launch process has been failing. You can load the file into Notepad or WordPad and scan through it to see any loading exceptions. Most importantly, you can examine the end of the file to see which driver was the last one that Windows tried to load. Frequently, this driver is the problem—the one that stopped the OS in its tracks. Using the Device Manager dialog box in System Properties, you can delete the driver, or, in the case of drivers for older products, you can edit the system files using the System Configuration Utility (click Start and choose Run, and then type **msconfig** and press Enter). By doing so, you can stop the offending driver or process from loading and, in many cases, allow Windows to launch without it.

After you've booted your system with the Enable Boot Logging option, Windows creates a log file named ntbtlog.txt. You can find this file in the main Windows directory (but again, only after you've used a Boot Logging startup). As you read it, you'll notice that the vast majority of drivers in the list are displayed as loading properly. But the log file stops at precisely the spot where Windows stopped the loading process.

Enable VGA Mode

Sometimes, the latest driver for your graphics card proves not quite ready for everyday use by causing unwanted video problems. If you've recently updated your video driver and Windows is displayed badly or not at all, try booting with the Enable VGA Mode feature from the Startup menu. In this mode, Windows uses the same video driver it uses when it launches in Safe Mode, but Enable VGA Mode (unlike Safe Mode) keeps all other drivers and registry settings active. You end up with a Windows that looks bad but performs just fine in every other regard. From here, you can uninstall the video driver, reboot, and either restore the old one yourself or let Windows attempt to do it for you automatically as it boots.

Last Known Good Configuration (Your Most Recent Settings That Worked)

Safe Mode represents the most important diagnostic tool in the Windows XP arsenal, but you have other startup options at your disposal when booting a malfunctioning Windows XP system. In fact, before you trying Safe Mode, call up the Startup menu and select the option labeled Last Known Good Configuration. Each time Windows starts normally, it saves the configuration information in the registry, updating it once again only when another normal startup takes place followed by a user login and a clean shutdown. If you install drivers or programs and immediately afterward Windows does not start properly, choosing Last Known Good Configuration rolls back the changes and, in many cases, allows Windows to boot properly.

Although Last Known Good Configuration resembles Safe Mode in its ability to help you get Windows XP running again, they work in considerably different ways. Safe Mode bypasses numerous drivers and registry settings in order to load a bare-bones version of the OS. By comparison, Last Known Good Configuration loads the full operating system, complete with all the drivers and registry entries you've created since first installing Windows; but instead of the most current version, Last Known Good Configuration loads the most recent one that booted successfully. Use Safe Mode when you need to make changes to your system; use Last Known Good Configuration when you want Windows to attempt to correct itself.

Controlling Your System with Task Manager

Back in the days of MS-DOS, if you wanted to reboot your computer you either pressed the Reset button on your computer case or, as many people quickly discovered, you gave your PC the three-fingered salute. This term, oddly enough never officially adopted by Microsoft despite its widespread use, referred to the Ctrl+Alt+Delete combination that resulted in a restart (called a warm reboot) of the operating system. Ctrl+Alt+Delete was used, quite simply, when you could do nothing else but start over.

Ctrl+Alt+Delete lives on in Windows, albeit with a somewhat different function. These days, the three-fingered salute results in the Windows Task Manager appearing on screen, one of whose functions remains, indeed, to shut down the system when you can't do so through the Start menu. Rather than initiating a brute-force, all-or-nothing shutdown, however, the Task Manager lets you shut down each program individually, indeed even some open windows within a particular program individually. Because it interacts directly with the Windows XP system, Task Manager has the capability to close programs and windows you cannot close through the usual methods, such as clicking the Exit button or choosing Close or Exit from the File menu.

You can launch the Task Manager by pressing the Ctrl+Alt+Delete key combination or by right-clicking the Taskbar and choosing Task Manager. Figure 6-8 shows the Task Manager Applications tab on a system running several programs simultaneously. To close a program in the list, select it and click the End Task button. If the program is currently busy, a dialog box asks if you want to shut it down immediately; if the program has been causing problems by acting strangely or running slowly, say yes to unload it from memory. The Task Manager helps you most by letting you shut down programs that have crashed; they appear in the window with the status Not responding.

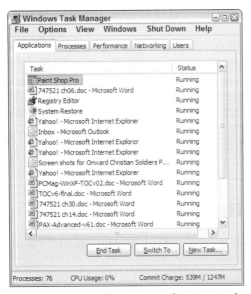

Figure 6-8: The Task Manager Applications window.

Figure 6-9 shows the Processes tab of Task Manager. Here you can see the computer processes currently active in your system. All programs run processes, as do numerous elements in the operating system itself. As with the Applications tab, you can click on any process shown here and stop it by clicking the End Process button. One of the main benefits of the Processes tab is that many items appear here that do not appear as full programs on the Applications tab, and you can learn quite quickly which processes you can shut down to save memory. If you don't work regularly with Acrobat reader, for example, terminate the Acrobat.exe process (near the top of the window in Figure 6-9). Similarly, if you're not planning to use the DVD drive to play movies, you can terminate cine-tray.exe. Before doing so, however, check the System Tray to see if the icons for these programs appear there, and close them normally instead. Ending a process via the Task Manager can result in program crashes and even complete system crashes. But when all else fails, with your system behaving erratically or extremely slowly, try ending some recognizable services and see if doing so clears up the problem.

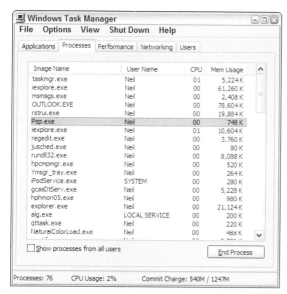

Figure 6-9: The Processes tab in Task Manager.

Sorting Out Problems with Virtual Memory

As your hard drive begins to fill up, Windows frequently starts running more slowly. The reason for this is quite simple. Windows continually swaps data from the hard drive into system memory and back again, and it needs part of your hard disk to work with in this manner. Windows calls this disk space *virtual memory*, and it calls the file to which it saves and extracts data a *paging file*. As you work with Windows, the paging file expands and shrinks as the operating system requires, but as you fill up your hard drive, you can render the paging file less and less useful.

Windows rarely tells you when the paging file gets too small. It does, however, inform you when your hard drive is nearly full, and it tells you if it cannot perform a task because it has run out of memory. Sometimes these messages are related; your paging file has reached its minimum size because your hard drive has filled up and Windows needs more memory than the paging file allows in order to run its programs. When you see this warning, keep in mind that not only will you soon run out of disk space (usually when you're trying to save the most important document of your life), but you are also affecting the performance of everything on your system.

You can help your virtual memory's cause in a number of ways:

- Remove programs from your system by accessing the Add/Remove Programs utility on the Control Panel.

- Remove data from the hard drive to give the paging file more disk space.

- Change the default size of the paging file to ensure that you never shortchange Windows.

- Move the paging file to a location you won't touch.

- Delete the paging file and let it reconstruct itself.

With the first option, cleaning unneeded items off your hard drive, you help yourself in numerous ways. You get more disk space and so does the paging file. Chapter 22 discusses various methods of reducing the data on your drives, but nothing replaces the good old Delete key. If you don't want to delete the files and folders, and if you have another partition (or another hard drive) with space available, move the files to that partition. Windows ties the paging file to a specific drive, and as long as that drive contains enough room for the paging file to act as a memory store, it continues to work just fine.

To work directly with the paging file, open the System Properties dialog box by right-clicking on My Computer and choosing Properties (or pressing Winlogo+Break). Click the Advanced tab, followed by the Settings button in the Performance area. Click the Advanced tab on the resulting Performance Options dialog box and look at the Virtual Memory area at the bottom. Here, you see the current size of the paging file, as well as a Change button if you want to reconfigure it. Clicking Change yields the Virtual Memory dialog box shown in Figure 6-10.

This dialog box shows all the partitions on your system, as well as an interface for changing the size of the file. Unless you have a reason to set the initial and maximum size of the file, click the System Managed Size radio button to let Windows XP control the size of the file on its own, increasing and decreasing it as required by current memory needs. Figure 6-10 shows a paging file set to 768MB as the initial size (roughly 1.5 times the amount of system RAM in the PC), with a maximum size of twice that amount. The benefit of setting the initial file size is that this size acts as the minimum size as well; when Windows controls the paging file, it will let it get much smaller. But Windows also uses maximum size to the best possible effect, so if you have plenty of hard disk space, the System Managed Size option remains the best.

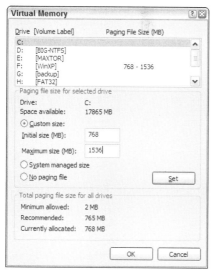

Figure 6-10: Configuring the paging file.

If you have a large hard drive, you can deal with the paging file extremely effectively by creating a separate partition 3–4GBs in size and assigning a system-controlled paging file to that partition (see Appendix A for details on creating partitions). Unless you install over 2GB of RAM in your system (unlikely today but possible by the time the next version of Windows appears), you'll never need a larger paging file. Because it's on a separate partition, and assuming that you can avoid actually using that partition for data storage, your paging file will work as well as it possibly can in a Windows XP system. Once you have a partition available for the paging file, you can assign the paging file to that partition via the Virtual Memory area of the Advanced tab of the Performance Options dialog box.

If you experience numerous out-of-memory messages or low-virtual-memory messages, your paging file might have become corrupted. Locate the file named pagefile.sys (typically in the root folder of C: drive), delete it, and then reboot your PC. Windows automatically generates a new page file during the boot process, this time without the corruptions.

Using the Automated System Recovery Wizard

The Windows XP Backup Utility contains a little-known feature called the Automated System Recovery Wizard. Using this feature, you create a backup of your system files on CD, DVD, or other backup media of the system partition. If you later experience a major system crash, you can effectively put Windows XP back in working order the way it was, albeit without any programs or data files you might have lost because of the crash.

To create this backup, open the Backup Utility from the System Tools folder by clicking Start and choosing All Folders→Accessories. On the resulting Welcome screen of the wizard, click the Advanced Mode link. Figure 6-11 shows the Welcome page of the Backup Utility, with the Automated System Recovery (ASR) Wizard displayed as the third option on the screen. Clicking the ASR Wizard button takes you into the wizard itself.

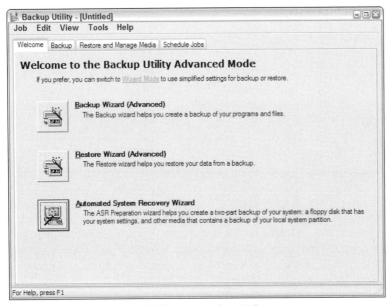

Figure 6-11: The choices available in the Backup Utility.

Click Next on the wizard's Welcome screen and browse for the location where you want to store your backup—a CD-R or CD-RW disc, an external hard drive, a tape drive, and so on. Click Next to begin the backup process. The Backup Utility requests media during the backup (CD-ROMs, DVDs, and so on), so be sure to have them ready.

If your system crashes and you can no longer load Windows, use this backup to make the necessary repairs. Locate the disk you just created, as well as the media for the backup itself. Finally, find your Windows XP installation CD. Put the Windows installation CD in the CD-ROM drive, turn on your computer, and press a key when prompted to start the installation from the CD. When you see the notice on the Setup screen to press F2 for an Automated System Recovery session, do so. Put the disc in your CD or DVD drive when instructed, and follow the process to recover your system.

Establishing Security with EFS

The Encrypting File System (EFS) offers an exceptional degree of security for your data. While the Windows XP firewall protects your PC from external intrusion, if someone does manage to break in the EFS renders any stolen data effectively useless. When you encrypt a file, you apply an encryption algorithm to it — EFS uses both expanded Data Encryption Standard (DESX) and Triple-DES (DES3) for its encryption — and in order to use that file, it must be decrypted. Once you've enabled EFS for a folder or file, Windows XP performs these actions behind the scenes, encrypting when you save the file to disk and decrypting when you load the file into a program. If you hold an Administrator account for a PC (or several PCs), you can enable EFS for the good of everybody without anyone even noticing it's there.

Note

The Encrypting File System works only on NTFS formatted disks. In fact, if you copy or move a file from an NTFS disk to a FAT32 or FAT disk, you remove the encryption entirely. For that reason, it makes little sense to use a FAT32 partition as a backup location for an NTFS partition that contains EFS-enabled folders and files, unless you can remove the FAT32 partition from the PC (as in the case of an external hard drive).

The EFS works through a trio of keys. Each file contains its own *file encryption key*, assigned when first encrypted and required to decrypt the file later. For further security, EFS encrypts the file encryption key as well, and anyone wanting to use the file needs the *public key* of the user who created the file or of any other users specifically authorized to do so (not even computer administrators can access another user's encrypted files without this authorization). The person who then tries to decrypt the file can do so only with a *private key* that matches the public key. In effect, the private key unlocks the public key, which in turn unlocks the file encryption key. Only with all the locks removed can the person use the file in an application.

Encrypting and Decrypting Data

To encrypt a file or folder, follow these steps:

1. Open Windows Explorer or My Computer, and navigate to the file or folder you want to encrypt.

2. Right-click on the file or folder, and choose Properties.

3. Click the Advanced button on the resulting Properties dialog box.

4. On the Advanced Attributes dialog box, check the Encrypt Contents to Secure Data option and click OK. See Figure 6-12.

5. Click OK on the Properties dialog box to begin the encryption process.

After clicking OK, another dialog box appears. If you apply the encryption to a folder, you get the Confirm Attribute Changes dialog box (see Figure 6-13).

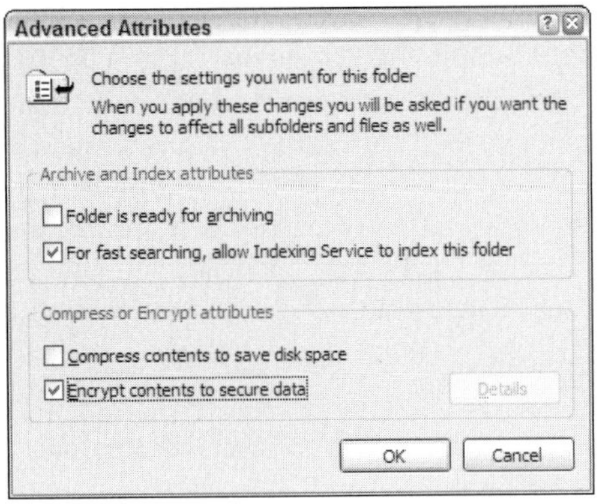

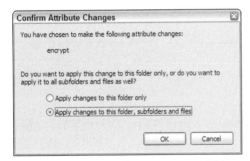

Figure 6-12: Enabling encryption for this resource.

Figure 6-13: Choices when encrypting a folder.

This dialog asks if you want to encrypt the folder only or, as a default, the folder and everything inside it — all files and all subfolders as well. When you apply encryption to a file, the Encryption Warning dialog box appears (see Figure 6-14), explaining that if you encrypt the file but not the entire folder, whenever someone modifies that file the encryption could disappear.

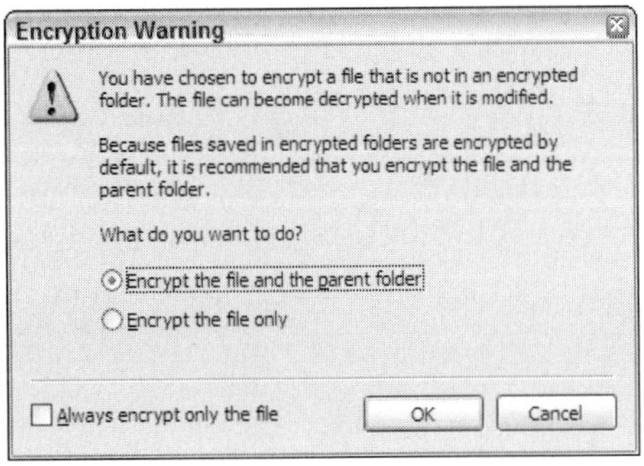

Figure 6-14: Choices when encrypting a file.

As both dialog boxes make clear, EFS works best when applied to entire folders rather than individual files. When you encrypt a folder and all its contents, you instruct Windows to encrypt all files you place in that folder from that point on, whether by copying them, moving them, or saving them from a program. By contrast, if you encrypt only a file, you strip the encryption by modifying the file, and you give up the full control provided by encryption at the folder level. The moral is this: Encrypt folders, and let the folders encrypt the files for you. For both dialog boxes, therefore, accept the default selection to encrypt the folder and all its files.

Windows indicates an encrypted folder or file by displaying its name in green. If you encrypt a folder, it automatically changes the folder name and all filenames to green, making it easy for you to see, in Windows Explorer or My Computer, which items operate under EFS. If you encrypt only the file, the folder name itself gives no indication that it contains encrypted files. This is another reason (albeit a less important one) to choose folder-level encryption.

If for any reason you want to remove the encryption from a resource, right-click on it and choose Properties, click the Advanced button, and uncheck the encryption option from the Advanced Attributes dialog box.

Note

You cannot use EFS on compressed folders. For that reason, on the Advanced Attributes dialog box, you can choose either "Compress contents to save disk space" or "Encrypt contents to secure data," but not both. (Of course, from an interface design standpoint an either-or selection always calls for radio buttons rather than check boxes, so this is one for the "Who designed this?" document.) Furthermore, you cannot encrypt entire hard drives, nor can you encrypt files bearing the System attribute.

Establishing a Recovery Agent

As you might have guessed by now, the powerful encrypting capabilities of EFS can cause access problems not just for the bad guys. If an employee encrypts folders and files and then leaves the company, unless you can access that user's account, you can't access the encrypted files and folders. This danger is especially acute if you lose access to the Windows XP installation entirely. Even if you reinstall Windows (see Appendix B for details), giving you access to the folders and files in the previous installation, you still cannot access the encrypted files. For this, you need a Recovery Agent.

Caution

If you do not establish a Recovery Agent and you lose access to the Windows installation, you cannot access files on that system encrypted through EFS. You might as well delete them (EFS doesn't stop you from doing that) because you have no way to access them at all.

Creating a Certificate

To create a certificate for use in adding a Recovery Agent, follow these steps. This process assumes a username of jones, but, of course, yours probably differs:

1. Open a command box by clicking Start, choosing Run, typing **cmd** in the Open field, and pressing Enter.

2. Notice the current folder, which is displayed in the path at the top of the command box. Write this down so you can locate the certificate once you've created it.

3. Engage EFS's cipher utility by typing **cipher /r: jones** and pressing Enter.

4. Windows prompts you for a password. Type it and then retype it to confirm, pressing Enter each time. Windows tells you it has created two files, `jones.cer` and `jones.pfx`.

5. Open the MMC (click Start and choose Run, then type **mmc** into the Open field and press Enter).

6. Choose File → Add/Remove Snap-in.

7. On the Add/Remove Snap-in screen, click Add and click Certificates on the resulting dialog box. Click Add.

8. Choose My User Account, and click Finish. Click Close on the Snap-in dialog box and OK on the Add/Remove Snap-in screen.

9. Click OK. The console shows the Certificates – Current User tree. Right-click on the Personal folder, and choose All Tasks → Import. This starts the Certificate Import Wizard. Click Next.

10. Click the Browse window, and in the Files of Type menu, select Personal Information Exchange. Double-click the `jones.pfx` file in the main window, and click Next in the File To Open window.

11. Type the password you decided on in step 4, and click the Mark This Key as Exportable option. That way, you'll be able to export the certificate (to another computer, for example) for safe-keeping.

12. On the Certificate Store screen, choose the top radio button, Automatically Select the Certificate Store Based on the Type of Certificate, and click Next. Click Finish to complete the import.

13. Now it's only a matter of telling Windows to use this key for the Recovery Agent. In the MMC, choose File → Add/Remove Snap-in, click Add, and choose Group Policy. Click Finish to add the Group Policy snap-in, and click OK on the Add-Remove Snap-in window.

14. In the MMC, locate the `Encrypting File System` folder by expanding the following items in the Console Root tree: Local Computer Policy, Computer Configuration, Windows Settings, Security Settings, and Public Key Policies. Right-click on Encrypting File System, and choose Add Data Recovery Agent. Click Next.

15. In the Select Recovery Agents window, click Browse Folders. Locate the `jones.cer` file you just created, and double-click it. Click Next and then Finish to complete the process.

When users without authorization try to access an encrypted file, they get a message telling them, in a rather terse manner, that they cannot do so. Double-clicking on the file icon (even inside an encrypted folder, the files themselves are clearly visible) results in the message, without letting the user know why they can't access it. The user simply knows that it's not available and can draw on all the conspiracy theories he or she wishes as a result.

The Recovery Agent *can* access these files, however. You create a Recovery Agent through the Group Policy Editor (outlined in Chapter 27). Open the editor (choose Start → Run, type **gpedit.msc**, and press Enter), and navigate to the Encrypting File System folder, located inside Local Computer Policy\Computer Configuration\Windows Settings\Security Settings\Public Key Policies. Right-click on the Encrypting File System folder, and select Add Data Recovery Agent. The Add Recovery Agent Wizard appears, guiding you through the process. If you do not have a certificate, you can create one using the instructions in the "Creating a Certificate" sidebar in this chapter.

When you have the Recovery Agent in place, that person can access any encrypted files and folders, as long as the certificates for that user are installed on that machine. For this reason, you should export the certificates to another location (ideally another computer) for later import should something go wrong. For example, in the case where you have an inaccessible Windows XP installation on one partition of your PC and you install Windows XP on a new partition, you can import the Recovery Agent's certificates and, once they're in place, gain access to the encrypted data. You can encrypt the certificate files on the second computer, but you run the risk of making it inaccessible if, in turn, you lose the keys for that second PC.

You now have a Recovery Agent in place. You should now back up your certificates by right-clicking on them, choosing All Tasks → Export, and storing them in a safe location.

Summary

Windows XP provides a number of extremely useful methods for recovering from the problems that can result from your daily computer use. As long as you have taken a snapshot of your installation using System Restore, and as long as you have backups of your most important data files, along with installation media for Windows XP itself and for your most-used programs, you can recover your system in a variety of ways. But even if you simply need to determine why Windows won't start or why you keep getting messages indicating low memory, you have ways to recover. Keeping these methods in mind gives you a sense of peace, knowing that you can get your PC up and running again even if the problem does happen — as it is wont to do — on a Sunday evening when all the computer stores are closed.

Part II

Utilities

iven the importance of guarding against data loss and system crashes, it makes sense to explore this group of backup utilities immediately to ensure that your system is protected against intrusion, viruses, spyware, and other unsavory malware. The products covered here help you back up your data, back up your entire system, and turn back the clock to a previous version of your system.

Windows XP itself contains utilities to handle two of these functions: Backup Utility handles data back up, including backing up important system files. System Restore is a capable time-turner. As with all other utilities, however, those included in Windows XP have fewer features than dedicated products, so be sure to check out several of the following. Here, we've included information on some of the more reputable data backup and ghost imaging products. Especially with the data backup group, however, these are only a few of the many solutions available out there.

Data Backup Utilities

You'll never run out of data backup utilities; then again, after you discover one you like, you won't have much cause to check out any others. As discussed in Chapter 4, the crucial components of data backup utilities are the capability to use a variety of media and multiple discs, to add incrementally to existing backups, to back up automatically according to a schedule, and to restore data in a highly user-friendly way. If you desperately need a folder back, the last thing you want is a clumsy interface.

Tanagra's Memeo (www.tanagra.com) is certainly a product to consider. For roughly $25, you get a full-featured backup program that sets itself up to capture the most easily missed files — such as your Internet Favorites — and lets you customize to include whatever you want. It also lets you back up to pretty much any kind of media, including not only the usual CDs, DVDs, and internal and external hard drives but also Internet backup sites such as FTP sites and the company's own Internet Disk service. Restoring is particularly user-friendly; hence we highly recommend it.

Other well-regarded products abound. LockStep Systems' Backup-for-One or Backup-for-Workgroups (www.lockstep.com), both of which provide a full suite of backup features and focus extensively on verifying that individual files are fully and reliably recoverable (very good features).

NovaStor's NovaBackup Professional (www.novastor.com) clocks in a bit high in price (about $80) but offers support for a huge variety of media and is friendly to use. SimpleTech's StorageSync (www.simpletech.com) offers the best price of the bunch — the Standard edition is free — and gives you all the features you need for regular backups. One of the most respected products for small businesses in this field is Dantz's Retrospect Backup, designed for server backup as well as desktop backup, and with an extremely strong focus on disaster recovery.

And what about online backup services? Well, they're definitely out there. Xdrive (www.xdrive.com), Iomega iStorage (www.iomega.com), @Backup (www.backup.com), and more. These services synchronize with your hard drive and let you send your data to their servers, which store the data for as long as you have your account. They're a superb idea for backing up your most important files, but they're quite costly for large backups. Xdrive's price of $5.95 per month for 5GB is the best I found. That's not bad, but if you took the $70 you'd spend in one year and doubled it, you'd get a far larger internal or external hard drive. Still, the benefit of these services is that they keep your data in a highly secure server environment that won't be affected by your PC breaking, being stolen, or being caught in a house fire, and for that reason you might certainly consider it.

For relatively small files, consider Yahoo! Briefcase (briefcase.yahoo.com), which gives you 100MB for absolutely zero dollars and which makes a superb choice for uploading files from your home that you can later access at work. And it's a pretty good secondary storage area to boot.

Ghost Imaging Utilities

Ghost imaging software, also called cloning software, creates an image of the contents of a hard drive (or one of the drive's partitions if you prefer). Essentially, it captures everything on the hard drive, and then, when you want to restore the contents of the drive, the software puts it all back in place exactly as it was before.

Although ghosting can be used to back up your data, and in fact is attractive as a data backup tool, the main reason to use ghosting software is to back up entire systems. This is especially useful for companies that want each user to have identical software environments: One PC is fully configured, a ghost image taken of that PC's drive, and the image is copied onto the drives of all the other PCs. Some, but not all, ghosting software is capable of restoring the image to PCs that do not have an operating system currently running, hence its usefulness in this regard. If you need to perform an installation on a drive that needs formatting and partitioning, be sure to shop for those particular features.

Ghosting differs from the System Recovery tools in that it does not restore only selected files to their previous state as, for example, Windows' System Restore does. System Restore and utilities of its ilk turn back the clock to delete drivers or programs installed since taking the restore point, leaving data files alone. When you restore a system using a ghost image, you wipe out anything you've done since the image was captured. However, as with data backup products, most ghosting software lets you take incremental images, modifying the original image so that you don't need to keep imaging your entire drive.

Norton Ghost (known as Symantec Ghost in the enterprise edition) is one of the best-known ghosting products and is available as a standalone product or as part of Symantec's Norton SystemWorks

Premier suite (www.symantec.com). Symantec's acquisition of PowerQuest Corporation put an end to one of its competitors, PowerQuest DriveImage, but any image created with DriveImage works with Ghost as of version 9. Ghost does not contain drive-formatting or -partitioning utilities. For that, you'll need your own additional utilities, and the company quite naturally, recommends its Partition Magic program, another acquisition from PowerQuest.

Acronis TrueImage (www.acronis.com) also lets you take incremental images, thereby helping you save time in backing up your system, but in general it runs faster than Ghost does. It also contains drive-formatting and -partitioning software, giving you considerably more flexibility in establishing your images on other PCs. TrueImage's interface is somewhat less user-friendly than Ghost's is, and it tends to assume that you have a decent command of PC terminology. Then again, you own this book, so no problem, obviously.

Both Ghost and TrueImage save the image to a variety of media types, including hard drives, CDs, DVDs, and external USB and FireWire drives.

Image for Windows (www.terabyteunlimited.com) is an inexpensive ghosting package (less than $30) that covers the same ground as Ghost and TrueImage do. Also included in the package is Image for DOS, which lets you perform an image restore on a PC without a working Windows partition.

Part III

Taming the Internet

Chapter 7

Connecting to
the Internet

onquering the Internet begins with connecting consistently and reliably to the Internet in the
first place. Windows XP embraces the Internet in many ways, and you have numerous options
available to you for connecting, reconnecting, and improving and repairing connections.

This chapter covers a variety of Internet connections, demonstrating how to set up the three most
common types for residential use: dial-up, cable, and DSL. In addition, the chapter looks at the benefits of using a router as well as the Windows XP feature of automatic connections.

Internet Connection Basics

For your PC to be connected to the Internet, it has to meet two criteria. First, it must connect to
other computers on the Internet using TCP/IP (Transmission Control Protocol/Internet Protocol).
Second, it must bear its own unique IP (Internet Protocol) address.

Note

IP addresses are numeric. For example, the IP address for microsoft.com is 207.46.250.119. Each computer on
the Internet has its own IP number, although a local area network (LAN) can assume a single IP number and
parcel out data to other computers on the LAN, each of which has its own private IP number (this is the basis
of Dynamic Host Consideration Protocol (DHCP) networks, covered in this chapter). From the Internet's perspective, however, only the public IP numbers exist, so the entire local area network (LAN) consists of only
one official address.

You can connect to the Internet through several different methods:

⬛ **Dialup:** The slowest connection, dialup uses a standard telephone modem and transmits
data through the same telephone cable bandwidth as telephone conversations themselves.

Its primary selling feature has long been price, but cable and DSL connections have recently decreased in price to the extent that unlimited dial-up access is now attractive primarily to those who have no other access type available, rural users in particular. Dialup remains of strong interest to anyone needing only a few hours of access each month; in such cases, a limited-hours account is often less than $10 per month.

■ **DSL:** An abbreviation for digital subscriber line, DSL increases the speed over standard modems by 10 times or more, although providers now offer slower DSL connections at lower prices than full DSL. DSL is one of the two major forms of access (along with cable) known as *broadband* or *high-speed*. DSL comes in several different forms (asymmetric digital subscriber line (ADSL), High bit-tate Digital Subscriber Line (HDSL), and so on), but when ordering Internet access, you won't likely need to know the difference. Indeed, you won't likely have a choice because your telephone company (or a third-party company that essentially sells the phone company's DSL service) will typically have only one technology available. DSL's great potential comes from the fact that it uses the same lines as the telephone service that comes into your home, so your house needs no additional wiring. Unlike dial-up access, however, DSL traffic uses a different portion of the connection and does not interfere with voice traffic, so you can use the Internet and talk on the same phone line simultaneously.

Note

DSL suffers a disadvantage in requiring filters to eliminate noise stemming from the differences between data traffic and voice traffic, but because DSL providers typically include several filters in the package, that disadvantage is small. The chief disadvantage of DSL lies in the overall topography of a DSL networking system; to receive DSL service, your home or office must be physically located within a specific distance from the closest endpoint, with the result that it's entirely possible for your house not to have service, while your neighbor's house down the block does.

■ **Cable:** Because cable services already carry TV signals, it makes sense that they could carry Internet data as well. By connecting a cable modem to your computer, you can receive cable Internet at a speed similar to DSL, 10 times or greater than the speed of dial-up service (but as with DSL connections, less expensive limited-speed cable accounts are available). The benefit of cable is its widespread availability in urban areas, but its disadvantage is the reverse: outside of population centers, cable simply doesn't exist. When working at its peak, cable Internet tends to exceed DSL in speed, but many users report that cable speeds slow down during times of peak television use in their immediate area (Sunday evenings, for instance). Cable Internet providers continually argue against this viewpoint, but the perception remains. Theoretically, cable connections also suffer from the standpoint of security because they do not shut down (you can set DSL connections to time out after a specific period of inactivity) and because many users share a single cable line instead of DSL's standard of a separate line for each connection. This security point, too, cable companies deny, and certainly the separation of user accounts through a single cable has improved significantly since the advent of cable Internet. Cable is the other major form of broadband or high-speed access (along with DSL).

Satellite: Many satellite television providers offer satellite-based Internet service as well. They have succeeded in large part because of the geographical limitations of cable and DSL: Satellites provide TV signals to nonurban areas, and they provide Internet service to those same areas. Download speeds approach or match those of cable and DSL services, but upload speeds tend to be slower because in many cases you upload through a dial-up modem. Satellite connections tend to be considerably more expensive than DSL or cable connections, but if you don't have cable or DSL available where you live, your only other choices are dialup or the emerging broadband wireless.

Wireless: Wireless connections take several forms. You can connect a wireless network to your wired LAN at home or in the office, enabling mobile users to connect without cables. The same principle holds for commercial establishments such as coffee shops and book-stores offering wireless access for their customers. Popularly known as *Wi-Fi* (wireless fidelity), these connections make use of networking technologies under the IEEE 802.1x banner. 802.11b has been the standard, with the newer 802.11a offering higher speeds but little compatibility with 802.11b. 802.11g offers the best of both. Another form of wireless Internet connection is the cellular phone system, which lets you connect to the Internet in a manner similar to dial-up modems without the cables. Cell access tends to be slow, but because the tiny LCDs so far offer primarily text, speed is of much less concern than with standard notebook and desktop PCs.

Broadband wireless: The emerging broadband wireless standard combines the best of satellite Internet service with public Wi-Fi service. Targeted to nonurban areas, broadband wireless works via a series of antennae that provide a high-speed wireless signal to which users can connect. To become a force, broadband wireless must solve the twin bugaboos of Wi-Fi technology: security and reliability. But the promise is significant.

T1 and higher: Larger organizations requiring bandwidth greater than standard DSL access can turn to a number of technologies, ranging from the venerable but still suitable T1 through T3, Dedicated Private T3 (DS3), OC3 up to OC48, and more. Prices range from approximately $300 per month for a fractional T1 connection (a portion of a T1, shared with other organizations or departments, for example) through approximately $50,000 per month for an OC3 connection. Higher-speed OC connections run into several hundred thousand dollars per month.

Table 7-1 shows the relative speeds and approximate prices of the various Internet connections. All prices are approximate.

Table 7-1 Speeds and Costs of Internet Connection Types

Connection Type	Connection Speed	Approximate Cost
Dial-up	56 Kbps and higher	$10–$22 per month for unlimited use, lower costs for limited hours. (MSN is $21.95/month.)
DSL	1.5 Mbps through 3 Mbps download speed, 128 Kbps and higher upload speed	Starts at $30–$50 per month, higher cost and higher speeds for business accounts.
Cable	1.5 Mbps to 3 Mbps and higher download speed, 128 Kbps and higher upload speed	Starts at $30–$50 per month, higher cost and higher speeds for business accounts.
Satellite	500 Kbps download speed, with upload speed determined by additional dial-up connection if required	Starts at $60 per month, plus equipment purchase or rental (sometimes free with one-year contract). Some satellite services require the additional purchase of a monthly dial-up connection for outgoing data.
Fractional T1, T1, Fractional T3, T3	128 Kbps up to 44 Mbps	$300–$20,000 per month plus local loop costs up to $3,000 a month.
OC3, OC12, OC48, OC192	155 Mbps–9.6 Gbps	$40,000 to more than $100,000 per month plus local loop costs up to $10,000 per month. Also may require additional setup cost.

This book explicitly covers only the first three types of Internet connections: dial-up, DSL, and cable. Many of the principles of these Internet connections, though, apply to other types as well. Still, if you work with an OC3 connection or above, you'll have a professional, dedicated support staff in charge of overall and local connections, in which case you're not likely to get involved with connecting your PC at all. They just won't let you.

An interesting new type of connection is making its way into test markets as this book goes to press. Broadband over Power Line (BPL) will make use of existing standard electrical wiring to deliver broadband services to homes and businesses, especially useful in areas where DSL and cable services are unavailable. It's been possible for some years to use your home's electrical wiring as a means of sharing an Internet connection, but offering full broadband services over the electrical services is of potentially strong value.

Your first step in connecting to the Internet consists of activating the TCP/IP protocol on your PC. Fortunately, when you install Windows XP in the first place, you install and activate TCP/IP with it. To confirm its activation, open My Network Places, click the View Network Connections option in the Network Tasks pane, right-click the dial-up and/or LAN connection icon, and choose Properties. On the General tab of the Properties dialog box, you should see a check box for Internet Protocol (IP). By default, this box is checked.

If not, click the Install button near the middle of the dialog box, highlight the Protocol item in the resulting Select Network Component Type dialog box, click Add, and choose Internet Protocol.

Note

In Windows XP, unlike previous versions of Windows, the only reason you'd have to install TCP/IP manually is if the original setup was a nonstandard installation.

Setting Up Internet Connections

To get an Internet connection, you need an Internet service provider (ISP). Your local telephone company will almost certainly offer Internet service, both dial-up and DSL (broadband), as will your local cable provider. Connections are available from other ISPs as well, including MSN, AOL, NetZero, Juno, and a host of other national, regional, and local companies, who make use of existing telephone or cable systems in order to provide this service (sometimes with exclusive arrangements that can limit your choices). If you can't get satisfaction from your telephone company, see if you can hook up with a satellite provider.

No matter which service you choose, your ISP will almost certainly provide you with installation software and setup instructions. With Windows 9*x*/Me, you often needed the special software to configure your PC for access. With Windows 2000/XP, you're frequently better off working directly with the operating system's connection utilities instead, unless your service provider makes it mandatory for the purposes of connecting to its specific services, as is the case with America Online, for example.

The following sections describe the typical steps for each type of connection under Windows XP.

Establishing Dial-Up Connections

To connect to the Internet through dial-up access, you need a standard modem, a telephone line, and a telephone cord running from the phone jack on the wall to the telephone line input on the modem. The modem itself is usually already installed inside the PC, even more frequently as part of the motherboard itself; in these cases, simply look for the phone port at the back or (with some laptops) the side of the PC. With these ready, do the following:

1. If it's not internal or already connected, connect the modem to your PC either by installing it in an available slot on the motherboard inside the case (for an internal modem) or by using the appropriate cable to connect the modem to the serial port or USB port on your PC (for an external modem).

2. Open My Network Places, and choose View Network Connections in the Network Tasks pane.

3. Click the Create a New Connection link in the Network Tasks pane of the Network Connections window. The New Connection Wizard starts. Click Next.

4. Select the Connect to the Internet radio button, and click Next.

5. Choose either Set Up My Connection Manually or Use the CD I Got from an ISP on the Getting Ready window. This book assumes the former, a manual connection. Click Next.

6. Select the Connect Using a Dial-Up Modem radio button.

7. Type a name for your connection. You can use any name you'll later find memorable.

8. Drawing on the information provided by your ISP, type the local phone number your ISP has instructed you to use.

9. Again drawing on the ISP's documentation, type the username and password your ISP assigned to you. Determine if you want to use the account name you've just typed for everyone who uses your PC to dial in to that ISP (families often use this kind of arrangement), and if you want this connection to be the default Internet connection (see the "Understanding Automatic Connections and How to Turn Them Off" section later in this chapter). Finally, decide if you want the built-in Internet Connection Firewall provided by Windows XP to be turned on automatically for this connection. The firewall increases Internet security but tends to make some activities, particularly those related to video cameras and audio transfer (such as talking over the Internet with other users) much more difficult to configure.

Note

In increasingly rare cases, the username and password will have no effect if entered in the Internet Account Information window. If your ISP instructs you to dial in first and then establish a terminal window in order to enter the username and password, leave this window blank and refer to the "Dial-up connections through a terminal window" sidebar.

10. Click Finish to complete setting up the connection.

11. To connect to the Internet, open the Network Connections folder and launch the icon for the connection you've just created. For added convenience, place a shortcut for the icon on your desktop or pin it to the Start menu.

Setting Up DSL Connections

DSL connections come in two main types. With the basic connection, you connect the DSL modem directly to the PC. For added firewall security, however, and to share the DSL connection among several computers, you can connect through a DSL router. The following sections examine both types of connection.

Dial-up Connections Through a Terminal Window

Early Internet providers often required you to connect through a combination of dial-up modem and terminal windows. You rarely find such systems these days, but universities and other research institutions still sometimes employ this method. To connect through a terminal window, create the dial-up connection as described in the "Establishing Dial-Up Connections" section, but leave the username and password fields blank as you encounter them in the wizard.

When you've completed the wizard, right-click on the icon for the connection you've just created and choose Properties. You have two choices of terminal windows. If you need to open a terminal window before the modem connects, click the General tab and then the Configure button under the modem name. In the resulting Modem Configuration dialog box, check Show terminal window and click OK until the dialog boxes disappear.

More frequently, you need to open a terminal window *after* connecting. In this case, click the Security tab of the Properties dialog box, and check the Show terminal window option in the Interactive logon and scripting area. If your ISP has provided you with a logon script, specify it in the check box and field immediately following. Click OK until the dialog box disappears, then launch the connection icon, following the instructions your ISP gave you when the terminal window appeared.

USING DIRECT DSL CONNECTIONS

For a direct DSL connection, you need to purchase a DSL line from your phone company or other DSL provider. You also need a DSL modem, which you can usually rent from the phone company at a monthly rate or purchase from your computer store. Before buying one, however, check with your DSL provider to make sure that the modem is compatible with its service. Then do the following:

1. Connect the DSL modem to the phone line using a standard telephone cord, and run an Ethernet cable from the modem's Ethernet jack to the Ethernet connection in your PC. If you have a DSL modem with a USB connector, run a USB cable from the modem to a USB port on your computer. Do not connect both the USB and Ethernet connections simultaneously unless your ISP specifically instructs you to do so.

2. Open My Network Places, and choose the View Network Connections item in the Network Tasks pane.

3. Click Create a New Connection in the Network Tasks pane of the Network Connections window. The New Connection Wizard starts. Click Next.

4. Select the Connect to the Internet radio button, and click Next.

5. Choose either Set Up My Connection Manually or Use the CD I Got from an ISP on the Getting Ready window. This book assumes the former, a manual connection.

6. Select the radio button labeled Connect Using a Broadband Connection that Requires a User Name and Password, and click Next.

7. Type a name for your connection. You can use any name you'll remember later. Click Next.

8. Drawing on the ISP's documentation, type the username and password your ISP assigned to you. Determine if you want to use the account name you've just typed for everyone who uses your PC to dial in to that ISP (an arrangement often used by families) and if you want this connection to be the default Internet connection (see the "Understanding Automatic Connections and How to Turn Them Off" section later in this chapter). Finally, decide if you want the Internet Connection Firewall that's built into Windows XP automatically turned on for this connection. The firewall increases Internet security but, as previously mentioned, it tends to make some activities, particularly those related to video cameras and audio transfer (such as talking over the Internet with other users), much more difficult to configure.

9. Click Finish to complete the procedure, and then double-click the icon you just created to connect to your ISP.

Tip

Don't toss away the documentation you received from your ISP. For whatever reasons, some ISPs assign usernames and passwords that are extremely difficult to remember, and while you can often change the password, you can rarely change the username. Write down the username in several places, and be sure to keep the documentation so you'll have it later if you need to set the connection up again. This is true of all types of connections, but it seems especially true of DSL connections.

USING DSL CONNECTIONS THROUGH A DSL ROUTER

Using a router with your DSL connection increases both the security and the convenience of the connection. Not only do you get a built-in firewall guarding you against Internet intrusions, you also can easily share the connection with other computers in your house or office. To use a DSL router, follow these steps:

1. Connect the DSL modem to the phone line using a standard telephone cord, and run an Ethernet cable from the modem's Ethernet port to the DSL input jack on the DSL router. Run a second Ethernet cable from one of the output ports on the router to the Ethernet port on your PC.

2. Using your Web browser (or sometimes separately installed software), open the configuration screen for your router. For browser-based configuration screens, this means typing an IP number into the Address bar of the browser. A fairly typical URL for these settings is 192.168.0.1, but different routers require different numbers. Microsoft's DSL router, for example, uses 192.168.2.1. You can find this number in the manual that came with your router. You can also find it in the support section of the manufacturer's Web site, but the Catch-22 here is the need for an Internet connection, which, of course, you don't have yet. Another good reason to have friends.

3. Locate the section in the configuration screen that lets you configure the PPPoE (Point-to-Point Protocol over Ethernet). It might also be more simply labeled DSL connection settings or something similar. In the PPPoE settings fields, type the username and password that your ISP provided in the documentation.

4. The configuration screen also contains an area, usually close by, where you determine disconnection behavior. You can keep your PC connected at all times to your ISP, or you can have the router automatically disconnect from the ISP at specified intervals. You can also have the router automatically connect whenever you request Internet traffic, so that you don't have to reconnect manually, a feature that's often called *Connect on Demand*.

Tip

Having your router automatically disconnect provides a useful level of security. When you're disconnected, nobody can hack into your machine. Even if you use the Connect on Demand feature, the router connects only when it sees traffic coming from the PC, not from the outside.

Establishing Cable Connections Directly or through a Router

Cable ISPs typically provide the easiest method of connecting to the Internet. Connect the coax cable coming from the wall into the cable modem and run an Ethernet cable from the Ethernet output of the cable modem to the Ethernet port on your PC. Turn on your PC, and you're on the Internet. Only in rare cases do cable ISPs require any form of username and password verification for connection.

Like DSL connections, you can run your cable connection through a router. In this case, connect the coax cable to the cable modem as before, but run the Ethernet cable from the Ethernet output on the cable modem to the cable input on the router. Run a second Ethernet cable from one of the output ports on the router to the Ethernet port on your PC. Unlike DSL connections, you don't need to set up the PPPoE username and password feature because cable connections do not use the PPPoE technology. In some cases, however, and increasingly rarely, you might need to load the router's configuration screen and fill in one or more fields. Check your cable company's Web site to determine how to do this, but again, any such adjustment is rarely necessary.

Caution

As you've no doubt guessed, the fact that you don't need a username/password combination with cable connections renders these connections potentially insecure. You should use a firewall for *any* Internet connection, but especially with a cable connection. If you do not, whenever you leave your PC on, it is fully connected to the Internet, and hackers can have a field day. Indeed, they do . . .

Why Use a Router?

You don't need a router to connect your DSL or cable connection to the Internet. But using a router gives you two primary advantages over a standard cable/DSL system. First, you can share the connection with as many computers as your router has Ethernet ports. Many cable/DSL routers have four ports, so you can have four computers connected to the Internet and perform Internet activities simultaneously (see Chapter 26 for details on sharing an Internet connection). In fact, you can have more if you daisy-chain routers.

Second, the router provides greatly enhanced security against intruders from the Internet. Virtually all routers contain their own firewalls, and if you combine the router's firewall with the Windows XP firewall and any third-party firewall you have, you greatly minimize the possibility that intruders will crack your PC. In today's intrusion-happy Internet environment, a router is practically a necessity.

However, it is possible to share Internet connections without using a router, by bridging the LAN and the modem. This book does not cover that possibility (for one thing, it's a less secure connection), but you can learn more about bridging connections in Chapter 25.

Understanding Automatic Connections and How to Turn Them Off

The Internet Options utility in the Control Panel provides a means for establishing an automatic Internet connection. With the automatic connection enabled, you don't need to connect to the Internet manually by using the connection icons created with the New Connection Wizard. Whenever you perform an Internet-based task, such as checking for email or opening your Web browser and clicking on a hyperlink (or simply opening the browser and having it attempt to load your default home page), Windows connects to the Internet automatically using the default connection.

To establish an automatic connection, launch the Internet Options utility and click the Connections tab. In the Dial-Up and Virtual Private Network Settings area, you see all the connections you've created. Click on the connection you want to use as your default (you might only have one, of course), and choose one of the options beside the radio buttons below the window. You can have Windows dial your default connection every time you use an Internet program or determine first if the PC is already connected and dial only if not.

If you use a cable connection or a DSL or cable connection with a router, you have no use for the automatic connection feature. The cable connection is always enabled, while the router enables the DSL connection for you through the Connect on Demand feature. In both cases, you should disable XP's automatic connection feature.

To disable this feature, choose the Never Dial a Connection radio button. This is especially useful when you have a cable or DSL connection but you have also established a dial-up connection. If you don't disable automatic connection, you'll find yourself having to cancel the dial-up connection whenever you perform an Internet task and your broadband connection has even a few seconds of inaccessibility.

Proxy Servers

One of the connection settings that sometimes causes connection difficulties is the Proxy Server. By enabling the Proxy server setting in Internet Options, you instruct Windows to look for a proxy server when connecting to the Internet. Like a firewall, a proxy server sits between your PC and the Internet, intercepting requests either to filter them — you can configure a proxy server to disallow requests to specific Web sites, for example — or to answer the request (if possible) without sending it through to the PC. While certainly no substitute for a firewall, proxy servers help with the overall process of guarding your PC, and they perform one other significant function as well: for a specified amount of time, proxies store frequently requested resources, such as Web pages, in order to speed up subsequent downloads of those pages.

To enable the proxy server, open Internet Options from the Control Panel, click the Connections tab and then the LAN Settings tab, and check the Automatically Detect Settings option. If your ISP runs a proxy server (and the vast majority do), Windows attempts to locate that server, along with other Internet settings, when you perform an action (such as clicking a hyperlink) that causes a resource request. If you know the address for the proxy server attached to your LAN, fill in the details in the Proxy server section of the dialog box.

The problem with enabling the proxy server setting is that often it slows things down, at least during the first few resource requests. Sometimes in practice, indeed, Windows can't seem to connect to them at all, in which case you have no choice but to toggle the setting off until later. Still, until you experience difficulties, by all means run your system through your proxy server.

Tweaking the Registry to Speed Up Connections

If you believe that you should be getting faster Internet connectivity on your PC, why not go straight to the heart of the matter and tweak the settings under your computer's hood? In Windows XP, that means editing the registry, a task not to be taken lightly. In fact, if you start changing or deleting registry settings without knowing what you're doing, you can render Windows partially or wholly inoperable, to the degree that you must reinstall it from scratch (in which case, see Appendix B).

But enough with the warnings. You've decided that you want the fastest possible connection, and you're willing to do whatever it takes to ensure that you have it. Keep a few things in mind, however. First, the faster your current connection, the less you'll notice any changes. Second, the speed of the Internet depends on the speed of the weakest link in the connection chain; if you're downloading files from a slow server, or across a slow connection, no amount of tweaking will help you.

Several registry editors are available via download, but Windows XP ships with a perfectly decent utility of its own. You can load Registry Editor by clicking the Start button, choosing Run, typing **regedit** in the Open field, and clicking OK. The Registry Editor opens, ready for, well, editing the registry.

Caution

Back up the registry before editing even a single character. The best way to do so is by opening Windows' Backup Utility (found by clicking Start → All Programs → Accessories → System Tools), and clicking the Advanced Mode link on the wizard's startup screen. From the resulting Welcome screen, click the Backup Wizard icon, then the Next button. On the What to Back Up screen, choose Only Back Up the System State Data. This choice backs up the registry, the boot files, the Windows system files, and more. Another highly useful thing to do before editing the registry is to set a restore point using System Restore so that you can roll back your entire system if something goes wrong.

Note

The instructions that follow enable you to experiment with under-the-hood settings for increasing your connection speed. However, there's a perfectly reasonable chance that you could try everything listed here and experience no speed increase or indeed discover that you've actually *decreased* your speed. Even if you do increase your speed, it's often hard to tell, given the extremely uneven speeds experienced by Internet users constantly. So have fun playing, but don't expect magic.

You can tweak the registry in a variety of ways to get your connection to maximum speed. However, the following list outlines the most typical settings. This list assumes that none of these registry keys already exist on your system; look for them first and, if they're already in place, edit them rather than create them.

1. With Registry Editor open, locate the following registry key:

   `[HKEY_LOCAL_MACHINE\SYSTEM\CurrentControlSet\Services\Tcpip\Parameters]`

2. Right-click in the pane on the right and choose New → DWORD Value.

3. Create a DWORD Value and give it the following name: **TcpWindowSize**. Double-click the name and, in the Edit DWORD Value dialog box, choose Decimal and type **32767** in the Value Data field. If this seems to make no difference in speed, you can edit the key and try each of the following values instead for TcpWindowSize: 93440, 186880, and 256960.

4. Following the same procedure, create the following DWORD values shown in Table 7-2.

Table 7-2 DWORD Values

DWORD Name	Value	Description
EnablePMTUDiscovery	"1"	Enables TCP protocol to attempt to automatically discover the Maximum Transmission Unit (MTU) over the path to the remote computer
EnablePMTUBHDetect	"0"	Prevents TCP from unnecessarily detecting black hole routers
TcpMaxDupAcks	"2"	Sets the number of duplicate acknowledgment packets to be received
SackOpts	"1"	Toggles on support for Selective Acknowledgment
Tcp1323Opts	"1"	Enables support for large TCP receive windows (for example, to receive large amounts of data at one time)

Once you have your DWORD values in place, close Registry Editor and restart Windows. You can test the speed of your connections using a variety of free tools on the Internet, including such sites as www.broadbandreports.com. Figure 7-1 shows the results of a scan at this site, with the results specifying that the connection is in good order.

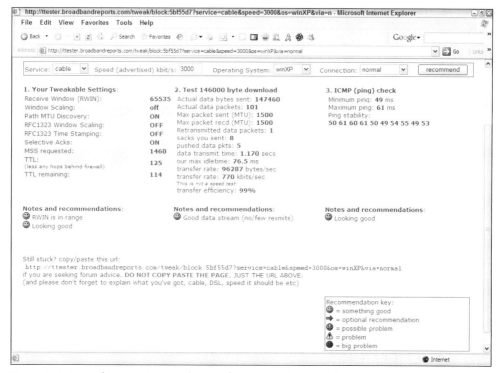

Figure 7-1: A speed testing site provides a useful service when tweaking your connection.

Summary

Your Internet experience begins with your choice of Internet connection. If you select an inexpensive dial-up connection, you'll discover quite quickly that the majority of today's Web sites are clearly designed for faster connections, and the volume of email, particularly unsolicited spam, means long downloads. For efficient use, broadband connections have become almost necessary, and Internet content designers continue to push the limits of their bandwidth capabilities as well.

Chapter 8

Putting the Internet to Work for You

Windows XP contains so many Internet features that simply knowing about all of them is a challenge. In fact, until you start digging through the mountain of configuration dialogs and setup menus, you'll miss out on a huge array of possibilities. This chapter outlines many of the possibilities, but a full description of all of them would require a book of its own.

Setting Your Default Internet Programs

As part of its settlement with the U.S. Department of Justice, Microsoft added a new utility to Windows XP with the release of the first service pack (SP1). The Set Program Access and Defaults (SPAD) utility installs with SP2 (and SP1) on the Start menu. The purpose of the new utility is to allow you to establish default Internet programs of your choice in place of the Microsoft-only configuration originally assigned by Windows. You can, for instance, set Netscape Navigator or Opera as your default Web browser and Eudora or Netscape Mail as your default email program.

The utility allows you to customize the following program categories:

- Web browser
- Email program
- Media player
- Instant messaging program
- Virtual machine for Java

This utility is not necessary, strictly speaking. You have always been able to configure Windows to use whatever programs you wanted as your default Internet programs. The problem was in what you had to go through to make these changes happen — and getting the changes to stick after you made them. To change defaults, you had to open numerous configuration dialogs, sometimes from within the alternative programs themselves. Set Program Access and Defaults gives you this control from one dialog box.

The SPAD dialog box consists of three (possibly more if your computer manufacturer has configured it differently) radio buttons, each of which, when selected, offers a distinctly different view. Figure 8-1 shows the expanded dialog box after the Microsoft Windows option has been clicked. Here, you see all Internet programs set to their Microsoft defaults, with email the only exception. Because the PC used for this figure contains both Outlook and Outlook Express, Microsoft lets you choose which one you want to use as your default. But because Microsoft produces only one Web browser, one media player, and one instant messaging program, you can't increase the selections available in those categories. If you have installed non-Microsoft products in these categories, they show up beneath the category title against the Enable Access heading. This designation means that you can access all non-Microsoft products (and additional Microsoft products) from the Start menu and All Programs.

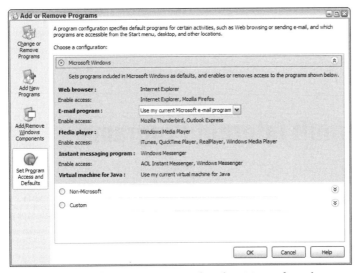

Figure 8-1: The default Internet options based on Microsoft products.

Changes start to happen when you click the other two radio button options. Choosing the Non-Microsoft radio button reveals a similar interface to the Microsoft Windows radio button, but with a few noticeably different features. First, for each non-Microsoft product installed on your system, you can choose that product from the drop-down list that accompanies every category. If you install Eudora, America Online, and Netscape Mail, for example, you can choose any of these from the drop-down list as your default email program. Programs such as QuickTime, RealPlayer, and iTunes appear in the Media Player drop-down list, and ICQ, AOL Messenger, and Yahoo Messenger all appear in the Instant Messaging list.

Tip

The number of programs in the Non-Microsoft and the Custom lists changes as you install and uninstall programs on your PC. To choose non-Microsoft programs, you must install those programs on your system. Windows will not install them for you, nor will it tell you how to do so.

The most interesting change — and the most obvious demonstration of Microsoft's fulfilling the DOJ demands — is the Remove Access line beneath the menu for each category. Here SPAD shows you which Microsoft programs *you can no longer access* in the menus of your system. Choosing the Non-Microsoft option not only tells Windows to use an alternative program as your default software for that category (see Figure 8-2), it also tells Windows not to let you use the Microsoft counterpart any longer. You can't even select the Microsoft counterpart in the drop-down menus.

Note

Excluding the Microsoft counterparts is precisely how SPAD differs from the standard methods of choosing default programs. With those methods, you choose the program either from the Programs tab of the Internet utility in Microsoft Windows or from the configuration areas of the individual programs (or you reply Yes when the program asks, upon launching, if you want to use it as the default for that purpose). In all those cases, the Microsoft programs are still available. Here, they are not, at least not from the Start menu and All Programs menu.

The final option, Custom, lets you mix and match Microsoft and non-Microsoft default programs and also lets you determine which programs will continue to be accessible and which will not. As Figure 8-3 shows, the Custom option shows each of the categories as a heading, with a radio button and an Enable Access to This Program check box beside each Internet program installed on your system. Click the radio button beside the program you want to use in each category, and check or uncheck the boxes beside all the others, depending on whether or not you want them to be accessible. Happily, you can't set your chosen default program as inaccessible, although it would be fascinating to figure out how to use the Internet if you could.

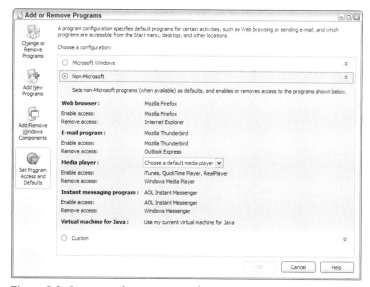

Figure 8-2: Setting up the non-Microsoft Internet options.

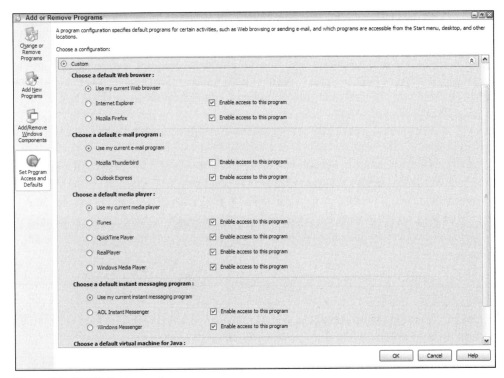

Figure 8-3: SPAD's Custom option.

Your system might not display the SPAD choices precisely as outlined here. Much depends on the computer manufacturer's configuration as well as the programs installed on your PC.

The Nearly Hidden Features of Outlook Express

Like Internet Explorer (covered in Chapter 9), Outlook Express (OE) is installed along with Windows XP. OE is packed with features; although not as complete as some free email programs, such as Netscape Mail and Mozilla's Thunderbird program, it still offers a wide array of useful possibilities. Indeed, it has as many basic features as pretty much all other email programs. Many users prefer Outlook Express over its bigger sibling, Microsoft Outlook, the email component of Microsoft Office (or, as it's called with the 2003 release, Microsoft Office System), because Outlook offers information management features such as appointment and contact management at a level that few people actually need. OE offers one other benefit over Outlook as well: OE handles newsgroups, while Outlook does not.

Many of OE's features aren't apparent when the program is first launched. These range from specific settings for individual messages to the capability for multiple users and multiple accounts.

Outlook Express, for example, offers security options in the form of virus protection, image blocking, and email encryption with digital signatures. It also offers the capability to check specific accounts for messages automatically, to log server messages, and to set up accounts using the IMAP protocol. Take a look at all the configuration menus of OE and IE as you work with them to get a sense of how to personalize them for your specific uses.

Working with Identities

With OE's Identities feature, you establish separate email access and folders for multiple users of the program. Multiple users can mean more than one person, as in the case of a PC shared by family members, or, and possibly more useful from a Windows XP standpoint, multiple identities for yourself in order to separate the messages you receive from different email accounts. For example, if you have an email address at work and another for private email, you can separate them into two identities, assigning each identity to one of your accounts.

Tip

Because you're using Windows XP, you can separate email data among users much more completely by assigning each user a separate Windows account rather than by creating separate identities in OE. Windows automatically creates a separate set of folders for each account and a subfolder in that account's Documents and Settings folder. Logging on to the account provides access to the email data for that account. Many people, though, like to use a single account for Windows, and this is where Identities comes into play to separate one user's email from another's.

To set up a new identity, follow these steps:

1. Open Outlook Express.

2. Choose File → Identities → Add New Identity.

3. The New Identity dialog box appears. Type the name you want for the new identity.

4. If you want to password-protect the new identity — this obviously makes more sense for multiple OE users than for multiple identities of a single user — check the Require a Password check box. When you do, the Enter Password dialog box appears. Type the new password and confirm it.

5. Click OK to complete the new identity. A dialog box appears asking if you want to switch to that new identity immediately. If you indicate that you do, the Internet Connection Wizard opens, and you can provide the details for the email account, including incoming and outgoing servers and email password verification.

After you've set up your identities, you can switch to them whenever you want. Choosing File → Switch Identities summons the Switch Identities dialog box, from which you choose the identity you want to work with, type in the password, and click OK. You can configure OE to start with a specific identity by opening the Manage Identities dialog box (File → Identities → Manage Identities) and choosing the identity from the drop-down box under the Use This Identity When Starting a Program check box.

Windows stores the data for OE identities inside the Documents and Settings folder of the main hard drive (typically the C: drive). To see these folders, open Windows Explorer or My Computer and navigate to c:\Documents and Settings*username*\Application Data\Identities. You need awareness of these folders only to avoid losing email when reinstalling your system (see Appendix B) or to get rid of data — such as newsgroup information — you don't want on your hard drive (see the section "Using OE for Newsgroups" later in this chapter).

Using OE for Your Hotmail or MSN Account

Nobody who has used a full-featured email account actually likes Hotmail (although its most recent revision is certainly better), but many users have Hotmail and MSN accounts anyway. There are reasons for this. They're free (once you figure out how to make your way past the screens begging you to sign up for the paid version), you can get to them whenever you have Web access (sometimes slowly, to be sure, but at least they are there), and, in the case of Hotmail especially, sometimes non-Hotmail email doesn't play nicely with Hotmail email, so you have no choice.

If you have a Hotmail or MSN account, however, you don't have to put up with Hotmail's interface. You can use OE to work with your Hotmail account, gaining all of OE's features and still having Web access to Hotmail and MSN. Here's how:

1. With OE open, choose Tools → Accounts to open the Internet Accounts dialog box.

2. Click the Add button followed by the Mail option.

3. In the first screen of the resulting Internet Connection Wizard, type the name you want to appear on your Hotmail or MSN messages and click Next. Note that this is not your Hotmail address itself, but rather whatever you want to appear in other people's email programs beside the address. Your real name is fine if that's what you want people to see.

4. In the Internet Email Address dialog box, type your full Hotmail or MSN email address, complete with the hotmail.com or msn.com portion, and click Next. Example: jim_smith2003@hotmail.com.

5. On the resulting Email Server Names screen, choose the HTTP option from the My incoming mail server drop-down menu, and Hotmail or MSN from the My HTTP mail service provider is drop-down menu. Click Next.

6. Type your Hotmail or MSN password on the Internet Mail Logon screen and verify that the Hotmail address is correct. Click Next, click Finish, and then close the Accounts dialog box.

OE now asks if you want to download mail from the mail server you've just added. Click Yes. This action causes OE to synchronize with the Hotmail or MSN account. Whenever you access this account from within OE, synchronization occurs. You can manually synchronize the two accounts by clicking the Hotmail or MSN entry on the Folders list at the left of the OE interface and clicking the Synchronize Account button.

Configuring OE's Email Settings

After you have set up an account, you can modify the settings of Outlook Express's email function so that it behaves precisely as you require. In fact, OE offers a huge array of configuration options, many of which are *not* in place when you first start the program and set up an account. Not only does adjusting these options make OE more useful but doing so can also save you both time and annoyance.

To access the Options dialog box, choose Tools → Options. The dialog box defaults to the General tab, and even here some of the options are important. The most useful options throughout the various tabs are provided in the following list. They are toggled on when the box beside the feature's description is checked:

- **Send and receive messages at startup (General tab):** Simply put, turn this one off. If you don't, every time OE starts it logs onto your mail server and downloads messages — and (more significantly) if you have messages in your Outbox, it automatically sends them. Sometimes you just don't want that.

- **Check for new messages every *xx* minutes (General tab):** If you want your messages downloaded automatically, leave this option checked and specify the frequency by using the Minutes drop-down box. You can also determine if you want your computer to connect to the Internet automatically in order to do so, usually a consideration only for dial-up users.

- **Make Default (General tab):** If OE is not your default email program, clicking the Make Default button will make it so. The default email program is the one that opens when you click an email link on a Web page. You can also make OE the default when you open it; if it is not the default program, a dialog box appears asking if you wish to make it the default. However, that dialog also offers a check box to stop it from automatically appearing, in which case the Make Default button is your only option from within OE itself.

- **Fonts (Read and Compose tabs):** You're not stuck with OE's default fonts for either reading or writing messages. At the bottom of the Read tab is a Fonts button; click it to choose the font for messages that use proportional fonts, messages that use fixed-width fonts, and the relative size of both (very small through very large). The Compose Font section of the Compose tab lets you set the defaults for outgoing messages.

- **Receipts (Receipts tab):** The Receipts tab lets you configure OE to request a receipt for all your outgoing messages. Uncheck this option unless you have a need for annoying all your contacts to distraction. More usefully, you can tell OE what to do when you receive a message that requests a receipt. You can have it never send a receipt, inform you if there's a receipt request, and let you determine what to do on a message-by-message basis, or always send a receipt except for mailing list messages. Generally, the best option is the second one, which is also the default; receipts can be important, but too often they're not.

- **Save copy of sent messages in the "Sent Items" folder (Send tab):** This option automatically saves a copy of all your outgoing messages. It's useful for keeping track of your correspondence, but it uses up disk space — especially since attachments are saved with the messages. Still, saving them is a good idea, especially if you routinely visit the Sent Items folder to delete what you no longer need.

▪ **Send messages immediately (Send tab):** Toggle this one off. If it's on and you compose a message and click the Send key, the message is gone, with no opportunity for you to edit or delete it. With the option off, the messages are stored in the Outbox folder until you click the Send and Receive button.

▪ **Empty messages from "Deleted Items" folder on exit (Maintenance tab):** When you delete a message in Outlook Express, you don't actually delete it. Instead, it transfers to the Deleted Items folder. You can automate the deletion process by checking this option; from that point on, when you close OE, the deleted messages disappear. Unless you know you'll want to find items in that folder, and unless you have sufficient self-discipline to empty your Deleted Items folder periodically, consider toggling this feature on.

▪ **Store Folder (Maintenance tab):** By default, Windows saves your OE messages deep inside the Documents and Settings folder. Not only is it difficult to find, but it can get deleted if you have to reinstall Windows. By clicking the Store Folder tab, you can change the location where these messages are stored. One useful suggestion is to move it to My Documents, perhaps in a subfolder called My Mail. That way, you'll always be able to find it.

▪ **Block images and other external content in HTML email (Security tab):** Leave this option checked if you want only the text of a message to appear when you read a message. It's a good option to use because external content can consist not only of pictures you might not want to display on your screen but also malicious code. You can choose to display the graphics on a message-by-message basis.

▪ **Get Digital ID (Security tab):** Clicking this button takes you to the Microsoft Digital ID Web area, from which you can move to sites that offer Digital ID certificates. Once you have an ID, you can digitally sign your outgoing messages (one at a time or all automatically), providing security that email otherwise does not have.

Using OE for Newsgroups

Despite problems with spam, hostile postings, and numerous other social and technological plagues, newsgroups retain some of the popularity they once had on the Internet. At one time, newsgroups were *the* forum for group message exchange, and even today you can find a newsgroup for just about any topic you can think of. If not, you can start one of your own.

OE is a fully featured newsgroup client. Indeed, Windows configures it on installation as its default newsgroup program. To view newsgroups, either click on any hyperlink you find on a Web site that refers to a newsgroup (the link starts with news:// rather than the Web's standard http://), or add a news account to OE.

ADDING AND WORKING WITH A NEWSGROUP ACCOUNT

To add a newsgroup account to OE, choose Tools→Accounts, click the Add button, and choose News. Follow the Internet Connection Wizard until you come to the Internet News Server Name screen. Here, you type the name of the news server, as provided on the Web page you were visiting (many software companies offer newsgroup forums, for example) or by your Internet service provider. Virtually all ISPs offer newsgroup access, although most are selective about the newsgroups they actually provide.

In many cases, especially with the newsgroups provided by ISPs, you need username and password authentication to access the groups. Still on the Internet News Server Name screen, check the My News Server Requires Me to Log On check box, click Next, and provide the username and password combination on the resulting screen. Click Next, click Finish, and then close the Accounts dialog box to get started with the newsgroups.

Tip

To put this as mildly as possible, you would be unwise to post your real name and email address on some newsgroups. In these cases, use a completely fake name and a completely fake address (the newsgroup system doesn't check for valid email addresses). If you have some newsgroups to which you want your name posted legitimately and others to which you do not, create separate identities to hold each one, and give them different properties.

OE starts the process by asking if you want to download newsgroups from the account you just added. This process can take a bit of time because Usenet (the server system that contains the newsgroup system) contains tens of thousands of newsgroups. In this stage, OE downloads the names of the newsgroups, not the messages themselves, and lists them in a dialog box called Newsgroup Subscriptions.

As Figure 8-4 shows, you can use this dialog box to subscribe to newsgroups. When you subscribe to a newsgroup, OE keeps the name of that newsgroup in the Folders pane beneath the name of the news account itself and continually monitors the group to determine if new messages are available for reading. To see the newsgroups available, either scroll through the list or — this is much more practical — type a keyword in the Display Newsgroups Which Contain: field and wait until the list refreshes. To subscribe, highlight one or more lists (hold the Ctrl or Shift key while selecting newsgroups to include multiple groups) and click the Subscribe button. Once you've completed the subscription request, the newsgroup name appears in the Folders list at the left and the message headings appear in the main window. Click on any heading to read the message.

Tip

You don't have to subscribe to a newsgroup. Instead, you can read the current messages to see if you're interested. To do so, highlight the newsgroup you want to examine and click the Go To button. When you exit OE, the newsgroup disappears from the list. This is a very good way to examine newsgroups without anybody knowing you've been examining them — which you may want to be the case with some of the, oh, less universally accepted topics that Usenet contains.

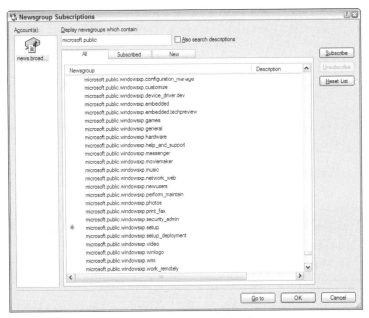

Figure 8-4: OE's Newsgroups Subscriptions dialog box.

Here are a few things you can do with OE's news client:

- With your newsgroups active, right-click on messages and group names to explore the options available to you.

- Ignore complete threads (conversations) or mark them to follow their progress.

- Mark all messages as read by right-clicking the newsgroup name and choosing Catch Up.

- Combine messages in order to decode attachments.

- Reply either to the initial sender of a message or to the entire group.

GETTING RID OF NEWSGROUP FILES

When you read messages in newsgroups, OE eventually deletes them from your system. You can set the schedule for deletions via the Maintenance tab of the Options dialog box, accessible by choosing Tools → Options. As shown in Figure 8-5, OE deletes newsgroup messages after five days by default, but you can change this setting to whatever you like.

Even with this feature active, however, OE retains evidence of your newsgroup activity. Specifically, OE creates a folder for each newsgroup from which you've downloaded attachments, and while you can delete the files using the Options menu, doing so does not delete the folders. The folders reside in the Identities folders; to see them, open My Computer or Windows Explorer and navigate to c:\Documents and Settings*username*\Application Data\Identities. There you'll see the folders you've created from your newsgroups. You may delete any or all of them from there.

Figure 8-5: The Maintenance tab of OE's Options dialog box.

Turning to the Command Line for Quick-and-Dirty Jobs

For its first two decades and more (the Net got its start in 1969), accessing the Internet meant learning command-line interfaces instead of today's graphical user interfaces (GUIs). There were no GUI-based email programs or newsgroup programs; you downloaded files using the character-based FTP commands, and there was no World Wide Web. As much as things have changed over the past decade, the command-line utilities remain, and Windows XP contains a good selection of them. You can still do a great deal of Internet work with these utilities, and sometimes, when everything else seems to break down, they can become the only Internet programs that actually work.

To use these commands, click Start → Run (or press Winlogo+R), type the command name into the Open field, and press Enter. Alternatively, you can open a Command window (a.k.a. DOS box) by typing **cmd** in the Open box and pressing Enter, then typing the commands at the DOS prompt. You can close the command window by typing **exit** at the prompt and pressing Enter.

Note

In virtually all cases, the old Internet commands and protocols bore names in lowercase text only. FTP is really *ftp*, Telnet is really *telnet*, and so on. In some cases this book uses uppercase characters to make reading much clearer, all the while recognizing and even revering the spelling of the original names. At least nobody used today's ubiquitous internal uppercase (camel case) system, such as PowerPoint, SystemWorks, and iTunes, with capitalization designed to stymie anybody's attempt to get it right. But enough ranting.

Here are some of the command-line utilities you can access in Windows XP:

- **telnet:** Long the most common method of logging into a remote account, Telnet lets you access a Unix or Linux account on another machine. To start a Telnet session, click Start and choose Run; in the Open field, type **telnet** and either the name or IP number of the server and press Enter. For example, **telnet dragon.uwaterloo.edu** connects you to the server named dragon.uwaterloo.edu and opens a command box with a username prompt. Type your username, press Enter, and type your password and press Enter. You can now proceed to work inside your remote account from there. Telnet has several more secure versions, most popularly SSH, but these are not built into Windows.

- **ftp:** Still the fastest downloading and uploading system available, FTP (File Transfer Protocol) is now built into Web browsers. You can access an FTP site by typing **ftp://server.name/** (replacing *server.name* with the real Internet name, of course) into the address bar of a browser and pressing Enter. If the server requires a username and password, the command will be **ftp://username@server.name**. The latter option results in a dialog box asking for your password, after which you enter the FTP site and treat the browser window as if it were any other My Computer window. You can still access FTP sites the original way, by choosing Start → Run, typing **ftp**, and pressing Enter. In the resulting command box, type **open *server.name*** and wait for the User prompt. Once in the account, you work with the files using the standard Unix-based FTP commands.

- **ping:** The `ping` utility lets you see if a resource is online. Actually, it lets you see if it's online and accepting `ping` requests (many addresses no longer do). But even here `ping` can be useful because it shows you the IP number of the Internet address you're trying to reach. Open a command box (click Start, choose Run, type **cmd**, and press Enter), type **ping *server.name***, and press Enter. The first line of the response shows the name of the server as you typed it, as well as the four-part IP number of that resource. For example, **ping microsoft.com** results in

  ```
  Pinging microsoft.com [207.46.245.214] with 32 bytes of data
  ```

  You now know the IP address of the server named `microsoft.com`.

- **ipconfig:** A Microsoft utility rather than a traditional Internet command, `ipconfig` gives you a view of your Internet status. To use it, open a command line (click Start and choose Run), type **ipconfig**, and press Enter. The resulting command box shows the IP addresses of your various Ethernet connections. This information is of immense value for trouble-shooting. If you have trouble with your Internet connection, your ISP will almost certainly ask you for the details showing in this window.

- **tracert:** A command that lets you trace the route (hence the command's name) between Internet servers. For example, typing **tracert microsoft.com** in a Command box and pressing Enter yields a list of servers that show the route your command has followed to reach the Microsoft servers, as well as the time taken to do so.

Summary

In addition to the Internet programs discussed in this chapter, you can, of course, download an enormous amount of additional Internet software for Windows from the Internet, including email programs, Web browsers, FTP clients, network-monitoring utilities, news readers, chat and messaging programs, search software, games galore, and much more. Indeed, if you're the type of user who feels that you can't ever have enough software, working with Internet packages will make you extremely happy.

Chapter 9

Tailoring Internet Explorer 6

When you install Windows XP, you also install Internet Explorer (IE) version 6 — Microsoft's long-controversial Web browser. And despite the trend of a great many users toward alternative browsers, especially Mozilla's Firefox, IE 6 works well. Indeed, it remains the only browser capable of accessing all the features on virtually all Web sites out there, although certainly Firefox is closing the gap. As for which browser you should use for your daily browsing, well, that's not a difficult question to answer. Why not just use them both? They're both free, they both have their positives and negatives, and it looks pretty promising that they're both here to stay.

Still, this chapter isn't about reviewing Web browsers. Instead, it's about tailoring the one you automatically get with Windows XP — Internet Explorer 6. And, to be sure, it works just fine straight out of the box. As long as you've established your Internet connection, you need only launch IE to start navigating the World Wide Web. But like pretty well everything else in Windows, you can tailor IE to suit your particular style of Web use, emphasizing the browser's strengths and avoiding possible pitfalls.

Indeed, IE comes with almost as extensive a set of configuration options as Windows XP itself. Strictly speaking, IE is not part of Windows, and you can use the Set Program Access and Defaults utility to render it (almost) inaccessible if you wish. But most users have IE installed on their systems, even if they use another Web browser in its place. For many Web designers, moreover, IE has become the de facto standard, even if — as many critics have pointed out — IE itself strays from the standards set by organizations such as the World Wide Web Consortium (W3C). It makes sense to configure it to suit your needs precisely.

This chapter covers some of the most important configuration options available in Internet Explorer, focusing especially on security and program associations.

Internet Explorer 6 and XP Service Pack 2

As discussed in Chapter 1, Windows XP Service Pack 2 adds some important security enhancements to Internet Explorer 6. To users, the most obvious enhancements are the capability to block pop-up windows and to provide warnings about possibly dangerous downloads. In addition, however, SP2 helps you control IE add-ons, provides stronger security zones, and stops Web sites from repositioning or maximizing IE's windows without your permission.

And what's the big deal about blocking popups? First of all, they're annoying. They not only interrupt what you're doing by simply appearing (seemingly) out of nowhere, they also slow down your browser considerably. Furthermore, if they originate on slow servers, they slow you down even more as they load their multimedia files (most popups are multimedia-heavy). Finally, they consume some of your system's memory, especially those (truly annoying) popups that load *behind* the windows on your desktop. You don't even know they're there, but they continue to take up memory. If you use your desktop for designing graphics, video, or sound, they can slow Windows down dramatically.

And what happens if you use SP2's pop-up blocker with other pop-up blockers? Certainly there's no lack of pop-up blockers out there, some of which are free. The Google and Yahoo! toolbars include pop-up blockers, for instance, as does the software available from numerous ISPs. One of the questions I've been asked repeatedly is whether it's okay to run two or more pop-up blockers simultaneously.

The answer is . . . sure. Whatever popup one of them misses might very well be taken care of by one of the others. The only problem is that each blocker takes up a small portion of memory, so each can slow down your system slightly while it does its work; but this will rarely be a problem.

The details behind the use and configuration of SP2's pop-up blocker are covered in Chapter 1. This chapter is designed to cover IE's built-in configuration possibilities.

Establishing Security and Privacy

By far the greatest number of configurable IE settings deals with security and privacy. This has always been the case. But as concerns about data, privacy, and security breaches on the Internet have grown over the past few years disproportionately to the technology itself, so have Microsoft's attempts at providing a means to defeat these breaches. To be sure, the crackers seem to keep winning the battles, but with a careful application of IE's security features — especially when combined with firewalls and other anti-malware programs — at least you have a fighting chance.

Controlling Cookies

Cookies are small files placed on your hard drive as a result of visiting a Web site. In the vast majority of cases, they are not only harmless but actually helpful; they customize your Web experience so that you can retain specific settings for specific Web sites. For example, the shopping cart of your favorite bookseller or electronics store is cookie-based, allowing you to place items in the shopping cart, leave the site and even turn off your PC, and come back to the site with the items still in the cart. But despite their relatively benign nature, many people distrust them, so IE lets you control them. Keep in mind, however, that if you delete or disable cookies, you might very well have to reenter information when you return to a site. Cookie removal can be a double-edged sword.

To manage cookies, open the Internet Options dialog box by choosing Tools → Internet Options. Click the Privacy tab to reveal the current cookie settings. As you move the slider, the setting changes, as does the accompanying explanatory text. At the one extreme, IE blocks all cookies from all Web sites and, furthermore, blocks all sites from reading cookies already stored on your hard drive (until you readjust the privacy setting). At the other extreme, IE accepts all cookies and all requests for existing cookie data.

Except for these two extremes, you can change cookie settings for individual sites. Click the Edit button near the bottom of the Privacy tab, type in the URL of the site, and click Block or Allow. These per-site settings are especially useful when you use the High setting, thereby blocking most cookies. When you encounter a site whose cookie you need in order to move further into the site, you can manually allow it by editing the per-site privacy.

No matter how you configure the Privacy settings, you can erase all cookies from your hard drive whenever you wish. Choose the General tab of the Internet Options dialog box and click the Delete Cookies button. When you do so, IE asks if you wish to delete all cookies in the Temporary Internet Files folder; but this question is somewhat misleading. IE stores cookies in the Cookies subfolder of each user folder within Documents and Settings, whereas pointers to these cookies are stored in the Temporary Internet Files folder (inside the Local Settings folder within each user account folder), because are cookies applicable to your current IE session (these are called *session cookies*; those in the Cookies folder are called *persistent cookies*). Using the Delete Cookies button gets rid of the cookies in both folders; clicking the Delete Files button deletes only the cookie information in the Temporary Internet Files folder, leaving the actual persistent cookies intact.

Tip

If you adjust the Privacy setting to a lower setting in order to receive cookies from which IE has restricted you, check to see if you have third-party privacy software, such as a firewall, running on your computer. Firewall utilities such as Zone Labs' ZoneAlarm provide an additional level of security against cookies, and in some cases, you have to shut down this software to receive a cookie. This behavior can occur even if you temporarily disable the cookie settings on the third-party utility, so the best idea is to close the firewall completely for a short period of time.

Controlling History

The Internet Options dialog box provides control over other areas of privacy as well. One such area is the History list, a set of URLs maintained by IE and displayed when you click the History button on the toolbar. The History list is especially useful when you click the History button in the IE toolbar; all the site names and corresponding URLs appear in the History pane to the left of IE, segregated by date visited, and you can return to any of them by expanding the folder for the specific day on which you visited the site and clicking on the site name.

However, the History feature also leaves a trail of URLs that anyone can follow, letting any curious user know your browsing activities. To clear this list, go to the General tab, and click the Clear History button. To stop IE from maintaining the list in the first place, use the drop-down menu beside the Days to Keep Pages in History heading to set the number of days to 0.

Controlling the Browser Cache

Even with the History list cleared or disabled, IE still tracks your activity. The browser cache, known as Temporary Internet Files, saves the content of visited Web pages on your hard drive. That way, when you revisit a Web page, the page doesn't have to be downloaded again but can be loaded much more quickly from the hard drive. By default, IE sets aside many megabytes of disk space for this function (the actual amount depends on the size of your drive), but you can reduce the size of or even eliminate the cache. To change the default size, click the Settings button in the Temporary Internet Files section of the General tab. Use the slider or the drop-down menu to decrease the amount of cache space to its lowest setting or, to be completely safe from prying eyes, to zero. But because the cache really does save download time—even with high-speed connections—you should give yourself 25MB or so to work with. If you're concerned about other users examining your IE cache, however, set a reminder for yourself to delete the cache every day or at least once every few days by clicking the Delete Files button in the Temporary Internet Files section of the General tab.

Controlling AutoComplete

Convenience also works against both activity tracking and security with the AutoComplete feature. This feature works with IE's Address bar and with Web-based forms, saving you time and typing by filling in the fields for you (that is, automatically completing them, hence the name). It derives its information from a store of URLs, usernames, and passwords; as you type, it performs pattern matching against this store to come up with possible completions. Whenever you type a URL in the Address field, you add to this store. Whenever you reply Yes to IE's asking you if you want to save the username and password for a Web form, you also add to this store. After that, when you type part of the name in the Address field or select a username in a form field, IE completes the URL or, in the case of the form, fills in the password field as well.

Caution

This is obviously extremely convenient, but it also means that anyone who uses IE to surf to that site will have access to your password as well!

To change the AutoComplete settings, click the Content tab on the Internet Options dialog. Now click the AutoComplete button. The resulting AutoComplete Settings dialog box offers several adjustments:

- **Web addresses:** By unchecking the Web addresses item, you tell IE to stop filling in the URL in the Address bar as you type. Note that clearing this box does *not* stop IE from storing addresses you visit and from offering them on the Address bar's drop-down menu; you must delete the browser history (on the General tab) to do so. But anyone using your browser will no longer have the address filled in automatically.

- **Forms:** Unchecking the Forms item tells IE to stop listing possible entries in a field on a Web form. For example, if you've typed your postal code in a form with this option checked, the next time you begin to type it, AutoComplete suggests a completion. Clearing this button stops that behavior.

■ **Username and passwords on forms:** Here is a *major* privacy and security concern, with dangers firmly related to identity theft. It's extremely convenient to have IE save the usernames and passwords you enter in Web forms, especially if these identifiers are unusual (for example, a partially numeric username or a password you did not choose yourself). But when you store these items on your hard drive, you open yourself to theft, either directly from the hard drive (in the case of online intruders) or by someone logging in to your account and using IE to call up the URLs to which those username/password combinations belong. Clearing this check box stops IE from giving you a list of usernames and from filling in the passwords for those usernames.

■ **Clear Forms and Clear Passwords:** These two buttons clear IE's store of forms information and passwords. For obvious reasons, clicking these buttons every so often helps your security efforts. But it also means that you won't automatically access some Web sites that require usernames and passwords, including newspaper sites, blog sites, and discussion sites. Once cleared, you must reenter the information for these sites.

Configuring Security Zones

Internet Explorer's Security tab gives you extensive control over IE's interaction with Web sites. Applying these configurations takes time and effort, but doing so will most certainly make your Web activity more secure.

IE offers four distinct security zones, as shown in Figure 9-1.

Figure 9-1: The four IE security zones.

You can assign specific sites to specific zones in order to control them. As you use IE to navigate the Web or other online resources, IE checks each URL or resource against your security zone settings. When a site meets the criteria you've established for these settings, IE displays it according to the behavior you've set for those criteria and displays the site's zone in the far-right portion of the browser's status bar. The four zones are as follows:

- **Internet (Default: Medium):** Everything else. If a Web site does not meet the Local Intranet, Trusted Sites, or Restricted Sites criteria, IE treats it as an Internet site.

- **Local intranet (Default: Medium-Low):** This zone includes resources for which security is relatively unimportant, typically those accessed only through your local network. Your company's intranet represents the primary focus of this zone, but it can also include other network connections. Clicking the Sites button lets you choose which resources to include.

Tip

You can configure IE to bypass the proxy server — a server operated by your ISP that stands between the Internet and your PC — at all times via the LAN Settings button on the Connections tab. Doing so does *not* stop IE from distinguishing between intranet and other zones. It's a good thing, too, because many users routinely disable proxy servers because of their tendency to bog down connectivity.

- **Trusted sites (Default: Low):** As you come to trust specific sites, click the Trusted Sites icon and then the Sites button to add those sites manually to this zone. If you become extremely concerned about security, you can set your Trusted Sites zone to Low security and all others to High security, thereby assuring yourself that only the sites in your Trusted zone will be able to do anything besides present the page for viewing. (You could, for example, enable sites in your Trusted zone to run scripts.) You can feel safe downloading files or allowing cookies from your trusted sites, and you need not feel concerned about what these sites are attempting to do.

- **Restricted sites (Default: High):** This zone represents the opposite of the Trusted zone. Add URLs to this zone (via the Sites button) when you know you don't want to allow them to do anything but display content.

The whole point of assigning resources to zones is to allow you to control the behavior of each zone. IE assigns a default security level to each zone (as shown in parentheses in the preceding list) and displays the features of that level in the dialog box when you click the icon for each zone. For example, in Medium setting (the default for the Internet zone), IE does not download unsigned ActiveX controls but prompts you when it encounters signed ActiveX controls. In Medium-Low, IE does not download the controls but also does not prompt for signed controls. In the High setting, it disables all ActiveX controls, signed or not.

To customize the behavior of the security zones, click the Security zone's icon and then the Custom Level button. Figure 9-2 shows the file download portion of the resulting Security Settings dialog box in its default configuration for the High setting. Nearly everything is disabled. Scroll through the settings and change those you want more or less restricted. In most cases, however, you'll find that the preconfigured settings — Low through High — will provide you with all the detail you need. The real trick in using IE's security zones is to keep adding URLs to the Trusted and Restricted zones and gaining control as a result.

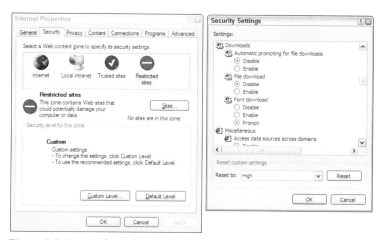

Figure 9-2: Forget about downloading files with the security setting on High.

Tip

Double-click the globe or the word *Internet* in the lower-right side of the status bar for quick access to the zones.

Changing Program Associations

Like all Web browsers, IE has grown increasingly capable of displaying different types of files over the years. It can't do everything, though; in fact, by itself, IE can't handle several important file types found in hyperlinks on the Web. For example, IE on its own is neither an email nor a newsgroup reader (although Outlook Express ships and installs with IE and is technically part of the IE package). Web sites, however, frequently contain mailto:// links, from which you can send email, and news:// links, which point to a newsgroup on a particular topic. To work with these files, IE must launch a separate program, and you can establish which programs will handle which file types.

You have two mechanisms for setting file associations: IE's Programs tab and the File Types tab in Windows XP's Folder Options. We cover both here because changing them comes into play most readily when launching these files from Internet hyperlinks rather than from standard programs.

Internet Explorer's Programs Tab

You can configure only a limited number of external programs from within IE itself, but depending on your uses, you'll find the possibilities significant nevertheless. With IE open, choose Tools → Internet Options and click the Programs tab. Beside each of the four functions listed next, you can choose the default program for that function by clicking the down arrow and choosing the program you want. IE lists all programs installed on your PC that are suitable for that function. The following list describes the available options:

- **HTML editor (responds to IE's Edit command and the Edit toolbar button):** While viewing a Web page in IE, you can load that page into your favorite Web-creation program for editing. To do so, either click the Edit button (which appears if you have installed particular Microsoft programs) on IE's standard toolbar or choose File → Edit. When you choose File → Edit, you see the full name of the default HTML editor on the Edit command. Clicking the toolbar button activates the icon for that same default HTML editor (as long as your default editor is a Microsoft program). Next to the button, IE includes a drop-down list for other installed HTML editors, letting you choose from among them on the fly. But you can set the default program — thereby including its name on the File menu — by selecting it from the drop-down list under the Programs tab. You have to restart IE for this change to take effect.

- **E-mail (responds to email `mailto://` hyperlinks):** When you click an email `mailto://` hyperlink on a Web page, IE opens the selected program. The menu lists all email programs installed on your PC, including those built into AOL, Netscape, Mozilla, and other multipurpose applications.

- **Newsgroups (responds to newsgroup `news://` hyperlinks):** When you click a newsgroup `news://` hyperlink on a Web page, IE opens the selected program. Unfortunately, the menu does not include all capable newsgroup programs. AOL, Netscape, and Mozilla do not automatically appear.

- **Internet call (responds to `callto://` hyperlink):** IE loads the selected collaboration program when you click a `callto://` hyperlink. Only Microsoft NetMeeting is fully supported.

You can also set default programs for calendar and contact functions; but in both cases, IE responds only to Microsoft Outlook.

Folder Options' File Types Tab

The File Types tab in My Computer's Folder Options gives you far more control than IE over which program opens when launching a specific file type. From this dialog box, you control the file associations of all programs in your Windows environment — not simply those that perform Internet functions. From here, you decide which program to open when, for example, you double-click a JPG, .Doc, .Wav, or other file type, which program launches when you click a PDF or an MP3 hyperlink, and which icon is displayed for a .Zip or TIFF file.

To change or add a file association, go to My Computer or Windows Explorer and choose Tools → Folder Options. Or click the Start menu and choose Settings → Control Panel → Folder Options. Then in the Folder Options dialog box, click the File Types tab to see the current associations. As Figure 9-3 shows, the file extensions appear in the left column of the Registered File Types window of the dialog box, with the associated file type in the column immediately to the right. Below that window, in the extension details area, the dialog box shows the program currently configured to open that type of file. You can change the associated program by clicking the Change button (or the Advanced button if Change is grayed out) and locating the program of your choice in the resulting Open With folder. If you don't see the program here, click Browse and find the .exe file for the program on your hard drive. Usually, you can find these files in the subfolder named for that program within the Program Files folder on your main XP drive.

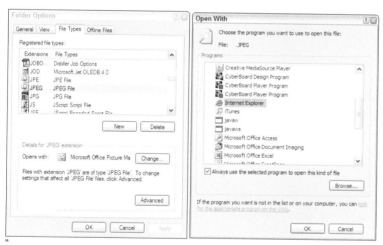

Figure 9-3: The File associations system in Folder Options.

You can change the programs for Internet activities directly from this dialog box instead of using the Internet Options dialog box in Internet Explorer. Scroll down the list until you see the group of file types beginning with (NONE) followed by URL (these are near the top of the list); each has a separate program associated with that protocol when encountered in a Web browser. To configure the browser's associated email program, for example, click the URL: Mailto Protocol item and then click the Advanced tab. In the Actions window, click the Open action and then the Edit button. The resulting dialog box shows the path for the associated program in the Application Used to Perform Action field. To effect a change, click the Browse button, navigate to the .exe file of the program you want in its place, and click Open. Click OK to set the new application in place. You can repeat this action for each Internet activity, including several not listed on the IE Programs tab, such as Gopher and Telnet links. If a specific URL is not listed among the file types, you can add it by clicking the

New button, then clicking the Advanced tab on the resulting Create New Extension dialog box, and locating the specific URL in the Associated File Type drop-down box (these are in the U's, near the bottom of the list).

While you're at it, you might as well tailor the file associations even further, giving you even more options when dealing with specific file types, albeit not in Internet Explorer. Specifically, for each file type, you can tailor the context menu that appears when you right-click on a file of that type in a Windows XP folder. For example, if you have more than one graphics program (as most people do), you can give yourself a choice in the context menu of opening the file with any of them.

To do this, locate and click the JPG extension (as an example) in the Registered File Types window under the Folder Options File Types tab. Click the Advanced tab and then, in the resulting Edit File Type dialog box, click the New button. Type a name for the action, something like **Open with Photoshop**, in the Action field, and click the Browse button to locate the .exe file for that program. Now when you right-click a JPG file icon, you see two items for launching the file inside a program: Open (which opens the default graphics program) and Open with Photoshop. You can add as many of these as you wish for each file type.

Caution

If you make a mistake while changing the default program for Open, you may do yourself more harm than good by possibly attempting to launch a program incapable of opening that specific file type or choosing a program that no longer functions on your PC. To get around the problem, instead of using the Change button to select a new default program, use the Advanced button to add a new program capable of opening that file type, set it as the default (press the Set Default button), and then, if it doesn't work properly, return to the Advanced dialog box to reset the default to the original program.

Summary

Internet Explorer currently remains the most popular Web browser of all, but you have choices if you want them. The venerable Netscape browser still exists, as does the more experimental client on which it is based, Mozilla. Opera is yet another choice. In the future, the once-fascinating browser wars could resurface, with Microsoft no longer offering IE as a separately available download (it will still ship only with Windows itself). So, it makes sense to give others a try now, in part because they make your Internet experience different and a bit fresher.

Chapter 10 completes your look at the built-in Internet technologies of Windows XP by examining the two remote control features, Remote Desktop and Remote Assistance.

Chapter 10

Controlling Windows from Afar

Windows XP ships with two features designed for remotely controlling one computer from another. Both allow you to take control over another computer on the network (LAN or Internet), but they differ in their purpose and their capabilities. Remote Desktop gives you the capability to work on a remote PC as if it were the machine in front of you. Remote Assistance lets you do the same thing but expands on this notion by including interaction with the user of the remote machine. Remote Assistance lets one user help another from a distance with troubleshooting or training by offering a variety of interactivity options, whereas Remote Desktop is a simple remote control feature, dispensing with interactivity entirely.

Of these two features, only Remote Assistance is actually new. Windows NT 4.0 and Windows 2000 already allowed remote control of a networked computer, albeit not as easily, through the separately installable Terminal Services feature (indeed, both remote features are Terminal Services applications). The two features have different requirements. For Remote Assistance, both computers must be running Windows XP Professional; by comparison, Remote Desktop must be *initiated* by a computer running Windows XP Professional, but the remote PC simply needs the Remote Desktop client software installed atop Windows 95 or later. You can install the Remote Desktop client from the Windows XP installation CD or by downloading the client from the Microsoft Web site at www.microsoft.com/windowsxp/pro/downloads/rdclientdl.asp.

This chapter compares the features of Remote Desktop and Remote Assistance, outlines how to get these features up and running, and describes how to use them to their best advantage. Both, unquestionably, are highly useful features.

Remote Desktop: Being in Two Places at Once

The Windows XP Remote Desktop feature provides an easy means for people with two or more PCs to gain access to one of them while working at another. In one classic scenario, you have a desktop PC at work and another at home, and while working at home you need access to your work machine. In another, you have a desktop PC in your study and a notebook you carry from room to room, and while working on the notebook you need access to the desktop.

Of course, in the latter scenario you could just walk to the study and do what needs doing, but in many cases that would be inefficient; in other cases, you actually want two machines at your disposal rather than just one, especially in the case of testing different configurations or different types of software. In both scenarios, you might very well find that using Remote Desktop is easier and more consistently reliable than the Windows networking features — even for simple tasks such as trading files.

Microsoft offers two versions of Remote Desktop: the standard version and the Web Connection version. With the standard version, you can use any version of Windows (Windows 3.1 or later, that is) to connect to and take control of a PC running Windows XP Professional (not the Home version). The Web Connection version gives you the same features, but you control the host machine (i.e., the machine running Windows XP Professional) through Internet Explorer by way of an ActiveX control, instead of through the separate Remote Desktop client program. Windows XP Professional can host a Remote Desktop Web Connection, but so can Windows 2000 and Windows NT 4. The Internet Information Services (IIS) Web server software version 4 or higher must be running on the host PC for the client PC to connect.

Note that the *host* computer is simply the PC running Windows XP Professional; the *controlling* computer is the one from which you connect to the host.

Note

In this chapter, we look at the standard version of Remote Desktop only because this book is about Windows XP and we can assume a Windows XP host. In addition, experience with both has shown that the standard version operates somewhat more speedily than the Web Connection version — even across precisely the same broadband connection. Furthermore, many users have their PCs configured to deny ActiveX controls, a configuration that renders the Web Connection version unworkable. But this is not to deny the convenience of an IE-based Remote Desktop or its importance as a remote control program for PCs running Windows NT 4 or Windows 2000.

Setting Up Remote Desktop

To get Remote Desktop up and running, you need to configure your remote Windows XP machine as a host. On that machine, open the System Properties dialog box, either from the Control Panel or by right-clicking the My Computer icon and choosing Properties (or use Winlogo+Break). Click the Remote tab and then click the Allow Users to Connect Remotely to This Computer check box in the Remote Desktop section of the dialog box. Figure 10-1 shows the dialog box and the resulting information box. This information box explains the need for using passwords on the remote machine in addition to the requirement for opening the correct port if your remote machine is protected by a firewall.

The central premise of Remote Desktop is that you log on to the remote PC as a user of that particular PC. If you don't have a user account on the remote machine, you can't access it. But because this chapter (like the Remote Desktop feature itself) presumes that such an account exists, you can work with Remote Desktop as soon as you've enabled the feature from the Remote tab of System Properties. If you wish, however, you can further restrict access by clicking the Select Remote Users button and choosing the specific user accounts that may use Remote Desktop to access the PC. For example, if you share your remote PC with multiple users, but you want only yourself and one other user to be allowed access from home, you can configure the feature to accept only these two users. In all cases, however, all users belonging to the Administrators group have access as soon as you enable the feature.

Now that you've configured the host PC to accept Remote Desktop connections, leave that computer powered on, move (physically) to your other PC — this will be the *client* PC — and fire it up. On the client PC, click the Start button and choose All Programs → Accessories → Communications → Remote Desktop Connection (you'd almost think Microsoft doesn't want you to find this, wouldn't you?). Alternatively, you can press Winlogo+R and type **mstsc**. In the resulting Remote Desktop Connection dialog box, type the network name of the computer (its IP number, its name on the local network, or its URL), and click the Connect button. Windows XP connects to the host PC, opens a separate window on your local client PC, and displays the host PC inside that window, beginning with the Log On dialog box. Note that it displays the Log On dialog box even if you have the host PC configured to use the Windows XP Welcome screen.

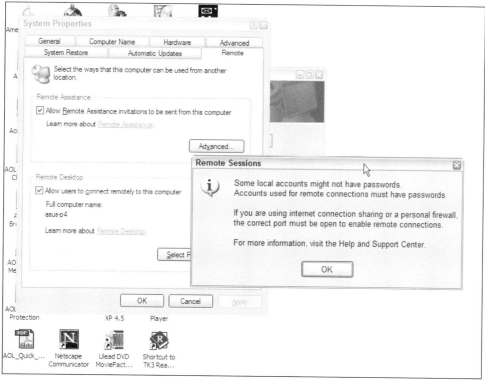

Figure 10-1: The Remote Sessions information box.

Tip

If you have the host PC configured to AutoHide the Taskbar, you'll find Remote Desktop easier to use if you unselect that option, allowing the Taskbar to be fully visible at all times. Otherwise, accessing the Taskbar can prove both slow and cumbersome.

To save time with your connection and to configure the connection for other purposes, you can customize the Remote Desktop Connection dialog box. Launch Remote Desktop, and click the Options button in the dialog box. On the General tab, type your username and password (for the remote machine, not the local machine) and, if applicable, the host's domain. Click the Display tab, and choose the desktop size and color quality for the remote display, keeping in mind that the larger and more colorful the display, the slower the response. You can adjust this response further by clicking the Experience tab and telling which of the following items you want to allow or disallow:

- **Desktop background:** If you don't need the background, leave this option turned off.

- **Show contents of window while dragging:** When you drag a window, Windows continually redraws the screen to display the contents. Turning this feature off (the default setting) stops the local machine from having to constantly download the redrawn screen.

- **Menu and window animation:** Again, Windows continually redraws the screen with these features, so leave them off.

- **Themes:** The fewer the graphics, the faster the connection, but if you get rid of themes, you also change the way your remote machine looks and feels to you.

- **Bitmap caching:** Toggled on by default, this feature saves images on the remote machine to your local hard drive so that they are displayed without downloading the next time they appear on the host.

From this dialog box, you can also choose your connection speed, but all this does is reset the options. Leave it at modem speed for optimal performance.

You can adjust two other important features. On the Programs tab, you can configure a program to load automatically when you connect to the remote PC — an option of particular use if you always load the same program (such as your word processor, spreadsheet program, or Web design tool) every time you access the host. On the Local Resources tab, you can choose whether you want to hear the remote PC's sounds on your local system (useful if you rely on sounds for your interface features), as well as whether the Windows keyboard combinations operate on the local machine or the host machine. Finally, and most important, you can configure Remote Desktop to provide access to the disk drives, printers, and serial ports of your *local* PC. This way, you can save data from a remote program to your local PC, print documents locally, and use serial port–based devices. Figure 10-2 shows this tab.

Figure 10-2: The Local Resources tab of Remote Desktop.

To save yourself from setting all these options again, click the General tab, click the Save As button, and save your configuration to a file.

Using Remote Desktop

Figure 10-3 shows a Remote Desktop window on a local PC. The window displays the host PC the way it would look if you were sitting in front of it, and you can perform precisely the same functions you would if you were there. You can work in full-screen mode to maximize the experience, or you can access multiple remote PCs and keep them all in individual windows.

Accessing Remote Desktop from Linux

If you use a Linux machine at home and a Windows XP machine at work — or vice versa — you can still use the Windows Remote Desktop feature. Because Remote Desktop works with the Remote Desktop Protocol, other clients can be designed to work with it (as indeed Microsoft's own clients for other Windows versions do). One such Linux client is rdesktop (www.rdesktop.org); although it doesn't provide quite the same video quality as when you link two Windows XP machines, it still lets you control the Windows XP host as you would from a Windows XP client. Other utilities designed for remote control include Symantec's PCAnywhere (www.symantec.com) and direct file transfer services such as www.gotomypc.com, although these do not use Windows' remote connection software per se.

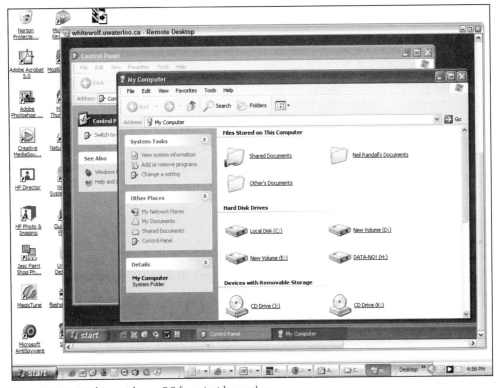

Figure 10-3: Working with one PC from inside another.

Tip

If you use the TweakUI Desktop Manager utility, you can even set up individual desktops, each with its own Remote Desktop window, and switch back and forth to control your various PCs (see Chapter 18 for more information about TweakUI).

Providing Help and Training through Remote Assistance

As its name suggests, Remote Assistance (RA) gives you a way to provide computer help to a user sitting at a remote computer. Remote Assistance lets you connect to the remote machine over the

Internet and fix technical problems, demonstrate how to use programs, or simply observe the user's actions to help him or her become more proficient.

Using Remote Assistance

In Remote Assistance lingo, the two computers on the connection are called Expert and Novice. The Expert PC is the computer that can see and take control over the other PC, while the Novice PC loads only the specific tools that allow the Expert user to communicate with the Novice user. Once the connection is established, both users can type chat messages back and forth or converse through a headset, and they can also send files to one another. There are two key differences between the two computers, however. First, the Expert PC can take full control over the Novice PC. Second, throughout the session, the Expert user can see every action the Novice user takes on the Novice PC. In effect, the Expert user is sitting at the Novice user's desktop, watching, commenting, and, when necessary, demonstrating by taking control of the mouse and keyboard.

On connection, the Remote Assistance interface appears on the Expert's desktop, while a smaller window appears on the Novice PC. Both function as chat windows and central controls (see Figure 10-4). Users can chat, or they can initiate activities such as sending a file to the other user, initiating a talk session using headsets, or disconnecting the session. The Expert sees the Novice's desktop in the viewing window of the Remote Assistance interface, and buttons along the top allow the Expert PC to take control of the Novice PC. In such a case, the Expert's mouse and keyboard are activated in the viewing window, allowing the Expert PC full remote control over the Novice PC. The Novice's keyboard and mouse are still active, but Microsoft recommends that the two users don't operate them simultaneously. The Novice might use them, however, to stop the control, end the session, or type a chat message.

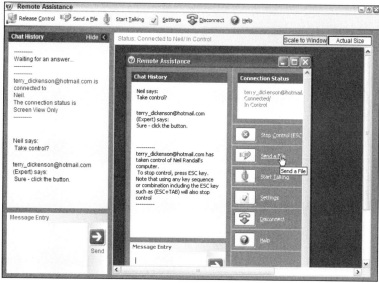

Figure 10-4: The multiple windows of Remote Assistance.

Interactivity and permission lie at the core of Remote Assistance. A typical session begins with the Novice requesting remote assistance, at which point the Expert can accept or decline. If the Expert accepts, the Novice receives a message asking if it's okay for the Expert to connect to the computer for the purpose of viewing the screen and chatting. If either party decides to send the other a file or to invoke voice communication over the network, the other party is presented with a dialog box to grant or deny permission. Similarly, the Novice must grant permission if the Expert wishes to take control of the Novice PC and can terminate the remote control by simply clicking the Stop Control icon in the RA window. At any time, either party can disconnect the session without permission from the other.

Invoking Remote Assistance

You can start a Remote Assistance session in three ways: through Windows Messenger, via email, or by sending a file. Messenger offers the easiest way, but it requires that both parties have Windows Messenger installed. Using Messenger, either party can invoke the Remote Assistance session either by right-clicking the user's name in the contact area of the Messenger window or by choosing Tools → Ask for Remote Assistance. In the latter case, the Novice can request a Remote Assistance session from anyone on the Messenger contact list or by choosing Other and specifying the email address of another MSN/Hotmail/Passport user. The Expert can use the Invite menu to ask the MSN/Hotmail user to allow a Remote Assistance session to begin, use Tools → Send an Invitation to perform the same task, or send a request to an MSN/Hotmail user not in the contact list.

Invoking Remote Assistance through email or file transfer takes place via the Help and Support screen, which is accessible by clicking Start → Help and Support or simply by clicking on the desktop and pressing F1 (or, from anywhere, Winlogo+F1). Clicking the first item under the Ask for Assistance heading — Invite a Friend to Connect to Your Computer with Remote Assistance — begins the process of initiating a Remote Assistance request. When you click this item, you have the option of inviting someone to help you or, alternatively, checking the status of a previous request. If you click the former, the next screen (shown in Figure 10-5) gives you a choice of selecting a Messenger contact, typing an email address and sending the request through your default email program (the address book of that program is available from here to help you), or saving the invitation as a file.

To proceed with the email method, click the Invite This Person link, fill in the email message form, and click Continue. The final screen lets the Novice set the point at which the invitation is to expire (it can stay open for up to 99 days). The actual invitation consists of a file attachment named RAInvitation.msrcincident, followed by an incident number in parentheses. This is precisely the same file created if the Novice invokes Remote Assistance by saving the invitation as a file, but in the latter case the Novice must send the file to the Expert in another way — via FTP or on a disk or CD, for example. In either case, the Expert opens the file in order to launch the Remote Assistance session, a procedure that sends a message to the remote PC to accept the connection and thus start the session.

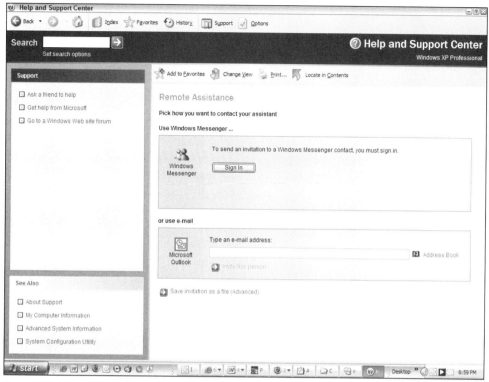

Figure 10-5: Using the Help and Support Center to request assistance.

Special Considerations for Remote Desktop and Remote Assistance

Both remote features work well in Windows XP, and both offer strong capabilities. But together they generate their share of peculiarities and special considerations, including possible connection difficulties and a sense of user confusion. This section discusses the most important of these issues.

Connections through Firewalls and Network Address Translation Devices

Increasingly, broadband users who want to share their Internet connection with other computers in a local area network — a typical situation for small offices or multi-PC homes — do so through cable/DSL routers. These routers use NAT (Network Address Translation) technology to assign separate local IP numbers — usually in the 192.168.*x.x.* address range — to each of the sharing PCs.

These separate IP numbers are necessary so that each PC sharing a single cable or DSL account can be treated as a unique host. NAT combines with Dynamic Host Configuration Protocol (DHCP) to route the responses to Web, email, FTP, and all other communication responses to the PC that made the request to preserve the illusion in each case of an independent connection to the Net (otherwise, specific routing would be impossible).

Note

Windows XP Service Pack 2 (SP2) has modified the built-in firewall significantly, but the procedure to open specific ports remains similar to that described in the following steps. You have greater flexibility in port modification with SP2, and indeed upon installation SP2 clears up a number of earlier problems with these connections. But if you cannot connect after installing SP2, or if you're still running SP1, open the firewall properties available from the Control Panel and adjust accordingly, or turn the firewall off.

To use Remote Desktop or Remote Assistance through a firewall, you must open port 3389 on your host machine. All activities for these two features happen through that port. If you use the built-in Windows XP firewall to protect your host PC, open the port by following these steps:

1. Open the My Network Places folder. (Alternatively, you can use Winlogo+R, **control firewall.cpl** to skip the first four steps.)

2. Click the View Network Connections link in the panel on the left. (If you don't see the link, click the Folders button to show the task pane.)

3. Right-click the icon representing your Internet connection, and choose Properties.

4. Click the Advanced tab of the resulting Properties dialog box, and then click the Settings button.

5. Click the Exceptions tab, and in the Programs and Services section (see Figure 10-6), check the Remote Desktop item.

6. Click OK until you've dismissed all the dialog boxes.

This sequence opens port 3389 in the Windows XP firewall (although it doesn't actually say that it does so). If you use this firewall in conjunction with another firewall, either hardware or software, you must open all 3389 ports. However, that port need not be open on your client machine, only on the machine you want to control remotely (that is, the host).

Neither remote feature functions if both the Expert and the Novice computers are operating behind a NAT device. Quite simply, it cannot make the connection. If the Novice connects through a NAT device, however, and the Expert has a direct connection (that is, a non-local IP address), the connection can be made and Remote Assistance can continue. This is true whether the TCP/IP configuration on the Expert computer specifies a fixed IP number or, as is the case of many cable and DSL connections, allows the ISP's DHCP server to assign that IP. As long as the Expert PC is identified by a non-local IP number, the Remote Assistance link can usually be made (ISP proxies and local firewalls can block this). To determine the current IP address of your Windows XP machine, open a command prompt by clicking Start and choosing Run (or use Winlogo+R), typing **command** or **cmd** in the box, and pressing Enter. Then type **ipconfig** at the prompt and press Enter once more. You'll see your IP address in the resulting Ethernet adapter information. If that address begins with 192.168., your PC has been assigned a local IP by a NAT device and will not be able to act as the Expert machine. You can, however, still be the Novice.

Another option for getting the connection to work is editing the RAInvitation.msrcincident file sent from the Novice PC via email or as a separate file. The file consists of XML code that you can edit in an text editor such as Notepad. If the problem is that one of the parties is operating behind a NAT device, you can examine the code for the embedded local IP number and change it to the public IP number. Depending on the NAT device, the connection might now work. Other factors, however, such as proxies and firewalls at either end, can still block access.

If you want to experiment with advanced configuration of your cable/DSL router or another network hub, the main point is that Remote Assistance functions through port 3389. Opening this port on the Expert machine can alleviate problems with establishing RA connections, but even this might not work on a cable/DSL router. If you're attempting to establish RA capabilities across the Internet through your company's hub, contact your system administrators to see if they're willing first to allow RA connections and second to open port 3389 in order to do so.

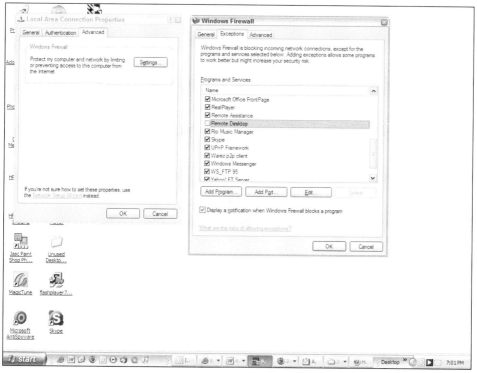

Figure 10-6: Controlling ports in the Windows XP firewall.

Using These Features with Multiple Monitors

Because each of these remote features runs in its own window, they become especially effective on systems with multiple monitors. Indeed, they have been designed to fully support Windows' Multimon feature. When you connect with another computer via either remote feature, the remote machine automatically appears as a maximized window on the secondary monitor. Such a display allows you, in effect, to work as if you had two separate computers, one on each monitor. Not only does this arrangement let you work more easily with your local PC, but it also eases the potential for confusion that can occur on a single-monitor system with the remote machine appearing as simply one window among several. In fact, if you use Remote Assistance from a single-monitor system, we recommend that you close all other windows to prevent such confusion.

You can run multiple instances of Remote Assistance, a situation most effective on a system with even more than two monitors. Obviously, any potential for confusion increases with each instance, but this arrangement allows you several useful options. If one Novice PC is connected through a standard modem, for example, you can assist a second Novice user while you wait for the first to transfer the necessary data. As another example, if your company tends to configure its users' computers similarly, and if one Novice user invites you into an RA session, you could, in turn, offer an RA session to another Novice user, take control over both machines, display each on a separate monitor, and solve the problem by determining how the two PCs differ.

Despite the advantages of using multiple monitors with Remote Desktop and Remote Assistance, there is one drawback to consider. If you view your remote machine at a different resolution than the resolution at which it is actually set — for example, you use 1280 × 1024 resolution on that machine, but you access it using 1024 × 768 resolution on your own PC — you will change window placements and possibly other graphical elements on the remote computer. The remote PC responds precisely as if you had changed resolutions, even though you haven't actually done so. So be prepared to return to your remote PC and see some differences.

Remote Control and Information Technology Policy

The inclusion of the Remote Assistance and Remote Desktop features in Windows XP brings remote control into the mainstream. If your company has not already developed a policy guiding the use of remote control by systems administrators or help desk operators, adopting Windows XP demands that you do so. There's a fundamental difference between telephone assistance and actually viewing or taking control over an employee's computer, and your policies must demonstrate an awareness of that difference. This is obviously true of Remote Desktop, which allows an administrator to control a remote machine with or without the permission of that PC's user, but Remote Assistance, despite its required granting of permission, raises some interesting issues as well.

The whole point of using RA is to let one user see the desktop of a second user while the second user is physically at that PC, but this arrangement creates unexpected concerns. For example, if Clark requests an RA session with help desk employee Lois, and Lois uses the RA session to send Clark a large file, Lois can watch everything Clark does on his desktop during the file upload, including multitasking activities. Unless Clark knows how RA works, he might be completely unaware of this fact, and Lois can, in effect, look over Clark's shoulder. Even if you discount the possible issue of Clark using the PC for personal use, there remain issues surrounding the right to monitor an employee's activities and, more simply, the problem of a help desk employee seeing documents and email messages that are legitimately private or even classified.

Note

None of this is to suggest that remote control has not been available before the release of Windows XP. Remote control packages have been available to IT departments for years, long enough indeed for Symantec's PCAnywhere to reach version 10 (and PCAnywhere works with other versions of Windows, too). But whenever Microsoft adds a feature to Windows itself, the feature suddenly takes center stage.

Summary

With most PC users using some form of Internet connection today, it makes sense for an operating system to provide a variety of techniques for making use of the fact that remote computers are so readily accessible. Remote Desktop and Remote Assistance represent two extremely useful examples of the kinds of tools that have made the Internet more than just a massive information source by actually letting you control PCs directly in order to configure them, perform tasks on them, repair them, or train others on them. Use these features even once and you'll begin to see their potential.

Part III

Utilities

In no category will you find more utilities available than in anything to do with your Internet life. A huge array of programs lets you control every aspect of your daily Internet use, from browser configuration to every email function imaginable. Here, I cover only a smattering, but all of them useful.

Alternative Browsers

You probably already know that you're not stuck with Internet Explorer for your Web-surfing needs. Several other browsers are out there ready for use, and each of them has its own advantages. The primary advantage over Internet Explorer is simply the fact the IE's huge market share, as well as a general dislike among hackers for everything that has to do with Microsoft, has made this popular browser the target of seemingly endless security hits. Get a different browser and many of these problems — although certainly not all — go away. But one of the problems is that Web designers frequently construct Web sites specifically for IE, meaning that some of them might not be fully compatible with other browsers. Still, it never hurts to give them a try, especially since most are free. And you don't need to uninstall IE in order to try them.

If you're an America Online customer, you already have an alternative browser, although AOL seems to change its mind fairly often about exactly what to offer. The latest buzz has them providing a newly modified version of Internet Explorer, one that loads when you access the Web from within AOL. For a time, the service wanted to use non-Microsoft products, but the ongoing bugaboo of Web site compatibility with non-AOL browsers kept rearing its head.

The most popular non-Microsoft browser comes from the Mozilla Project (www.mozilla.org), the original developers of the first popular browser in Web history, Netscape. Netscape itself is still available (www.netscape.com), and it uses the Mozilla browser as its core technology. Mozilla, a full suite of Internet software, including an email program, a newsreader program, and the Mozilla browser, can be downloaded from www.mozilla.org, as can its even more popular browser, Firefox. Firefox has come as close as any browser yet to disrupting IE's hold over the browser market, to the degree that it, too, has recently been undergoing security hacks. Firefox is regularly touted as being somewhat faster than IE in downloading pages and displaying them, and it has a tabbed interface that lets you have only one instance of the browser open with each page having its own tab. Whether or not you intend to use Firefox regularly, you owe it to yourself to download it and give it a try. Firefox has hundreds of free extensions that add almost any feature you could want to the program. So, the core program is simple, but with extensions, very powerful. The full Mozilla suite is also free and similarly worth your while.

Opera Software produces another highly regarded browser alternative, Opera for Windows. Opera has a free download (www.opera.com), but eventually you'll have to decide if you want to pay its $39 price — certainly not exorbitant, but it might very well seem that way given the fact that IE and Firefox/Mozilla/Netscape are free. Opera's free version is supported by small ads. Opera's paid version includes email. Everything in Opera can be done through the keyboard. It has a truly unique Zoom In and Out. Opera is an extraordinarily fast browser and uses a fully implemented tabbed interface. It even contains a voice interface feature that not only lets you control it with your voice but also reads Web content to you as listen on your headphones or through speakers. As with Firefox, this one is absolutely worth trying.

If you want to take IE itself to a different level, consider Avant Browser (www.avantbrowser.com). Avant is a free add-on to IE, providing support for three-button mice, a full-screen mode that dispenses with toolbars and displays only the Web content, built-in Google and Yahoo! search engines, and (very nicely) an automatic restore feature that reloads the Web pages you had open when the browser or your system crashed. Also included is a Flash animation filter, designed to block Flash advertising.

Other recommended free browsers include Ace Browser (www.aceexplorer.com), Slim Browser (www.flashpeak.com), and Maxthon (www.maxthon.com).

Email Programs

You won't find as many email alternatives as you could six or seven years ago, but there are more than enough to keep you occupied trying to find the one you like best.

Aside from Outlook Express, Microsoft Outlook itself is probably the most popular email client — a favorite among businesses and with anyone who owns Microsoft Office. It owes its popularity to its wealth of features, but primarily because it functions not just as an email program but also as a personal information manager. With it, you can keep contacts, appointment calendars, notebooks and journals, and much more. The biggest single problem with Outlook, aside from its sheer size as a program (and such annoyances as the fact that it doesn't have a standalone mail checker) is the fact that it is the target of by far the most viruses and other malware. If you use Outlook, you absolutely *need* a virus-checker for incoming and outgoing email.

The Mozilla suite (www.mozilla.org) comes with its own email program, which has been spun out into a standalone program, Thunderbird. While Thunderbird and Mozilla do not function as personal information managers, they're correspondingly smaller than Outlook and as fast and reliable as Outlook Express. Mozilla and Thunderbird import messages and account information directly from Outlook Express and Outlook, so you can get up and running quickly and with no loss in productivity. Additionally, Thunderbird has many free extensions. Interestingly, Mozilla (like Outlook Express) can be used for newsgroup reading, while Firefox cannot, but given the lack of interest in newsgroups these days, that doesn't matter unless you still need that capability.

Poco Systems (www.pocosystems.com) offers two useful email programs, Barca and PocoMail. The former operates as an email reader as well as a personal information manager, so it's close to Outlook in functionality, although unlike Outlook it does support newsgroup reading. PocoMail is simply an email program, but it has an advantage for those concerned about malware by not running scripts written in JavaScript or VBScript, both of which can be used to distribute viruses.

Qualcomm's Eudora (www.eudora.com), probably the most used email program early in the Internet's popularity, continues development and remains popular. With a strong message-filtering system and better Outlook import features than it had before, and with its continuing fast email management capabilities, this program is still worth trying. It's available in three modes: Paid mode (you buy it, you get all the features, and you get no ads), Sponsored mode (the full program but with an ad bar that isn't nearly as annoying as it sounds), and Light mode (no ads, but not quite as capable). Start with Light mode and see how you fare.

One of the more popular third-party programs today is RiTLabs' The Bat (www.ritlabs.com). The Bat connects with Microsoft Exchange servers, thereby letting you work with it instead of Outlook, and along with its templates and forms, and its highly sophisticated filtering and sorting systems, this feature demonstrates its ties to the business community. But it's also of considerable use on non-business PCs, particularly if you grow tired of Outlook (or don't want to buy Outlook).

Password Managers

One of the more important utilities to consider when using the Internet is a password management tool. Not only can such a utility help you keep track of your passwords but it can also help you create passwords that are hard to figure out, simply because you don't have to remember them yourself.

Password Manager XP (www.cp-lab.com) is about as full-featured as you could ask for in this category. You can create multiple databases, each with its own password and with whatever type of encryption you choose (indeed, multiple algorithms per database if you want), with each database storing passwords, PINs, credit card info, and any other sensitive data you need to protect. When you need a password or other code, you can access the database and retrieve it, and you can even install the utility on removable drives such as thumb drives for easy portability. It never creates unencrypted temporary files, it clears out memory immediately after use, and it can be set to turn itself off after being idle for a specific amount of time.

PassCrypt (www.seamistsoftware.com) offers encrypted databases and links to fill-in forms, helping you keep that data both handy and secure. A similar program is the popular RoboForm (www.roboform.com), which allows automatic logons to Internet sites again with secured data. Both programs memorize your passwords and fill in data as you type it the first time, much the way your browser does but with far greater security.

Part IV

Letting Windows' Hair Down: The Creative and Entertaining Side of Windows XP

Chapter 11
Imaging Central: Working with Digital Scanners and Cameras

Chapter 12
Working with Video Files

Chapter 13
Unleashing Your Inner Spielberg: Making Videos

Chapter 14
Playing, Ripping, and Recording Music

Part IV Utilities

Chapter 11

Imaging Central: Working with Digital Cameras and Scanners

Out of the box, Windows XP lets you work directly with digital cameras and scanners, two of the most popular types of imaging hardware. The Scanner and Camera Wizard takes you step by step through the process of scanning documents from your scanner and transferring photographs from your digital camera to your hard drive. But beneath the hood lies the single most important element of this support: the automatic recognition of scanners and cameras when you plug them into a USB port. You don't even have to keep these items connected to your computer; just plug them in when you need them, and Windows either sets them up instantly or walks you through the procedure necessary to get them working.

As with all hardware devices, Windows needs your scanner's or camera's drivers in order to work properly. Even here Windows XP eases the process. The operating system ships with drivers suitable for an extremely wide selection of hardware, and hardware vendors, along with Microsoft itself, continually post new drivers to the Windows Update site. If you buy a new device that comes with a CD containing a driver and you're in a hurry, plug in the device before even considering the CD; often, Windows installs a driver that, while possibly not the most recent version, lets you work with the device immediately. You can always upgrade later.

Quite possibly, however, the drivers and associated software that comes in your imaging product's package will support more and different features than the drivers found in Windows XP do, so by all means give them a try. As always when installing software, use System Restore to create a restore point, then follow the installation instructions in the package.

This chapter covers the features built into Windows XP for working with digital cameras and scanners. These features include automatic connection with cameras, controlling cameras from within the imaging software in Windows XP, and using your scanner effectively in Windows XP.

A Thousand Pictures Are Worth a Gazillion Words

With a digital camera you can take an unlimited number of pictures at any time and for any purpose whatsoever. At some point, however, either because you run out of memory in the camera itself or because you want to work with the pictures and view them or print them, you need a way to transfer the pictures from the camera to your PC. Windows XP gives you several alternatives to capture them to your drive and a range of possibilities for working with them once you do.

Controlling Your Camera from within Windows

When you plug your camera into the PC via the USB port (or, with some cameras, the IEEE 1394 port), Windows recognizes the camera and opens the Removable Disk window (see Figure 11-1). The window offers several options, the actual number of which depends on the photo viewing, editing, and collecting software you have installed on your PC. This chapter, however, considers only the options built into Windows XP, not those of third-party installations.

Figure 11-1: The Removable Disk window offers many choices.

If you want simply to view the pictures on your camera, choose View a Slideshow of the Images Using Windows Picture and Fax Viewer, and click OK. Windows then switches into a full-screen window showing the first picture in the camera. Click on the screen at any time to move to the next picture. Right-click to display the context menu (see Figure 11-2) that enables you to rotate the picture, set it as the desktop background, or load it into a photo editor. At the top right of the window is a command bar from which you can start the slide show or move to the next or previous picture.

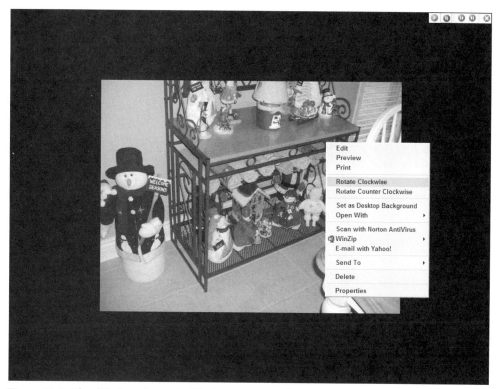

Figure 11-2: The slideshow feature in Windows Picture and Fax Viewer includes a helpful context menu.

You can also view and work with the pictures on the camera by selecting the Open Folder To View Files Using Windows Explorer option in the Removable Disk window. Because Windows sees your camera as simply another storage device, no different from a floppy disk or CD-ROM, you can treat each picture on the camera as a separate graphics file in Windows Explorer. You can use Explorer's various views to see the files, selecting, moving, and copying them as you would any other files.

Tip

Whatever method you choose to transfer pictures from your camera to your computer, pay attention to the filenames associated with the pictures. Your camera's proprietary software, like Windows itself, will create generic filenames, often along the lines of photo-001.jpg, photo-002.jpg, and so on. To work with your pictures, it can help a great deal to change the filenames, using Windows Explorer, as soon as you copy the pictures to your hard drive. That way, when you return to your pictures folders to fine a particular photo, you'll be much more likely to locate it.

One the most useful of these views is the Filmstrip view. Figure 11-3 shows the Filmstrip view of the pictures on the digital camera. The File and Folder Tasks on the left let you choose the options you want to perform.

Figure 11-3: The pictures on the camera in Filmstrip view in Explorer.

While you can work with your picture files individually using these methods, transferring them from the camera to the PC one by one and only as you require them, and deleting them from the camera one by one as well, you can use the Scanner and Camera Wizard to copy all the pictures at once to your hard drive (this should be what you do most of the time) and then delete them all from the camera files unless you want to store them on the camera so that you can copy them to other PCs as well (or just view them on the camera itself). This wizard is especially useful if you fill up your camera rapidly. You can offload your pictures, offloading them to the hard drive, and deleting them from the camera, and then so that you can use the camera again immediately. The wizard's design assumes that your primary activity for photographs is to get them off the camera and onto the hard drive.

After the pictures are copied to your hard drive, unplug the camera and turn it off, to save batteries if nothing else. The pictures are on your hard drive, and you can view them as a slideshow, as thumbnails, and with the Filmstrip view, and organize and edit them any way you want.

From the Removable Disk window, choose the Copy Pictures to a Folder on My Computer using the Microsoft Scanner and Camera Wizard option, and click OK. Click Next on the Welcome screen of the wizard to reveal the Choose Pictures to Copy window. This window features a check box in the top-right corner of each photo thumbnail, and by default all pictures are checked. If you want to copy them all to your hard drive, click Next. Otherwise, uncheck the ones you don't want to copy. You can select only a few to copy by clicking Clear All to remove all the check boxes and then checking only the pictures you want to copy. Click Next.

The Picture Name and Destination window (see Figure 11-4) opens. Type a name for this group of pictures and choose a folder in which to copy them. By default, the wizard displays the folder you most recently used for this purpose along with a drop-down menu that lists all your recent folder selections when using the wizard. Once you've chosen a destination folder, decide if you want to delete the pictures from the camera. Click the check box if you do, and then click Next.

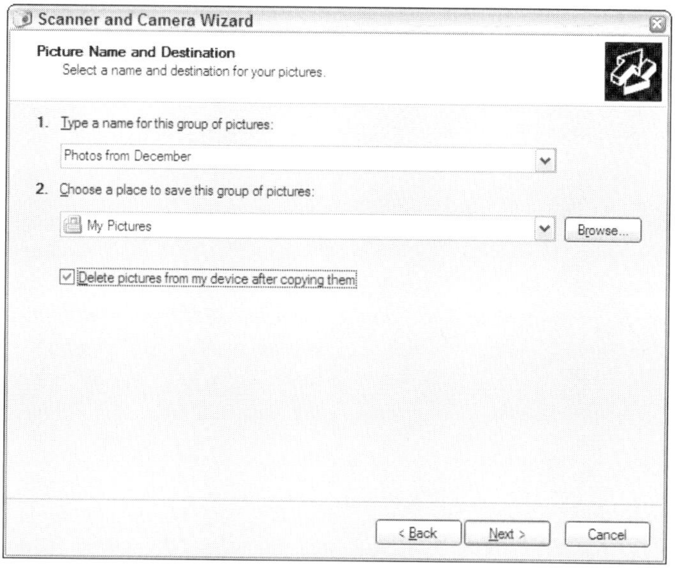

Figure 11-4: Decide where to save your pictures.

In the wizard's final stage, Copying Pictures, Windows transfers the photos to the destination folder and, after doing so, deletes the pictures from the camera if you so choose. Your pictures are now stored on your hard drive, ready for editing, printing, or simply viewing.

If you did not choose to delete the pictures from your camera in the wizard, you need to delete the pictures from your camera now to create room for new pictures. You can delete pictures by using the software built into your camera or through the imaging feature of Windows XP.

If you use a digital camera to take pictures while traveling, you practically need a notebook computer or a hard drive–based personal digital assistant (PDA) or audio player with you as a place to store your pictures so you clean them off your camera and prepare to shoot more. Today's hard drive–based audio players, for example, frequently double as portable hard drives and are ideal for this purpose. The drives, however, tend to be significantly smaller than notebook drives.

Tip

Once you have your pictures saved onto your hard drive, you can view them regularly via XP's My Pictures Slideshow Screensaver. From Control Panel, launch Display Properties, and click the Screen Saver tab. In the Screen Saver pull-down menu, choose My Pictures Slideshow. From now on, when your screensaver kicks in, you get a slideshow of the picture files stored in the My Pictures folder.

Editing and Altering Photographs

Windows XP provides a couple of useful tools for editing photographs. You won't confuse these tools with a full-featured photo-editing suite (packages such as Adobe Photoshop, JASC Paint Shop Pro, or Ulead PhotoImpact) any time soon, but until you acquire one of those — they often come with printers and digital cameras, even if only in "Lite" versions — you can make do with the utilities included with Windows.

USING MICROSOFT PAINT

The primary Windows photo-editing tool is Microsoft Paint. This program has accompanied Windows for more than a decade, and Microsoft has done little to enhance it during that time. Strangely enough, even with all the advances in third-party software, Paint remains a useful little tool for minor editing tasks. Paint is in the Accessories folder — on the Start menu, select All Programs → Accessories. Open it, and then load the photograph into it. Alternatively, locate the photograph in My Computer, right-click it, and choose Edit. Paint opens with the photograph displayed.

Note

You can also open Paint by clicking the Start button, choosing Run, typing **mspaint** into the Open field, and clicking OK. You can open it from a Command box by typing **mspaint** and pressing the Enter key.

You can use Paint to set the photo as your desktop wallpaper, to rotate the image or flip it vertically or horizontally, and to resize it with the Stretch and Skew dialog box (you need to increase each dimension by precisely the same amount). You can add text and various shapes to the image, provide a bit of airbrushing, and crop it to avoid printing unwanted areas. To crop, use the Select tool to frame the area you want to keep, right-click on that area, and choose Copy. Choose File → New and then Edit → Paste to paste the cropped photo into a new file.

WINDOWS PHOTO-EDITING UTILITIES

You can perform some editing functions directly from a folder, without the need to load a separate program such as Paint. To do so, open My Computer and navigate to the folder containing your photos. Right-click on a picture file, and examine the options. From this menu you can rotate the pictures clockwise or counterclockwise, print them, or open them in a specific editing program.

USING MICROSOFT PHOTO EDITOR AND MICROSOFT OFFICE PICTURE MANAGER

However helpful the included Paint program might be, they can't compare with dedicated editing software. Indeed, Paint is more useful as a screen capture utility and a graphics file converter than a photo editor. But if you own any version of Microsoft Office beginning with Microsoft Office 97, you have at least one built-in picture editor with far more features than Paint. Office 97, 2000, and XP all contain the highly useful Microsoft Photo Editor, while Office System 2003 features the Microsoft Office Picture Manager. Because of the popularity of the Microsoft Office suite, and the fact that it often comes bundled with Windows XP systems, let's take a quick look at Photo Editor.

To launch Photo Editor, either locate the icon in the Microsoft Office folder (or the Tools folder in Office XP) or, more easily, right-click on a picture file in My Computer (such as the My Pictures folder) and choose Microsoft Photo Editor from the Open With submenu. If neither the option nor the menu item appears, Photo Editor might not be installed on your system. Insert your Office CD, step through the setup process, and install Photo Editor from the Shared Tools menu.

Inside Photo Editor, you have a significant variety of editing possibilities. You can do the following:

- Smudge or sharpen the photo by choosing the desired effect from the Tools menu.

- Change the size of the photo precisely to your liking using the Resize dialog box.

- Use the Crop dialog box to crop the photo or apply special effects, such as a corner curl (called Ear, in Photo Editor) to the corners of the cropped picture.

- Adjust brightness, contrast, and color using the Balance dialog box.

- Apply special effects ranging from giving the picture a stained glass or watercolor look to creating a negative image of a selected portion of the picture.

If you do get a chance to work with Microsoft Office Picture Manager, the photo-editing component of Office System 2003, you'll discover that it contains fewer features than Photo Editor. It makes strong use of the task pane of the Office suite to provide easy access to the features as you work with the pictures. From a user interface standpoint, the Office task panes are modeless, in that they do not require input (as do many dialog boxes, such as the Save As boxes in Office) for the user to dismiss them.

Several freeware or shareware photo editors are available if you don't have access to the Microsoft utilities discussed here.

Tip

When you determine which graphics programs you want to work with frequently, consider adding them to My Computer's Send To menu. To so do, open the Send To folder by clicking Start → Run, typing **sendto** in the Open field, and pressing Enter. Now, drag the icon for your desired program from any other folder, or from the Start menu, Quickstart menu, and so on, into the Send To folder. When you right-click your picture file, you can choose Send To and your newly added program and have the file load in that program.

Printing and Publishing Your Pictures

No matter which photo-editing program you use, you will be able to print your pictures from it. But Windows XP includes a printing feature with which you can print quickly and easily without a separate program. This feature, the Photo Printing Wizard, steps you through the printing task.

PRINTING YOUR PICTURES FROM WINDOWS

To use the wizard, open My Computer, and locate the folder that contains the picture file you want to print. Select that picture, and click the Print This Picture item in the File and Folder Tasks panel at the left. Click Next on the Welcome screen of the resulting Photo Printing Wizard. The next screen shows all of the pictures stored in that folder, with the selected one highlighted and displayed at the top left of the Picture Selection screen. Check any additional pictures you want to print, and click Next. The Printing Options screen appears. Choose your printer (or install a new one) and configure the printing task to suit your needs by clicking the Printing Preferences button. This button leads to the standard Properties dialog box for that printer from which you can perform any function that you normally would in that dialog box.

Tip

To print multiple pictures using the same printer and settings, highlight all the files you want to print before clicking the Print This Picture link. To select all the pictures in the folder, click the link before selecting any individual pictures; by default, the wizard opens with all of them checked.

ORDERING PRINTS ONLINE

Windows provides a variation on printing your own pictures. Clicking the Order Prints Online link in the Picture Tasks pane of the folder launches the Online Print Ordering Wizard, which steps you through the process of sending your picture files (along with your credit card information) to a professional printing company to receive high-quality prints. You select the photos from the folder precisely as you did for printing on your own, but this time clicking Next takes you to the printing company selection screen, with the choices Microsoft has built into this feature (one assumes the companies paid a bundle to get there). At this point, the wizard turns into a Web browser, downloading a shopping cart and order form from the selected printing company's site. Figure 11-5 shows part of this screen, including the price per unit for specific sizes of prints.

The remainder of the wizard consists of the actual ordering form, with form fields for your name, address, and credit card data.

Of course, you can also take your CDs and memory cards to an increasing number of printing locations to get good quality prints for a reasonable cost, especially large prints (which are often a problem with inexpensive home printers). Wal-Mart offers such services, and so do many supermarkets. As you're out shopping, take note of these locations and visit them when you have special printing needs.

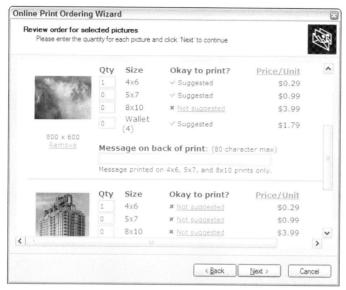

Figure 11-5: You can order prints of your pictures online.

Caution

Apart from sending your credit card information over the Internet, always a somewhat risky venture, be careful what photos you actually send. No matter how good your prints look on the screen, in many cases they simply don't have a high enough resolution, or a rich enough color depth, to make good prints. A good photograph will look reasonably good even when printed on a monochrome laser printer, so first try printing a copy yourself. Doing so also gives you a sense of how large the photo will be when you get it back from the printers. Your first few times, you might very well discover that that full-page photo actually takes up only a small section of the page. In other words, be careful that you don't simply waste your money.

PUBLISHING YOUR PICTURES

Of course, what's the point of taking all those pictures if you can't show them to your friends, relatives, and anyone else you feel has unlimited time and endless patience? Microsoft has thought of this need and has included a means of publishing your pictures to an MSN Web site.

Open a picture folder in My Computer, and select the pictures you want to publish. In the File and Folder Tasks pane at the left of the folder, click the Publish This File to the Web option (in the case of multiple pictures, this option changes to Publish the Selected Items to the Web). This launches the Web Publishing Wizard, where you can choose additional pictures from the folder if you want and then step through the subsequent screens to place them on the MSN servers. You can publish them to a private server (and later direct people to the URL so they can view them), or you can create a new MSN group where you and others can share pictures.

Figure 11-6 shows the screen in the wizard where you can choose to upload documents and/or pictures to this site, after which you choose whether you want the pictures to appear as small (640 × 480), medium (800 × 600), or large (1024 × 768). The larger the picture, of course, the longer it takes to upload, and you have only three megabytes available to you on the MSN servers. The wizard then initiates the upload and, after it has finished, steps you through the creation of an MSN account or, if you already have one, lets you log into it and perform the upload.

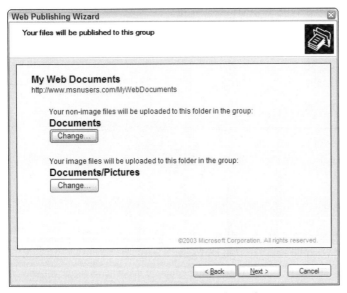

Figure 11-6: It's easy to post your pictures to the Web.

Getting the Most from Your Scanner

To Windows, your digital camera and scanner are very much alike. Both fall in the category of imaging hardware, and both are image capture devices. Indeed, Microsoft bundles the two together in the Scanner and Camera Wizard, with similar functions available to both. Many people buy scanners and digital cameras for precisely the same reason: to work with photographs. In the case of the camera, you create new pictures; in the case of the scanner, you digitize existing prints.

Scanning Images

With the Scanner and Camera Wizard, you can import pretty much any physical document into Windows as a graphics file. You can use your scanner as a photocopier in this way, scanning a page as an image file and then sending it to your printer, or as a fax machine by scanning the document and sending it to a recipient as a fax. You can also use the scanner to store copies of documents (typed, handwritten, illustrated, whatever) by scanning them and saving them as graphics files in an organized folder system.

To scan an image, first place the item in the scanner. After that, you have several options, depending on the software you've installed. First, you can use the Import or Acquire commands in your graphics software (in MS Paint, this command is on the File menu and it's called From Scanner or Camera). Second, you can load the Scanner and Camera Wizard (which in fact many graphics programs use anyway) by launching it from Start → All Programs → Accessories. Click Next on the Welcome screen; the Choose Scanning Preferences dialog box opens. Choose your picture type: color picture, grayscale picture, black-and-white picture or text, or custom (grayscaling converts color or black-and-white images to shades of gray, resulting in a smooth image suited for printing in black and white). Figure 11-7 shows the result of clicking the Preview button, which activates the scanner and loads the result into the Preview area.

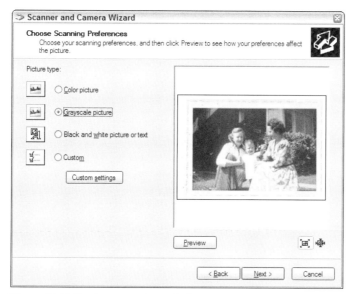

Figure 11-7: Preview your picture before you scan it.

By default, the wizard scans the image at a resolution of 150 dots per inch (dpi). You can increase or decrease this resolution by clicking the Custom Settings button. In the resulting Properties dialog box, use the arrows to change the resolution and the sliders to adjust the brightness and contrast.

Note

In a rather questionable decision, Microsoft has provided an image on the Properties dialog on which to base the brightness and contrast settings (which is a good thing), but not the image you're actually working with (a less good thing). Surely, it would have been more useful to show the actual picture.

Click Next. The Picture Name and Destination screen lets you choose the name of the scan (badly named as "group of pictures" because it's the same screen used for transferring photos from a digital camera), the folder in which you want to store it, and the file type. Four file types are available: BMP (excellent quality but large files), JPG (good quality, much smaller files, the most common type on the Web), TIF (high quality, larger files, excellent for printing), and PNG (much like JPG, suitable for the Web). Click Next to perform the scan.

Once you've scanned the image and saved it as a file, you can do anything with it you want: print it, publish it to a Web site, edit it, attach it to an email message, load it into photo album software, incorporate it into documents, and more. If you use images a great deal, your scanner can quickly become one of your most important peripheral devices.

Scanning Text

The Scanner and Camera Wizard provides a setting for text, but it captures text as an image without any provision for converting it into text. It lacks, in other words, Optical Character Recognition (OCR) capability. If you want to scan paper documents into your PC and convert them into text, tables, and multicomponent productivity files, you must buy third-party OCR software. Many scanner manufacturers bundle OCR software with their scanners, even if only a reduced-feature version of their standard OCR software, but if you are buying a scanner for this purpose, instead of the more common purpose of scanning photographs, illustrations, and images, be sure to look for bundled OCR software.

To get the most out of OCR software, look for the following features, at the very least:

- **Accuracy:** Even when converting the clearest and most noise-free paper document possible, OCR software will probably make one or more errors during the conversion. An accuracy rating of less than 95% renders the process almost unworkable; on a 2,000-word white paper, 95% means 100 errors, which you have to catch by hand later. Higher accuracy, indeed, is often what you pay for when you buy more expensive OCR software.

- **Form and table conversion:** When you scan a paper document containing a form or a table, you want the OCR software to recognize them as such and convert them into spreadsheet or word processor versions, with formatting intact. All OCR software touts this feature, but if your goal is to digitize your forms and tables, try it out first to avoid frustration.

- **Document component recognition and conversion:** While you want your OCR to convert forms and tables, you also want it to recognize other features, such as images and drawings, and convert them to like elements within your digital documents. An image should feed into your word processing software as an editable image, a chart, ideally, as an editable chart.

- **PDF conversion:** The Adobe PDF standard has grown successful precisely because of the similarity of PDF files to paper documents. But PDFs are difficult to edit, and their information is difficult to capture. Your OCR software should be able to perform the conversion for you, so that you can edit the PDF file with your productivity software.

Fortunately, most OCR software makers provide downloadable trial versions (time-limited rather than feature-limited) from their Web sites. Microsoft includes OCR software as part of the Microsoft Office Document Scanning feature of its Office XP product and the Microsoft Office Document Imaging feature of Office System 2003. If you do not see the software in Start → All Programs → Microsoft Office Tools, you can install it from the Shared Tools section of the Office installation CD.

If Your Camera Doesn't Work

A number of things can prevent your digital camera from operating correctly in Windows XP. Here is a simple troubleshooting checklist:

- Check the batteries in the camera. If you are not working with your camera through a power cable, you might simply have lost battery power.

- Make sure that the battery is turned on and set to its photo-viewing setting (playback setting), whatever that setting happens to be on your particular camera.

- Check that the cable between the camera and the PC has not somehow lost the connection. Many cameras have tiny USB ports, and they tend to stand up less well to even the smallest pull on the cord. The easiest thing to do is to unplug the cable and plug it in again each time you use the camera.

- If the Removable Disk window fails to appear, check to see if you have customized third-party software to handle transfers automatically. Right-click on the Removable Disk icon in My Computer, and examine the properties. On the Autoplay tab of the Properties dialog box for the camera, you can also see if AutoPlay for the camera is turned off; if so, toggle it back on. You can also set up Autoplay by right-clicking the Removable Disk icon in My Computer and selecting Autoplay.

- Ensure that your USB or IEEE 1394 ports work properly. These ports fail, temporarily, far too often and usually for reasons difficult to trace. If you've used your camera (or scanner) successfully before and suddenly it no longer works, open the Device Manager section of the System Properties dialog box, locate and expand the Universal Serial Bus Controllers section, and see if any appear as malfunctioning. If so, reboot your computer and see if the problem fixes itself (despite advances, this procedure remains the best way to repair temporary problems in Windows). If not, follow the guidelines for troubleshooting USB and IEEE 1394 connections in Chapter 23.

Moving beyond Windows

As you get more serious about working with your photographs, you'll want to expand beyond Windows XP itself into additional software packages, ranging from Microsoft's own Picture-It to JASC Paint Shop Pro and Adobe Photoshop. Third-party photo management packages such as ACD

Systems' ACDSee, JASC Paint Shop Photo Album, and Adobe Photoshop Album enable you to organize your photos in a variety of ways, letting you enhance them and share them easily. Two excellent free packages are Picasa (www.picasa.com), which lets you edit photos and organize them, and Irfanview (www.irfanview), a powerful image editor.

If you want better results with optical character recognition, you can turn to third-party software such as IRIS's Readiris Pro and ScanSoft's venerable OmniPage Pro.

Summary

Windows XP provides everything you need to use your digital camera and your scanner effectively. It recognizes cameras and scanners when you plug them in and automatically launches the software you need to control them. It also provides features in Windows Explorer itself that let you view images as thumbnails or slideshows, and save them as various graphics file types. Enhanced with additional software, your Windows XP system can solve even more of your imaging needs.

Chapter 12

Working with Video Files

In much the same way that giving people a GUI word processor with fonts turned everybody into a desktop publisher, the readily available combination of camcorder and video-editing software has everyone making movies. In both cases, the results rarely get confused with the same work done by a professional, but in both cases the enjoyment, challenge, and sense of creative freedom compensate more than adequately.

Windows XP contains three programs for use with video:

- **Windows Media Player:** Watch video files; also encode, create, and convert movie files.

- **Windows Movie Maker:** Import and edit video as a means of creating a finished video file for viewing on a PC, a DVD, or videotape.

- **Windows Media Encoder:** Convert, capture, and broadcast video files.

Together, these three programs demonstrate Windows' increasing emphasis on multimedia viewing and production.

This chapter covers Windows Media Player and the Windows Media Encoder. Chapter 13 features Windows Movie Maker and the creation and editing of videos.

Best known as a general-purpose audio listening tool, Windows Media Player also does some reasonably impressive video work. In fact, Windows Media Player Version 10, the most recent version, contains features that very few people seem to know about, and on which Microsoft doesn't seem to place a great deal of emphasis. Then again, even fewer people appear to know about Windows Media Encoder, so perhaps most Windows XP users listen to or watch multimedia files rather than create them. For those users who do, and for those who eventually will, both programs are well worth attention.

Using Windows Media Player

When it comes to video, by far your most common activity in Windows Media Player (WMP) is simply watching. To this end, Media Player works well, combining a variety of viewing options with support for numerous types of video files. Open WMP by clicking Start and choosing All Programs → Accessories → Entertainment → Windows Media Player, or by clicking its icon on the Quick Launch toolbar. After it's open, you can load a video file to view.

Choosing Video File Types

You can configure WMP as the default player for specific kinds of video files. To do so, choose Tools → Options, and then click the File Types tab. Check any video files that you want to associate with WMP; you can choose from among the following types:

- **ASF (Advanced System Format):** A video format especially suitable for streaming over the Internet and other high-speed download systems that WMP has, at least in part, been designed to handle. Covers .asf, .asx, .wm, .wmp, and .wpl extensions.

- **WMV (Windows Media Video):** The standard compressed file format used by WMP and Movie Maker. Covers .wmv and .wvx extensions.

- **AVI (Audio Video Interleaved):** A cross-platform compressed video file format noted for high-quality but large files. Covers .avi extensions.

- **MPEG (Moving Pictures Expert Group):** Cross-platform and extremely common video file format, noted for the high quality of both video and audio, and efficient and effective compression. Covers .mpeg, .mpg, .mpe, .mp2, .mpv2, and .mpa extensions. (.mp3 is an audio format, not a video format).

Watching DVDs

Media Player also works as a DVD player, but not in and of itself. To play DVDs, you need DVD decoder software, which you can purchase from a number of vendors and install yourself (purchasing and installing practically any standalone DVD-viewing software package will also give you what you need). If you bought a DVD player with your computer, you almost certainly have a DVD decoder already installed on your system that Media Player will recognize and use. If not, download and install a program such as Cyberlink's PowerDVD or Intervideo's WinDVD to get the decoding technology you need.

With the decoder in place, use the View menu to select from a variety of DVD-viewing options, including playing the movie at different screen sizes (View → Video Size), accessing the Root or Title menus (View → DVD Features), and changing the camera angle (View → Video Features) for DVDs that support such features. The control area at the bottom of the Media Player interface lets you perform standard DVD operations such as pausing, muting, and skipping forward or backward from scene to scene. If your video card and your DVD decoder support video mixing rendering (which you can turn on via Tools → Options → DVD tab → Options button), you can use the View → DVD Features menu to capture the current frame as a still image. Even so, WMP lacks a number of useful features provided by dedicated DVD players, including the capability to move ahead in the movie by tiny increments to watch scenes frame by frame (this feature is extremely useful for teaching purposes), but for the most part it will support your needs.

Other Video Players and Why You Need Them

Despite its obvious strengths, Windows Media Player doesn't do it all. If you want to play QuickTime movie files (with a .mov extension), download the free QuickTime player from Apple (www.apple.com). If you want to play RealVideo files, download the free version of the RealPlayer from Real Networks (www.real.com). And if you want to play files generated by the specialized software that comes with your video card, use the video player the manufacturer provides for best effect.

Why do you need these other players? First, WMP doesn't handle all video files. It handles neither QuickTime nor Real files, for example. And it sometimes has trouble with certain files for no apparent reason. If that happens, having a different video player can prove a godsend; try loading the file (an AVI video file, for example) in QuickTime instead of WMP, and you might well discover that it plays just fine. In the same way, WMP sometimes plays files that Real or QuickTime has trouble with. You can't predict this behavior; it just happens. In the world of computers, you never regret having two programs that ostensibly perform the same functions. Sooner or later, one of them will work when the other doesn't.

Using Windows Media Encoder 9 Series

Much less well known than Windows Media Player, the Windows Media Encoder 9 Series (there is no Media Encoder version 10 as of this writing) provides a number of highly useful features for working with video files. Together, the Encoder and its utilities provide a small, but effective, set of tools to capture, convert, encode, edit, and stream video files.

Media Encoder 9 Series is available as a separate download from Microsoft. The URL is too long for inclusion here, but you can find the software by going to Microsoft's home page (www.microsoft.com) and typing **Windows Media Encoder** in the Search field at top right. Among the first resulting links you'll find the direct link to the download page. Click it; then, from the resulting Encoder 9 page, click Continue. You need to go through a brief Windows validation sequence in order to proceed to the Encoder Download page, at which time pressing the Download button starts the downloading and installation process. Installation also adds a Windows Media menu to your All Programs menu, from which you can launch Windows Media Encoder and its utilities.

Opening Media Encoder, or choosing File → New, yields the New Session dialog box shown in Figure 12-1. You can click either the Wizards or the Quick Starts tab to begin your session, choosing from among the wizards or Quick Starts scripts to perform the function you want.

Converting and Capturing Video

The Convert a File Wizard converts a video file to Windows Media Player format. You can choose any file that WMP itself can play (AVI, MPEG, etc.) and convert it to WMV format for later use in WMP. Windows Media Encoder performs the conversion in several passes, displaying the video as it converts it. You can choose to convert the file for viewing on a PC, a DVD or CD device, a Pocket PC, or a streaming or progressive download. Each choice leads to its own Encoding Options dialog box (see Figure 12-2) from which you can further select the quality of video and audio you want in the converted file.

Figure 12-1: Select either tab in the New Session window.

Figure 12-2: Encoding options for streaming Windows video conversion.

Using a wizard very similar to the Convert a File Wizard, you can use Media Encoder to capture the incoming signal from a video device attached to your PC. Click the New Session button, and double-click the Capture Audio or Video option. On the Device Options screen, specify the video and audio devices you want to capture; the drop-down menu pertaining to each type of device (that is, video and audio) lists all installed options available, separated by device. You can customize each device by clicking its Configure button. The resulting dialog box gives you control over the input type, input level, and other relevant properties, including, for TV tuner cards, the input channel from antenna or cable.

Stepping through the wizard, choose the most appropriate quality of the content (depending on its ultimate purpose), and after that the encoding options for both video and audio. Video-encoding options range from low-bandwidth video to live-broadcast video and DVD-quality video, while audio options start with voice-quality radio and proceed through CD-quality sound and higher.

After setting optional author and title information, which viewers can see by enabling the captions feature in WMP, Media Encoder begins the capture.

In addition to the wizards, Media Encoder provides two Quick Starts for capturing video and a third for converting it. All are available from the Quick Start tab of the New Session dialog box. The Capture Live Content for Local Playback Quick Start captures from your attached video device and saves the file with settings appropriate to viewing it on a PC. The Capture Live Content for Streaming Quick Start option creates a file best suited for streaming over the Internet for recipients using WMP or another streaming video viewer. The Convert Film Content to Video Quick Start is specially designed to capture video recorded on film (such as from a VCR) and rendering its attributes suitably for recording onto a DVD or a CD.

Capturing Screen Actions

The Screen Capture Wizard lets you capture whatever activities you perform on the screen during the capture as a video file. While you could create a capture video for many purposes (such as reminding you later how you accomplished a particular task), the primary purpose of this feature is to demonstrate how to do things with Windows itself or with a program. You can use the resulting video in meetings, training sessions, program demos, self-help products, or simply as a means of showing friends and colleagues how to solve a particular problem.

To create a screen capture video, launch the wizard, and choose whether to capture a specific window, the entire screen, or a region of the screen that you select for yourself. If you choose the specific window option, clicking Next opens a screen in which you select from among the currently open windows. If you choose the region option, clicking Next takes you to the Screen Region dialog box shown in Figure 12-3. Click the selection button and use the mouse to outline the area you want to capture, or enter the coordinates of the top-left corner of the desired region and the region's width and height. Click Next. The wizard asks for the name of the output file and, after you click Next again, the quality of the video. Choose low quality for a smaller capture file and high for the best possible picture.

After filling in the optional title and author information on the next screen, Media Encoder is ready to capture your screen movements. Click Finish to begin the capture and to minimize the Encoder window. After you've performed the actions you want to capture, restore the Encoder window (from the Taskbar or via the Alt+Tab menu), and click Stop. Media Encoder displays the results of the encoding and lets you play the output file in Windows Media Player.

Broadcasting Live

The Broadcast a Live Event option in the Wizards window lets you use video devices attached to your PC as a means of broadcasting across the Internet. To make the broadcast work, you need access to a Windows Media server and possibly a Windows Server 2003 system with video streaming already established. This means, of course, that the live broadcasting feature isn't for everyone, but if you do have access to the servers, either through your organization or by renting space from a service provider, you can broadcast meetings, talks, classes, or anything else for which you have video and/or audio equipment.

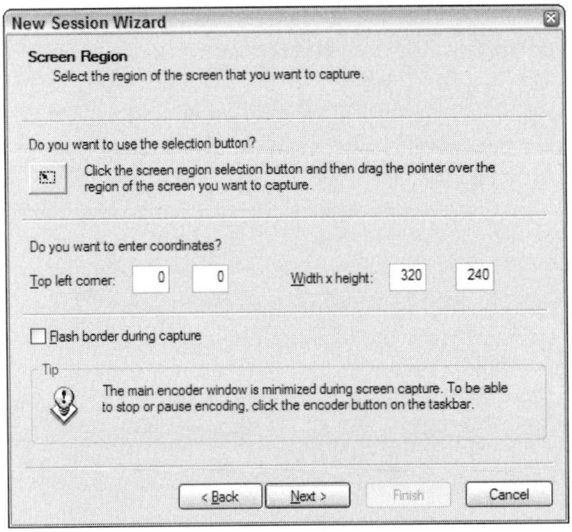

Figure 12-3: Select a region to capture.

To broadcast live, either you push the content from Windows Media Encoder or you have the recipients pull the content to their own encoders. *Pushing* content, in which you distribute it without a request from a remote machine, provides the closest to an actual broadcasting scenario because that's how the broadcasting industry — television and radio — distributes content (that is, they don't wait for requests, they just send it out and people tune in as they want to). *Pulling* content works in the opposite way; you place the content on a server, and the recipients use their client software to request it. Pushing works best for large distributions; pulling works best for smaller distributions.

To push, you need to distribute the content from a Windows Server 2003 with Windows Media Services 9 enabled. Pulling can happen from any server with Internet Information Services (IIS) enabled, but only five clients can view the content at a time using Windows Media Encoder. If you are distributing from a Windows 2003 Server environment, you can add a publishing point to the content, so that the broadcast begins only when the first client connects. That eliminates unnecessary traffic between the encoder and the server.

You make the decision to push or pull on the Broadcast Method screen of the wizard. If you choose Push, clicking Next yields the Server and Publishing Point screen (see Figure 12-4), in which you enter the name of the server and the publishing point or location.

Click Next, and then set the audio and video bit rates for the content and whether you want to archive the broadcast as a file for later access. Finally, click Next and you have the choice of adding up to three files to the broadcast: a welcome file, an intermission file, and a goodbye file. Media Encoder adds each of these files to the broadcast, and you can switch to them when you're ready to do so. Configuring a pull session works much the same way, except that instead of establishing a server name and publishing point, you simply specify the server URL and port through which the recipients can access the stream.

Understanding Constant Bit Rate and Variable Bit Rate Encoding

No matter which wizard you use in Windows Media Encoder, you eventually come upon the Encoding Options screen, where you need to make a choice from a list of video- and audio-encoding types. The names of the choices in the drop-down menus usually provide enough information to let you make a good guess, but nowhere does the wizard go out of its way to explain the difference between CBR and VBR, even though it uses the two terms frequently.

Constant Bit Rate (CBR) encoding assigns essentially the same number of bits to all portions of the content, without taking into consideration whether the content is complex or simple. The complex portions, therefore, receive more compression than the simpler portions, resulting in the most complex portions having lower quality than the simpler portions. Variable Bit Rate (VBR) encoding is always the preferred type because it works specifically with the dynamics of the data. Complex portions of the content receive more bits to work with than the simpler portions, so that you compress complex information less than simple information. The result is a more consistent compression from a quality standpoint, with the additional nice touch of an output file that is typically much smaller than one that undergoes CBR encoding. CBR encoding, however, works better than VBR for streaming, precisely because of the consistency of compression, so for this purpose it is the recommended method.

You can also engage the push method of broadcasting by using the Broadcast Company Meeting Quick Start option. This script simply steps you directly into the Windows Media Server Publishing Point screen of the New Session Wizard and requires that you run the broadcast through a Windows Media Server with a publishing point already in place.

Figure 12-4: Specify a publishing point.

Summary

Windows Media Player and Windows Media Encoder together offer a significant suite for working with video. When combined with Windows Movie Maker, the subject of the next chapter, you have a production suite for decent homemade video, complete with the capability to create simple sound-tracks or narrations and even to broadcast the video or share it over email, via the Web, or on DVD.

Chapter 13

Unleashing Your Inner Spielberg: Making Videos

Windows XP ships with Windows Movie Maker 2.0, Microsoft's second attempt to create a general-purpose video creator and editor. Version 1.0, which originally shipped with Windows XP, suffered from numerous problems ranging from frequent crashes to lack of features, especially when comparing it with the Mac OS's classy little iMovie—as Apple Macintosh owners frequently did. The good news for Windows fans is that Movie Maker 2.0 runs rings around version 1.0 in both features and stability. If you don't have version 2.0, you can download it from the Microsoft Web site or though Windows Update. Version 2.1, a minor upgrade from 2.0, is also available via Windows Update. This chapter deals exclusively with version 2.1.

Tip

If you download Windows XP Service Pack 2, you automatically get Movie Maker 2.1 with it. You don't need to install version 2.0 before 2.1; you can upgrade directly from 1.0 to 2.1.

Windows Movie Maker 2.1 (hereafter just Movie Maker) offers all the power you need to get started making videos. You can import video from a camcorder, VCR, or DVD player; chop it into individual clips; set transition effects between the clips; add titles and narration; and save it to a variety of different file types with a variety of different compression algorithms. As an introductory movie creator with features that dip into the intermediate level, you simply can't go wrong with this program. It works, and it works well.

This chapter shows you how to use Movie Maker to construct a complete video. In addition to editing and compiling video, it covers the various camcorder types available for shooting video, how to capture video to your PC, and how to add audio tracks.

What You Need to Get Started

First of all, of course, you need Windows Movie Maker 2.1. If you bought a Windows XP machine recently, launch Windows Movie Maker (usually in Start → All Programs → Accessories or down another level in the Entertainment menu). After the program loads, choose Help → About. The version of the software appears immediately above the paragraph about licensing — don't confuse it with the Windows version, which also appears on this window. If the version number does not begin with 2.0, download the latest version from the Microsoft site (www.microsoft.com/windowsxp/moviemaker/downloads/moviemaker2.asp) and install it.

Tip

Before installing Movie Maker 2.*x*, you should manually uninstall version 1.0 by using the Add/Remove Programs utility in Control Panel. Numerous users have reported problems launching version 2.*x* when they simply installed it over 1.0.

Next, you need video, which you can acquire in a number of different ways:

- **VHS tapes:** If you have a bunch of VHS tapes lying around — and many of us do — you can capture them in Movie Maker, edit them, and either view them from your hard drive or store them for recording back onto tape. The primary purpose of this kind of capture is to convert your home movies into edited video files to send to friends, family, or colleagues, or for storing as DVD videos. Of course, you could also edit all your favorite *Happy Days* episodes down into, say, three or four short ones, but because of copyright law you can't actually show them to anyone, so there seems little point.

- **Digital camcorder:** Digital camcorders offer enormous advantages over everything else as a source of video. Movie Maker not only captures from digital camcorders, it also controls the camcorder's playback, rewind, and speed-up functions and even finds the start and end points you specify. The question, though, is which digital camcorder to get. See the "Which Camcorder?" sidebar for a brief guide.

- **Analog camcorder:** Although Movie Maker prefers digital camcorders, it works perfectly well with all those good old VHS and 8mm camcorders. The quality of digital recordings is superior to analog recordings, but besides that the only real difference between the two in Movie Maker is the need to control the analog camcorder manually. The program's play/rewind controls do not appear when you connect an analog camera.

- **Webcam:** For low-quality video at equally low expense, you can't beat a Webcam. Some offer surprising results when used as standalone video cameras instead of for real-time video over the Net, and they definitely provide a way to get started, especially because many PCs ship with them. But if you want video anyone might actually want to watch, a Webcam won't take you very far.

- **Television:** Television provides video 24 hours a day, so why not capture some and learn Movie Maker with it? The program lets you capture directly from TV tuners, providing a

Properties dialog that gives you control over the channel you wish to record, the NTSC or PAL video standard, and more. One superb way to learn Movie Maker is to edit the commercials out of your favorite sitcom or, as you get more experienced, capture a game by your favorite sports team and edit it down to a 10-minute highlight video. Copyright laws forbid you from distributing or sharing these videos, but they work extremely well for self-training purposes.

 Web sites and existing video files: If you have video files stored on your PC, you can possibly import them into Movie Maker and edit them. The word possibly refers to the formats Movie Maker can import. It can handle AVI, MPEG, WMV, and ASF, but not other popular formats such as MOV (an Apple standard). To use other formats, you must first convert the file to one Movie Maker can work with, and the program itself does not provide that function. You can also download videos from innumerable locations on the Internet, but here again, keep in mind that copyright laws forbid almost all distribution or showing of the content except to yourself.

Which Camcorder?

You can use any camcorder with Windows Movie Maker. As long as the camcorder has a video output jack (RCA, USB, FireWire, or anything else) and you have the correct cable to run from that port to the video card, you can import video into Movie Maker. But if you're in the market for a camcorder and you intend to use it primarily or even significantly for creating video to edit on your PC, you should consider the quality of the video you want to create and the ease with which the PC and the camcorder communicate with one another.

PC-camcorder communication becomes less of an issue with each generation of camcorder. Today's camcorders are made with digital video editing in mind, so they offer appropriate interfaces. These interfaces include not only the ability to control the digital camcorder from within video editing software such as Movie Maker, but also fast, reliable transfer connections with either or both FireWire and USB 2.0. If you are buying your first camcorder, however, watch which type of transfer connection the camcorder supports. At this point, only FireWire provides all the benefits, with USB 2.0 coming along quickly. Older, slower USB 1.1 or 1.0 connections will frustrate you not only with the poor transfer speed for video but also with the lack of control over the camera from within the program. Recent USB-connected cameras, however, have offered sophisticated support for USB streaming, in which the computer imports the video as a stream.

Of greater concern is the video format your camera supports. Two primary digital formats are now available, DV (and the related MiniDV) — DV stands for Digital Video — and Digital-8 (the latter introduced by Sony). Older-style VHS and 8mm camcorders still exist, along with the better-resolution Hi8mm, but DV and Digital-8 record in digital format, with far better preservation of signal when transferring between camera and PC. DV recorders use either specialized tapes or built-in disk-based storage, while Digital-8 recorders use Hi8mm or even regular 8mm tapes and record a digital signal onto them. The benefits of Digital8 are the ability to use less expensive tapes, along with compatibility for your existing 8mm and Hi8mm tapes. Ultimately, DV gives you better quality, and if you're serious about producing digital video you should consider a DV camcorder carefully, but Digital8 camcorders are also extremely appealing for many reasons.

In addition to the video itself, you need some items that, in all likelihood, came with your computer if you bought it within the last few years or that you've accumulated over time. First, and obviously, you need a video card, and while you do not need the most expensive or technologically advanced card, you should aim for a card with a minimum of 64MB of video memory (128MB is even better) and, ideally, an AGP 2X (or higher) interface. The reason for this is performance: You can create videos with a less capable video card, but you'll quickly notice that Movie Maker's responsiveness suffers along with the quality of what you've captured. Closely related in terms of performance issues is the CPU of your system; here, too, the more powerful the processor, the better your system's performance with *any* video features, not just Movie Maker. At this point, you should count on a 2.8GHz Pentium 4 processor or above, although certainly you can use Movie Maker with less. You should also work with at least 500MB of system RAM in order to give Movie Maker the room it needs to process video, but here, too, you can do with less as long as you're willing to put up with slow response. The problem is that the response can get *extremely* slow, so be prepared if you choose to go this route.

One thing you must look for in a video card is the ability to import video signals from external devices. To this end, you need either a video input jack or, if you plan to work with only VCRs or TV signals, the coaxial jack that TV tuner cards have. Many video cards possess neither and contain only a monitor port, so be sure that you have input capabilities. If not, you can buy a reasonably good video card for not much more than $100 that will contain everything you need. Some cards, in fact, offer an extension component that plugs into the video card and contains jacks for audio, video, and often USB or FireWire input. You can also buy separate TV tuner cards that fit into a vacant PCI slot on your motherboard and work in conjunction with the video card to capture TV signals. TV capture hardware is also available for external attachment via USB, USB 2.0, or FireWire ports.

Unless you plan to produce nothing but silent movies, you also need a sound card. Here, too, however, you probably already have one because all PCs ship with sound capabilities, either as a separate peripheral card or built into the motherboard, unless you specifically request that they do not. You can work with two different audio sources in Movie Maker — the audio captured during the filming itself, which you cannot separate from the video, and an entirely separate audio track, which you can create separately using audio- or music-editing programs and import into Movie Maker. You can use a microphone to narrate the video, but you can't have both a separate audio track and narration at the same time. In other words, if you want musical background for your video, the only way to add narration is to cut the audio track into sections and record narration between them. See the "More On Audio" sidebar for a way to compensate for this shortcoming.

Finally, you need the cables necessary to connect the video and audio sources to the sound and video cards. Things can get tricky here because the connections on your sound card frequently differ from those on the other equipment. For example, to capture video from a VCR, you need both a video and an audio cable; the video cable has an RCA-style plug at both ends, while the audio cable has two RCA-style plugs at one end — one for each stereo channel — and a mini-stereo plug at the other. Other situations demand different kinds of cabling. You can get all the cables you need at your local computer or electronics store; take the product manuals for your sound and video cards with you when cable shopping. (For that vast majority of PC users who have no idea where those manuals might have disappeared to, you can usually find PDF versions in the support section of the manufacturer's Web site.) You can also buy a wide array of adapter cables, in case you have one type of connector on one device and another on the other device. One such adapter cable lets you connect S-Video connectors to RCA jacks, allowing you greater flexibility in choosing a multimedia card.

More On Audio

You can add only one audio track to a Movie Maker video in addition to the audio recorded with the video file itself (that is, while the recording was taking place). Unfortunately, having only one track of audio limits your options considerably, especially given the very real fact of the importance of sound in movies. Movie houses keep investing in better and better sound systems for a reason: sound and music, they realize, are very nearly as important to the viewing of a movie as the pictures themselves — in some cases, maybe even more important.

The best way to create a separate audio track is to use third-party multitrack-recording software, of which numerous packages are available. These programs range in cost from under $100 to over $800, but you can do almost as much with the cheaper ones as you can with the expensive ones. As an example, Magix Music Studio 2005 offers a full-featured multitrack recording studio for about $100, and while Cakewalk's Sonar 4 Producer Edition offers more features and more precise control, at roughly six times the price you have to be a serious musician to consider it. Both programs include video-editing software, however, and Cakewalk 4 Producer Edition has generated considerable enthusiasm for the way in which its audio- and video-editing capabilities work together.

These programs let you record audio (typically WAV) and MIDI files as a series of tracks. If you are recording music, for example, you record a drum track first, then a bass track, then a guitar track, and you follow it up with a main vocal track and some harmony vocal tracks. If you're not satisfied, keep adding tracks of various instruments and sounds until you're finished. You can add numerous sound effects, ranging from the standard reverb to bizarre items that make it sound extremely spacey, and you can fiddle with the equalization and settings to your heart's content.

When you've finished your recording, you combine the tracks into one (the term is track bouncing) and record it as a single audio file, usually in WAV format or MP3 if you want a smaller file. You can then import the track into Movie Maker's single audio track and have a full, rich sound on your video.

Of course, the problem then becomes synchronization. Unless you're providing only some generic background music or sound effects, where the timing of the sound does not matter, you want to synchronize the sounds and music in the audio track with the events of the video track. You can do this in numerous ways:

- Using your music-recording software, create multiple audio files. Import them all into Movie Maker as a separate collection called, say, Audio Files, and drag each item onto the audio track as needed. Use the timeline to split or clip the audio segments in order to synchronize them with their corresponding video elements.

- Create a single audio file with your music recording software, import it into Movie Maker, and drag it to the audio/music track on the timeline. Play the movie to the point where you need to make adjustments, pause it at that point, and split the audio track. Continue this process until you have as many splits as you need, and then resize the newly created clips to correspond with the video elements.

Continued

More On Audio *(continued)*

- Buy music-recording software that includes a video import feature. Create the video in Movie Maker, and import it into the recording software. Now, create your music and sound tracks using it as the basis. The benefits to this approach are flexibility and precision; the video track is only one of a potentially unlimited number of tracks (depending on the recording software), and you can use the software's extensive features for audio fading and resizing to match the audio precisely to the video.

The question, as always, is how much work you want to put into your project. But with a combination of Movie Maker and good audio software, your videos are certain to be more impressive than ever.

Digital camcorders connect to PCs via FireWire (IEEE 1394) or, increasingly, through USB 2.0 ports. To capture video, you need both the matching connection on your PC and the appropriate cable to connect the two together. To be safe, buy a PC with both FireWire and USB 2.0 ports, but if you have only one of the two and your camera requires the other one, you need to purchase a peripheral board for your desktop PC or a PC card adapter for your notebook. If you're not sure whether your computer has the appropriate ports, open Device Manager from the Hardware tab of the System Properties dialog (you'll find System Properties in Control Panel, or use Winlogo+Break) and look for sections labeled IEEE 1394 Bus Host Controllers and Universal Serial Bus Controllers. Your PC must have these devices installed for them to appear in Device Manager.

Making Your First Movie

The sequence here steps through the process of creating a movie using Movie Maker 2.1 along with both an older 8mm camcorder — specifically a Sharp ViewCam Hi-Fi Monaural — and a newer digital camcorder, a Sony Digital-8, connected to an ATI All-In-Wonder Radeon 8500DV video card. As you can tell by the screen captures, beginning with Figure 13-1 a bit later in this chapter, the video is nothing fancy, just a home movie of a small wedding shot last year on a hot August day. But that's precisely the kind of video that so many people have sitting around waiting to be edited — hence its inclusion here. The steps are as follows:

1. Plan your video.

2. Collect your tools and resources.

3. Connect the video source to your computer.

4. Launch Movie Maker.

5. Capture the video from the source into Movie Maker.

6. Wait for Movie Maker to create the video clips.

7. Drag the clips to the storyboard in whatever order you wish.

8. Edit clips by splitting them and/or altering their duration.

9. Insert transitions between clips.

10. Edit clips for special effects such as fades.

11. Add titles.

12. Import audio files into Movie Maker.

13. Drag the audio clips onto the timeline to create the sound/audio track.

14. Edit the audio clips by splitting them and/or altering their duration.

15. Set audio volume and properties.

16. Create the movie file.

To be sure, this list seems extensive. You'll quickly discover, though, that the stages quickly become almost second nature because once you start using Movie Maker the logic of the sequence stands out. You actually *require* only a single video track consisting of one or more video clips; you add the rest of the steps to create a video worth watching (and hearing). Once you get the pattern of dragging clips to the storyboard or the timeline, then editing the clips and adding effects, titles, and audio to enhance those clips, the process seems to require fewer steps than those listed here.

Planning Your Video

As with anything else in the world of creativity software, you don't actually have to plan. You can simply gather your materials, fire up Movie Maker, and go to town. You'll end up with a video, and it might be wonderful, but in all likelihood you'll find yourself editing further. In fact, video professionals, like movie professionals, will tell you that a successful product is all about planning. Videos and movies undergo careful, precise crafting.

Of course, your home videos need much less of this crafting because you already know you'll have a mostly sympathetic audience. Even so, you can increase everyone's enjoyment, including your own, by following at least some of the planning items listed here. Keep in mind, though, that these items assume that you already have the video footage, so the list does not include planning and staging the actual shooting. Storyboarding your shots and directing the production are far beyond the scope of this book.

Here are the major items to consider when planning your video:

■ Decide what you want to say. You don't need an overarching epic story or even a consistent narrative thread. But even if you decide to show your audience something as simple as "our wedding was beautiful," you have a place to start. You want to focus on the events, people, and places that made it beautiful, and you omit, shorten, or deemphasize the rest (like Uncle Billy getting drunk and passing out in his food). In a business video covering new procedures, a production that clearly states how the new procedures will streamline tasks not only speaks more strongly to the audience but also provides a sharper focus on what to include.

▪ Watch the video and note the 10 most important moments, keeping in mind your decision about what you're trying to say. Watch it again, and cut that number to five. Watch it one last time, and decide on the three absolutely essential moments. Now you're ready to build your video with a sharp focus. All other moments remain important, but you now know where you wish to direct your audience's attention through careful use of the Movie Maker editing capabilities.

▪ With a pencil and paper, storyboard the video. Draw four rows of five boxes, with each box having enough room for notes, and draw a line beneath each row on which to note the timing of the boxes. In the first box of the second row, write the name of the first of the three most important moments you determined beforehand. Write the name of the second in the first box of the third row, and the third in the first box of the last row. Fill in the first row with items in the video that lead toward the first moment, fill in the remainder of the second row with items leading to the second important moment, and so on. By the time you've finished, you'll have a useful little storyboard to refer to as you edit.

▪ At the end of the line beneath the last row of boxes, write down the endpoint of the video in minutes. For example, if you want a 30-minute video, write 30. On the line below each row, note the approximate time at which each box will occur, keeping the total length of the entire video in mind. This procedure helps you time your important moments and then, with those decided, the remaining events and sequences.

▪ Write down anything else that comes to mind that you want in your video, including music, narration, the types of transitions, and titles, text, and credits. Where you can, note the location of each of these on the timeline.

Obviously, you can plan much more by expanding the number of boxes and specifying numerous events on the timeline. But even if you follow only the processes in this list, you'll start your editing session with an excellent idea of what you're trying to accomplish.

The Movie Maker Process

Creating a movie consists of two stages: capturing video and editing it. Here are the steps for both stages, with explanations of how each step proceeds.

STAGE ONE: CAPTURING VIDEO

If you don't have video, you can't edit it. Unless you use preexisting video files, which you can simply import into Movie Maker and edit from there, you have to bring in video from another source. The steps here assume a capture from a camcorder, but the process from a VCR and other sources is practically identical.

1. Connect the camcorder to the video card and turn the camcorder on.

2. Load Movie Maker. Click the Capture From Video item in the Movie Tasks pane. The Video Capture Wizard loads.

3. On the Video Capture Device screen, select the appropriate device (you might have only one). Also set the input source for the video by choosing Composite, TV Tuner, or SVideo from the drop-down menu. Composite refers to the standard video input jacks on your video card, but if your card and video device let you work with the higher-quality SVideo connection, by all means do so.

4. In the Audio section of the screen, shown in Figure 13-1, choose the audio device you want to use (often your sound card is the only option listed here) and the input source of the audio data. Usually you select the Line In option because the Line In jack acts as the primary nonmicrophone input for sound cards. This is most certainly true of camcorders, VCRs, DVDs, or TVs; to capture the audio portion of the tape, you run your cable from the output of the camcorder or VCR to the Line In jack on your card. You can, however, create an audio track entirely separate from the video by choosing a different sound source, such as your computer's CD player. In this case, you bring no audio from the video source at all, so don't use this separate sound source option unless you know you don't want the audio portion. One benefit of this approach is that, in effect, it gives you two audio tracks separate from the video: the audio you capture while capturing the video, and the audio you capture later to place on the audio/music track.

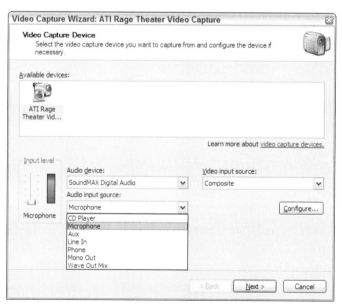

Figure 13-1: Setting the video and audio capture devices.

5. If you wish, you can configure the camera settings, video settings, and TV tuner from this screen as well, by clicking the Configure button. Of particular note is the Camera Settings button that appears after you do so, which itself yields the Properties screen, one tab of

which is shown in Figure 13-2. Under the Video Decoder tab, you can see the number of lines of resolution detected on your tape (the higher the better), but more important, you can adjust the way Movie Maker processes the video during the capture. Under the Video Proc Amp tab, you can adjust the brightness, contrast, hue, and saturation, and with some input devices other attributes as well, but in doing so keep in mind that you cannot undo these settings. Still, if you are trying to create a bright, richly contrasted video from a sub-standard original, experiment with these settings. In addition to the camera settings, you can adjust the settings for your TV tuner from this screen, setting the television channel you want to capture (TV Tuner button), the input source if you have more than one (main screen), and whether you wish to capture in NTSC (North American) or PAL (European) configuration (Video Decoder tab). Once you've made all your selections, click OK for each of the individual dialogs, to get back to the initial wizard screen, and then click Next to move to the next stage of the wizard.

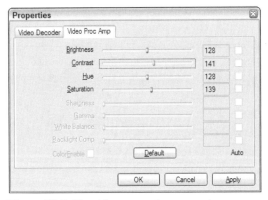

Figure 13-2: The video-processing properties.

Caution

Be careful not to overadjust the video-processing settings. Sliding the brightness control even a short distance to the right increases the picture's brightness considerably, and sliding it all the way over makes even a dark video far too light. Even worse, sliding any one of these controls by half the distance to the left or right can cause Movie Maker to crash, especially with analog camcorders.

6. On the resulting Captured Video File screen, you give the file a name by which Movie Maker can later refer to it and decide on a location in which to store the file on your hard drive. By default, Movie Maker uses the My Videos folder, a subfolder within My Documents, but to keep your projects separate you should click Browse and create a new folder for each project. Click Next when you've finished this step.

7. The Video Setting screen (see Figure 13-3) provides a crucial set of options. The Movie Maker default, the Best Quality for Playback on My Computer option, configures the video according to the technical capabilities of your PC. In most cases, you end up with a video with a size of 320 x 240 pixels at 30 frames per second, with a variable bit rate and a relatively low file size. If you intend to distribute the video instead of simply playing it on your own PC, click the Other Settings radio button and choose one of the numerous options from the drop-down menu. These options change depending on the video source. Figure 13-3 shows the menu that appears with the Sony Digital-8 camcorder attached to the PC, while the older Sharp analog camcorder dispenses with the DV-AVI option as well as the two options for video with local playback (NTSC).

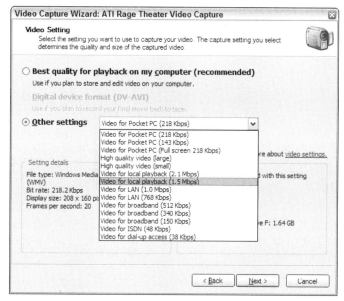

Figure 13-3: Video-editing options.

As you click on each option, the Setting details area of the dialog box shows the display size, bit rate, and frames per second properties associated with that selection. Simultaneously, the Video File Size area changes to reflect the amount of disk space required for each minute of video along with the space available on the hard drive. You will find this information extremely important because of the speed with which video chews up disk space. This is especially true if you select the DV-AVI format (click the middle radio button under the Video Setting heading), which is designed to let you copy the edited video back onto tape. As Figure 13-4 shows, this setting offers the highest video quality, with a bit rate of 25 Mbps and a display size of 720 × 480 pixels, but it eats a whopping 178MB of your disk for *each minute* of video.

8. After you've decided on the video setting, click Next to get into the real action. The Capture Video screen (shown in Figure 13-4) gives you a preview window showing the video,

along with a Start Capture button, a Stop Capture button, and, in the case of a digital video camcorder, a set of DV camera controls. The DV camera controls do just that: They let you control your DV camcorder from the Movie Maker interface instead of from the camcorder itself. With an analog camcorder, by comparison, you have to use the controls on the camcorder, with Movie Maker providing only the capture capabilities. The Capture Video screen also gives you the options of muting the computer's speakers (Movie Maker captures the sound, but you don't hear it during the capture), of automatically splitting the video into clips (otherwise, it creates a single long clip), and of setting a capture time limit. Only automatic clip creating appears as a default; for your first movie leave it checked.

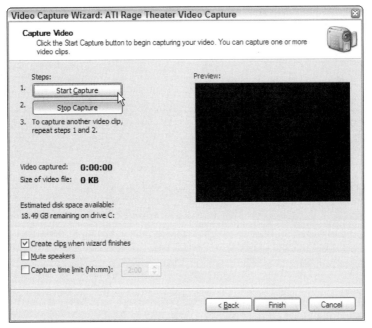

Figure 13-4: The Capture Video screen.

9. Click the Start Capture button. If you're using a non-DV camcorder, press the Play button on the device. Movie Maker is now capturing your video. If you have a DV camcorder, initiating the capture opens another screen, as shown in Figure 13-5. This Capture Video screen lets you choose to capture the entire tape automatically, in which case Movie Maker rewinds the source video to the beginning and begins the capture, or to capture manually by cueing the tape yourself and clicking the Start Capture and Stop Capture buttons according to the video you wish to capture. This screen also provides an option to prevent the video from appearing in the preview window during capture, a choice that guarantees the best-quality video but also somewhat lessens the usability of the Capture Video screen (if capturing manually, you have to view the video on the camcorder). Make your choice, and click Next.

Caution

Watch the Size of Video File display for the first few minutes of the video capture. When using an analog camcorder, Movie Maker sometimes fails to perform the capture, even though the preview window displays the video in progress. If the video file size does not rise, Movie Maker has probably stopped working properly. In this case, click Stop Capture and then Finish, or just Finish by itself, which results in a Windows error message and the loss of your work so far. Even if the video file size does seem to work correctly, test a short capture before launching into a long one.

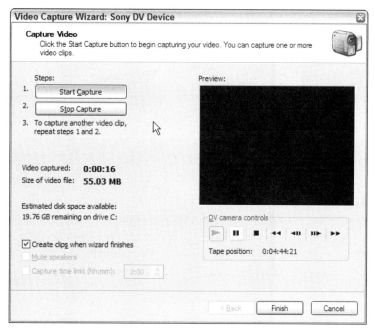

Figure 13-5: The DV capture choices.

10. When you've captured the video you want, click Stop Capture. If you want to capture additional video, cue the source video to the desired location and repeat the Capture process. When you've finished capturing, click Stop Capture (if it is not already stopped) and then the Finish button. Movie Maker takes a few minutes to create the clips and then displays them in the Collection area of the main Movie Maker window. Figure 13-6 shows the wedding video with two clips appearing in the Collections area.

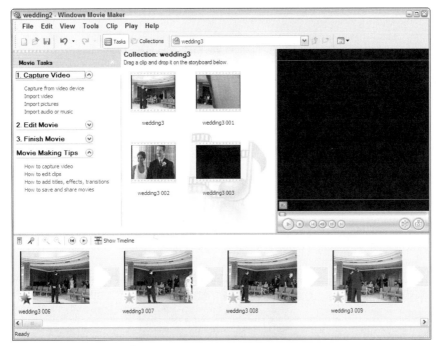

Figure 13-6: The result of all that capturing.

STAGE TWO: EDITING THE VIDEO

Editing is the whole reason for Movie Maker's existence. From this single streamlined interface, you drag the captured video clips onto the storyboard or the timeline, add a few bells and whistles (literally, if you want), and tell Movie Maker to create the video file. Here are the steps.

1. Click on the first clip and preview it for a few seconds (or as long as you want) by clicking the Play button below the preview window.

2. Now get used to the controls. Click the Stop button to halt the video and return to the beginning. Slide the Seek bar, located just above the controls, to any location in the movie. Click Play to view the clip from that point. While viewing the video, click the Next Frame button (fourth in line from the Play button) to pause the video; click it again several times to move ahead one frame each time. When you've reached a frame you like, capture it as a still image by clicking the Take Picture button. The Save Picture As window opens, letting you save the still as a JPG file in whatever folder you wish. The photo also appears instantly in the collection.

3. With the first clip still selected, drag it to the first placeholder on the storyboard (that is, the square on the far left). The clip now exists both on the storyboard and in the collection. Clicking on the clip places it in the preview window, from which you can view it as before. You can also play it by clicking the Play Storyboard button in the storyboard toolbar.

4. Drag the second clip to the second storyboard placeholder and the third clip to the third placeholder. You now have a three-clip movie ready for viewing (see Figure 13-7). Clicking the Play Storyboard button plays the three clips in succession; the currently playing clip is highlighted on the storyboard, and this highlight changes as the movie moves to the next clip. As the movie plays in the preview window, clicking on a clip moves the Seek slider to the start of that clip and plays the movie from that location; similarly, as you move the Seek slider, the highlighted clip on the storyboard changes to reflect that move. In part, this is what makes Movie Maker easy and quite powerful: Its various components interact so completely.

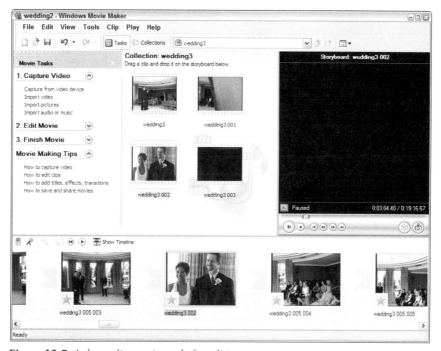

Figure 13-7: A three-clip movie ready for editing.

5. Split the existing clips into additional clips. This step is unnecessary if you already have a large number of clips, but if Movie Maker created only a few, you can add more in two ways. First, you can play the video to the point where you want a new clip to start, then click the Split button on the preview window's control bar (the button lies immediately to the left of the Take Picture button) or choose Clip → Split. This process splits the clip into two clips and lets you work with each independently. Second, you can have Movie Maker create additional clips automatically by right-clicking the clip in the Collections area and choosing Create Clips from the menu. This process gives you many additional clips, and you essentially start your storyboard over again. If you wish, you can continue to split and create clips, breaking your footage into smaller and smaller segments.

6. Edit out unnecessary footage. Much unedited video has a great deal of unnecessary footage, at least from the standpoint of the intended audience. You can eliminate excess footage in two primary ways — first, by deleting clips and, second, by decreasing their duration. You can delete clips from either the storyboard/timeline or the collections window by right-clicking the appropriate item and choosing Delete; you can decrease their duration by trimming them. To trim a clip, click the Show Timeline button just above the storyboard, click the appropriate clip in the timeline, move the pointer over either end of the clip until it turns into a double red arrow (see Figure 13-8), and drag the clip either left or right, depending on whether you want to eliminate footage from the beginning or the end of the clip.

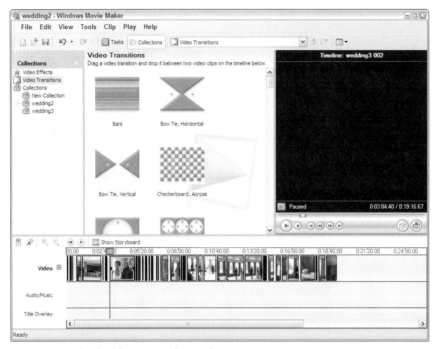

Figure 13-8: The double arrow in the timeline.

7. Add effects to individual clips by right-clicking the clip and choosing Video Effects. Figure 13-9 shows the Add or Remove Video Effects dialog box atop the movie interface, with only the first clip, at the far left of the storyboard, selected. Click the effect you want, and then click the Add button. When you've finished adding them, click OK to put them into effect. You can also add effects by choosing Tools → Video Effects, clicking the icon for the desired effect in the resulting Video Effects window, and dropping it onto the clip. When you've applied a video effect, the Effects icon at the bottom-left corner of the clip (in the storyboard) becomes highlighted, and you can hover the pointer over that icon to see a list of the effects for that clip.

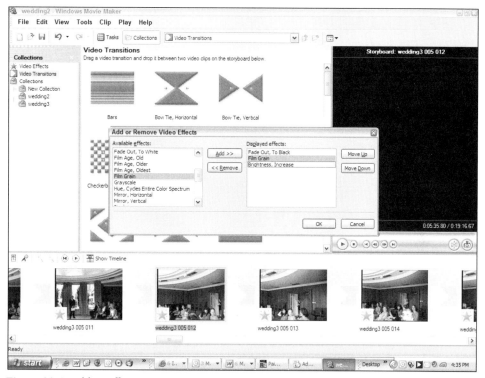

Figure 13-9: Adding effects.

8. Add transitions between clips, especially when an edit or trim has produced discontinuity. To add a transition, choose Tools → Video Transitions to display the Transitions area. Click on the Transition icon you want and drag it to the small square on the storyboard just in front of the clip into which you wish to transition. The transition creates an artificial link between the clips, adding a special effect that acknowledges the discontinuity but prevents jarring the viewer by making it obvious. Movie Maker includes transitions ranging from upward and downward wipes to page curls, shatters, dissolves, checkerboards, pixelation, and even a keyhole (see Figure 13-10). The transition appears briefly in the video to help your audience make the switch from clip to clip easily.

Tip

Transitions can be extremely effective, but if you use too many of them they quickly come to seem amateurish to an extreme. Use them only when you need to give your viewers' eyes something to focus on between the clips. They provide an excellent means of switching from one location to another in your video, such as from the final scene in the wedding ceremony to the opening scene halfway into the reception later in the day.

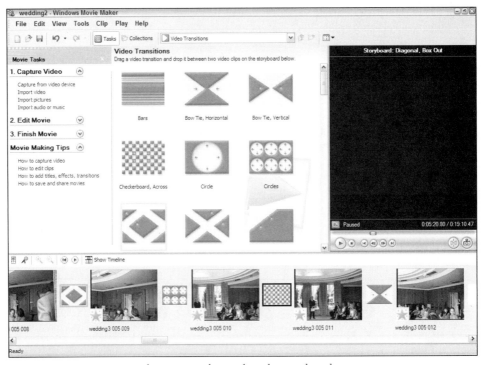

Figure 13-10: Transitions in the main window and on the storyboard.

9. Click the Rewind Storyboard icon just above the storyboard to rewind to the beginning of your video. Click the Play button, and watch the movie all the way through, stopping to make additional changes as you see fit.

10. Click the Show Timeline button to reveal the timeline. Here, you can see the Audio/ Music track and the Title Overlay track. If you want to add narration to your video, plug a microphone into your sound card (or whatever audio device you have configured in Movie Maker), and choose Tools → Narrate Timeline. Click the Start Narration button in the Narrate Timeline area, perform the narration, and click Stop Narration when you've finished. Movie Maker adds a clip in the Audio/Music track, showing the beginning and ending of the narration. You can add music clips and other sounds to that track as well.

11. To add titles, credits, and other text overlays, choose Tools → Titles and Credits. Figure 13-11 shows the result: a number of hyperlinks that change the interface once more when you click them, allowing you to add the textual elements precisely where you wish. To add an overall title, probably the choice you'll want most frequently, click Add Title at the Beginning of the Movie and fill in the cells. To add text between clips or on top of clips, click the appropriate link and fill in the cells once again. At the bottom of the Enter Text screens are two important links that let you change the animation for the title, including

fading, mirroring, and paint-dripping effects, and that also let you change the font along with its color, size, and transparency level. Click the Done link to add the text elements to the video.

Figure 13-11: The interface for textual elements.

12. Save your project in two ways. First, throughout the creation and editing, save it as a Movie Maker project by choosing Save → Project. When you've finished all your editing, choose File → Save Movie. You have several options for saving a video, ranging from saving it to a CD to saving it to a DV camera. Saving to a CD means that you can play it on any compatible video CD player, which includes most newer standalone DVD players. Saving to the Web requires a hosting location. Saving in order to send by email results in the smallest possible file and the lowest available quality.

Tip

You can save yourself a great deal of time and effort by using Movie Maker's AutoMovie feature, accessible in the Tasks pane. AutoMovie will create a movie with the clips you give it, adding transitions, effects, and fairly substantial edits. The result is always pretty good, but you're better off in the long run controlling the process yourself.

Summary

Congratulations! You've completed your first movie from start to finish. Get a bit of practice at this, and before long you can set up a ticket booth and a concession stand, wait for nobody to show up to watch it, and then complain bitterly about the prejudice of the movie industry against films that really matter. More seriously, once you've mastered the beginnings of Movie Maker, you can start digging into its numerous capabilities, such as precision placement of clips, additional special effects, and downloadable add-ons. Clearly, this program excels at usability, and its results are amazingly good, so get the most out of it before even considering advanced video software.

Chapter 14

Playing, Ripping, and Recording Music

Windows XP ships with Windows Media Player. It is best known as a multimedia file player, but it's surprisingly adept in other areas as well. Surprisingly, that is, because most people know Media Player as a music and video player only. Pop an audio CD into your CD drive, and Media Player starts and plays the music, unless your PC's manufacturer has changed the Windows XP default to launch a different program instead. Click on a Windows Media link on a video site, and Media Player lets you view the video. Even if the program doesn't actually start when you insert a CD, it always appears as an option in a menu of choices along with any other music software you've installed on your system. Thanks to its inclusion in Windows, Media Player is all over the place.

But the program does more than just play music and video files. In fact, it offers a range of advanced features that give you control over numerous multimedia tasks, including: listening to the radio, burning CDs, transferring playlists to portable devices, and purchasing music online.

This chapter covers the variety of music-related activities possible with Windows Media Player, from playing songs and acquiring album information to ripping and burning CDs. To follow the details in this chapter fully, you need version 10 of Windows Media Player. If you don't have version 10, you can download and install it via Windows Update or from the Microsoft site at microsoft.com/windows/windowsmedia/mp10/default.aspx. Alternatively, by installing Service Pack 2 (see Chapter 1), you get version 10 automatically.

Incidentally, lest you think I'm advocating particularly violent actions in your musical computing, *ripping* (in CD-land, anyway) means copying songs from a CD to your hard drive, while *burning* means copying data to a CD. Just another couple of charming computer terms, nothing more.

Note

Many who use Media Player recommend against installing version 9 or 10, first citing problems with stability and then decrying the Digital Rights Management (DRM) features built into it (see the DRM sidebar later in this chapter). Both issues are valid for certain users, but many users have also reported no stability problems, and many either do not know about or have no problem with DRM making its way into entertainment presentation software. This chapter examines version 10 because it offers the latest features, but if either of these items concern you, feel free to stick with Media Player 8 or earlier, whatever you already have on your PC. If you do, though, be aware that some of the instructions in this chapter won't do you a lot of good.

Playing Music

In all likelihood, you've already discovered that Media Player plays music. It does so very well, automatically, and painlessly. But inside the Media Player interface lies a plethora of features that few users ever bother to learn. Then again, it also has limitations that many people overlook. As an example of the former, Media Player contains a built-in graphic equalizer with three different modes of operation, giving you full control over the tone of your music (see the "Sound Enhancements" section later in this chapter). As an example of the latter, Media Player does not, in and of itself, work completely with two of today's primary digital formats: MP3 and DVD.

If you want to record MP3 files (Media Player plays them just fine) or watch DVD movies, you have to install add-ons. In the case of MP3 encoding, this usually means purchasing new software (often inexpensively, but it's still a purchase). In the case of DVD viewing, you can also purchase an add-on, but first check your DVD movie collection. Many DVD movies come with their own DVD decoder for your PC (insert the DVD into your DVD drive to find out), and this can help you overcome that limitation. But back to music.

You can play almost all popular music formats in Media Player. A summary of digital music formats appears later in this chapter; but for now, you can assume that Media Player will play whatever you offer it, including audio CDs, .wav files, MP3 files, .wma files, and more. It cannot, however, play your RealAudio files (including RA, RM, RPM) or Apple iTunes files (AAC format). So, if you get your music via iTunes, stick with the iTunes player.

To play a music track in Media Player, you have several choices:

- Open Media Player, choose File → Open, use the Open dialog box to navigate to the music file, select the file, and click Open.

- Use My Computer or Windows Explorer to navigate to the music file, right-click on the filename, choose Open With from the menu, and click on Windows Media Player. If the file bears the Media Player icon, you can simply double-click it to play it with Media Player; if you've assigned that file type to another music program (some programs, on installation, make it hard not to do this), the file will have that program's icon. In this case, you'll have to use the right-click method.

- Use My Computer to navigate to the music file. Select it and click the Play All item in the Music Tasks area on the left (this item becomes Play Selection if you choose multiple tracks).

- Launch Media Player and insert a music CD in the CD drive.

- Without Media Player or any other music program running, insert a CD in the CD drive and wait for the Audio CD dialog box to appear. Choose the Play Audio CD using Windows Media Player option. If you want Media Player to load automatically whenever you insert a CD, click the Always Do the Selected Action check box and click OK.

In all these cases, the music file begins playing. The Seek bar, located just above the Play controls at the bottom of the screen, indicates the current location in the track. You can slide the Seek control forward to jump ahead in the song or backward to rewind it. To see information about the song itself, click the Now Playing button on the toolbar.

Note

Although you can use Media Player without being connected to the Internet, the first time you play a CD you must have an Internet connection in order for Media Player to download the album and track information for that CD.

Using the Info Center

By default, this action shows one of a number of possible Info Centers designed to display the information about the track such as artist, song title, album title, and more (see Figure 14-1). The Info Center view that actually appears depends on which music store or information site you've selected via the Choose Online Store button at the top right of the Windows Media Player interface. This chapter uses MSN Music for the sake of demonstration. But as I discuss later in the chapter, under the "Using Media Player's Online Stores" heading, you have a wide range of choices available. Each online store provides a different Info Center view.

Figure 14-1: MSN Music's Info Center in Windows Media Player.

Like the view itself, the actual information you get from the Info Center depends on which store you've selected. Figure 14-1 shows the result of clicking the album cover for the currently playing CD using the MSN Music Info Center. As you can see, the only information here is about the album itself, how to buy tracks from it, and CDs you might also like (the list on the right). Other Info Centers (such as Puretracks) give you more information about individual tracks. The Walmart Music Downloads view of the Info Center provides a short text write-up of the current CD, but nothing else other than a link to buy it.

All of which brings up the question, "Who thought this was a good idea?" In Windows Media Player 9, the Info Center was still related to purchasing the product (there was a link to do so), but it also provided useful links to artist information, lyrics, similar music, and more. In other words, the Info Center actually had *information*! Obviously, Microsoft figured it was time to link directly into the sales of music — commendable in that nobody should be downloading music without paying for it — but why penalize the potential purchasers by providing even less information than before? The result is a poorer Media Player than before from an information standpoint, but a richer one for purchasing online. A fair trade-off? No, I don't think so.

Using Media Player's Online Stores

Media Player 10 makes it easier than ever to spend your money on music. In addition, you can spend your money on movies, radio, and even Court TV (I'm not making this up). Figure 14-2 shows the result of clicking the Browse All Online Stores item in the Online Stores drop-down box at the top right of the Media Player's interface.

Figure 14-2: Choose your online store.

There are several ideas at work here. In the case of music, you purchase either individual songs or entire albums and download them into Media Player's library. Then you listen to them on your PC, make them available via your networked media player, or burn them to a CD. Movies work much the same way. Radio purchases give you access to multiple stations, while TV access gives you access to various programs. MLB Baseball, for example, offers a $14.95 package that lets you listen, via Media Player, to live audio broadcasts of every game on the schedule; for this price, you also get archives. For $79.95, you can watch televised broadcasts of games taking place outside your local area (again, with archives); $99.95 gets you both.

When it comes to making purchases, or gleaning information about the products, don't expect all the online stores to work the same. Each has its own interface, and each looks like a Web site rather than part of Media Player itself. In fact, Media Player basically acts as a Web browser for these stores; the only difference between buying items here and over the Web is that the files download directly into Media Player's library and are instantly ready for use. Which, by itself, is obviously a useful feature.

After selecting a store, click the Now Playing button to get the Info Center view specifically designed for that store.

Enhancements: Audio and Visual

When you first open Media Player, you see the Now Playing area (the large, central portion of the window), the All Music list (which becomes the title of the CD if you insert an audio CD) on the right, and the Mini Player toolbar at the bottom. You don't actually need any other elements to listen to music. You can, however, gain much greater control over the actual sound of the music by bringing other elements of the Media Player interface to the screen, especially a set of additional areas called Enhancements. You'll quickly find some of the sound-oriented Enhancements indispensable for a complete listening experience, because they provide methods of adjusting the music file or CD precisely to match the capabilities of your speakers and your sound card and the vagaries of your listening moods.

You can access each of the Enhancements separately by choosing View → Enhancements and choosing the one you want. Alternatively, choose View → Enhancements → Show Enhancements to reveal the Enhancements pane, and then click the back and forward arrows at the top of the pane to move among them.

SOUND ENHANCEMENTS

From the standpoint of Media Player as a playback vehicle for your music, the most important enhancements are those that let you change the sound of the currently loaded track. And make no mistake, these enhancements do their job. You can thoroughly alter the sound of the song you're listening to, in effect creating a different experience each time out.

As with even the cheapest stereo, tone controls provide the greatest single difference in sound (well, technically volume controls do because you can silence the music completely or blow out your ears and your windows, but we'll stick with tone controls here). Media Player goes beyond the standard bass and treble controls, however. Instead, you get a full 10-band graphic equalizer (see Figure 14-3), giving you pinpoint control over the full range of frequencies. Not only that, but you can control these frequencies in three different ways. The equalizer represents Media Player's true tour de force from a listening standpoint — a true enhancement.

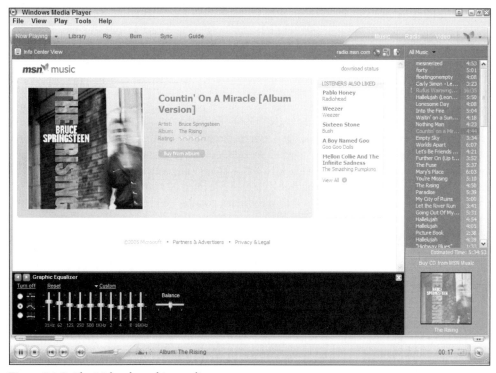

Figure 14-3: The 11-band graphic equalizer.

Choose Graphic View → Enhancements → Equalizer. Activate the equalizer by clicking the Turn On link near the top of the Enhancements pane (it should be on by default). Now, play some music and slide the controls up and down. The slider on the far left controls the lowest bass sounds; the one on the right, the highest treble sounds. Between those two extremes lie the remaining frequencies, with midrange — in which you find the majority of vocals, guitars, and middle-range piano — occupying the middle three to five bands. If you love bass at the expense of everything else, drag the treble sliders down and raise the bass; if you want only midrange booming bass, emphasize the second and third sliders from the left. If you want to emphasize high-hats, triangles, piccolos, and other high-end instruments, raise the sliders near the right extreme. And so on.

You have several ways to adjust these settings. The three radio buttons to the left of the sliders give you the following modes of control (from top to bottom):

- **Independent:** Each slider moves independently of the others, thereby providing precise control over each frequency range.

- **Loose Group:** Moving one slider affects all the others, but only to a limited extent, with the frequencies closest to the slider being moved undergoing the greatest change.

- **Tight Group:** Moving one slider moves all the other sliders to a significant degree, with the cluster of nearby sliders undergoing the greatest change.

These options provide an extremely useful variety of methods for adjusting the tone. If you know precisely which frequency you want to change, click the Independent button. If you have a pretty good idea, but you want to make sure by adjusting similar frequencies, click the Loose Group button. Finally, if you want a general change, something closer to the standard Treble and Bass controls on a stereo, use the Tight Group option.

If you prefer, simply choose the sound you want and let Media Player perform the actual adjustments. This option appears in the form of a menu when you click the Custom link just above the sliders. From this menu, you can choose from a variety of configurations with the frequency adjustments preset to genres of music such as rock, grunge, opera, classical, blues, and more. Click the one you want, and watch the sliders readjust.

Also available on the Graphic Equalizer Enhancement pane is the left and right balance control.

The SRS WOW enhancement (not pictured in Figure 14-3) also significantly affects tone. A combination of technologies, SRS WOW simulates a surround-sound experience, with more powerful bass and enhanced midrange sounds, especially good for listening to quiet tracks, in quiet environments, or, on the other extreme, for locations where you need to get additional power from your speakers. Click the Turn On link to activate this feature, and then click the speaker link beside it to customize the sound for large speakers, normal speakers (the default), or headphones. Slide the TruBass control to the right for stronger bass or left for weaker, and the WOW Effect slider to enhance the surround-sound simulation.

Two additional enhancements change the listening experience (again, not pictured in Figure 14-3). Quiet Mode helps when you need to keep the volume turned down by evening out the differences in volume between loud and soft passages in the music (in music lingo, this process is called *normalization*). Turn the feature on and specify the result you want: medium difference for a moderate amount of normalization or little difference for maximum normalization in which loud and soft passages will be as close to the same volume as possible. The Crossfading and Auto Volume Leveling Enhancement pane provides two more controls. Auto Volume Leveling works somewhat like normalization, but instead of leveling out the volume differences in a single music track, it levels out the volume differences between tracks, a problem particularly acute when downloading music (purchased albums are mastered to ensure balanced volume levels). Crossfading makes Media Player sound like a radio station by overlapping the end of one track with the beginning of the next. Note that both Auto Volume Leveling and Crossfading works only with downloaded files or files ripped from audio CDs, not with audio CDs themselves.

OTHER ENHANCEMENTS

While the sound enhancements affect your listening, you can influence the appearance and performance of Media Player in other ways as well:

- **Skin Mode:** Not related in any way to listening to music while unclothed, choosing Skin Mode shrinks the size of Media Player dramatically, configuring it as a small, stylish-looking device that's easier to keep out of the way of other windows. Figure 14-4 shows the result of clicking the Skin Chooser item on the View menu: Click on each item on the Skin list to see what each skin looks like. When you've decided on one you like, click the Apply Skin item just above the main windows. From this point on, when you choose View → Skin Mode in the standard (Full) version of the player, the player will take on the look of this skin.

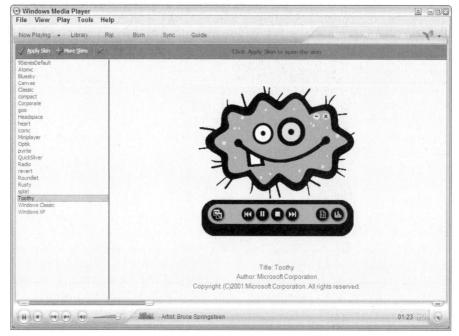

Figure 14-4: The Skin Chooser window in Media Player.

In Skin Mode (see Figure 14-5), right-click the player and choose Switch to Full Mode to return to the standard player. In fact, while in Skin Mode the right-click menu becomes in many ways your best friend, offering all Media Player options.

Figure 14-5: Media Player using the Canvas skin.

- **Color Chooser:** This Enhancement pane lets you set the hue and saturation of the standard player or choose black as the background color.

- **Play Speed Settings:** This Enhancement pane, available with only downloaded or ripped tracks, lets you speed up the audio without changing the pitch. Use it when you want to listen to a track but want to get through it more quickly, or if your offspring want to listen to music that wouldn't sound very different when sped up by, say, double.

- **Video Settings:** This Enhancement pane gives you control over hue, saturation, and brightness/contrast of videos. It works best with downloaded items such as music videos.

- **Visualizations:** On the theory, pushed hard by MTV and its spin-offs, that one cannot possibly concentrate on music without something to look at simultaneously, you can play visualizations — primarily colorful animations — in the large Now Playing area of Media Player. They range from the genuinely pretty to the bizarrely psychedelic.

Tip

While in Skin Mode, the player is much smaller, and it's quite easy to lose on a crowded desktop. You can keep it always on top by opening the Options dialog (Tools → Options in the full player, or right-click and choose Options in Skin Mode). On the Player tab, choose Keep the Player on Top of Other Windows.

Working with the Media Library and Playlists

You can listen to your commercial and burned CDs in Media Player, but it truly comes into its own as an endlessly flexible music environment with its music organization features: the Media Library and playlists. Together, they complement one another, with the Media Library encompassing all your music and each playlist containing a portion of it. Put another way, the Media Library separates your media files from the rest of the files on your PC, while the playlists divide up the Media Library. Once you've set Media Player loose finding all your media files and have separated some of them into a half-dozen playlists or so, you have a much greater degree of control over the potentially widely scattered music files on your PC. In fact, you might well discover songs you'd forgotten you'd ever downloaded or ripped from CDs.

To populate the Media Library, load Media Player and either press the F3 key or choose Tools → Search for Media Files. In the rather clumsily named Add to Media Library By Searching Computer dialog box (in somewhat less than concise style), you can search all your drives, all folders except those containing programs, the My Music folder (a subfolder of My Documents), any of the specific drives on your system, or, by clicking the Browse button, any folder or subfolder on your PC. By opening the Advanced Options area, you can tell Media Player to ensure that all the tracks added to the Media Library undergo the volume-leveling procedure so that when you create playlists, all songs will play at roughly equivalent volumes. If you choose this procedure without significantly restricting the search and want to compile the Media Library while simultaneously performing volume leveling, expect a long process.

Tip

You can configure Media Player to add items to the Media Library automatically. Choose File → Add to Library, select the By Monitoring Folders option, and click the Add button to browse for additional folders to monitor. Then click OK. By default, Media Player monitors My Music only.

Once you have items in the Media Library (see Figure 14-6), you can start organizing them into playlists. To do so, you can choose from several different methods. The first method is to right-click on any file in the Media Library and choose Add to Playlist, an action that opens the Add to Playlist dialog box, which contains a list of your playlists. Choose the playlist to which you want to add the file and click OK or create an additional playlist by clicking New. You can select multiple songs in Media Library and add them all to a playlist with a single action of this type. The second method is to expand the folder list on the left-hand side of Media Library, and right-click on one of the elements in the Artist, Album, Genre, or Other Media folders and choose Save as New Playlist. Another method is to drag songs and albums from the Media Library to the playlist. The final method is to choose New Playlist from the File menu, create the playlist, and then locate songs in Media Library to add to it.

When you have created a playlist, you can play the entire collection in sequence by right-clicking on it and choosing Play. At any time, you can drag and drop the songs in the playlist to have them play in the order you like.

Figure 14-6: The Media Library filled with songs and playlists.

Tip

You can create and populate playlists from any Windows folder, not just from the Media Library in Media Player. Open a folder on the desktop or inside Windows Explorer, locate the song files and select them, either individually or as a multiple selection, right-click, and click Add to Playlist. This action opens Media Player (if it is not already open) and also opens the Add to Playlist dialog box.

A Guide to Digital Music Formats

This section takes you on a tour of digital music formats. Understanding these formats and how to use them is indispensable for working with music files on a PC. Few things are more frustrating than downloading a file and discovering that you can't do anything with it. This section explains why that happens and what you can do to give yourself the maximum flexibility possible. This section is not specifically about Windows Media Player, but it is very much about using Windows XP itself. You will encounter these files around the Internet, and you need to know how to handle them.

Media Player itself can play several of the file types covered here. If you choose Tools → Options to open the program's Options dialog box (see Figure 14-7), you can see the list by clicking the File Types tab. Specifically, Media Player can play the following straight out of the box:

- Apple audio file (.aiff)
- Audio CD (.cdda)
- Microsoft/IBM audio file (.wav)
- MIDI (.mid)
- MPEG Layer 3 audio (.mp3)
- Windows Media Audio (.wma)
- Windows Media Video (.wmv)
- Windows Media File (.asf)
- Sun audio file (.au)

Raw music takes up a great deal of hard disk space. A commercially produced audio CD, for example, can typically hold 74 minutes of music. Because the same CD could hold roughly 650MB of data, each minute of music consumes close to 10MB of the CD. If you own music simply to listen to it, the size of the files poses no problem. Seventy-four minutes of music on a CD is more than enough for most of us, especially because most musicians seem unable to produce more than 20 minutes of even remotely memorable music with each new release.

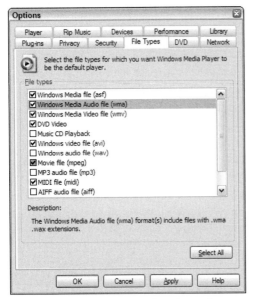

Figure 14-7: The File Types tab in the Media Player Options dialog box.

If you want to store songs on your hard drive, put them on small units that use flash memory, or send them across the Internet (legally, we mean), 30MB for a three-minute song is far too much data. For those purposes, you need a compressed format that shrinks the size of the file dramatically, ideally without losing any — or at least not very much — of the sound quality. Different compression technologies have appeared over the lifetime of the personal computer, each technology claiming different benefits and many having their 15 minutes or more of fame. The Sun Audio format, for instance, had a heyday in the Internet's early years as the only file you could realistically download over a dial-up modem. In the past couple years, the most famous audio format of them all, MP3, has fulfilled that same purpose and more.

The following sections briefly describe the major formats.

WAV

By far the most common file format among Windows music developers, WAV (which stands for Waveform sound), was a joint development of IBM and Microsoft. Although you can run into programs that don't play certain types of audio files, *every* piece of sound software in the Windows world plays .wav files. It is the standard, bar none.

Like the files on a commercial music CD, .wav files are uncompressed. Because of this, they sound practically identical to CD audio. Indeed, when you rip a song from a CD with many CD ripping programs, the default result is a .wav file; playing the two back to back reveals no discernable difference (Media Player rips CD tracks to WMA format, however). Professional recording software routinely uses WAV as the primary audio format, burning the .wav files directly to CD when the recording and mastering is completed.

.wav files use an average bit rate of 1,411.2 Kbps (that is, 1,411.2 bits per one second of audio). By comparison, the bit rate of MP3 is 128 Kbps, hence the difference in file size.

WMA

As you can probably guess by its name, Windows Media Audio is a Microsoft design and implementation and was supported at first only by Windows Media Player. When you consider that everyone running Windows owned Windows Media Player, however, and that ripping CDs using Media Player reformatted the tracks as .wma files, it's no surprise that .wma files began to proliferate on the Net. Indeed, they have, to the extent that many portable MP3 players now support both MP3 and .wma files, a trend that will not only continue but also grow.

Fortunately for music buffs, WMA provides a genuine alternative to MP3. WMA promises equivalent sound quality to MP3 files (near CD quality in both cases) at half the file size, by using 64-bit rather than MP3's standard 128-bit encoding. However, to get equal quality in the real world, you should use WMA's 128-bit encoding, at which point WMA sounds at least as good as MP3, but at which point the file size is significantly larger. That leaves one major advantage to WMA: Because of its built-in DRM capabilities, and the resultant deals between Microsoft and entertainment companies, you're likely to start finding more WMA than MP3 audio files before long.

AIFF

An acronym for Audio Interchange File Format, AIFF does for the Macintosh what WAV does for the PC. Uncompressed and of the highest quality, AIFF files are synonymous with Mac music and sound.

MP3

As a perfect example of how technology can become an almost overnight standard, with its name (or at least its acronym) becoming part of everyday language, look no further than MP3. The full name for the format is actually MPEG-1 Audio Layer 3, but with the possible exception of the engineers of the Motion Picture Experts Group, nobody calls it that. Today we have MP3 software, portable MP3 players, and MP3 support on standalone CD and DVD players. The MP3 acronym makes the news regularly because of the fight between the music industry and the zillions of people who convert CD tracks into MP3 format and trade them over the Internet. MP3 is hot, big time, and shows no sign of relinquishing its lead.

Actually, MP3 did not spread overnight. Developed by a German research institute, MP3 was patented way back in 1989, and the Motion Picture Experts Group brought it into its standard a few years later. So it's anything but brand new. But only its adoption by Internet users, empowered by MP3 decoders, brought the format into the mainstream. Then came Napster, whose horribly slow speed demanded small files, and MP3 became king.

MP3PRO

Developed by Coding Technologies and supported by, among others, Intel, mp3PRO combines MP3 with spectral band replication (SBR) technology. SBR is necessary because in compressing the file to roughly half the size of standard MP3 files, mp3PRO loses high-frequency sounds. In the mp3PRO scheme, MP3 technology handles low frequencies, while SBR takes care of the highs. The result is a music file that sounds as good as — and often better than — the MP3 file itself, but which takes up less space.

All You Ever Wanted to Know about MP3s but Were Afraid to Ask

The way MP3 works demonstrates how ingenuity can improve the way we experience technology. This compression technology (like others) works by acknowledging the way human beings filter out certain sounds or, in fact, can't hear them at all. Specifically, the human ear doesn't hear all the sound available to it; it either cannot pick it up because the volume is too low or the frequency is out of hearing range, or it effectively blocks the sound by replacing a softer sound with a louder sound. This replacement process is known in psychoacoustics research as *masking*, and it provides the basis for MP3 compression.

Psychoacoustics research studies the limits of the ear's ability to perceive sounds. Psychoacoustic software, of which MP3 compression is an example, excludes sound in the audio signal rendered unnecessary by the fact that we won't hear it anyway. It's the principle we encounter in everyday life when one sound — talking to someone near an airport, for example — gets drowned out by another sound — like that of an airplane taking off. A pure digital translation of the event leaves both noises in the signal. A psychoacoustic translation essentially gets rid of the conversation, as much as it can, because our ears do not perceive it.

MP3 compresses files according to the following process:

1. It removes sounds with frequencies beyond the range of human hearing (roughly 20 Hz to 20+ KHz).

2. It removes sounds too quiet for humans to hear.

3. It removes masked sounds.

With all these sounds removed, the size of the file shrinks by over 10 times. So, that five-minute song that clocks in at over 50MB as an uncompressed sound file can be less than 5MB with MP3 compression applied. Other audio formats, such as Microsoft's Windows Media Audio, compress the data even further, resulting in a file size roughly half of MP3s. The question then becomes one of sound quality.

MP3 and WMA use *lossy* compression; the file shrinks through a loss of data. By comparison, CD music files (CDDA format) and their counterparts — WAV in the Windows world and AIFF in the Mac world — provide no compression of this kind at all. *Lossless* compression technology does exist in the audio world (it's well known in the digital image world), such as Free Lossless Audio Compression (FLAC) and Lossless Predictive Audio Compression (LPAC). But because their file sizes remain high, they haven't caught on for Internet audio and we don't cover them here.

To date, the industry hasn't exactly jumped on the mp3PRO bandwagon because of the ubiquity of MP3 itself. But mp3PRO provides a full range of DRM encodings and has the full support of industry giants such as Intel. So, expect this format to start showing up in large quantities. In fact, Gracenote, the company that maintains the enormous database of music your player accesses whenever you put a music CD in your CD-ROM drive, encourages the use of mp3PRO because of the ease in which song and album information can be encoded into the audio file itself. This support alone should guarantee the format's success.

MP4

Developed in the late 1990s by Global Music One, the MP4 file format offers one significant improvement over the MPEG-4 standard on which the format was based. Specifically, MP4 embeds a player into the audio file so that people downloading an MP4 file don't have to worry about whether their audio software can play the song. The company used this format to distribute audio with its Global Music Outlet service, but today its focus is on wireless applications. Still, you'll find MP4 files in various locations, and you know you'll have a player for them.

QUICKTIME

At times, you may come across audio files bearing the .qt or .qt3 extension. These are QuickTime audio files, designed for play in Apple's free QuickTime player. But QuickTime isn't a separate audio format; in fact, these files bear encodings as AIFF or WAV. Most major audio players recognize these files as QuickTime files, but if you try to play a .wav file, for instance, and your player tells you it has an invalid file format, try to play it in QuickTime instead. Often, it works.

RA, RAM, RPM

RealNetworks has developed its own proprietary audio format designed specifically for streaming. Part of RealSystem G2 multimedia technology, the RealAudio format uses lossy compression through psychoacoustic methods to achieve the best possible size-to-quality ratio and then encodes streaming instructions into the file. You don't usually find RealAudio files as downloads like MP3 or WMA, but rather as hyperlinks on Web pages that open the RealPlayer and stream the audio so you can listen as you download.

MIDI

Unlike all other files listed here, MIDI files contain no audio data at all. Instead, MIDI files, which bear the .mid extension and are extremely small, contain instructions for your MIDI synthesizer — either a separate MIDI device (typically a keyboard) or the synthesizer built into most PC sound cards. Many notebook PCs do not have MIDI synthesis as part of their sound system, so don't get frustrated if the MIDI file does not play.

Ogg Vorbis

Originally going by the charming name of Squish, Ogg Vorbis is not the name of a bizarre species in *The Hitchhiker's Guide to the Galaxy*, but rather an audio format designed to provide a money-free, license-free, and patent-free technology to music creators and collectors alike. *The Hitchhiker's Guide to the Galaxy* notwithstanding, the name Vorbis does come from a book — Terry Pratchett's *Small Gods* — while Ogg comes from the old network sci-fi game Netrek. In the software itself, however, Vorbis refers to the compression technology, while Ogg refers to the format.

Ogg files have not yet reached the mainstream, at least not as separate music files. But that's coming. Electronic Arts has used Ogg files in some of its games, as has Epic Games. Record companies are paying attention as well because, unlike MP3 and WMA, Ogg Vorbis use does not require licensing fees. The primary drawback for music distribution, however, is Ogg Vorbis's lack of support for DRM. Whether this changes remains to be seen, especially given the general contempt of the Open Source community (of which Ogg Vorbis is proudly a part) for anything protection related. But given that many people claim Ogg Vorbis files sound better than either MP3 or .wma files, and given the support for Ogg Vorbis in the growing Linux community, surely some form of DRM will happen before long.

Digital Rights Management (DRM)

Copyright means *the right to copy*. With some exceptions, such as the highly limited use of material in classrooms, only the holder of the copyright on an item may copy that item. Copyright laws work well as long as material is difficult to copy (which is why copyrights on printed matter held so well before photocopiers came along), but they break down when copying — and subsequent distribution — become easier.

Digital Rights Management (DRM) goes hand in hand with copyright and licensing. Because digital content is so easy to copy, and copying has become so widespread, industries based on the ownership of these materials (of which the music and film industries have garnered the most press) have worked to develop restrictions. DRM technologies cover the identification, copying, and monitoring of content by letting companies and individuals build licensing, usage restrictions, and encryption into their files.

Two of today's major audio formats, WMA and AAC, support a full range of DRM features. Microsoft has added extensive DRM capabilities to WMA, while the DRM features of Apple's AAC format provide the foundation for the company's iTunes service. You can copy an iTunes file to any iPod you want, but only to three computers, and each computer must be authorized with your Apple ID and password and confirmed over the Internet before it will play the song. You can burn to CD a playlist containing protected AAC files only 10 times, after which you must change the playlist. WMA's DRM works similarly and can be encoded directly into digital content by using Windows Media Encoder, freely downloadable from the Microsoft site.

The major players in DRM right now are the music and film industries, with the Recording Industry Association of America (RIAA) recently grabbing headlines — and usually not very flattering ones — for suing people who share music files extensively. As Hollywood films start using the Internet for distribution (apparently by 2006–2007), expect strong DRM built right into the products. QuickTime file formats already contain DRM features, and Real Networks, the company behind the ubiquitous RealPlayer, has introduced DRM for its MPEG-4 and MP3 offerings. Most current MP3 files, however, continue to lack DRM settings, a fact that has the majority of file-sharing services still choosing MP3 as a dominant format. Not having DRM makes things easier.

Ironically, the computer industry itself was the first to feel the effects of easy copying. In the 1980s, programs would often ship with *dongles*, small items that attached to a port on the computer and controlled whether the program ran. Other forms of copy protection proliferated, including the now standard CD key. Indeed, Microsoft's much maligned Product Activation is another form of DRM.

AAC

Short for Advanced Audio Coding, AAC is actually further abbreviated from its full name, MPEG-4 AAC. While three music services have used this format as the basis for protecting and delivering their content — AT&T, Global Music, and Liquid Audio — AAC has become the single biggest player in paid music services today as the file format supported by Apple's famous iTunes. AAC offers higher quality than MP3 at lower bit rates, and in addition — and this is crucial — it supports a full range of DRM properties. Apple has also built AAC into its QuickTime software at both the developer and end-user level. So for Macintosh systems, it has become, in effect, the standard audio format. iTunes for Windows also uses ACC files, and portable players in addition to Apple's iPod have started to appear that support the AAC format in addition to MP3 and (in most cases) WMA. In numerous tests, AAC files have outperformed both MP3 and .wma files from the standpoint of sound quality. Other tests, however, have shown conflicting results, as these kinds of tests tend to do. The fact is that as iTunes becomes more successful, AAC might very well become *the* Internet audio standard. So, keep your eye on it and watch it grow. For the time being, though, MP3 continues with great strength, and WMA is the format of choice for services such as Napster and MusicMatch.

ATRAC

The file format used by Sony's MiniDisc players, ATRAC is a lossy compression algorithm with a standard bit rate of 285.3 Kbps. From a sound quality standpoint, ATRAC and MP3 are remarkably similar. Those who own MiniDisc players, however, naturally tend to prefer ATRAC, and it tends to perform a little better than MP3 and WMA in genres such as classical music with its great dynamic range.

Media Player, CDs, and Portable Audio Devices

In addition to its role as the center of your music listening experiences, Windows Media Player provides a solid set of CD ripping and burning capabilities. Specifically, you rip songs from a CD by clicking the Copy from CD item on the Features toolbar, and you burn songs to writable CDs via the Copy to CD or Device item. Both areas of Media Player are reasonably straightforward—easy enough, in fact, that Media Player functions well as everyone's first CD-creation program.

To rip songs from a CD, click the Rip button at the top of Media Player. As Figure 14-8 shows, this screen provides a list of songs on the CD with a check box beside each one. Check the songs you want to store as media files on your PC, and click the Rip Music button, located on the title bar immediately above the main screen. The first time you copy music in Media Player, a dialog box appears explaining that you can choose to include copy protection with the copy, or choose not to include it if you prefer. In either case, you can continue only by checking the box to confirm that you realize that copyright laws apply.

Once you are past these decisions, you next have to decide to retain your current preferences for creating the music file or change them via the Options dialog. If the latter, open the Options dialog from the Tools menu. Here, you can choose to copy protect music you rip, and you can decide to rip CDs whenever you insert them into the CD drive (although it's hard to figure out why anyone would do this) and (more reasonably) to eject a CD once you've copied it. You also choose on this dialog box the default location for your ripped files.

Tip

Consider ripping your music to a shared folder so that everyone on your home network has access to it and so that you have access to it yourself from a different PC (such as when you're sitting on the deck with your notebook and your Wi-Fi connection).

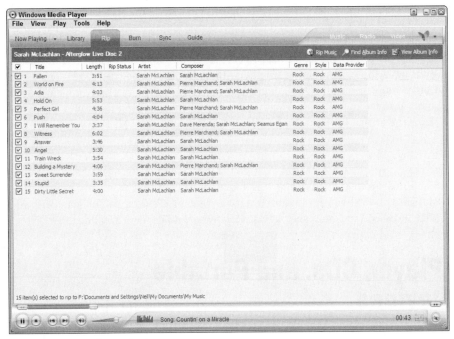

Figure 14-8: Song list in the Rip area.

The most important item on the Options dialog is the Format drop-down menu. By default, Media Player gives you a choice of three formats. Select each of them in succession and watch the Audio Quality slider below the menu to see the differences among the three:

- **Windows Media Audio:** Stores an entire CD (depending on the number of minutes of music) in 50–60MB of hard disk space. Records at 128 Kbps. You can adjust the Kbps downward to save space, but below 64 Kbps you'll notice a significant loss in quality.

- **Windows Media Audio (variable bit rate):** Variable bit rate represents the most efficient means of storing data, so feel free to experiment with this option. If you do, however, move the slider up for better quality from its default of 40–75 Kbps. You needn't go too far up for good results.

- **Windows Media Audio Lossless:** .wma files achieve their small size (as do MP3s) through lossy data compression. In this compression method, a considerable amount of data is removed from the file with very little compromise in quality. Media Player's third option lets you store files without data loss, but a long CD will consume close to a gigabyte of hard disk space. For your most important music, however, use this option.

You can add more format types to Media Player's ripping capabilities through plug-ins. For example, if you want to save files in MP3 format (and who doesn't?), you need MP3 encoder software. On the Options dialog box, clicking the Learn More About MP3 Format link takes you to the MP3

Creation Plug-ins section of the Windows Media Plug-in pages on the Web. From here, you can order one of three plug-ins, each selling for roughly $10. Buy and install it, and the MP3 option appears in the Format drop-down menu. You can now rip from CD to MP3. However, since most of today's audio players play .wma files, and WMA is free, there's little reason to do so. Only if you specifically need MP3 format do you need to install an MP3 creator.

To burn songs onto a CD, click the Burn button at the top of Media Player. Figure 14-9 shows the two-pane window that lets you perform this action, the left side listing the songs you wish to copy and the right side showing items already on the CD-R or CD-RW. Fill the left side with the songs you want on the CD (you can copy .wma, MP3, and .wav files) and then press the Start Burn button. Media Player shows you the progress of the copying and tells you when you can eject the CD.

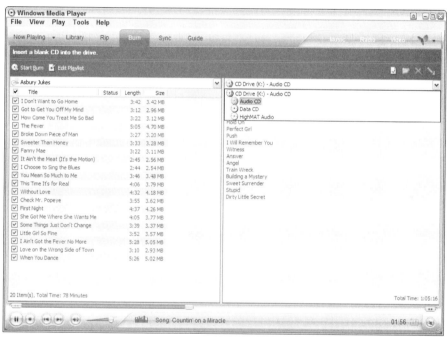

Figure 14-9: An album full of songs ready to burn onto a CD.

Copying music to portable audio devices such as MP3 players follows the same process. As long as Windows recognizes your device as a storage unit, you can copy songs to it. In this case, the Copy to CD or Device window displays the device on the right-hand side instead of the writable CD. You simply copy the songs between the two windows.

Now, back to playlists. As useful as your playlists can be when it comes to listening to music on your computer, they're even more useful when it comes to burning your own CDs and copying songs to portable devices such as MP3 players. As Figure 14-10 shows, the drop-down list immediately below the Start Burn button pane displays your entire Media Library, including any playlists you've created. Choose a playlist from this list, reorder the tracks as you want them, and copy the playlist to the CD or device. In the case of a portable player, you can develop an entire series of playlists, rotating them onto your device, depending on your mood or needs. Media Player can quickly become a central gathering of music, ready to copy to external devices whenever you want.

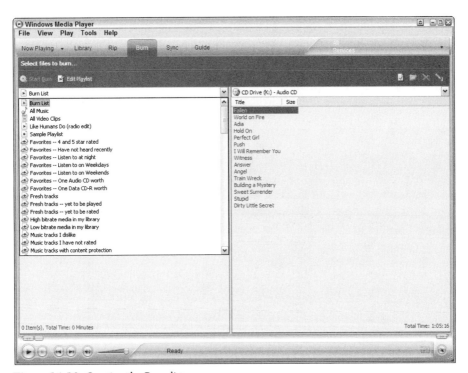

Figure 14-10: Creating the Burn list.

Tip

When burning music to CDs, you should consider using a burn speed less than the default or the maximum for your recorder. Although your own mileage will vary, tests have repeatedly shown that burning at 8X speed, sometimes even 4X, offers the best possibility of a CD that sounds good and lasts a good long time (most burned CDs eventually start losing the audio data). You can adjust the speed in Media Player before you begin the burning process.

Summary

Nothing in the entertainment world has felt the personal computing revolution more profoundly than digital music. Your options for listening to music, copying it, recording it, modifying it, and carrying it with you are stronger now than at any time before, and those options continue to expand. It would be nice if the open-mindedness of record companies would expand accordingly so that they would sign more acts that offered alternatives to the me-too sameness of so much music today. But perhaps digital music will help in that regard, as well, giving artists greater access to new and specialized audiences. Whatever happens, rest assured that your PC will be along for the ride, with Windows offering solid, useful, and well-featured programs like today's Windows Media Player. But look past Media Player as well, to players, rippers, and organizers from other companies. If you're into music, you'll want to find the best possible programs for your needs.

Part IV

Utilities

The utilities covered here include a range of products that install onto Windows XP and give you a wealth of creative power. I've isolated only the products I've actually used (as in all the other Utilities sections), and I fully realize every one of you might have a preferred product in each of the major categories. I've also tried to stick with programs that clock in at under $100, realizing that the lower the price, the more likely it is that you'll give them a try. If you haven't used some of those described here, you might want to consider them.

Photo Editors/Graphics Programs

Where to start? There are so many excellent graphics packages available that even this list could take an entire chapter of the book. Adobe Photoshop (www.adobe.com) is, of course, at the top of the heap, the graphics choice of professionals everywhere, but to my mind amazingly difficult to use. Then again, I'm not especially good at graphics manipulation beyond the basics, so that could be why. But there are alternatives, in fact a broad range of them.

Corel's Paint Shop Pro (formerly by Jasc at www.corel.com) started out as a superb shareware program, and in fact the final shareware version, 4.0, is still around and being used by those wanting a fast, capable little graphics program. Today's Paint Shop Pro is much larger and much more feature-laden, but it still works quickly (well, as quickly as graphics programs ever work; they're pretty slow as a rule.) It offers a range of useful features for touching up everything from individual artwork to digital pictures. Noise removal, scratch removal, one-click photo fixes, and a wide array of effects make this one worth trying.

I've mentioned PhotoShop, but Adobe also offers a free program called PhotoShop Album, downloadable from the Adobe site. This one performs actions only on photos, and it does it well, although, it's not an image editor per se. By the time you get to the point where you need more power than this, you'll have manipulated so many photos that you'll know which features you need to look for. And free is good, obviously.

Ulead Systems offers a series of photo-, graphics-, and video-editing programs, of which PhotoImpact is the flagship product (www.ulead.com). This one has a particularly appropriate set of tools for editing pictures and comes complete with PhotoImpact Album, a picture sorting and orga-nizing utility. Roxio's PhotoSuite 7 (www.roxio.com) is a good, if not spectacular, program on its own, but as part of the still-inexpensive Easy Media Creator suite, which includes CD and DVD cre-ation programs, a sound editor, and much more, it's an excellent deal.

Other worthwhile programs that handle many of these same tasks include Amazing Photo Editor (www.silvereaglesoft.com), PaintBuster (www.softbusters.com), Picture Trail Photo Editor (www.picturetrail.com), and Focus Photoeditor (www.new-world-software.com). All of these are well worth downloading in their trial versions and putting through their photo-editing paces.

Some photo-editing programs remain free. Photobie (www.photobie.com) is one of these, a use-ful editor although with limited features. FastStone Image Viewer (www.faststone.org) is a decent editor but excels as an image file converter. Brush Strokes Image Editor (www.pabird.supanet.com/~pabird/freesoftware/brushstrokes) lets you work at the pixel level effectively. The Gimp (gimp.org) has long been an image editor of choice for the Linux crowd, and it is equally effective as a free Windows tool, well worth the downloading and more.

Music Players and CD Creators

This is another huge list of possibilities, but again I'll restrict it to programs that I've actually used. I've already mentioned Roxio's Easy Creator suite, which includes programs to create and burn CDs, edit sound files, import music from tape and vinyl albums (for which you need a tape player and a turntable, of course), a CD copier, and a full-featured music player. Real offers its always popular RealPlayer as part of numerous program installations, including the full Mozilla suite (www.mozilla.org), and it plays practically every form of music file available. QuickTime (www.apple.com) is an extremely popular player as well, ubiquitous on the Macintosh platform but an excellent choice for Windows users as well.

Other players worth considering include Media Center (www.mediajukebox.com), an exception-ally strong program that offers playlists, full music file organization, and more. Along the same lines is JetAudio (www.jetaudio.com), the Pro version of which includes an MP3 encoder (usually avail-able only at extra cost). And then there's the venerable WinAmp (www.winamp.com), a free player (basic version) that offers all the music capabilities you'll ever need.

As for CD burning, you almost certainly have a program that came with your CD burner (or your PC) — that is, something other than Windows Media Player. Cheetah CD Burner (www.cheetahburner.com) is a well-focused program that gives you what you need to organize and burn audio and data CDs, while Nero (www.nero.com), bundled with numerous CD burners but also available as a sepa-rate product, is the CD burner many people swear by, with an endless array of possible configura-tions and possible applications. If you want a free CD burner to try out, Instant CD & DVD Burner (www.albumgalaxy.com) should do the trick. A simple interface and a limited feature set lets you get the job done without getting mired in options.

DVD Players and Burners

Not to be outdone by the CD player and creator crowd, DVD players and creators have come fully into their own over the past few years, as DVDs themselves have gained ubiquity. The Cheetah people offer a DVD player to go with their CD player, while Burn4free (www.burn4free.com) offers one of the very few free DVD burners (burns video as well as data DVDs). DVD Wizard Pro (www.dvdwizardpro.com) provides a relatively easy interface for copying DVDs (including a good interface for converting VHS tapes to DVD).

DVD players are numerous, and most have a full array of excellent features. PowerDVD (www.gocyberlink.com) remains among the most popular, with 16:9 display support and the capability to deinterlace DVDs for better images. DirectDVD (www.orionstudios.com) looks on screen like a physical DVD player, and it features superb audio tools to get the best sound from your DVDs. NeoPlayer (www.mediostream.com) supports the displaying of dual subtitles on the screen as well as the capability to stretch audio without pitch distortion, letting you play back scenes in slow motion while still retaining proper sound and voice.

Part V

Changing the Interface

Chapter 15

Giving Windows a Facelift

When you look at the desktop of most PCs running Windows XP, you see almost exactly the same thing. First to strike the eye is the background image, by default the one labeled Bliss in the Display Properties dialog box. Next you probably notice the icons, sometimes scattered around the desktop, other times lined up neatly. At the bottom of the screen resides the Taskbar, with its dark blue background and its somewhat garish green Start button bearing white text and the famous pastel Windows logo. Nice sky, nice hill, nice icons, nice Taskbar. But what you need is a desktop and an interface that are all about you.

Of course, nobody is about to suggest that there's anything particularly wrong with the default Windows XP desktop. In fact, the only thing that comes to the fore is the surprising lack of individuality displayed by most of its users. The layout, content, and styles of the desktop are almost infinitely changeable, to the degree that every user's desktop can look completely different from every other user's desktop. For some reason, however, few people seem to make any changes at all to the default desktop, choosing to stick with the one Microsoft gave them. The surprising part about this is that customizing your Windows XP desktop makes every bit as much sense as customizing your office or your study, and this operating system offers numerous ways to make it your own.

This chapter focuses on changing the appearance of the Windows XP interface — colors, screen resolution, fonts, icons, and more — and on how to organize your desktop to make it more effective. By the end, you'll have all you need to create a desktop that suits your needs perfectly, and one that looks as elegant and organized — or for that matter as chaotic and gaudy — as you wish.

Why Fix It? Is It Broken?

Why would you want to change the default configuration of Windows XP? First, you work with XP's desktop every single day of your life, often for several hours during that day. Why not, at the very least, make it more pleasing to look at, more to your aesthetic taste? More importantly, you can alter it so that it suits your work methods, your preferences, and your needs. The Windows XP desktop works fine out of the box, but until you customize it precisely to your individual requirements it won't reflect your work methods as well as it could. On the default desktop some of the elements may well be in the wrong place for optimal usability for you, while others can get in your way, and still others can simply look different from the way you'd like them to. You owe it to yourself to make the entire desktop better for *you*.

In all likelihood, you won't want to make all the changes outlined in this chapter. But, then again, you might. The most effective Windows interfaces are those in which the user has explored every possible alteration and in many cases *made* every one of those alterations. The interesting part is that once you make your changes, you'll probably find everyone else's desktop somewhat clunky to use.

Caution

By definition, customizing your Windows XP desktop means that it's no longer the standard version. Many organizations frown on customization, in fact, because of the potential difficulties it creates for IT personnel and because moving from one machine to another requires readjustment. Some organizations specifically disable the capability to make certain changes (as you may discover). Unless you frequently move from machine to machine, however, it makes more sense to tailor your most frequently used environment to your own needs. Besides, it doesn't really take all *that* long to readjust to the default XP desktop.

Figure 15-1 shows the initial XP desktop in all its uncustomized glory. Prepare to say goodbye to it.

Figure 15-1: The ho-hum default Windows XP desktop.

Choosing between the Logon Screens

Before you even get to the main XP desktop, you have to pass through the Logon screen (on a machine with more than one user, unless you use TweakUI to automatically log on). When run for the first time, XP presents you with the standard blue Welcome screen (see Figure 15-2), with colorful icons representing each user account. Click on an account icon, type in the password (if required), and you're on your way to that account's desktop.

Tip

Turning off the Welcome screen option can provide a significant security benefit in that you can configure it to force users to type in their usernames and passwords in order to log on to the PC. In addition, unlike the Welcome screen, the old Logon dialog box does not automatically display the already existing user accounts. When you use the Welcome screen, by contrast, anyone can simply click one of the user icons and then attempt to guess the password, and if you haven't enabled passwords for all accounts (an option in XP), you make it fairly easy for outsiders simply to force their way in. Of course, some degree of security still exists, but it's harder to guess both the username and the password than the password alone.

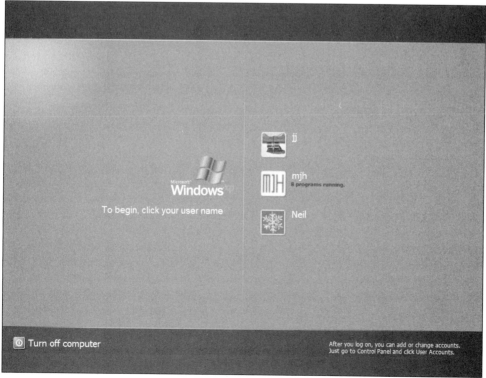

Figure 15-2: XP's standard blue Welcome screen greets you with icons for each user account.

But XP's roots lie in Windows 2000, whose Logon screen looked nothing like Figure 15-2. Microsoft chose the more colorful desktop screen to make XP more visually appealing—and less intimidating for newcomers —but the previous Logon screen remains available to you (indeed, if your PC is part of a network domain, you have no choice: Windows switches to the older Logon screen automatically). To switch to this screen, do the following:

1. Click Start and then Control Panel to open the Control Panel folder.

2. Double-click the User Accounts icon.

3. Under Pick a Control Panel icon, double-click User Accounts.

4. Under Pick a Task, choose the option Change the Way Users Log On or Off. Figure 15-3 shows the result.

Note

If you uncheck the Welcome screen option, you also automatically disable the fast user switching option. You can't use fast user switching with the pre-XP-style Logon screen.

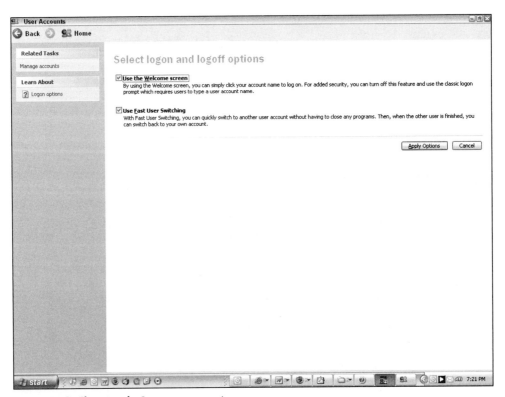

Figure 15-3: Changing the Logon screen option.

5. Uncheck the option labeled Use the Welcome Screen.

6. Click Start, click Log Off, and then click the Log Off icon. After logging you off, XP presents the older Logon dialog box, in which you type your username and password.

Changing the Desktop: Backgrounds, Resolution, and Color Quality

Once past the Welcome or Logon screen, you come to the desktop itself. This is where you can make the most noticeable changes to the XP interface because for many users the desktop *is* the interface, providing access to programs, files, and more. When you consider that Windows essentially began (with version 3.0) as nothing but a desktop, a set of clickable icons with no Start button or Taskbar whatsoever, the tendency to work strictly from the desktop makes sense.

But you don't have to leave the desktop as you find it. If you want brighter colors or no colors at all, go for it. If you want huge icons with huge fonts, go for that as well. If you want a background image showing the Milky Way galaxy, Fenway Park, or Elvis, go right ahead. These options, and many more, including a completely blank desktop or one displaying your own artwork, are readily available to you.

Changing Backgrounds

Windows XP *backgrounds* consist of images displayed on the desktop (this used to be called *wallpaper*). All users can have their own settings and background. XP provides a fairly wide variety of backgrounds, but if you don't like any of them, or if you just get bored with them all, you can create your own. If you're graphically challenged, the way I am, you can head out onto the Web and download as many as you want from any number of sites. Many are free; otherwise, the site charges a (usually) small fee.

Backgrounds are images. Some are large images, while others are small image files that combine to create a background pattern through repetition, called *tiling*. Figure 15-1 shows the default XP background called *Bliss*, (although farmers might very well call it *Work*, and it's probably entirely *unblissful* for hay fever sufferers). The Bliss background consists quite simply of an image, bliss.bmp (found in the folder \windows\web\wallpaper), that XP loads every time you log on to that account. You can find all of XP's large background images in the same folder. You can see the smaller background images, from which XP creates its background patterns, in the main \windows folder itself (look for the BMP files). You can use any small image to create your own background. If you choose not to tile it, it will simply occupy a small square at the center of the desktop. Figure 15-4 shows the background named Zapotec, a single image tiled to cover the entire screen.

You can change your background image in two fundamental ways: through the Display Properties dialog box or by assigning any image you find in My Computer, Windows Explorer, or Internet Explorer as the desktop. Any popular image type will do, with BMP, JPG, GIF, and PNG being the most common.

Figure 15-4: A small image tiled to cover the desktop.

CHOOSING BACKGROUNDS IN DISPLAY PROPERTIES

To gain the most control over your background selection, use the Display Properties method. You can open the Display Properties dialog box either by double-clicking the Display icon in Control Panel or, more easily, by right-clicking on the desktop itself and choosing Properties from the context menu (or use Winlogo+R, **control desk.cpl**). Because you need to right-click an unused part of the desktop, you'll probably find the Control Panel route easier if open windows already fill your desktop.

Tip

Whenever you want to see your desktop uncluttered by open program and document windows, click the Show Desktop icon on the Quick Launch toolbar on the Taskbar (the blue-edged icon is supposed to look like a desktop blotter — how nineteenth century). This action minimizes all windows; you can restore them all to their previous state by clicking the Show Desktop icon a second time. If you don't see the Quick Launch toolbar (it's disabled by default), right-click an empty area of the Taskbar and choose Toolbars and Quick Launch. Or use Winlogo+D to display the Desktop (and again to restore previously open windows).

With Display Properties open, click the Desktop tab (the Themes tab is discussed a little later in the section "Saving Your Interface Adjustments as a Theme"). Figure 15-5 shows the result, with the default Bliss desktop already selected.

Figure 15-5: Preview the background before choosing it.

Tip

In a nice gesture, XP lets you preview the background before you choose it. The preview area is extremely useful when choosing all your interface options.

Click each of the icons in the Background area of this dialog box to see which one you want. When you've decided, choose it, and click Apply or OK. Your desktop immediately takes on that image.

Stretch, Tile, and Center

As you click through the selections, take note of one difference between the full images and the patterns. When you choose a full image, such as Autumn, the Position drop-down menu to the right shows Stretch. When you choose a pattern, Position shows Tile. A third option in the Position menu is Center, although none of the images defaults to this choice.

▪ **Tile:** When you choose Tile, you instruct Windows to display multiple copies of the image, with each copy adjacent to the next, in a pattern of squares or rectangles covering the screen. You can tile any background image, but Microsoft has designed the pattern images specifically with tiling in mind, so they fill the screen properly. Each of the full background images already fills a screen with a resolution of 800 × 600 pixels (the images are 800 × 600 in size), and tiling has no apparent effect unless you choose a higher resolution. Once you do, the tiled image results in four adjacent copies of the image across the screen, as you can see in Figure 15-6.

■ **Stretch:** To compensate for the differences in screen resolution, XP provides the Stretch option. This option dynamically changes the size of the image to match the resolution you've chosen. You can stretch any image in this way, but if the image is small, stretching it will cause the image to become *pixilated*; all images consist of pixels, and when you display a low-resolution image at a higher resolution, the pixels themselves become visible. XP uses background images specifically suited to stretching (800 × 600 resolution at 96 dpi), something to keep in mind if you want to create your own backgrounds.

■ **Center:** As its name suggests, choosing the Center option centers the background image on the desktop. As you increase the screen resolution, the image stays the same size as before and, therefore, covers less of the desktop. Choose Center when you have a background image that neither tiles nor stretches well.

Figure 15-6: Tiling the Bliss background at a resolution of 1024 × 768.

Choosing Your Own Background Image

If you don't like any of the backgrounds XP provides, or if you simply want to look at something new when Windows launches, you can choose another image entirely. With the Display Properties dialog box open, click the Browse button. XP takes you directly to your My Pictures folder, which is located inside \Documents and Settings\YourUsername. To demonstrate this feature, Microsoft has stored four possible background pictures, all in JPEG format, inside the folder called Sample Pictures: Blue Hills, Sunset, Water Lilies, and Winter. Click any of these pictures to bring it into the Background area of the Display Properties dialog box, and then click Apply or OK to accept it.

Note

The Sample Pictures folder is actually a shortcut to another folder, located in \Documents and Settings\All Users\Documents\My Pictures. When XP is installed, it creates a shortcut to this folder in the My Pictures folder of all user accounts so that all users have access to them.

ACQUIRING A BACKGROUND IMAGE FROM THE WEB OR ANOTHER PHOTO PROGRAM

If you find an image on a Web page you want to use as your background, you can do so directly from your browser. Virtually all modern browsers—such as Internet Explorer, Mozilla, Mozilla Firefox, Netscape Navigator, and Opera—offer a command to make this happen. (Keep copyrights in mind when you select an image to use. You should never use these images for any purpose other than enjoyment on your personal machine unless some other use is clearly permissible). When you see the image you want in your browser, right-click it and choose Set as Background (Internet Explorer) or Set As Wallpaper (Netscape, Mozilla, and Firefox). The image immediately becomes your background, and you can stretch, tile, or center it as you can any other background (it is centered by default). Open Display Properties, click the Desktop tab, highlight the generic name of the image— Internet Explorer Wallpaper, Netscape Wallpaper, and so on—and choose the options you want. Figure 15-7 shows the Background list with an image selected in the Firefox browser.

You can also choose background images from some photography software packages. For example, XP includes two graphics programs, the venerable Paint and the newer Windows Picture and Fax Viewer. When you have an image file open in Paint, you can set the image as your background by choosing File → Set As Background (Tiled) or File → Set As Background (Centered). If you open an image in the Windows Picture and Fax Viewer, the default viewing program in XP, right-click the image and choose Set as Desktop Background from the context menu.

For the ultimate background toy, go to www.microsoft.com/downloads and search for Wallpaper Changer. This gives you a link to a free program (wallpapertoy.exe) that automatically changes your wallpaper at a set period (minutes or hours); you can tell it to use pictures from any folders (such as your vacation shots in My Pictures).

Where Did My Background Image Go?

One of the questionable design choices in XP is its handling of externally selected background images. Whether you choose an image from somewhere else on your PC or from a Web site, XP treats it as a temporary choice. In each case, once you choose the new background image, XP displays it in the Background area of the Display Properties dialog. If you chose a file from your PC, XP shows the file's name; if you chose an image from the Web, XP displays the generic name Wallpaper, along with the name of the browser you've used (Internet Explorer, Netscape, Mozilla, etc.). But as soon as you choose a different background, these images disappear from the list. To choose them as background images again, you have to go out and find them.

To prevent this disappearance, copy the file into the folder that contains the built-in background images: \windows\web\wallpaper. This way, you have access to the image whenever you open Display Properties. If you've chosen the background from the Web, you'll need to give it a unique filename, so the best idea is to save the image into that folder directly from your browser. If you don't give it a new name, it will be overwritten by the next wallpaper image you choose from your browser. This is a good folder to view using Thumbnails (View → Thumbnails).

Figure 15-7: All options are available for all background images, no matter where you acquired them.

Changing Your Screen Resolution

While changing your background image makes the most obvious visible difference to your desktop, adjusting your display resolution makes an even more dramatic difference to the way you work. Your resolution determines the amount of working area you have on your desktop, to the extent that the desktop itself effectively changes size. The higher the resolution, the larger the desktop, the more windows you can have open, and the more you can see inside each window. In order to make this happen, everything must be smaller to fit the fixed area of the monitor.

Screen resolution is expressed as the number of *pixels* (short for *picture elements* — a single dot) across the display by the number of pixels from top to bottom. A resolution of 640 × 480 (the original Windows resolution), therefore, means 640 pixels horizontally by 480 pixels vertically. By comparison, today's graphics cards and monitors routinely support resolutions of 1600 × 1200 pixels, 1920 × 1440 pixels, and even higher. A resolution of 1600 × 1200 packs roughly six times as many pixels onto the screen as 640 × 480, and 1920 × 1440 gives you close to nine times as many. Because everything you see on the screen is made up of pixels, the more pixels you crowd into each square inch of the screen, the denser — and thus the less choppy — the image. The smoothness of images and fonts depends entirely on the density of the pixels, so a higher resolution means a smoother-looking desktop.

To see this difference at work, take a look at Figures 15-8, 15-9, and 15-10. All show the same browser window. They differ, however, in the amount of information available to the user. Figure 15-8, with its resolution of 800 × 600, demonstrates a fully serviceable window. But if you like to work with numerous programs at the same time, say with multiple windows of a single program or with programs that function best with multiple interface elements open, a larger monitor with a higher resolution answers those needs.

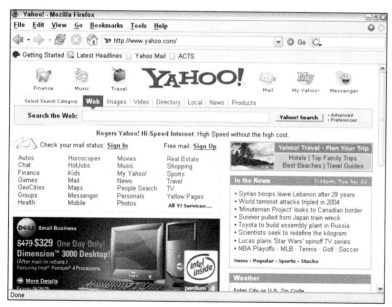

Figure 15-8: A window at 800 × 600 resolution.

Clearly, the screen in Figure 15-10 offers considerably more room than the other two screens. It also provides more information at a glance — that is, without the need for moving the windows or scrolling them — than any of the others.

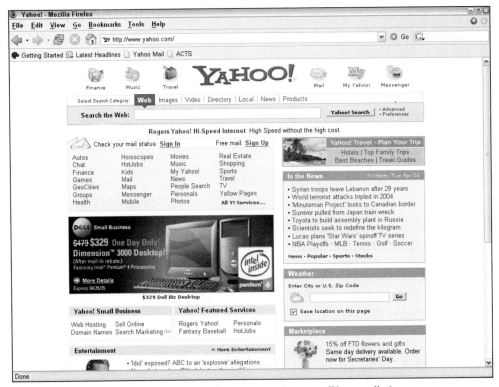

Figure 15-9: The same window at 1024 × 768 resolution (more stuff but smaller).

So, why not always choose a high resolution? Well, for several reasons:

- In many cases, it's harder to read text at higher resolutions. A high resolution on a small monitor means small fonts in documents, in menus, and throughout all interface elements. Even on a larger monitor, lower resolutions can be much easier on the eyes than higher resolutions.

- The quality of your monitor helps determine the suitability of resolutions: some monitors are simply made better than others.

- Higher resolutions take more processing power to render, so lesser-powered PCs and graphics cards will slow down when set to these resolutions. In some cases, a higher-resolution desktop can even look like it's flickering.

Only by trial and error can you determine which resolution is correct for your system and your personal preferences. However, when you first install Windows XP, the operating system chooses the best resolution for your hardware, a choice you can later change via Display Properties.

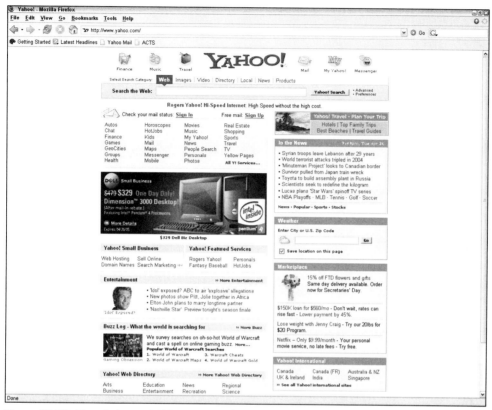

Figure 15-10: The window at 1600 × 1200 resolution.

Follow these steps to change your screen resolution:

1. Open the Control Panel and double-click the Display Properties icon.

2. Click the Settings tab. Notice that this system has two monitors that can be configured differently.

3. In the area labeled Screen Resolution, move the slider toward the right for a higher resolution or to the left for a lower resolution. As you move, watch the resolution measurement below the slider, and watch the view area (the monitor) in the space above. The view area gives you an idea of how the resolution affects the size and position of the Display Properties dialog box.

4. Before clicking OK to set the new resolution, click the Advanced button to set the behavior of XP whenever you change the resolution or color settings. In the compatibility area, choose one of the three options:

   a. Restart the computer before applying the new settings

b. Apply the new settings without restarting

c. Ask me before applying the new settings

In most cases, the second option (b) works just fine. If you experience problems when changing resolutions or colors, which typically occurs only with older programs, choose option (c), which presents you with the dialog box shown in Figure 15-11 every time you alter these settings. Only if you really enjoy waiting for XP to restart should you choose the first option.

Figure 15-11: You can check the Don't Ask This Question Again check box to tell XP to revert to option (b) in the Compatibility area of the main dialog box.

5. Click OK until you exit the Display Properties dialog, at which point the XP desktop changes to your chosen resolution.

CHANGING COLOR QUALITY

The term *color quality,* as it appears on the Settings tab of XP's Display Properties dialog box, is something of a misnomer. Color *quantity* would be more accurate, given that the term refers to the *number* of colors XP has available for its displays. The greater the number of colors, the richer the display (the richness is where the term *color quality* comes in). Just as with screen resolution, however, the higher the color quality, the slower the rendering. That said, pretty much all recently purchased PCs sport a powerful enough graphics card to support the highest color setting easily, so you'll find few reasons not to choose this setting. Then again, unless you work extensively with high-quality graphics, such as photographs, you'll find very little visual difference between the 24-bit color and 32-bit settings. Do some experimenting to determine which works best for you.

To change the number of colors on your display, double-click the Display icon in the Control Panel and click the Settings tab on the resulting Display Properties dialog box. In the Color Quality area, choose your preferred setting from the drop-down menu. Depending on your PC's video subsystem (graphics card and monitor), you might have two, three, or even four choices. The setting labeled Medium (16 bit) enables your PC to display roughly 65,000 colors, while High (32 bit) gives you over 16 million and Highest over 4 billion. Depending on your system, you might also have settings for 256 colors, once considered the standard for PC displays and still very often the quality of images on the Web, and maybe down as far as 16 colors. If you set your PC to 256 colors or lower, you'll definitely notice a visual difference on graphics-rich programs, and even on the basic XP display. Photographs at 256 colors appear blotchy and at 16 colors downright ugly.

One more recommended change in this area, especially if the monitor seems to bother your eyes: from the Display Properties Settings tab, click the Advanced button; then choose the Monitor tab. The choice for Screen refresh rate may already be correct. However, some users find increasing the refresh rate above 60 hertz better for their eyes (be sure the Hide modes box is checked).

CHANGING RESOLUTION AND COLOR SETTINGS TEMPORARILY

The screen resolution and color quality setting on the Settings tab of Display Properties applies to your entire XP environment: the desktop and all programs. You can, however, set an individual program to run at low color quality and low resolution by adjusting the Compatibility settings on its Properties dialog box. You might need to do so in the case of some older programs (especially games and graphics or other multimedia programs) or to test designs — particularly for the Web — to see what your visitors will experience if they use systems set to those settings.

To change the settings of a program, locate the icon that launches that program. You can use an icon on the Desktop, the Taskbar, the Start menu, the All Programs list, or in My Computer or Windows Explorer in the folder where the program's files reside.

1. Right-click the program's icon.

2. On the resulting Properties dialog box, click the Compatibility tab.

3. In the Display Settings area, check one or both of the options Run in 256 colors and Run in 640 × 480 screen resolution. Figure 15-12 shows these settings selected.

Figure 15-12: Choosing compatibility options.

4. Click OK.

5. Launch the program.

When the program starts, XP changes to the color and/or resolution setting you've specified. It retains these settings until you exit the program.

Note that running the program sets the entire XP environment to those temporary specifications, not just the program itself. If you need to work with two programs with different specifications, you need to close and reopen the reset program as often as necessary. Still, this feature can come in extremely handy and tends to be much more convenient than readjusting the entire display.

Tip

If you want to isolate the program even further from all others, check the third option under Display Settings to disable the visual themes you've configured or selected, including changes to menu text, window borders, and so on. This change, too, lasts only until you close the program.

Setting Up Your Favorite Fonts

Like everything else on the XP interface, Microsoft has optimized the fonts to appeal to the widest possible audience. Less apparent, however, is the ability to customize the font choices throughout the interface, beginning with desktop icons and running through the menu bars, window titles, warning boxes, and other messaging subsystems. Not only that, you can also tailor the font colors and decorations, to the degree that you can render the interface as effective and appealing as you wish.

Your control center for customizing fonts is the Appearance tab on the Display Properties dialog box. Once there, you can perform a global font change by choosing one of the options from the Font size drop-down menu. The choices are Normal, Large Fonts, and Extra Large Fonts. In this global scheme, Normal means 8 point (or 10 point for window titles), Large means 10 point (14 point for window titles), and Extra Large means 12 point (17 point for window titles). These increases occur as soon as you click Apply or OK, affecting every font occurrence in the XP interface. The fonts in the display pane reflect the changes you make. You may find Large or Extra Large more useful *after* you increase screen resolution (see the earlier section).

Much of the time, however, you'll want finer control over your fonts and their sizes. To exercise that control, click the Advanced button on the Appearance tab, revealing the Advanced Appearance dialog shown in Figure 15-13. The trick to using this dialog box is to pay attention to the display pane, which changes to reflect the alterations you make to each interface component. Ultimately, you have to click OK to accept all the changes and to see what your customized desktop actually looks like, but while you design it, the display pane helps considerably.

To change fonts, open the drop-down menu by clicking the down arrow, choose the item whose font you want to change, and make the changes. For example, to change the font of the icon labels on the desktop, choose Icon from the menu and choose the font name and its size along the bottom row of menus on the dialog box (see Figure 15-13). On installation, XP sets the icon font to 8 point

Tahoma, but you can change it to any font installed in the Fonts folder of the operating system and any size your system accepts. You can also bold or italicize the font by clicking the appropriate button beside the icon size menu.

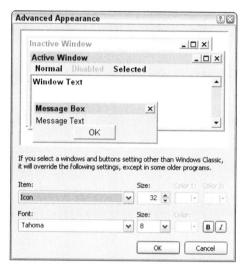

Figure 15-13: The Advanced Appearance dialog box.

Tip

You can change the size of the icon itself from this dialog box by choosing from the Size drop-down menu immediately beside the Item menu.

You can choose individual fonts and sizes for the following interface elements:

- **Active Title Bar:** The title of the currently selected window as displayed along the top of that window.

- **Icon:** The text label of icons on the desktop and in the My Computer and Windows Explorer folders.

- **Inactive Title Bar:** The titles of all windows except the currently selected window as displayed along the top of those windows.

- **Menu:** The text on all menus, including the menus of all programs.

- **Message Box:** The text included in a box containing a system message, including dialog boxes and warnings.

- **Palette Title:** The title of the small program-specific windows/toolbars known as palettes.

- **Selected Items:** You can assign a separate font and size to the currently selected item in a list, giving it an even greater distinction from the remaining members of the list.

- **ToolTip:** The explanatory text that appears when you hover the pointer over a button or icon. Many people appreciate being able to increase the size of this text (or change the font and color). Unfortunately, we can't increase the time it lingers on-screen.

Caution

While changing fonts and sizes tailors the appearance of the interface elements however you want them, you can easily create a fairly ugly-looking system. More important, you can create an interface in which some elements actually work against other elements. Start by changing one or two of the more obvious fonts — Icon and Menu, for example — and progress to a completely customized look.

Making Other Interface Adjustments from the Advanced Appearance Dialog Box

You can do much more with the Advanced Appearance dialog box than simply adjust fonts. The sizes and colors of the various interface elements are also at your disposal. For example, you can resize the scrollbars and change the spacing between the icons on the desktop, once again altering your display and the interface with it. Here are the remaining elements adjustable via this dialog box. To choose the size of the item, click the arrows of the Size menu to the right of the Item menu. To choose the color, click the down arrow and choose the color you want.

- **3D Objects:** The size of 3-D objects in the interface.

- **Active Title Bar:** The thickness and color of the strip, along the top of the active window, which contains the title of the active window.

- **Active Window Border:** The thickness and color of the border surrounding the currently selected window.

- **Application Background:** The background color of the windows belonging to your programs. For example, in a Word document, adjusting this color changes the color of the window into which you type the text.

Note

Be careful not to choose a background of precisely the same color as the text, or you won't be able to see what you type.

- **Caption Buttons:** The size of the buttons in the title bar of the window that allow you to minimize, maximize, and close the window.

- **Desktop:** The color of the desktop itself. Background images reside atop the desktop itself. If you use a background image that fills the whole screen, the only way to see the desktop color is to shrink the background image (try the Center option) or remove it by choosing None on the Backgrounds list.

- **Icon:** The size of the icon on the desktop and in XP's folders.

- **Icon Spacing (Horizontal):** The horizontal spacing between the icons on the desktop and in XP's folders. Increasing the size sets the icons at a further width apart from one another; decreasing the size brings them closer together.

- **Icon Spacing (Vertical):** The vertical distance between the icons on the desktop and in XP's folders. Increasing this size moves the icons further apart from each other upward and downward; decreasing the size brings them closer together.

Note

The closer you move the icons to one another, the greater the chance of abbreviating the icon labels. Moving them further apart results in your being able to read more or all of the icon labels.

- **Inactive Title Bar:** The thickness and color of the strip along the top of all windows not currently selected.

- **Inactive Window Border:** The thickness and color of the border surrounding all windows not currently selected.

- **Menu:** The thickness and color of the bar that acts as a background for the menus at the top of each window, immediately below the title bar.

- **Scrollbar:** The width of the scrollbar at the right of each window.

- **Selected Items:** The thickness and color of the bar that acts as a background for the currently selected item in a menu list.

- **ToolTip:** The color of the ToolTips, which appear when you hover the pointer over an icon or button.

- **Color:** The color of the window itself.

Why change these elements? The reasons, as always, are personal preference and — more important — usability. You might prefer a wider scrollbar, for example, if you typically have trouble positioning the pointer inside the scrollbar; you might prefer a narrower one if you decrease the screen resolution and no longer need the scrollbar's full width. The same holds true of menus: Increasing the size of the strip in which the menus reside can help with pointer positioning. Then, too, you might simply want a different interface experience from time to time.

Saving Your Interface Adjustments as a Theme

Once you've finished adjusting the interface elements, you can save them as a group in order to restore them whenever you wish. Each such collection of interface elements is called a *theme*. To save your current selections, click the Themes tab on the Display Properties dialog box, and click the Save As button beside the Theme drop-down menu. By default, XP targets the My Documents folder as your save location. Give your theme a name, and click Save to store it on your hard drive.

Once you've saved a theme, you can recall it by returning to the Themes tab of the Display Properties dialog box and then choosing it in the Theme drop-down menu. Because XP looks only in its system folders and the My Documents folder (for each user), you should always store your themes in My Documents. XP does not provide a way to browse for a theme.

Tip

You can use themes extremely effectively to build a collection of situational interfaces. If your organization demands that you create presentations using a particular desktop color, along with specific font sizes and colors for specific elements, you could create such a theme and then store it as a theme called Presentations. You might create another theme for the most effective use with a newsletter you regularly edit and another for working on spreadsheets and reports. By creating and storing three separate themes, you can recall the themes without the need to make individual adjustments each time.

Be Kind to Your Eyes: ClearType

Out of the box, set to a reasonably high resolution (at least 1024 × 768 but perhaps even higher) and Medium, High, or Highest color quality, Windows XP looks good. It gives you rich colors, smooth edges to its graphics, easy-to-read menus, and more. But XP contains a built-in feature called ClearType that makes fonts look even better. Designed specifically for laptop computers and LCD monitors, in general ClearType makes every bit as much difference to PCs with CRT desktop monitors. Essentially, ClearType fills in the gaps between the pixels of text characters, resulting in a much smoother display for typed documents and Web pages.

Figures 15-14 and 15-15 demonstrate the marked difference between a normal display and a ClearType-enabled display. The fonts on the normal display (see Figure 15-14) look choppy, almost spindly, when compared with the ClearType-enabled version (Figure 15-15). Look closely at the difference between the capital *C* and the lowercase *y* in the two examples; Figure 15-14 looks more jagged. On an LCD display, particularly for laptop computers, ClearType makes an even greater difference. Generally speaking, however, ClearType enhances usability—through increased readability—to an extremely significant extent.

Be Kind to Your Eyes: ClearType

Figure 15-14: This text lacks the smoothness of ClearType.

Be Kind to Your Eyes: ClearType

Figure 15-15: ClearType fills in the gaps between pixels, resulting in a display that looks much closer to the quality of print.

For reasons probably having to do with Microsoft's seeming paranoia about making changes that might not work on older PCs, ClearType is turned off by default when you install XP. Having it turned off is the safe thing to do, of course, because the non-ClearType display has proven its compatibility and usefulness over the years. But ClearType provides such an improved text display that the interface should at least offer to switch to it for you, both when you launch XP for the first time and then periodically as you work in the XP environment. As it stands, many people don't even know the option exists, when it could significantly assist them. XP confounds the issue even further by making the option somewhat difficult to find.

To turn on ClearType, double-click the Display icon in Control Panel. Next, click the Appearance tab. Once there, click the Effects button. In the drop-down list under the option Use the Following Method to Smooth Edges of Screen Fonts, choose ClearType. Click OK until Display Properties closes. XP immediately changes your display to reflect the ClearType technology.

Getting Rid of Desktop Clutter

Like real-world desktops, XP desktops tend to gather clutter. No question, you use many of the items, but others often have a barely remembered (or no longer relevant) purpose. And also as with real-world desktops, you can improve the functionality of your XP Desktop by occasionally cleaning it up.

First, you can delete any icon from the desktop by right-clicking it and choosing Delete or by highlighting the icon with your cursor and either pressing the Delete key or dragging the icon over the Recycle Bin icon and dropping it in.

Note

All of these options place the icon in the Recycle Bin, where it is available for recall if you later change your mind. That is, until you empty the Recycle Bin or the system does it for you. Be aware that if the icon is a shortcut (which runs a program installed elsewhere), deleting that shortcut does not uninstall that program.

Getting an Icon-Free Desktop

The most dramatic way to rid yourself of desktop clutter is to get rid of not just a few of the icons, but *all* of them. Early in the development of Windows XP, in fact, Microsoft seemed to want all of us to do precisely that, focusing attention instead on the revamped Start menu. But as with so many innovations over the history of Windows, the company made the empty desktop an option instead of a default. But the option remains in place, and many users find that hiding the desktop icons provides a cleaner desktop.

To change to an icon-free desktop, right-click an empty area of the desktop, choose the Arrange Icons By command, and uncheck Show Desktop Icons. The icons remain in place—the command doesn't delete them—but you can no longer see them.

Tip

XP provides ways to use your desktop icons even if you've opted not to show them on the desktop. Open Windows Explorer (Winlogo+E) and the Desktop is at the top of the folder list on the left. You can also right-click an empty area of the Taskbar and choose Toolbars → Desktop. This action places a Desktop button on the Taskbar, with a clickable arrow as part of that button. Click on the arrow to see the Desktop icons arrayed in a list. Choosing any one of these icons opens the program or file associated with the icon.

Arranging Your Icons for Easier Viewing

The Arrange Icons By command offers several other organizational possibilities for your desktop icons. The easiest choice is Auto Arrange, which allows XP to organize the icons according to its built-in programming. In fact, Auto Arrange does little more than snap the icons into line according to a vertical and horizontal grid (think of it as a table or spreadsheet), filling in any empty spaces (cells) by moving icons into those spaces. If you turn off Auto Arrange, you can still snap the icons to this grid by choosing Align to Grid, but unlike Auto Arrange this command does not automatically fill in the empty spaces.

Whether or not you use the Auto Arrange or Align to Grid commands, you can organize your icons further by choosing the Name, Size, Type, or Modified options:

- **Name:** Organizes the icons alphabetically (in descending order only) according to their names. If you have folder icons on the desktop, XP places these first, also organized according to their names.

- **Size:** Organizes the icons according to the size of the files they represent. This feature can be useful, to cite just one example, if you want to sort graphics or video files by size in order to determine which ones are suitable for including in email or posting to a Web site.

- **Type:** Organizes the icons alphabetically according to the file extension portion of the name of the files they represent. All program files sort under .exe (nearly all program files in Windows bear an .exe filename extension), while icons for Web pages are typically sorted under the extensions .htm, .html, or .asp. Multimedia files are sorted according to the extensions as well, not according to the multimedia categories we would normally recognize. XP doesn't sort the icons into graphics files and video files, for example, but rather according to their file extensions: .bmp, .gif, and .jpeg (graphics files) are interspersed with .au, .mp3, .mid, and .wav (audio files) and .avi, .mpeg, and .mov (video).

- **Modified:** Organizes the icons according to the most recent modification date. Use this option if you want to determine which file you changed most recently, particularly in the case of similarly named files.

Organizing Icons into Desktop Folders

One of the most useful organizational exercises for the desktop is to create folders for the various categories of programs and data files and move the icons into these folders. If you wish, you can take this a step further, creating folders within folders for further organization. For example, you could name a folder *Client Presentations* and create a folder for each client — or for each of your products or services — within that folder.

The trick to successful folder organization, indeed, is making the folders meaningful for the tasks you perform. If you organize your work according to clients, then create folders with your clients' names. If you organize your work according to days and months, create folders for the months and subfolders inside those folders for each week. If you work according to the project type, create folders with names such as *Word Processing Documents, Spreadsheets*, and so on. Think about the way you work and organize accordingly.

The reason you have to do this kind of thinking yourself is that XP doesn't do it for you. XP doesn't organize its desktop icons according to any useful system, and only a few elements of the interface make any such attempt. The Control Panel offers a category view, intended as a help for newcomers (but with many users never having accepted the change), and the new Start menu does a very useful job of organizing the various Windows functions. Windows XP also does a creditable job of organizing the programs you install with the operating system, into the Start menu folders such as Accessories, Administrative Tools, and Games (to use three examples). But, for the most part, Windows XP assumes that you want to work with programs rather than tasks, and it's up to you to provide whatever organization you need.

Note that most of what appears on the Desktop is also stored in a folder: c:\Documents and Settings\your user id\desktop.

Changing Your Display with Your Graphics Card's Tools

The Display Properties dialog box provides a comprehensive means of customizing your display. But many graphics cards, whether included with your system or purchased later, offer software that makes some of the alterations easier and quite possibly offers additional enhancements. Typically, graphics card manufacturers place their customization features in three locations in the XP interface: the System Tray, the Display Properties dialog box, and the Control Panel.

The System Tray resides at the far right of the Taskbar in the bottom-right corner of the display (unless, of course, you move the Taskbar itself), and it consists of one or more small icons that allow fast access to the program the icon represents, or at least some portion of the program (such as its Preferences or Properties dialog boxes).

In the case of graphics cards, you can usually right-click the icon on the System Tray and choose from a list of screen resolution and color quality settings. This feature eliminates the need to open the Settings area of the Display Properties dialog box, thereby reflecting the purpose of the System Tray itself, which exists solely for ease of access to important controls.

Tip

The System Tray is a great idea, and for purposes such as quick adjustment of display settings it works superbly. But far too many programs consider themselves more important than they should, placing an icon on the System Tray when you install them. Some even insist on drawing attention to themselves by flashing little messages to you throughout your work session. Make your System Tray effective by getting rid of any icons you don't regularly use. To do so, open the Preferences or Options dialog box in the associated program and locate the command or setting to stop the System Tray icon from appearing.

In the Display Properties dialog box, graphics card enhancements appear as part of the features of the Settings tab. Open Display Properties, click the Settings tab, and then click the Advanced tab. The graphics card's installation process adds more tabs to the top of the Advanced dialog box, reflecting the features of that particular card. Figure 15-16 shows the Advanced dialog box for an ATI 8500DV card. As you can see, the dialog box offers numerous tabs, each of which offers a display from which you can change a variety of settings (such as the choice of Open3D or OpenGL as shown).

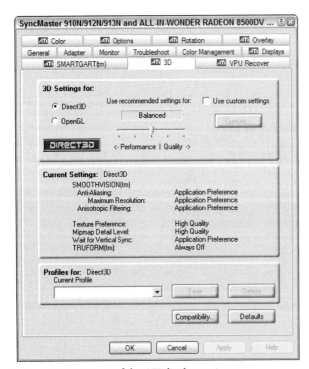

Figure 15-16: Some of the ATI display options.

Other popular graphics cards provide different configuration options. As one example, the NVIDIA series of cards, most popular for their GeForce name, offers tabs such as 3Deep and GeForce4 Ti 4200 (the name depending on the actual card in use). 3Deep refers to a feature included with NVIDIA cards that displays 3-D games with accurate lighting and shading. The GeForce Ti 4200 tab provides a menu with numerous subwindows, all accessible from the same area of the Display Properties dialog box. The bulleted list that follows highlights a number of these options in order to demonstrate the wealth of customization options available through a well-developed graphics card. NVIDIA's primary competitor in the graphics card industry.

Tip

As with any dialog box, you can get help with the contents of these windows by clicking the question mark icon beside the exit icon at the top right of the dialog box and then clicking the item you want to know something about. Or, you can click the right mouse button over the item and choose What's This? Well-constructed dialog boxes offer such help for all items that appear in the dialog box.

The NVIDIA configuration options are:

- **Technical Details:** You might very well find the technical details uninteresting, but they can be of significant use if you're troubleshooting your system with Technical Support representatives.

- **Multiple Monitors:** If you attach more than one monitor to your system, you can adjust the way the configuration works. This feature is important for NVIDIA cards because the majority of them have built-in dual display capabilities, with two monitor ports on the card.

- **Image Smoothing:** In this window you can choose between displaying your images at the highest possible quality or, at the other extreme, at the highest possible speed. The other two sliders, Antialiasing and Anistropic Filtering, provide additional smoothing effects for images. In each case, the higher the setting, the higher the quality but the slower the performance.

- **DVD and Video Adjustments:** The Video window lets you configure how your graphics card plays DVD and other video. If you have more than one monitor, you can choose which monitor will actually display the video. Numerous other video settings are available here as well.

- **Media Center and Desktop Manager:** The Desktop Utilities subwindow lets you display the icon for the NVIDIA Media Center on the System Tray for easy access to all the submenus of the Display Properties dialog box. You can also enable the Desktop Manager from here, enabling virtual desktops.

- **Display Rotation:** The NVRotate area lets you rotate your screen 90 degrees in either direction. While this is useful only for monitors that support rotation, you can give yourself or your colleagues an experience not quickly forgotten by rotating the display and figuring out how to deal with it.

Other NVIDIA-specific controls let you configure the display settings when running programs that use Direct3D or OpenGL. These technologies enhance three-dimensionality in displays, but often they require tweaking in order to function at their best with a specific graphics card and monitor. Often the program itself performs best with specific settings, and this subwindow lets you establish those settings.

Many graphics cards install a further set of interface enhancements on the Control Panel. Both ATI and NVIDIA, the two most popular manufacturers, provide such features. As an example, NVIDIA installs an icon called NVIDIA nView Desktop Manager in the Control Panel, and double-clicking it opens the nView Desktop Manager dialog box. Each of the 10 tabs on the resulting dialog box contains a range of features for customizing the XP interface, and taken together — even without the rest of the customizability discussed throughout this chapter — the features represent enormous interface possibilities. For example, under the Effects tab of the nVidia Desktop Manager dialog box, you can change the XP interface so that you activate windows by simply moving the pointer over them, by making windows transparent when you drag them, and much more.

The list that follows, outlines a few of the most dramatic interface enhancements available through the nVidia Desktop Manager. Naturally, depending on your hardware, your mileage is likely to vary.

- **Collapsible windows:** A button on the title bar of all windows makes it possible to collapse that window to show only the title bar on the screen.

- **Virtual desktops:** You can establish up to nine virtual desktops, including the ability to allow programs to run on all desktops or only a single one. Each desktop can have its own background image.

- **Shell extensions:** You can add a Windows Explorer and My Computer shell extension that lets you switch among desktops and drag windows from one desktop to another.

- **Transparent windows when dragging:** You can make the window transparent (to the degree you specify) when you drag it, so that you can see the other windows and accurately place the one you're dragging.

- **Transparent Taskbar:** Having a transparent Taskbar eliminates the need to hide it if you want to expand your applications to cover the full length of the screen.

- **Window colors:** Assign a different color to the title bar of each application and its associated windows for easy identification.

- **Hot keys:** Assign keystroke combinations to actions ranging from locating the cursor (useful on desktops) to switching desktops and making windows transparent.

- **Dialog box positioning:** On multiple monitor setups, you can center each dialog box on the monitor its application occupies.

Every one of these features — and the dialog box offers lots more — changes the Windows XP user interface. Practice by using them one at a time to get used to them, because they really do make a substantial difference in how you interact with your desktop and your applications.

Summary

With your color, font, and resolution adjustments taken care of, and your icons organized in folders to help you find your way to the resources you need, you're well on your way to a personally tailored Windows XP interface. In Chapter 16, you work with two essential interface elements, the Taskbar and the Start menu, to move your customization along even further. Chapter 17 takes you into the Control Panel to perform still more adjustments, while Chapter 18 outlines the remaining major methods for tailoring the interface: the Accessibility Options and TweakUI. Get through all four chapters, and your Windows XP interface will never again look like the one straight out of the box.

Chapter 16

Taking Control of Your Start Menu, Taskbar, and Folders

For some people, the icons on the desktop serve as the primary interface for Windows XP. But for the majority, the main interface consists of two elements that, unlike the desktop (which gets buried under the open windows), can always remain in full view: the Start menu and the Taskbar. The Taskbar runs along the bottom of the screen (although you can move it elsewhere) and contains any number of clickable objects, providing an instant overview of what you're doing and what you might wish to do. The Start menu, accessible by simply clicking the Start button at the left of the Taskbar, gives you access to everything else. Together, these two features give you access to almost anything you wish to do.

This chapter details the numerous options available for configuring the Taskbar and Start menu. By the time you've explored these options and tried out a number of them on your system, you'll have the Taskbar and Start menu set up precisely as you need them.

Starting, Not Stalling: Building a Better Start Menu

The Start button is well named: It provides a starting point for everything you do with Windows XP. Clicking it opens a collection of items that are collectively called the Start menu, and you can customize this menu to include whatever you wish. To make the interface truly your own, you should add what you need and delete what you don't.

The Start menu has fronted the Windows OS since its initial appearance in Windows 95, but with Windows XP, Microsoft has given it a new design. Larger and more inclusive than before, it functions more as a second desktop than as a menu, with several functions formerly on the desktop now available as part of a two-column display. In fact, you can think of the Start menu and the Taskbar as providing, together, a replacement for the desktop, and you can see this possibility at work if you hide the icons on the desktop. In such a case, the Start menu acts as a pop-up desktop and the Taskbar acts as a constantly available reference point.

NOTE

Over the years, Microsoft has gained a reputation as an implementer rather than an innovator of technology. Put another way, they do really well at taking concepts that are already out there and tailoring them to their own products. The graphical desktop, for example, saw its origins with Xerox PARC and its first popularity on Apple's Macintosh (although Commodore's Amiga computer had a color GUI before the Macintosh adopted one), but it has achieved its greatest success — from the standpoint of sheer numbers of users — on the various versions of Microsoft Windows.

With Windows 95, however, Microsoft might well have contributed the one interface element that will define its legacy. The Start button seems innocuous enough, but when you consider how it has fundamentally changed the way users access their computers' capabilities, you can see that adding this button to the interface was indeed an important moment of innovation. Its implementation remains imperfect, but the concept is dead on. Computers are complex, and without a clear and obvious place to start, most people will never realize what they can accomplish. So tip a glass to the Start button, and hope that Microsoft makes even one other usability contribution as strong as this one in the future.

What's in the Start Menu

Clicking the Start button reveals the Start menu (see Figure 16-1). The Start menu consists of three separate areas. The first two, the Pinned Items List and the Most Frequently Used Programs List (hereafter, MFU List), occupy the left half of the menu, with the Pinned List above the separator line and the MFU List below. These areas contain shortcuts that you place in them yourself or that your recent actions place in them. The right side of the Start menu, which we'll call the System Area, is made up of links to important folders within the Windows XP system.

When first installed, Windows populates the Pinned Items List and the System Area with items deemed (by Microsoft) the most useful to the largest number of users. The Pinned Items List includes a shortcut to the Internet Explorer browser and to the Outlook Express email program. If you install Microsoft Office, however, the more fully featured Outlook replaces Outlook Express. The System Area contains shortcuts to the following folders, most of which are stored under c:\Documents and Settings\username\ (including the Start Menu itself):

- **My Documents:** The default folder into which Windows expects you to save your data files. Each user account has its own individual My Documents folder. Note this folder's specific location is c:\Documents and Settings\username\My Documents.

- **My Recent Documents:** A list of links to the 15 documents you've most recently worked on. You can't customize how Windows establishes this list, so it's a bit limited in usefulness. Try pressing Winlogo+R (more about this in a second), and typing the word **recent** in the Run box (then press Enter) to open a window on c:\Documents and Settings\ username\Recent, where you'll find many more shortcuts to recently opened documents. Try sorting these by date (newest at the top) and View, Details or Thumbnails. Leave this window open when you shutdown, and it will be there when you start up as a quick way back to these documents (some will see this as a privacy concern).

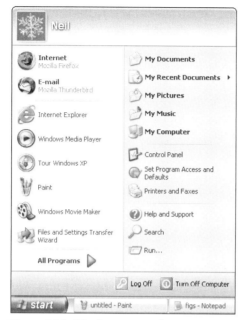

Figure 16-1: Windows XP's multipart Start menu.

My Pictures: The folder inside My Documents that contains image files. Windows XP populates this folder with a few pictures by default, and many graphics programs are configured to use it as the default folder for storing new images.

My Music: The folder inside My Documents that contains music files. Some programs, including the new Napster 2.0, use the My Music folder by default.

My Computer: A link to the folder called My Computer, from which you can navigate through all the drives and folders on your system. Clicking the My Computer icon opens the folder where you can begin navigating among your drives. Right-clicking a drive reveals several important options, including Explore, which opens Windows Explorer, and Properties, which opens the System Properties dialog box.

My Network Places: The folder containing icons for computers and folders on your local area network as well as Web sites on which you've recently published documents and FTP sites to which you've recently connected.

Control Panel: The Windows XP Control Panel, from where you can control the behavior of all aspects of Windows. You may use this often enough to want to try Winlogo+R, control to open it.

Set Program Access and Defaults: A link to the Set Program Access and Defaults utility, allowing you to specify the Web browser, email client, and other Internet programs you wish to use by default.

- **Printers and Faxes:** The Printers and Faxes folder, from which you can add and remove printers and set up Windows faxing.

- **Help and Support:** The Windows help interface.

- **Search:** A link to the Search folder, from which you can locate files, folders, and other resources on your system.

- **Run:** A link to the Run dialog box (shown in Figure 16-2), from which you can open a program or data file without locating the icon. This folder is especially useful for system programs such as telnet, regedit, and msconfig. You can also open a command prompt from here with cmd. Be sure to see what happens with each of the following (typed separately): recent, sol, calc, and mailto: (that's a colon right after mailto, no spaces); you'll learn others throughout the book. Run keeps a list of recently run commands, which can be very useful when you want to repeat something (start typing and a list will appear, or you can click to drop down a list). Convenient and, to some, a privacy concern.

Figure 16-2: Run programs directly from the Run dialog box.

ADDING TO THE PINNED ITEMS LIST

As the name says, the Pinned Items List consists of items that remain in place; the items are pinned there, if you will. You can add items to this list that you use regularly and remove those you use rarely. This way, the list remains constantly useful, reflecting the activities you typically perform.

NOTE

Keeping the Pinned Items List at a manageable level accomplishes another useful purpose as well: if you lower the screen resolution to 1024 x 768 or below, a heavily populated list will display only some of its items, but all items will be displayed if you keep the list short.

To add an item to the Pinned Items List, right-click that item's icon and select Pin to Start menu. You can perform this action on any icon on the Desktop, in a Folder, or on the list of most frequently used programs (the MFU List, discussed next). Once you pin an item to the Start menu, that item will no longer appear in the MFU List, no matter how many times you open it. Nor is there any need to place it in the MFU List, because you have ready access to it among the Pinned Items List.

If you want to remove an icon from the Pinned Items List, right-click the icon and select Remove From This List or Delete (doing so will not remove the related program). Once you've done so, the item will begin to appear again on the MFU List as soon as you use it.

Tip

One good use of the Pinned Items List is placing programs that do not otherwise exist inside a folder on the All Programs menu. For example, if you regularly make use of the Windows Registry Editor, you can make it readily accessible by using Windows Explorer to navigate to your main Windows folder, right-clicking the file called regedit.exe, and choosing Pin to Start menu. This technique is even more useful for older programs (such as still useful shareware programs that don't require installation) that you cannot simply load via the Run menu (as you can regedit.exe) and that you must launch from within their folders.

CONTROLLING THE MFU LIST

You don't have to do anything special to add a program to the MFU List. Windows XP does this all by itself, adding programs you use as you use them. You can delete programs from the list whenever you wish, however, by clicking Start, right-clicking the program's icon, and choosing Remove from This List. The program is still fully accessible from the All Programs menu; it simply no longer appears on the MFU List.

To remove all the icons from the MFU List, open the Taskbar and Start menu Properties dialog box either from the Control Panel or by right-clicking the Start button and selecting Properties. Click the Start menu tab and then the Customize button, and, in the Programs area, click the Clear List button.

Beside the Clear List button is the Number of programs on Start menu option with the default value of 6. This is the number of icons that appear on the MFU List, and you can change the number to anything from 0 to 30. Choosing 0 essentially disables the MFU List, while choosing 30 makes the list extremely long.

You can manually add programs to those the MFU List will not display. To do so, open the Registry Editor by clicking Start, then Run (or Winlogo+R), and typing **regedit** in the Open box and pressing Enter (or Return). Always be careful with regedit — you can make regrettable changes here. Navigate to the registry key HKEY_CLASSES_ROOT\Applications and then to the name of the file that launches the program you do not wish to appear on the MFU List. Right-click in the Values pane (the rightmost pane) of the dialog box and choose New → String Value. Name the String Value **NoStartPage**; then close the Registry Editor and restart your PC.

Caution

Working with the Registry Editor is *always* dangerous. Before changing anything in the registry, use the System Restore dialog box to set a restore point for your PC and back up your registry itself before proceeding. Indeed, you should avoid editing the registry unless you absolutely have to, but for some purposes it proves the only useful way of performing the task.

Why Some Often-Accessed Programs Don't Appear On the MFU

Windows XP adds most programs to the MFU List when you open them more than once, but not all. The goal is to give you quick and easy access to programs you use to get your work done, not to programs that Windows uses itself or that provide information rather than help you with your tasks. For this reason, Windows XP never adds the following programs to the list:

- Installation programs such as setup.exe or install.exe

- Uninstallation programs such as isuninst.exe, unwise.exe, unwise32.exe, St5unst.exe

- System files and programs such as rundll32.exe, explorer.exe, sndvol32.exe, realmon.exe, navwnt.exe, and so on

- Any item with a shortcut name containing the following text strings:

    - Documentation

    - Help

    - Install

    - More Info

    - Readme (or Read Me or Read First)

    - Setup

    - Support

    - What's new

Reverting to the Old Windows Start Menu

Much to Microsoft's dismay, not everybody likes the Windows XP Start menu. Some users prefer the Start menu they've been accustomed to while using Windows 2000, Windows Me, or Windows 9x. If this describes you, no problem: You can revert to the earlier Start menu style by opening the Taskbar and Start Menu Properties dialog box from Control Panel, clicking the Start Menu tab, and choosing the Classic Start Menu radio button. Click OK, and you've turned back the clock.

Cross-Reference

The Classic Start menu is covered in greater detail in Chapter 18.

Setting the Start Menu Options

In addition to the number of programs displayed in the MFU List, you can make several other changes to the Start menu in order to tailor it to your needs. To make these changes, open the Taskbar and Start Menu Properties dialog box by right-clicking the Start button and choosing Properties (or by double-clicking the relevant icon in Control Panel). Click the Start Menu tab and then the Customize button. All options are accessible from the two tabs on this dialog box.

Setting General Options

Your first choice on the General tab is whether to display large or small icons. There's nothing much to this except that small icons can be extremely helpful when you either reduce the screen resolution or increase the number of programs on the Start menu. In both cases, small icons let you see more of the shortcuts on the menu.

Also on the General tab, you can decide whether to display your default Web browser and your default email program. Check one or both boxes (or neither) to pin these icons immediately to the menu. When you check a box, you activate the selection menu to the right, from which you can choose which of the installed programs you want to display on the menu. Windows adds browsers and email programs to the respective menus as you install them.

SETTING ADVANCED OPTIONS

The Advanced tab of the Customize Start Menu dialog box (see Figure 16-3) consists of two major parts. The first contains settings for the Start menu and Recent Documents list. The second contains a lengthy list called Start Menu Items. All options directly affect the Windows interface, and thus you should consider each one carefully.

Figure 16-3: You can see more items in the middle area by using the scrollbar.

Mouse Hovering and Recent Documents

You have two choices available in the Start Menu Settings section of the Advanced tab. You can toggle them on or off by checking or unchecking their respective boxes. The Open Submenus When I Pause On Them with My Mouse gives Windows XP a kind of automation. With this option checked, each time you hover the pointer over an item that contains a submenu (as signified by a right arrow beside the item), you open the submenu associated with that item. You can still click the item if you wish; you just don't have to.

To cite a primary example, if you don't check this option, to see the All Programs menu, you have to click the Start button and then click the All Programs item. With this option turned on, you can click the Start button and simply hover on All Programs to summon the menu.

Tip

On desktop computers, enabling hover actions seems like a no-brainer. Why click twice, after all, when you need only click once? But on notebooks that use a touchpad for a mouse pointer — that is, where you tap the pad to activate the mouse click — you might very well prefer the feature off. Many users have difficulty with the touchpad taps, especially when the touchpad software is set to respond extremely sensitively to the touch of your finger. You can uncheck the Open Submenus option in cases like this.

If you spend significant gobs of your life installing and experimenting with new programs, the Highlight Newly Installed Programs option will probably appeal to you. When this option is enabled, Windows does the following:

- Highlights (in yellow) the icon for that program's folder on the All Programs menu.

- Highlights (in yellow) the icon for the program itself inside its folder on the All Programs menu, along with all other launchable elements of the program you have not yet opened.

- Places a message on the Start menu alerting you to the fact that you have installed new programs.

The highlighting and alert message last only until you actually launch the program from the All Programs menu. Well, actually, they're *supposed* to last only that long. Sometimes, however, the highlighting hangs around a bit longer, usually until you reboot your computer. Maybe some programs are just newer than others. . . .

The Recent Documents section of the Advanced tab contains the check box to turn off XP's listing of documents you've recently opened (it lists them in the My Recent Documents item on the Start menu). Alternatively, or additionally, you can clear the list of recent documents by clicking the Clear List button. Why would you want to disable this list? Well, the list can actually be a security or privacy risk. If you've recently worked on a file you don't want others to see, or if you've viewed files you don't want other people to know about, turn this feature off. Whether it's viewing photos, listening to music, or working on sensitive financial spreadsheets, the My Recent Documents list displays your activities to anyone who has access to your account. Just remember that even when this is unchecked, Windows is still storing shortcuts in c:\Documents and Settings\username\Recent.

Tailoring the Start Menu's System Area

Inside the Start Menu Items pane of the Advanced tab are the items you can add or remove from the System Area (the right side) of the Start menu. In some cases, you can also instruct XP *how* to display these items.

In addition, in one instance, Scroll Programs, you can specify how the entire All Programs folder behaves. Why Microsoft placed this single behavior option inside this list is a complete mystery because nothing else about the list works similarly, but we're sure it seemed like a good idea to someone at some point in the development of the interface. Then again, one other option, Enable dragging and dropping, controls your own behavior rather than the Start menu's, so clearly this list is an example of design by committee. Rather like the camel.

Several items offer a simple on or off check box, so you can toggle these items as you see fit:

- **Enable dragging and dropping:** Allows you to drag and drop items around the Start menu. Leave it on unless you want to ensure that you don't accidentally move items with your mouse. This option is on by default.

- **Favorites menu:** Displays a shortcut to the Favorites Menu from My Computer and Internet Explorer, with the submenu displaying the Favorites themselves. This option is off by default.

- **Help and Support:** Displays the link to the Help system. This option is on by default.

- **My Network Places:** Displays a link to the My Network Places folder. This option is on by default.

- **Printers and Faxes:** Displays a link to the Printers and Faxes folder. This option is on by default.

- **Run command:** Shows a shortcut to the Run command, from which you can launch programs without having to locate their icons. Uncheck this command if you don't want people to have easy access to such programs as regedit, msconfig, sol, calc, and text-based Internet programs such as telnet. This option is on by default. Note that even if you remove Run from the Start Menu, Winlogo+R will still open the Run dialog box.

- **Scroll Programs:** This somewhat confusing option lets you set up the All Programs menu as a single scrollable column instead of the default multicolumn list. An arrow appears at the bottom of the menu providing access to the remainder of the list. This option is off by default, and it is best kept that way for most users.

- **Set Program Access and Defaults:** Displays a link to the Set Program Access and Defaults utility. This option is on by default thanks to Microsoft's settlement of its antitrust trial with the U.S. Department of Justice and is available only with Windows XP Service Pack 1 and later.

Other items in the list — My Computer, My Documents, My Music, and My Pictures — provide a set of three radio buttons, letting you decide how you want the items to behave when you add them to the Start menu. You can choose from the following:

- **Display as a link:** Provides a single item in the menu, with no associated submenu.

- **Display as a menu:** Displays an arrow to the right of the item, providing access to a submenu of items inside the item's folder.

- **Don't display this item:** Keeps the item off the Start menu completely.

The final two Start menu items in the list offer their own unique options: You can display Network Connections as a standard link or as a Connect to menu from which you can connect your PC to network locations or Internet providers. You can also display System Administrative Tools as a folder on the All Programs menu only, on both the All Programs menu and the Start menu, or not at all.

Taking Windows to Task: Building a Better Taskbar

As you use Windows XP day after day, you'll find the Taskbar a true workhorse. In fact, you should get into the habit of looking at the Taskbar the same way you would the rear-view mirror in your car: Make sure that everything's there, take a look at anything new that appears, and respond quickly to whatever demands your attention.

You can configure the Taskbar in two ways: using the Taskbar itself and via the Taskbar and Start Menu dialog box.

Before you begin, however (and assuming that you're working with a new Windows XP installation), you need to unlock the Taskbar. Otherwise, you won't be able to configure it, and it will remain in its not especially useful default state. To unlock it, right-click an empty area of the Taskbar and uncheck the Lock the Taskbar option. You can lock it again later if you feel like it, once you have everything in place, but to make changes right now you need it unlocked.

Moving the Taskbar

Although most users never use this feature, you can move the Taskbar from its default position at the bottom of the screen. You can dock it (see the Note that follows) along the top, bottom, left, or right borders of the screen. To move it from its default position, click the Taskbar in any blank area or on the clock and drag it to the right, the left, or toward the top of the screen. The Taskbar snaps into place at the location you've chosen.

Figure 16-4 shows the Taskbar positioned against the right side of the screen. Note the significant differences from the look of the Taskbar in its standard position. Plan to take a few moments to get used to working with the Taskbar in this location; some of the elements are no longer exactly where you expect them.

NOTE

From this point onward, this book assumes that you will have the Taskbar in its default position. Any references to manipulating the Taskbar, such as resizing it or reordering its toolbars, use the default position as the reference. If you position your Taskbar elsewhere, please make the necessary adjustments to the instructions. For example, the "Resizing and Hiding the Taskbar" section a bit later in the chapter instructs you to drag upward to increase the Taskbar's size. If you dock the Taskbar at the top of the screen, you'll have to drag downward; if you dock it on the right side of the screen, you'll drag to the left, and so on.

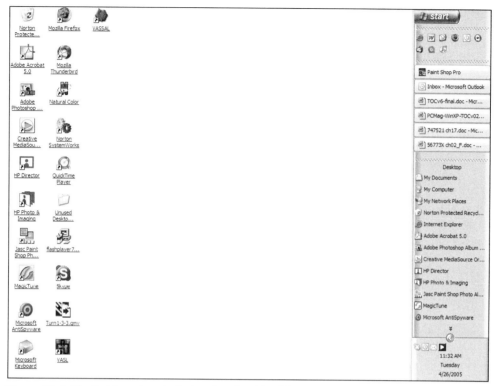

Figure 16-4: The Taskbar when docked against the side of the screen.

TIP

Docking a toolbar means positioning it against another interface element so that it snaps against that element. Most Windows programs offer toolbars you can move from position to position, docking them against the top, bottom, left, or right sides. Usually, you can choose to *float* these toolbars instead. A floating toolbar is detached from all other toolbars, and you can move it freely around the screen as you would any other window. You cannot float the Taskbar, however. You must dock it against one of the four sides of the screen.

Manipulating the Taskbar

When XP is installed, only the Start button and the System Tray appear on the Taskbar. The Start button, located at the far left of the Taskbar, opens the Start menu, while the System Tray, at the far right, holds the clock and a few other icons. As you install programs, both the Start menu and the System Tray expand, and you can get along reasonably well working only with those two interface elements.

Another part of the Taskbar expands as you work in Windows. When you open a program, the icon for that program appears on the Taskbar, in the area between the Start button and the System Tray called the Document Tray. With some programs, such as Microsoft Office XP and 2003, each open document appears by default as a separate icon on the Document Tray. Clicking an icon in this area minimizes the document's window (or restores it if already minimized). Right-clicking an icon opens a menu with options to Restore, Move, Size, Minimize, Maximize, or Close the document.

Resizing and Hiding the Taskbar

Once you open multiple programs, the Taskbar can start to get crowded. Icons automatically shrink as you add more to the Taskbar, to the extent, in fact, that you can no longer read them. Obviously, this pretty much defeats the purpose of the taskbar. This may be why some people move the Taskbar to one side or the other of a large monitor.

Fortunately, you can increase the size of the Taskbar to give its icons more room to breathe. To do so, move the pointer to the top of the Taskbar until it turns into a double-sided black arrow. Then drag away from the edge of the screen. The Taskbar resizes in increments (see Figure 16-5), and you can continue to increase the size until the Taskbar covers half the screen.

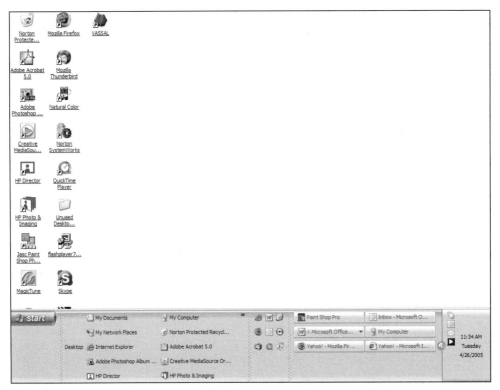

Figure 16-5: The Taskbar at triple its default size.

Caution

In another example of questionable interface design, you can easily shrink the Windows XP Taskbar to a size that's too small to use or even see. If you can't see your Taskbar, and if it doesn't pop up when you move the pointer to the bottom of the screen (as it would with the auto-hide feature turned on), then quite possibly you've shrunk it to its minimum size. This is remarkably easy to do by accident, and remarkably confusing and irritating when it happens the first time.

To undo the damage, move the pointer to the bottom of the screen until it turns into a double-sided, vertically pointing arrow. Now drag the Taskbar upward until it comes back into view. Once you know about this issue, it can actually become a useful tool, a method of temporarily hiding the Taskbar when you're working with large windows and you need another half-inch of screen real estate. But the first time it happens, it can be debilitating, especially because we all depend so heavily on the Taskbar. Note to Microsoft: A ToolTip, a periodic warning, or some other notification would prove extremely useful here.

Making the Taskbar Go Away

Of course, the more you enlarge the Taskbar, the less room you have on the desktop. Fortunately, XP offers a solution to continually resizing the Taskbar to move it out of your way. Turning on auto-hide tells the Taskbar to appear only when you move the pointer to the bottom of the screen, at which point the Taskbar pops up at whatever size you've made it. When you move the mouse away from it, the Taskbar hides itself once more, giving you back your entire screen.

To turn on auto-hide, right-click the Start button and choose Properties. Click the Taskbar tab, and check the Auto-hide the taskbar option. Click OK, and click anywhere on the desktop to cause the Taskbar to slide away.

When you combine an enlarged Taskbar with auto-hide, you create a truly new interface for yourself. It becomes, in effect, a mini-desktop all its own, filled with icons and toolbars and yet visible only when you want it to be.

Caution

Auto-hiding the Taskbar is an incredibly useful feature. Plaudits to Microsoft for including it. But brickbats to Microsoft for countering its usefulness by forcing the Taskbar to become visible automatically at certain times. When a program demands your attention — such as when a warning box is open — the Taskbar unhides itself and highlights the program's icon until you do what it's demanding of you. This behavior is *extremely* disruptive to your work and should never have seen the light of day. But it did, so be ready for it.

Adding More Toolbars to the Taskbar

The Taskbar has far more to offer than even these useful features. You can begin to see the possibilities by right-clicking the Taskbar at a spot away from any icons, revealing the context menu. Depending on where you click, the context menu offers you different options, but one constant option is the Toolbar's submenu, and this option can change the Taskbar greatly.

The Taskbar consists of the Start button, the System Tray, the Document Tray, and one or more toolbars. The toolbars expand the functionality of the Taskbar, giving it an even more central role in your customized interface. To add a toolbar, right-click the Taskbar (but not on the Start button), away from any icons, and choose the Toolbars item. From the resulting submenu, choose the toolbar you want to add. Figure 16-6 shows an enlarged Taskbar with all standard toolbars open.

Tip

If you can't seem to find a clickable area of the Taskbar, right-click the clock or enlarge the Taskbar until you see some empty space.

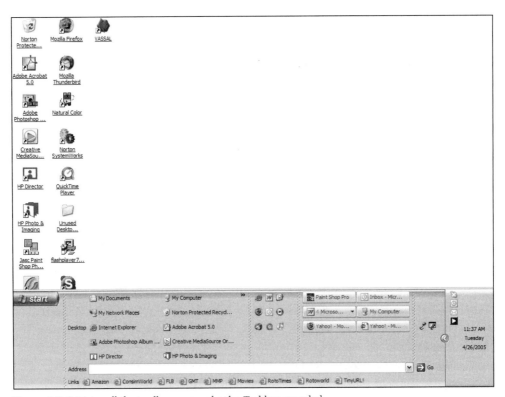

Figure 16-6: Using all the toolbars can make the Taskbar crowded.

You can add any of the following toolbars:

- **Address:** The Internet Explorer Address bar. This option lets you type Web addresses (URLs) directly from the Taskbar. The first address you type opens an Internet Explorer (IE) window; each subsequent address uses the same IE window, replacing the currently loaded Web page. This Address bar is precisely the same as the one in IE, so it includes addresses you've already visited; as long as you have the auto-fill feature turned on in IE, the Address bar on the Taskbar presents you with the same auto-fill possibilities.

- **Language bar:** The Language bar from Microsoft Office XP or 2003. This option appears only if you have installed Office XP or 2003, and even then only if you've installed the Speech elements of those programs. From this bar, you can activate speech commands and the Handwriting and Drawing applications that are part of the Office suite.

- **Links:** The Internet Explorer Links bar. This option replicates the Links toolbar on your Internet Explorer browser. Because you can configure the Links bar to give you access to frequently visited Web pages, displaying this toolbar on the Taskbar lets you access them from here instead. As you add items to the Links bar in IE, or delete them, the Links bar on the Taskbar changes to reflect these changes; the reverse holds true as well.

Tip

One benefit to adding the Address and Links toolbars to the Taskbar is that you can turn them off on IE itself, giving you a larger window in IE for the Web page itself.

- **Desktop:** The Desktop folder. Adding the Desktop folder to the Taskbar gives you easy access to all your desktop icons. If you've chosen to hide your desktop icons, adding this folder to the Taskbar effectively replaces what you've lost. The benefit to using this toolbar over the Desktop itself is that the toolbar is readily accessible even when windows cover the desktop. Compare this toolbar with Winlogo+R, desktop and Winlogo+E; each is different.

Tip

If you open the Desktop toolbar on the Taskbar, you can delete the Desktop icon from the Quick Launch bar. Its entire purpose is to give you access to the icons on the desktop, so the toolbar renders it unnecessary.

- **Quick Launch:** A collection of icons for programs you frequently use. The Quick Launch bar should be the first you add to the Taskbar. In fact, Microsoft should have placed it on the Taskbar by default. It really is that useful. When you first install XP, the Quick Launch bar includes icons for Internet Explorer, Windows Media Player, and the desktop. You can add icons to the Quick Launch bar by dragging their icons onto it, and you should do so for any program you use frequently. Because the icons on the Quick Launch bar remain visible at all times, they're even more convenient than those on the Start menu; you need click only once, not twice, to open the program. One program you should consider adding to the Quick Launch bar immediately is Windows Explorer, the extremely useful dual-pane file and folder utility. You can find it in All Programs → Accessories. Or use Winlogo+E anytime for Windows Explorer.

Tip

Many programs automatically add icons to the Quick Launch bar when you install them. You should monitor Quick Launch regularly and delete any program on it that you don't use regularly. Like the Pinned Item list on the Start menu, the Quick Launch bar is far more useful when you keep it efficient, displaying only the items to which you need ready access.

Tip

The Quick Launch bar gives you quick access to anything you need, not just programs. If you're currently working on a project with several data files, for example, you can create shortcuts on the Quick Launch bar to each of those files so that you can open the file and its associated program with one click of the mouse. When you've finished the project, delete the shortcuts and add new ones reflecting a new project. In other words, you can use the Quick Launch bar as a primary interface on a day-to-day basis.

Configuration Options for Each Toolbar

When you right-click each toolbar, you see the context menu for that particular toolbar. Many context menu elements are identical across the toolbars, but some are not. This list outlines the possibilities:

- **View:** The View option contains a submenu that lets you choose between large icons and small icons. By default, XP has small icons toggled on for all toolbars, but you can opt for large icons if you wish. Keep in mind, however, that increasing the icon size also decreases the number of icons visible on that toolbar as well as increasing the height of that toolbar (and thereby reducing screen real estate). Big icons can be kinder to the eyes, though.

- **Open Folder:** Each toolbar is actually an XP folder. This command opens the folder on the desktop, where you can work with the icons, add others, and do anything else you can do with a folder. The Desktop toolbar does not contain this option, even though it too is an XP folder.

- **Show Text:** With this option off, you see only the item's icon. With it on, you see the icon along with a text heading (a title, if you will) to the right of the icon. If you know what the icons mean, you should turn text off, allowing you to display more icons. In the case of the Links toolbar, however, turning text off may result in a group of identical Internet Explorer icons, rendering the toolbar meaningless.

▓ **Show Title:** Choosing the Show Title option causes the toolbar to display a title at the left side of the icon group. The Desktop toolbar displays the title `Desktop`, the Links toolbar displays the title `Links`, and so on. Once again, if you can do without the title, as you'll probably be able to with the Quick Launch and Address toolbars, you save space by not having it displayed. But the title can most certainly help, especially on a Taskbar with numerous toolbars open, so in most cases you should probably keep it on.

▓ **Close Toolbar:** This option removes the toolbar from the Taskbar. You can also close the toolbar from the Toolbars option, covered in the next bullet.

▓ **Toolbars:** The submenu for this option lets you open and close toolbars on the Taskbar. Checked toolbars are open; unchecked ones are closed.

▓ **Cascade Windows:** This option causes all open windows to cascade neatly from the top left to the bottom right of the screen. Figure 16-7 shows the windows cascaded in this manner.

▓ **Tile Windows Horizontally:** This option arranges all open windows adjacent to each other across the screen. The tiled windows appear as narrow rectangles two rows across by as many windows down as XP requires in order to fill the screen.

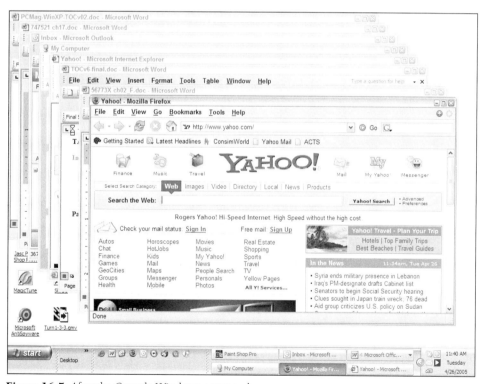

Figure 16-7: After the Cascade Windows command.

- **Tile Windows Vertically:** This option arranges all open windows adjacent to each other down the screen. The tiled windows appear more or less as squares four rows across by as many windows down as XP requires in order to fill the screen. Figure 16-8 shows the difference between horizontally and vertically tiled windows.

Tip

The more windows you have open, the less useful horizontal and vertical tiling becomes. These commands are most useful when you want to compare windows that have similarities to one another — such as two graphics files or two Web pages — or if you want to keep one or more windows on one side to use as references for the window(s) on the other. You may find it useful to minimize or close those windows you don't want to tile before tiling. You can also click one Taskbar item and hold the Ctrl key down as you click others, then right-click one of these to tile the group (or to close all the selected items at once).

- **Show the Desktop:** This command temporarily minimizes all windows, letting you see the desktop with its icons. Selecting it a second time restores the windows to their original position. Show the Desktop works exactly the same as the Show Desktop icon on the Quick Launch bar. You can execute the Show the Desktop command by using Winlogo+D; repeat to restore the minimized windows.
- **Task Manager:** This option opens the Windows Task Manager, with which you can close programs and processes manually and get technical details about the current state of your system.

Cross-Reference

For more on the Task Manager, see Chapter 6.

- **Lock the Taskbar:** This command locks the Taskbar in place. To move it, you must choose this option again to unlock it.
- **Properties:** This option opens the Taskbar and Start Menu Properties dialog box.

CREATING NEW TOOLBARS

XP provides a number of useful toolbars out of the box, but you can create as many new ones as you wish. Any folder can act as a toolbar, and placing it on the Taskbar gives it all the organizational and navigational features of all other toolbars, including the creation of an access arrow if you shrink the toolbar to the extent that it cannot display all the icons. These features make this method more useful than creating a shortcut for the folder on the Quick Launch bar or the Start menu, where you need to open the folder to access the items inside it.

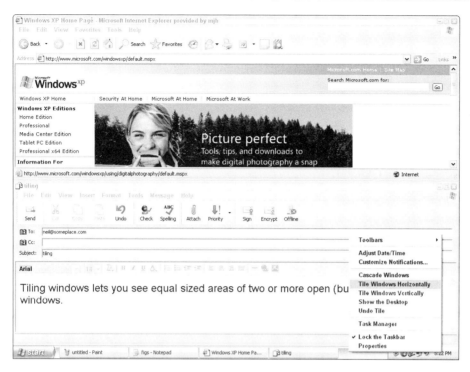

Figure 16-8: Notice the difference in appearance between horizontally tiled windows (top) and vertically tiled windows (bottom).

To create a new folder, right-click the Taskbar, choose the Toolbars option, and click New Toolbar at the bottom of the submenu. XP opens the New Toolbar dialog box, from which you can navigate to the folder of your choice. Highlight the folder, and click OK to add it to the Taskbar.

When you create a toolbar, XP adds the name of that toolbar to the Toolbars submenu accessed by right-clicking the Taskbar. The menu item, however, lasts only as long as you keep the toolbar open. As soon as you close it, the Toolbars submenu reverts to its original state.

Tip

You can use the Toolbar creation mechanism to add an empty toolbar that you can populate later with related items. For example, if you're a musician, you might decide you need a toolbar containing all your audio-editing programs and utilities so that you can access these programs without having to locate them in the All Programs menu or their own folders. To create such a toolbar, open the New Toolbar dialog box, highlight a location on your PC in which you want to create the associated folder, and click Make New Folder. Name the folder whatever you want the toolbar to be called ("Recording Tools" in this example), and click OK. The new toolbar appears on the Taskbar. To populate it with programs and other shortcuts, right-click the toolbar's name and select Open Folder. Drag any items you wish into the folder and close it. It now appears on the Taskbar as a fully functioning toolbar. Or just try dragging and dropping any item onto any toolbar and dragging those items to rearrange them.

REORGANIZING THE TASKBAR'S TOOLBARS

You can make the Taskbar even more effective for your specific uses by resizing and moving the various toolbars. Keep those you don't readily need smaller and mostly out of sight, with those you use constantly more visible and closer to one another. As with all of XP's interface elements, you should base the configuration on *your* way of doing things, not on XP's default structuring and ordering.

The first way to reorganize the Taskbar is to move the toolbars where you want them. To do so, click the title of any toolbar and drag that toolbar to the new location. From a usability standpoint, this technique sounds easier than it actually is because moving the toolbars can get tricky fast. Sliding one taskbar moves others as well, and you won't necessarily end up with any of them precisely where you wanted them, at least not on the first try. Furthermore, when you lock the toolbar, the slider grips disappear and the icons shift slightly, to the degree that you might no longer be able to see one you want. Be prepared to experiment a few times before getting the organization correct.

The second organizational technique is changing the size of the toolbars. Grasp the left-hand borders of a toolbar (the borders look like small perforations), and slide the border left or right to change the toolbar's size. In doing so, you also increase or decrease the size of bordering toolbars, a point to keep in mind as you make your adjustments. Enlarge a toolbar if you want more of its icons visible on the Taskbar; shrink those for which the expansion arrow provides sufficient access.

Moving and resizing taskbars can be extremely effective when you've increased the Taskbar beyond its default one-row size. With two or more rows to work with, you can display more toolbars and more icons from each of those toolbars. Careful adjustments can give you a thickly populated

Taskbar with precisely the icons you need to work with, and with ready access, through the expansion arrows, to numerous other useful programs, folders, and files.

TIP

Once you get your Taskbar fully organized, set it in place by right-clicking it and choosing Lock the Taskbar. Doing so prevents you from making accidental changes.

Floating the Toolbars

You don't need to keep the toolbars docked to the Taskbar. If you have a large enough monitor to maintain an area devoted to toolbars, you can detach any of the toolbars by dragging them from the Taskbar onto the desktop. You can then use them as individual program and document launchers, clicking on any item inside them to open it as a new window. Figure 16-9 shows an XP desktop with two toolbars floated on the right side of the screen. With multiple monitors, you can float or dock toolbars on different monitors.

Figure 16-9: Floating your most frequently used toolbars gives you ready access to them.

TIP

If you detach a toolbar containing numerous items, you might need to enlarge the window (by dragging the corners or the top/bottom) in order to see all the icons. This idea works, but it often makes the toolbar too large. All such folders automatically create an arrow, at the bottom of the toolbar, that you can click to open the toolbar further and see all the items. This is one primary reason to create toolbars from frequently used folders. If you simply open a heavily populated folder on the desktop, you can see all the icons only by scrolling the window. If you make the folder into a toolbar, XP automatically creates the pop-up arrow for you.

One problem with floating your toolbars is that you can lose them behind other windows. To stop this from happening, right-click on the toolbar's title bar and choose Always on Top.

NOTE

You don't have to float all your toolbars to make them accessible in this way. Instead, float one toolbar — it doesn't matter which one — and, when you need the contents of a different toolbar, right-click the toolbar's title bar, choose the Toolbars item, and select the toolbar you need. The contents of the floating toolbar change immediately to reflect the new toolbar's contents.

Adjusting the Taskbar's Properties

While you can set some of the Taskbar's options by right-clicking the Taskbar itself, the Taskbar and Start Menu Properties control panel presents a few other choices. Right-click the Taskbar, and select Properties in order to open this control panel (it's also in the Windows XP Control Panel). The choices are as follows:

- **Lock the taskbar:** This command sets the Taskbar and its current components in place. You need to uncheck this option, or uncheck Lock the Taskbar in the Taskbar's context menu, to alter the Taskbar.

- **Auto-hide the taskbar:** This is the single most useful option on the Taskbar tab of the Taskbar and Start Menu Properties dialog box. When you check this option, you cause the Taskbar to disappear from the screen whenever you click another area of the desktop. The result is more screen real estate to work with, which is especially important if you have enlarged the Taskbar to add more icons and toolbars. To use the Taskbar, move the pointer to the bottom of the screen; the Taskbar reappears exactly as you left it.

- **Keep the taskbar on top of other windows:** By default, the Taskbar is always visible (unless you auto-hide it) at the bottom of the screen. You can slide windows directly underneath it, and the Taskbar still remains on top. Disabling this option removes this characteristic, allowing windows to cover the Taskbar. In my opinion, the auto-hide feature is far better at achieving more screen real estate than this option, so you're better leaving this option checked.

Group similar taskbar buttons: Here's another option with major significance for the interface. Without this option checked, if you have several windows open for a specific program — numerous Web pages in Internet Explorer, for example — the Taskbar displays them individually in the Document Tray. For example, with several IE windows, several Word windows, and several Excel windows open at the same time, the items in the Document Tray quickly become unreadable as the increasing number of open windows causes the icons to shrink in size. With this option enabled, once you have more than four instances of the same application open (you can modify this number using TweakUI, as shown in Chapter 19), Windows groups them all together so that only one icon appears for that program; you can then access the individual documents belonging to that program via an arrow at the bottom of the icon. For example, you see only one Internet Explorer icon, and clicking on that icon reveals a menu of Web pages you have open. Choose one of them to switch the display to that document. When windows are grouped like this, you can right-click the button for the group to act on all at once to close or tile that group.

Show Quick Launch: Check this box if you want the highly useful Quick Launch bar to be visible at all times. I can't honestly imagine why you wouldn't.

Show the clock: By default, XP displays a clock in the System Tray on the bottom right of the Taskbar. The clock can be useful (including as a place to right-click for Taskbar properties), but if you don't need it, you can save some real estate by hiding it. Uncheck this option to do so.

Reducing Clutter by Hiding Taskbar Icons

Windows XP loves to give you information — whether you want that information or not. Fortunately, you can reduce the number of alerts and notifications you experience in your day-to-day work by checking the Hide Inactive Icons option at the bottom of the Taskbar tab of the Taskbar and Start Menu Properties dialog box. Checking the option and clicking OK will get the job done by itself, but you can further control these items by clicking the Customize button. Figure 16-10 shows the resulting Customize Notification dialog box. The idea here is to stop icons from appearing in the System Tray unless you truly want them there.

First, scroll through the list to see the wide range of items XP keeps track of. Click any one of them to activate the menu for that item, and click that menu's down-arrow to choose one of the three options: Hide When Inactive, Always Hide, and Always Show. The latter two options are obvious, but Hide When Inactive requires a bit more explanation. When you're not actually using the item, it is inactive and removes itself from the System Tray. When XP makes use of that icon by starting the associated program (your virus checker, for example), the icon reappears. After a further period of inactivity, it hides itself once more.

Figure 16-10: You can set the behavior of each of the icons in this list.

Summary

The Start menu and Taskbar serve the important function of keeping your programs and folders readily available even when windows cover the desktop. They also provide a strong organizational function, to the extent that tailoring the Start menu, adding toolbars to the Taskbar, and adjusting the components of both interface elements according to your liking gives you a truly customized interface.

Chapter 17

Changing Your Interface from the Control Panel

So far, I've pointed out a variety of ways to alter the Windows XP interface, by doing everything from changing the appearance of the entire desktop to tailoring the Start menu and Taskbar in a seemingly endless variety of ways. But your options for customizing the XP interface are far from depleted. This chapter outlines the numerous interface elements accessible via the utilities in the Control Panel, from accessibility enhancements to folder options. The Control Panel offers a wealth of customization features, and you should examine each utility closely to see what it can do for you.

Changing the Way Your Folders Look and Act

Folders lie at the core of the Windows XP experience. No matter what programs you use, no matter how much you accomplish through the Desktop, the Start menu, and the Taskbar, on numerous occasions you have no choice but to work with folders and their contents. XP provides workable folders out of the box; but as with everything else about this operating system's interface, you can change the way those folders look and act. You have two primary means for customizing your folders: the View menu and toolbar in the folders themselves and the Folder Options applet in the Control Panel.

Folder Views

To open a folder, first open My Computer either from the desktop or the Start menu. When you do so, you see the contents of the My Computer folder, including the standard XP folders and the drive icons. Clicking a folder opens that folder so you can see what's stored inside.

Tip
The fastest way to My Computer: Winlogo+E (for Explorer).

When you open a folder, by default you see a view called Tiles with subfolder icons arrayed in alphabetical order in the top portion of the window, and the files, each with its own relevant icon, lined up alphabetically below. Figure 17-1 shows a view of a My Documents folder.

This view is not the standard in all folders. In three of the subfolders within My Documents, XP automatically sets the default view to Thumbnails rather than Tile. These folders, My Pictures, My Music, and My Videos, use this view to emphasize the multimedia nature of their contents. XP's folders are designed to let you see and play multimedia files, and the Thumbnail view shows, to a certain degree, what each file contains. Figure 17-2 shows the Thumbnails view for the My Pictures folder.

In the case of My Pictures and My Videos, the Thumbnails view lets you see not only a small version of each individual picture (in the case of a video file, it's the video's opening frame), but a four-panel visual preview of the pictures inside the subfolders as well. You can see this useful aspect in Figure 17-2, with each subfolder showing thumbnails of the first four photos inside that folder.

The View menu of each folder shows the views possible for that particular folder. Each view changes the look of the folder considerably, and each view offers its own advantages and drawbacks. The Thumbnails view, for example, offers the obvious benefit of letting you see the pictures themselves — which is much more useful than seeing the filenames — but it also increases the size of the icons, thereby restricting the number of icons you can access without scrolling.

Figure 17-1: The standard Tile view in My Documents.

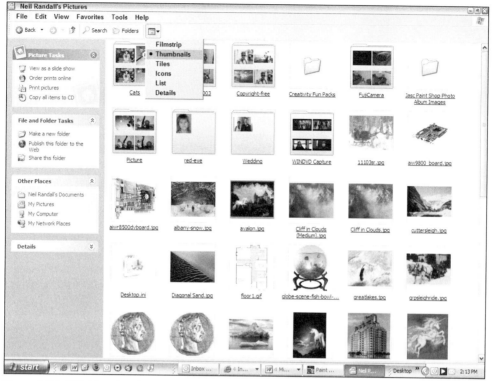

Figure 17-2: XP's Thumbnails view.

The following list details the various views and discusses the positives and negatives of each. The first five are common to all folders, while the rest are specific to certain folders.

- **Filmstrip:** The Filmstrip view (shown in Figure 17-3) arrays your graphics files as a single row of thumbnails along the bottom of the window, with the currently selected graphic displayed at a larger size above the row of thumbnails. As you select each graphic, the larger image in the middle changes accordingly. Below the larger image are tools for moving through the images and for rotating the selected image either clockwise or counterclockwise.

- **Thumbnails:** The Thumbnails folder uses large icons and therefore lowers the number of icons viewable without scrolling. But icons that represent pictures or videos show small previews of those items, so this is an extremely useful view if you need to locate a specific photo or video. If not, you're better off with the Tiles view.

- **Tiles:** The icons in the Tiles view are much smaller than those in Thumbnails, allowing you to see far more of them in a standard-sized window. As you can see in the Tiles view shown in Figure 17-1, however, you do not see a representation of photos or videos. So, if you need to work with images or videos, this view can hinder rather than help. The Tiles view does offer a limited amount of information about each file — its name, size, and type — offering a compromise between the Thumbnail view and the more information-rich Details view.

Figure 17-3: The Filmstrip view.

- **Icons:** In the Icons view, the icons get smaller still, and only the name of the icon appears with it. To get additional information about the icon, hover the pointer over it until the information ToolTip appears (the same holds true for all views). The primary advantage of this view is its combination of an uncluttered look and the display of numerous icons.

- **List:** The List view shrinks the icons even further. Once again, hover over an icon to get details about it. List view works well when the folder holds many icons, and you want to avoid scrolling as much as possible. Because of its usefulness in this regard, the List view is standard for the Open and Save windows of Microsoft Office and other productivity programs.

- **Details:** If you want to see extensive information about your files, choose the Details view. The Details view gives you the same small icons as the List view, but the icons are arrayed in a single alphabetical column. Beside the icons you get additional columns, each with a specific type of information about the file on that line. See the sidebar "Adding More Columns to the Details View" for information on adding more columns.

Adding More Columns to the Details View

By default, the Details view shows the size of the file, its type, and the date it was last modified. You can add even more columns by right-clicking the columns bar (immediately above the files) and choosing whichever new columns you want.

- **Date Created:** Sometimes you need to know at a glance not only when the file was last modified but also when it was originally created.

- **Attributes:** Here, you can see the attributes for each of the files, including information about whether the file is read-only (R), hidden (H), or a system file (S). You don't usually need this information, but it can help when you are trying to troubleshoot access to the file.

- **Owner:** The owner of the file according to the system ownership attributes. Ownership is determined according to the user account in which the file was originally created and the groups to which that user account belongs. You need to know the owner only if you have some reason to attempt to change that owner in order to gain access to the file.

- **Title:** Applicable primarily to Office documents, XP takes the title of the document from the Title field of that program's Properties dialog box.

- **Comments:** Also applicable to Office documents, XP takes the comments from the Comments field of that program's Properties dialog box.

- **Date Picture Taken:** Available by default only in the My Pictures folder, this column shows the date the photograph was originally taken, as captured from the information in the digital camera. This date can differ from both the Date Modified and the Date Created.

- **Dimensions:** Available by default only in the My Pictures and My Videos folders, this column shows the dimensions of the picture in pixels.

- **Duration:** Available by default only in the My Videos and My Music folders, this column shows the length of the video or audio file in seconds.

- **Artist, Album Title, Year:** Available by default only in the My Music folder, these columns display the respective information as contained in the Properties dialog box of the audio file.

- **Track Number:** Available by default in the My Music folder, this shows the file's track number on the CD.

Numerous other columns are available from the context menu as well. These include the bit rate of the audio file, whether the file is protected, and the model of the camera used to capture digital or video files. If you want to display even more columns, right-click the column bar and select More. Check whatever boxes you wish in the resulting Choose Details dialog box, and click OK to add them to the folder.

You can also change the order and the size of the columns. To change the order, click and hold the title of the column and drag it until the insertion point is where you want to place the column. To resize it, move the pointer to the separation between two column titles (it turns into a double-arrow), and drag the column border to make the column the size you want.

Tip

You can sort the contents of your folders in two main ways. In the Details view, you can click the title of each column to sort the icons according to the data in those columns — alphabetically in the case of Name, in order of size in the case of Size, and so on. (You can sort in the opposite direction by clicking on the column title a second time). You can also sort the icons by right-clicking an empty area within the folder and choosing the Arrange Files By option. The submenu gives you a variety of sorting options, including one — Show in Groups — that sorts the icons according to groupings. The groupings themselves change as you click the column titles. Clicking Name sorts alphabetically, with one group for each letter of the alphabet, while clicking Size organizes into groups with headings such as Zero, Tiny, Small, and Medium. Experiment to get the grouping you like best.

Tip

If you like the way your current folder looks, you can set all folders to look the same. With the model folder open, choose Tools → Folder Options and click the View tab. In the Folder Views area at the top of the resulting dialog, click the Apply to All Folders button. Presto! You've standardized your folders.

Folder Options

The other primary means of changing your folders is the Folder Properties Control Panel applet. To open it, double-click the Folder Options icon in Control Panel, or click the Tools menu of My Computer or Windows Explorer and choose Folder Options.

WARNING

As with desktop, font, and virtually all other interface settings, the settings you choose in the Folder Options dialog box apply only to the current user account. Each user can set these properties individually. It would be nice if XP restricted certain options to certain user types — such as administrators — but unless you configure the Group Policies (see Chapter 27 for details on how to do so), you can't stop users from configuring their folders in a way that might cause damage.

Two areas on the General tab of the Folder Options dialog box are of particular interest. In the Tasks area, you can choose between the folder style of older Windows versions (User Windows Classic Folders) and the newer XP style (Show Common Tasks in Folders). The newer style displays a task pane on the left side of each folder window; you can see this pane in all the figures shown so far in this chapter. The Browse Folders area lets you choose what happens when you open two or more folders in succession. By default, XP replaces the contents of the first folder with the contents of each one you subsequently open, but you might find it more useful to open each folder as a separate window completely.

Note that if you choose to open each folder in its own window, your desktop can become cluttered extremely quickly. On the other hand, this option makes copying and moving files between folders easier to accomplish, because you can place the folders side by side and drag files from one to the other.

Tip

If you need more than one Explorer window open, right-click a folder name and choose Explore (from the Folder pane) or Open (from the Task Pane). Alternatively, use Winlogo+E.

Tip

Don't overlook the task pane when you first start working with XP folders. What actually appears on the task pane depends on the type of folder you open. My Documents shows a different set of tasks from My Pictures, and My Music, My Videos, and My Computer are different again. My Computer offers a System Tasks area in the task pane, while My Documents offers a File and Folder Tasks area that includes such activities as publishing a file to the Web or emailing it to a recipient. My Pictures shows a Picture Tasks area with actions such as ordering prints online (using one of three built-in services), and My Music includes commands for playing all the files in Media Player, copying files to an audio CD, and shopping for music online.

The heart of the Folder Options dialog box is the View tab, from which you exercise the greatest control over your folders. Figure 17-4 shows this pane, with only part of its lengthy Advanced settings list in view. This list provides a broad range of configuration possibilities, each of which affects the interface with your folders:

- **Automatically search for network folders and printers:** XP goes out onto the network every few minutes to locate folders and printers accessible through your local network. The purpose is to add these items to My Network Places as other network users add them.

- **Display file size information in folder tips:** When you hover over an icon in a folder, XP displays the size of the file in kilobytes or megabytes in a small tip window.

- **Display simple folder view in Explorer's Folders list:** This option tells Windows Explorer to expand the folder listings (in the left pane of Explorer) to show subfolders, when you click on any folder, then contract that folder when you switch to another. Without this option, you must click on the plus sign to expand the folder, and clicking on another folder does not automatically contract it.

Figure 17-4: The extensive View tab options.

◾ **Display the contents of system folders:** By default, with this option turned off, Windows displays a warning screen in place of the folder contents when you try to open a folder that contains files needed by XP itself (such as your primary Windows folder). With this toggled on, XP allows you to see these folders without a warning.

TIP

You should keep the display of the contents of system folders toggled off, even if you're the only person using the computer. The warning screen is easy enough to get past (all it takes is a single click), and if it prevents you from accidentally deleting even one important file over the course of a couple years, it's worth the extra few seconds.

◾ **Display the full path in the address bar/title bar:** XP likes to simplify things, one way being to shorten the location information (the path) shown in the Address field of each folder (or the title bar of the file you have open). Turn this option off to display only the name of the current folder (the default); turn it on to display the full location.

◾ **Do not cache thumbnails:** The first time you turn on the Thumbnail view for a folder, XP loads each thumbnail into memory, allowing you to view it, and caches the thumbnails (retains some of their data in memory) so that, when you return to the folder, the images take less time to load. Caching can cause a few headaches if you change the contents of the folder because the cache does not match what's really there (you have to refresh the folder in such a case).

■ **Hidden files and folders:** Here, you have the choice whether to show the hidden files and folders on your system. You can set any file or folder to hidden status by right-clicking the item, choosing Properties, and checking the Hidden box in the Attributes section on the General tab of the Properties folder. When you hide a file, you prevent XP from displaying it in any folder display or via the command line's DIR command. You can instruct XP to display the hidden files and folders as a matter of convenience to yourself. If you do so, the hidden items bear a muted icon color indicating their hidden status.

■ **Hide extensions for known file types:** One of the strikes against MS-DOS and Windows (especially by people accustomed to using the Macintosh) is the use of the file extension, the characters after the filename that identify the file as belonging to a specific program (.doc for Word files, .exe for programs, .ppt for PowerPoint files, and so on). With Windows XP, you can prevent Windows from displaying these extensions, forcing you to identify files through their associated icons only (the icon reflects the program in which you created the file). Whether you want to see the extensions is purely a matter of preference, so choose as you like.

Note

If the file uses an extension that XP does not recognize, it will display the extension as well as the filename. Recognition depends on the file association system, which you can see — and set — by clicking the File Types tab in the Folder Options dialog box. Chapter 19 deals with setting and changing file associations.

■ **Hide protected operating system files:** The Folder Options dialog box calls this option "Recommended," and you'll get no argument here. Unless you have a very specific purpose, you do not need to work directly with system files, and keeping them hidden from view prevents you from accidentally deleting or moving them. Think of this option as an additional safeguard — hiding the contents of system folders is the other — against damaging your system by altering a critical file.

■ **Launch folder windows in a separate process:** This rather obscure feature instructs XP to load each folder window into a different portion of memory. It's similar to the option on the General tab Open Each Folder in its Own Window except that it isolates the folders from one another for the sake of protection from problems. The feature primarily benefits developers who might need to experiment with one folder while guaranteeing that others won't close down in case another crashes.

■ **Managing pairs of Web pages and folders:** You have three options here, all of which are covered in Chapter 9.

■ **Remember each folder's view settings:** Because you can change the settings of each folder individually, configuring them according to your needs, you want Windows to remember what you've done so that you don't have to reconfigure them each time you reboot. Check this option to have Windows retain the settings.

- **Restore previous folder windows at logon:** Windows XP automatically reloads any folders you had open on the desktop the last time you logged off, restarted, or shut down. This option is useful if you constantly work with the same folders, but one of the typical purposes behind rebooting is starting fresh with a clean desktop and all programs cleared out of memory, so most users will want to leave this option unchecked. Still, if it helps you get to work faster, by all means toggle it on. One worthwhile use is to have the My Recent Documents appear with each boot-up, helping you get up to speed quickly each session.

- **Show Control Panel in My Computer:** This option adds an icon to the Control Panel in the My Computer folder. Check the option only if you have hidden the Control Panel from the Start menu and you've chosen Windows classic folders on the General tab of the Folder Options dialog box. In such a case, you have no other Control Panel icon available. You might consider this procedure if you want to prevent users from opening the Control Panel and working with its configuration utilities.

- **Show encrypted or compressed NTFS files in color:** When you use an individual folder's Properties dialog box to compress the folder (see the "Working with Compressed Folders" section later in this chapter) or encrypt it using the Encrypting File System (see Chapter 6), Windows displays the former in blue and the latter in green. You can't choose to color one or the other; it's either both or neither. NTFS stands for NT File System; Windows XP uses the file system, although modified, begun in Windows NT and continued through Windows 2000. The other major file system for PCs is FAT32 (and the older FAT); FAT is short for File Allocation Table, and is far less customizable than NTFS.

- **Show pop-up description for folder and desktop items:** When you hover over an item on the desktop or in a folder, Windows displays a small pop-up showing details about the item. You can turn this feature off if you don't want to see the pop-ups. Some users find them annoying. Others find them highly useful.

- **Use simple file sharing:** This is another recommended item, and in most cases you should just leave it on. Chapter 25 covers the differences between simple file sharing and standard file sharing.

Setting the Folder Template and Icon for New Folders

To create a new folder, right-click an unoccupied place in the current folder and choose New → Folder from the context menu. Windows then creates the folder icon and gives the folder the rather obvious name New Folder. You should rename the folder before doing anything else to make it more useful to you; after you've done that, you can customize the folder significantly.

To customize the new folder, right-click the folder and choose Properties from the context menu. Click the Customize tab on the resulting Properties dialog box. Begin the customization by clicking the down-arrow beside the Template menu near the top of the folder. Windows provides the following templates, as shown in Figure 17-5:

- Documents (for any file type)

- Pictures (best for many files)

- Photo Album (best for fewer titles)

- Music (best for audio files and playlists)

- Music Artist (best for works by one artist)

- Music Album (best for tracks from one album)

- Videos

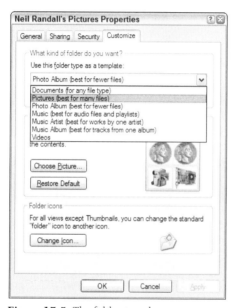

Figure 17-5: The folder template types.

The specialty folders within My Documents—My Pictures, My Music, and My Videos—have already been configured as templates: Pictures, Music, and Video, respectively. You can't change those folders, but you can add your own of each of those types and more to your folder collection. Once again, customization helps you create a tailored interface.

You can customize these folders in three other ways from the Properties dialog box. If you want to base all subfolders within this folder on the same folder template, check the Also Apply This Template to All Subfolders option. Furthermore, at the bottom of the Properties dialog box, you can choose the folder's icon by clicking the Change Icon button and scrolling through the resulting icon collection, as shown in Figure 17-6. (Mind you, it would be nice if Windows would associate specific icon types with specific template types so that you could give all your Picture folders the same icon as My Pictures by default, but perhaps that's asking a bit much.) Finally, you can select a picture to appear as the thumbnail graphic for the folder by clicking Choose Pictures in the middle of the dialog box and selecting the picture you want.

Figure 17-6: You can assign any icon to each folder.

Tip

The task pane for each folder depends on the template you assign to that folder. Pictures folders, for example, assume the same task pane as My Pictures, complete with the feature for running a slide show based on the images in the folder.

Working with Compressed Folders

Compressing folders or files reduces their size. File compression works by removing bytes that contain no data or, in the case of multimedia files, by eliminating redundant data. The primary function of file compression is to save disk space, but it has a separate (and for many users an equally important) function as a backup system.

In a move that simply seems determined to cause confusion, Microsoft has built two types of file and folder compression into XP:

- **Compressed (zipped) Folder:** This is accessible from within any Folder window.

- **Compress contents to save space:** This is an option in the Advanced Attributes sub-dialog-box within an individual folder's Properties dialog box.

Although these options may sound similar, they're two different things, as I'll show in the following sections.

Compressed (Zipped) Folders

Zip is the primary compression technology for Windows-based computers. You can download and/ or buy several zip utilities, but Windows XP contains its own. Overall, this utility offers significantly fewer features than a standalone zip program such as WinZip, but it has the benefit of being built right into the operating system.

To zip a file, open the folder in which it resides, right-click the file's icon, and choose Send to → Compressed (zipped) Folder. XP copies the file, compresses it, and then creates a folder into which to place it. The folder icon appears as a standard folder with a rather neat-looking zipper to its left. Often, it makes sense to zip several files together at once, both to compress them and to store them in a single folder. To do so, highlight all of them (by holding either the Ctrl or the Shift key while selecting) and compress them all using a single Send to command.

You can use this as a kind of backup system, storing copies of your important files in a zip folder, and you can also use it as a convenient method for sending files via email. Instead of attaching multiple files to an email message, you can zip them together and send the entire compressed folder. All the recipient needs to open the folder is a zip utility, which most users have either as part of Windows XP (or Windows Millennium Edition) or as a separate program such as WinZip.

Tip

If you use Compressed Folders as a backup system, you should move or copy the compressed folder to another location. A CD-ROM is perfect, as is a separate hard drive. Failing that, move it to a separate partition or even a different folder so that you can access it later if you need it.

Once created, a compressed folder works just like any other folder. You can open it and work with any of the individual files inside it. To make the files fully functional, however, you need to uncompress them. You can do this manually by copying or moving the file out of the Compressed Folder into an uncompressed folder, or you can uncompress all of them at once by clicking the Extract all files item in the Folder Tasks section of the compressed folder's task pane. This action launches the Extraction Wizard, the second stage of which appears in Figure 17-7.

By default, the Extraction Wizard creates a folder named for the first file in the compressed folder. Before compressing, you can change the location of the compressed files by typing a path or clicking Browse and choosing an existing folder in the resulting Select a Destination dialog box (where you can also create a new folder). Once you've decided on a folder, click Next to uncompress the files into that folder.

Kudos to Microsoft for the final screen of the dialog box. By checking the Show Extracted Files option and clicking the Finish button, you instruct Windows to open the folder into which you've extracted the files. While this feature might seem obvious—why force you to navigate to the new folder?—earlier zip utilities didn't offer it.

To see how the Extraction Wizard can help, here is an example. On the Web, say you come across a download called clipart.zip that contains several clip art files. Click the download link from within the browser to begin the download and save the file to your desktop. When the download is complete, double-click the icon on the desktop. This action opens the zip file as a compressed folder, where you click the Extract command to start the Extraction Wizard. Because you don't want the files scattered all over your desktop, you click Browse and create a new folder for them. Clicking Next extracts them to that folder, and clicking Next again opens the folder with the clip art files in full view.

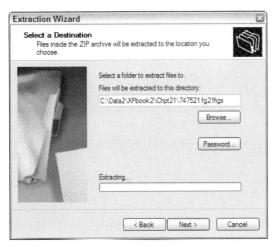

Figure 17-7: The Extraction Wizard uncompresses all files in the zip folder.

Caution

When you download a zip file from the Web, resist the temptation to choose Open instead of Save when the download begins. While choosing Open removes a step from the extraction process (you don't have to open the zip file separately), it also makes you more vulnerable to virus and other *malware* (that is, malicious software) attacks (such as Trojan horses). To be safe, store the file on your drive, run it through your virus checker, and then extract the files to a new destination. You might have to configure your virus checker to scan compressed (zip) files, because not all versions do so automatically. Check the Options or Preferences dialog box for your antivirus software.

If you install another zip utility on your PC (WinZip is an especially popular one), it will take over XP's built-in zip functions. You can still send your files to an XP compressed folder by right-clicking on them and making the standard choice, but when you double-click on saved zip files, they open in the new utility instead. Other utilities have many more features than XP's built-in zip, but it's up to you to determine if you need those features. If you don't, uninstall the new utility to have XP resume its default functioning.

Compressing with the Advanced Attributes Dialog BOX

The Compressed Folders feature does not actually save disk space; in fact, it uses more space. The reason is simple: sending a file to a compressed folder makes a copy of that file — in a compressed version, admittedly, but still a separate file. Unless you delete the original file from your system, you've used up even more of your hard disk.

XP does, however, provide a way to compress files and folders without first making copies of them. Right-click the file or folder and select Properties. In the Attributes area of the resulting Properties dialog box, click the Advanced button. Figure 17-8 shows the result, the Advanced Attributes dialog box. Check the option labeled Compress Contents to Save Disk Space, and click OK. XP asks if you want to compress only that folder or all subfolders as well, and then it compresses the files (it can take a few minutes, so be patient) and denotes the compression by changing the color of the file icons to blue so that you can easily recognize them. You can uncompress your files and folders by reversing this procedure.

Figure 17-8: Compress or encrypt files with this dialog box.

You can save even more disk space by compressing an entire hard drive. Open My Computer or Windows Explorer, right-click the drive's icon, and choose Properties. At the bottom of the Properties dialog box is a Compress Drive to Save Disk Space check box. Click OK to start the compression process. You can even compress your primary drive (C:) if you want, although this would likely slow down your computing experience.

Caution

Disk compression used to be an important tool in maximizing space on your hard drive. Today's storage methods and the continually lowering prices of hard drives have rendered compression much less useful, however. In general, you're better off not compressing an entire drive or even your most frequently used files and folders. Compressing them removes some possible features from them — notably the Encrypting File System, which does not work on compressed files and folders — and doesn't save you all that much space anyhow.

Saving Your Mouse Finger with the Single-Click Option

Back in the old days of 1984, the creators of the Apple Macintosh decided that, while people needed a mouse to interact with the interface, they needed a mouse with only one button. Apparently, more than one button would simply cause confusion among users. To be fair, most users had never used a mouse, so to some extent this decision had validity. But it resulted in the double-click, one of the most questionable designs in the history of human-computer interaction. Double-clicking is anything but intuitive, and for some people it's downright difficult.

The idea was this: You clicked once to select an icon, after which you could drag it, copy it, do whatever you wanted to do. What most people wanted to do with icons most of the time, however, was open their associated files. The double-click provided a solution to selecting the icon and then choosing the Open procedure. The first click did the selecting; the second-click, performed in rapid succession, did the launching. You couldn't allow a single-click to perform the launch because then you would have no way of selecting without launching.

Along came Windows. From the introduction of its GUI, Microsoft chose a two-button mouse as the standard rather than a one-button mouse (the Amiga and Atari ST had already used them). By the time Windows was ready for prime time (version 3.0, released five years after the first Mac, was the first truly usable version), the double-clicking routine had already become such an unshakeable standard that Microsoft adopted it. There was no reason to do so, however. With a two-button mouse available, the designers could have set the interface so that the right button selects and the left button launches, or some other combination. In the meantime, Unix systems adopted a three-button mouse as the standard, and users could customize the buttons as they saw fit.

Next came the Web. Here, single-clicking was the norm. You single-clicked on a hyperlink to open that page; you single-clicked on a file to download it, view it, or play it. If you wanted to select a file to work with it, you right-clicked it (Mac users needed to press a separate key on the keyboard while clicking). Everything made sense: the single-click had won.

When Microsoft introduced Windows 98, the first version of Windows to recognize the Web as a major focus, it also introduced the single-click option for regular desktop use. All icons would act just like hyperlinks; you clicked on them to open them. In the early beta versions of Windows 98, the single-click option was turned on by default. Who, the reasoning went, could possibly object to saving mouse clicks? Well, many people objected, for reasons known only to themselves, and Windows 98 — along with all subsequent versions of Windows including XP — offered the single-click interface only as an option.

The single-click interface saves mouse clicks, prevents the frustration of not double-clicking fast enough, and replicates the most usable interface of all computing history: the Web browser. For that reason, you should try it for a few days, after which you aren't likely to want to go back. But it has a few peculiarities, which are covered in the following sections.

First, turn on the single-click option. To do so, open the Folder Options applet in the Control Panel or from within a folder (by choosing Tools → Folder Options). On the General tab, select the Single-Click to Open an Item (Point to Select) radio button. If you want the descriptive text of all icons underlined (a bit unsightly for many), choose the Underline Icon Titles Consistent with My Browser suboption. If not, choose the second, which applies an underline only when you point at an icon. Click OK to apply the changes.

Selecting and Opening with the Single-Click Interface

Now, open a folder or view the desktop. Move the mouse pointer to an icon. Windows immediately highlights the icon label and, after a few seconds, automatically selects the icon and highlights it as well. This is how you select an item using the single-click interface: you point at it. You can even change the speed at which Windows makes the selection by using the TweakUI utility (covered in Chapter 18).

To open the item, click on it (you don't need to wait), exactly as you would a hyperlink in a Web browser. To access the context menus, right-click the icon as you would with the original double-click interface.

Single-clicking becomes tricky only when selecting multiple items. Because selection no longer depends on clicking, you have to teach yourself how to do this, and it takes a few tries to get it right. Hover over the first item until XP highlights it. Next, with the Ctrl or Shift key pressed down, as in all multiple selections, hover over the next item (the subsequent icon if you're using Ctrl, the final icon if you're using Shift). XP performs the selection again. You can now drag the icon group, delete it, right-click to use the context menu on it, or whatever you would normally do.

Tip

In only one other way does the single-click interface take some getting used to. Often, when you save a file using the Save As dialog box in your program, it's convenient to click on a previous file to use its name as a basis. Choosing this file places the name in the Name field, and you simply edit it to give your new file a different name. With the single-click option turned on, you do the same thing by hovering over the previous file, not clicking it. If you click it, you initiate the Save, which you then have to cancel (in the subsequent warning dialog box) to avoid overwriting the previous file. Again, this takes a few tries to get right.

The Single-Click Interface and Laptops

Many laptop computers use a touchpad to replace the mouse. When you first get your laptop, the touchpad usually simulates both the mouse pointer and the mouse buttons. You use your fingertip to move the pointer to the desired location on the screen, and then you tap the touchpad to simulate the mouse click.

You can turn the tapping function off, and many users do in order to avoid accidental mouse clicks. When using a single-click interface, the tapping function becomes even more difficult to control. After practicing for a while, the single-click interface actually enhances the tapping experience because double-tapping causes its own set of hand-eye coordination issues. But you really do need to practice.

Consider turning the tapping function off (your laptop has software that lets you do so) or decreasing the sensitivity of the tapping. Otherwise, you'll find yourself launching programs you had no intention of launching—not a bad thing, but often annoying. Figure 17-9 shows the options available for the Synaptics brand of touchpad in use on a wide range of laptops.

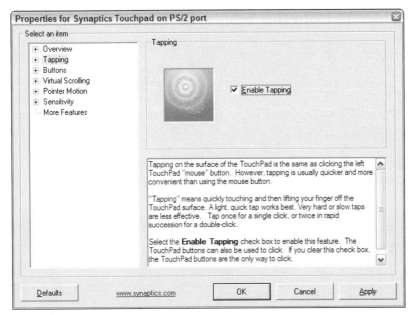

Figure 17-9: The Synaptics touchpad tap options.

Configuring Your Keyboard and Your Mouse

Aside from your eyes, your mouse and keyboard provide your primary means for interacting with the computer interface. Interestingly, however, many users seem unaware that, like the visual interface, you can also customize how your input devices work. For the most part, the mouse and keyboard work perfectly well out of the box, so there's no need to customize them. But a quick look at the options shows that you might very well want to do so. You can configure both devices from the Control Panel.

Tip

Many keyboards and mice offer special features that you can control using software included with these products. In many cases, the software changes the Mouse and Keyboard dialog boxes, sometimes dramatically. If you have a mouse with extra buttons or a keyboard with special keys, locate the special software for it either on floppy disk or CD-ROM, or go to the Support section of the manufacturer's Web site to see if you can download the software from there. Here, we deal only with the default Windows XP Mouse and Keyboard dialog boxes.

Setting the Mouse's Behavior

To configure the mouse, open the Control Panel and choose the Mouse icon. The first option on the Buttons tab in the Button Configuration section lets you switch the buttons so that the right button performs the selection and launches functions while the left button calls up the context menus. Obviously, the purpose of this option is to increase usability for left-handed users; but if you want to see how skilled you've become at mousing, switch the buttons one day and try to perform some typical actions. (Switching buttons also makes for a great practical joke, but you didn't read that here.)

Many PCs sold today include Microsoft's Intellimouse software. If your PC has this software, the Mouse dialog displays different options. Again, to configure the mouse, open the Mouse icon from the Control Panel. From the Buttons tab, as Figure 17-10 shows, you can choose the primary functions for each button and the wheel button. From the Activities tab, you can set the double-click speed, a useful feature if you've been having trouble double-clicking fast enough to open icons (many users experience this difficulty, so you're not alone). The ClickLock option at the bottom of the Activities tab lets you avoid holding the mouse button while dragging (another activity that causes difficulty for many people).

Also from the Buttons menu, you can set the double-click speed, a useful feature if you've been having trouble double-clicking fast enough to open icons (many users experience this difficulty, so you're not alone). In addition, the ClickLock option at the bottom of the dialog lets you avoid holding the mouse button while dragging (another activity that causes difficulty for many people).

Figure 17-10: The Buttons tab.

Note

You should choose neither of these last two options if you've switched to a singe-click interface, however; double-click speed is largely irrelevant, and ClickLock does not work.

The Pointers tab (see Figure 17-11) offers a series of mouse pointers for you to choose from so that you don't have to put up with the boring flat white ones Windows uses by default. Click on the Scheme menu to see the list and then on any of the schemes to see what the pointers for that scheme look like. Click OK to accept the new pointers. You can also place a shadow under the pointer for aesthetic purposes and to make the pointer easier to see.

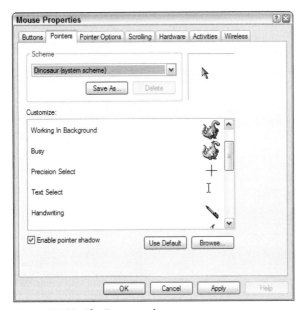

Figure 17-11: The Pointers tab.

On the Pointer Options tab, you can set the speed at which the pointer moves across the screen when you move the mouse, and you can tell XP whether to hide the pointer while you're typing. This option keeps the pointer out of the way while you type, and you need only touch the mouse to have it reappear.

TIP

Two options on the Pointer Options tab especially suit laptop use. Display pointer trails causes XP to show a trail behind the pointer as you move the pointer across the screen, thereby preventing the common occurrence of losing track of the mouse on a laptop display. Show location of pointer when I press the Ctrl key lets you use the Ctrl key to find your pointer, again an issue with many laptop users.

On the Wheel tab, you can set what happens when you roll the wheel on a wheel mouse. By default, rolling the wheel one notch scrolls the active document three lines at a time. You can change the number of lines to any number from 1 to 100, but keep in mind that scrolling a hundred lines at once is practical only on specialty programs and very large screens. You can also set the wheel to scroll one full screen with each notch.

Setting the Keyboard's Behavior

Open the Keyboard dialog box from the Control Panel, and you can see that you have fewer options for configuring the keyboard than you have with the mouse. You have only two choices: setting the repeat delay and the repeat rate. You activate the repeat delay when you hold down a key on the keyboard; once the delay has passed, the key types in a repeated fashion at the rate established in the repeat rate area. In other words, if you want to type a string of Xs in a document, you hold down the X key until the repetition begins, and the speed at which the Xs appear depends on the repeat rate setting.

Test your settings by clicking in the Click Here and Hold Down a Key to Test Repeat Rate field and then pressing a key until it repeats.

A final option on the Keyboard Properties dialog box lets you set the blink rate of the cursor, as you see it in various types of programs (such as your word processor). Move the slider until the cursor at the left blinks at the rate you want and click OK to set this new rate. If you don't want the cursor to blink at all, move the slider to None.

Setting the Date and Time

XP provides a clock whose icon resides at the far right of the System Tray. Double-clicking this icon opens the Date and Time Properties dialog box. From here, you can set the current time and date. To set the date, choose the month and year from the menus at the top of the Date area and click the correct day of the month. To set the time, which is expressed here in hours, minutes, and seconds, click the item you want to change (the hour, for example), and then move the arrow either up or down to make the change. Click OK when you've finished.

Note

No, you can't just move the hands on the clock to change the time. You should be able to, but you can't. Ask Microsoft why.

To set your time zone, click the Time Zone tab and choose a time zone from the drop-down menu at the top of the dialog box. If you live in a time zone with daylight-saving time, click the option below the map to have Windows change the time automatically on the appropriate date.

Note

No, you can't just click on the map to select your time zone. You should be able to, but you can't. Again, ask Microsoft why.

Figure 17-12 shows the Internet Time tab of the Date and Time Properties dialog box. Here, you can configure Windows to connect with a time server on the Internet to set the time and date for you. Time servers are synchronized to the computers of official time setting organizations, so you can be assured of having the correct time at all times. XP synchronizes with the selected time server once every week.

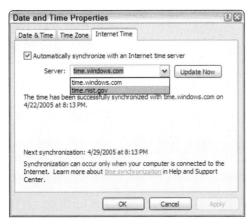

Figure 17-12: Let the Internet set your system time for you.

Summary

The Control Panel gives you what its name suggests — *control*. Control over your hardware devices, control over your software programs, control over your network connections, and, just as important, control over portions of the Windows XP interface. This chapter has demonstrated how to change the look of the folders and the operation of the primary input devices, the mouse and keyboard. Chapter 18 concludes the discussion of interface configuration, focusing on accessibility features and the TweakUI Power Toy.

Chapter 18

Taking Even Greater Control of Your Interface

As extensive as your options are for customizing the Windows XP interface — as you've seen so far — you can do even more to tailor your Windows experience to your needs, work habits, and preferences. This chapter explores ways you can cut down on the Windows interface rather than adding to it, and shows you how to set accessibility options for people with disabilities, even minor ones. Finally, the chapter covers the extensive customizability of the Microsoft downloadable Control Panel applet called Tweak UI, a utility that lets you change a wide variety of interface options.

Reverting to the Windows 2000 Interface

If you've come to Windows XP having used an earlier version of Windows, as a great many people do, you'll notice from your first boot-up that the Windows XP interface differs considerably from the interface on previous versions of Windows (including Windows ME, Windows 2000, Windows 98, and earlier versions). Microsoft planned it this way. It wanted the XP interface to supplant everything that went before it without alienating its customers too extensively. But, for people who don't like to change interfaces or companies that refuse to do so, the new interface proved alienating anyway. If you're one of these people, you'll be pleased to know that you can customize the XP interface to look and behave much like earlier Windows interfaces. This is particularly true for Windows 2000 users, but also to a significant degree, for Window 98/Me users as well. In this section, we look at Windows 2000 only.

Choosing the Classic Start Menu

The single most noticeable change in the Windows XP interface is the revamped Start menu (see Chapter 16 for complete coverage of this menu). Even though many people find the new Start menu more useful than the old, many don't. Fortunately, you can change back to the older style Start menu at any time. In fact, you can flit back and forth between the two if you like.

To make this change, go to the Control Panel and open the Taskbar and Start Menu Properties Control Panel applet (or right-click the Start button and choose Properties). Click the Start Menu tab, and then select the Classic Start Menu radio button. Click OK to finalize the change.

The primary difference between the two Start menus is the addition in the new version of the System Area on the right. In all likelihood, Microsoft designed this component to complement another new Windows interface option, the icon-free desktop. Many of the items available in the System Area are traditionally available via desktop icons, so it makes sense to have a Start menu that acts, to a degree, as a desktop replacement.

Note

Choosing the Classic Start menu for yourself does not change the Start menu in other user accounts. All users have the choice of the Windows XP Start menu or the Classic version.

Setting the Control Panel Back to Normal

The next step in configuring a retro interface is changing the Control Panel from the Windows XP Category view to the Classic view. Microsoft changed the Control Panel to help people more easily locate whatever utility they need to perform the task they're doing, but many users coming from earlier Control Panels find the new one more confusing than ever.

Open the Control Panel through the Start menu, Windows Explorer, or with Winlogo+R, **control**. To switch from the default Category view in Windows XP to the Classic view, click the Switch to Classic View link at the top of the Control Panel's task pane at the left of the window. To switch back, click Switch to Category View in the same location. If you don't see the task pane on the left, click the Folders button below the menu (if that still doesn't show the task pane, keep reading).

The new Control Panel (Category view; shown in Figure 18-1) offers a task-oriented interface that combines utilities according to what you want to accomplish. In effect, this version works like a wizard.

When you click a category, you get a new page that offers specific tasks along with icons to launch the various utilities. The old version (Classic view; shown in Figure 18-2) puts all the utilities in front of you and lets you choose whichever one you want.

In principle, the Category view is a good idea. Human-computer interaction theory tells us that any interface that emphasizes tasks rather than programs offers a more usable interface. As Microsoft and other software manufacturers continue to add utilities to the Control Panel (some graphics card manufacturers already do, for example), organizing the utilities into categories makes a lot of sense. However, at this stage, the Control Panel just isn't crowded enough to justify the extra step you have to take to get to the utility you want. So, for most people, the Classic view offers the most value.

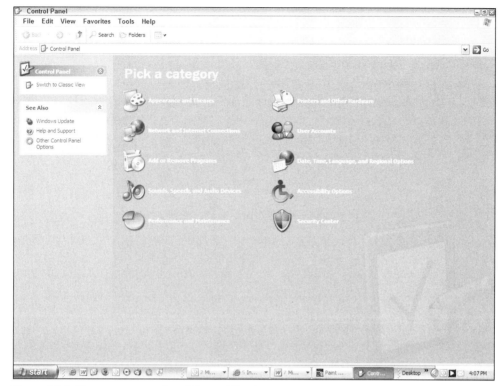

Figure 18-1: The new category-based Control Panel.

Tip

In one particular case, the Category view does work well — at least once you know enough to click the correct link in the first place. The Performance and Maintenance link (which probably could use a better name) opens a window that provides access to numerous useful utilities you can adjust to affect system performance and take full control over your PC. From here, you can work with your hard drives, set power options, and access the full suite of Administrative Tools. This window shows how the new Control Panel *should* work — even if the items don't quite fit a single category — but it's probably the only window that does.

Simplified Folders, ClearType, and More

Beginning with Windows ME (released after Windows 2000), Microsoft added the advanced folder view that was later adopted for Windows XP. In this view, folders display a task pane from which you can perform actions specific to the folder type you currently have open. For example, with a Pictures folder open, you can choose to display the photos in a slide show or publish them to a Web site. All these commands are accessible from that pane.

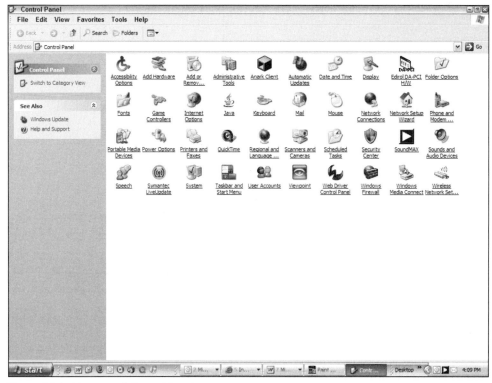

Figure 18-2: The original Control Panel.

Windows 2000 uses an older folder view, one without the task pane. To revert to this view, open the Folder Options dialog box. On the default tab, General, select the Use Windows Classic Folders radio button. Click OK, and the task pane disappears.

Caution

Unfortunately, when you revert to the old folder view, you lose some of the new features that Windows XP offers by default. When looking at a Pictures folder, you no longer have access to the View as a slide show or Order prints online commands. Furthermore, the Filmstrip option disappears from the View menu; the Filmstrip view shows the selected image file at a large size in the top two-thirds of the window with the remainder of the images in a row along the bottom. In a Music folder, you can no longer execute the Play all or Shop for music online commands. You would think these commands would appear in the main menu or the context menu, but they do not. Unfortunately, if you want a true Windows 2000–like environment, you have no choice but to go this route.

You'll need to turn off two other features if you want a true Windows 2000 environment. First, get rid of ClearType by opening the Display Properties applet in the Control Panel, clicking the

Appearance tab, clicking the Effects button, and choosing Standard in the Use the Following Method to Smooth the Edge of Screen Fonts menu. Next, open the Taskbar and Start Menu Properties applet in the Control Panel and, under the Taskbar tab, uncheck the Group Similar Taskbar Buttons check box. The first change turns off the font smoothing provided by the ClearType technology, whereas the second forces the Taskbar to display all icons separately instead of combining icons belonging to the same program (such as all Internet Explorer windows) under one icon with a selection arrow.

Obviously, you don't have to turn off all new features. You can make the Windows interface look mostly like the Windows 2000 interface without sacrificing some of the nicer touches, such as ClearType and button grouping. But, if you want the added features of Windows XP while working fully within the look and feel of Windows 2000, you'll have to sacrifice a few of the additions to Windows XP.

Working with Accessibility Options

Windows XP contains a number of useful adjustments for people with one or more types of disabilities. You can set some of these elements individually by using the Accessibility Options dialog box in Control Panel (Winlogo+R, **control access.cpl**), but, for the full range of accessibility possibilities, you should work your way through the Accessibility Wizard. This wizard combines the accessibility tools with a variety of other interface alterations to produce the best possible interface for your particular set of difficulties. The Accessibility Wizard brings together options found scattered through various Control Panels, including Accessibility, Display, Mouse, and Sound (each of which you may find yourself visiting instead of or after the wizard).

Even though the accessibility options exist primarily for the sake of people with disabilities, many people without disabilities find them useful as well, especially in specific circumstances. If you wear glasses, for instance, you've probably already discovered that no two monitors are alike and that lighting situations can render some monitors — especially notebook displays — extremely difficult to read. In other cases, you might also find that the desktop's mouse or the notebook's touchpad device doesn't work properly, rendering even the most rudimentary selecting, dragging, and menu access difficult and frustrating. In still other instances, your location makes typical actions hard, particularly if you're on an airplane. The accessibility options can help in these cases and more.

To launch the Accessibility Wizard, click the Start button and choose All Programs→ Accessories→Accessibility→Accessibility Wizard (or Winlogo+R, **accwiz**). This is an elaborate wizard that bears a bit of a resemblance to one of those 1980s-style Choose Your Own Adventure novels. As you click through the wizard, you encounter several choices, and, depending on the choice you make, the wizard continues along a different path. By the time you've finished the wizard, you can have a very different appearance and interface than you started with.

In the first step of the Accessibility Wizard after the Welcome screen, you choose the text size. The choices are as follows:

- **Use usual text size for Windows:** No change from the default
- **Use large window titles and menus:** Increases the size of the text in the window titles and on the pull-down menus
- **Use Microsoft Magnifier and large titles and menus:** Increases the size of the text in window titles and pull-down menus and activates the magnification utility

Caution

Unlike many other wizards, which typically wait until you've completed all of their steps before setting your selections in place, as you make choices in the Accessibility Wizard, your configuration changes immediately. From a design perspective, the instant changes work well because the person using the Accessibility Wizard might very well need to activate the alterations in order to complete the wizard, but the instant reaction can be a bit disorienting. You may want to set a restore point with the System Restore utility so that you can revert to the an earlier configuration if you need to. (See Chapter 6 to learn more about setting a restore point.)

Clicking Next takes you to the Display Settings stage. Here, you choose from the following possibilities:

- **Change the font size:** If you didn't choose to adjust the fonts in the first step of the wizard, you can do so now.

- **Switch to a lower screen resolution:** This decreases the screen resolution by one major step. You can also do this manually in the Display Properties dialog box.

- **Use Microsoft Magnifier:** If you didn't activate the Magnifier earlier, clicking the check box here activates it immediately.

- **Disable personalized menus:** Personalized menus hide infrequently used menu commands. To access the hidden items, you need to click on the down arrow at the bottom of the unhidden list. Disabling this feature makes all commands available without the need for special action.

After selecting these options, the variable section of the Accessibility Wizard comes into play. The heading titles that follow reproduce the check box labels from this screen of the wizard (see Figure 18-3), and the text under each heading outlines the wizard screens you see if you make that particular choice.

I Am Blind or Have Difficulty Seeing Things on Screen

Aside from increasing the text size for the menus and window titles, options available earlier in the wizard, the Accessibility Wizard also presents a series of choices for altering specific interface elements for easier viewing by those with poor eyesight.

In this section of the Accessibility Wizard, you first choose the width of the scroll bars. Next comes the icon size with the choices Normal, Large, and Extra Large. Again, because icons represent a crucial element in the interface, you should set these at the most appropriate configurations for you.

In the next window, you have a choice of five color schemes. You can keep your current scheme or choose from four additional schemes that emphasize strong contrast. Experiment with these, and choose the one you want. For many people, white text on a black background is much easier to read than the standard black text on a white background, and here you can make that choice.

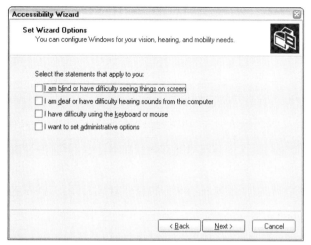

Figure 18-3: Each of these check boxes corresponds to one of the following four sections.

Click Next to choose the cursor style and color you want — again with the goal of making the cursor as visible as possible. Clicking Next again gives you the option of changing the blink rate of the cursor. In the subsequent stage of the wizard, review what you've done and then click Finish to set everything in place.

Note

The settings available in the various sections of the Accessibility Wizard that pertain to sight are subsets of the options available in the Display Settings dialog box and the Mouse utility in Control Panel. The wizard makes these choices easier to make with less need to dig through the configuration utilities and windows elsewhere in XP. However, you may want to use the Control Panel to fine-tune these and related settings.

I Am Deaf or Have Difficulty Hearing Sounds from the Computer

The Accessibility Wizard deals with hearing impairment by adding sounds and subtitles — the same way television does. In the first step of the wizard after you choose this option, you configure SoundSentry, the XP feature that displays a visual notification whenever the computer makes an event sound. The visual notification comes in the form of a rather off-putting flash. It's off-putting because it's so fast and abrupt; you might think, understandably, that your computer is slightly malfunctioning. But, it's certainly better than nothing.

Tip

You don't actually need sounds turned on in Windows XP to use the SoundSentry feature. Go into Control Panel, launch the Sounds and Audio Devices utility, click the Sounds tab, and look at the Sound Schemes menu. If the menu shows No Sounds, you're telling XP not to generate sounds, but the SoundSentry feature continues to flash your title bar, window, or screen.

Clicking Next on the wizard brings you to the ShowSounds dialog box. With this option turned on, programs with ShowSounds capability display captions for sounds or speech relevant to that program. The option is useful only if the software designers have programmed the application to support ShowSounds and developed the captions as part of the package. Because this is hit or miss, you'll find that turning ShowSounds on results in an inconsistent interface experience, but, if you know that the program you bought uses ShowSounds, the feature can help.

After you exit the Accessibility Wizard, you can choose which part of the screen to flash: the active window's title bar, the active window itself, or the screen. To make your choice, open the Accessibility Options dialog box from the Control Panel (use the Start menu or Winlogo+R, **control access.cpl**), click the Sound tab, and click the arrow in the Choose the visual warning menu. Make sure the Use SoundSentry box is checked, and click OK to activate your choice.

Tip

As with other accessibility options, you do not need to be hearing impaired to appreciate SoundSentry and ShowSounds. In an office with cubicles instead of real doors, the last thing the person besides you wants to hear is your PC making sounds (to say nothing of speech). The same holds true when you're working in your house late at night or in the family room during a quiet movie. Turning these options on at such times can help.

I Have Difficulty Using the Keyboard or Mouse

XP offers a series of options to help use the primary input devices—the mouse and keyboard. The design of keyboards and mice, like the design of most technological control devices, thoroughly reflects the belief among designers in a *typical* or *normal* mode of human action. Nothing's wrong with that; in fact, it's probably necessary. Unfortunately, many people don't fit that standard of normalcy. There is nothing whatsoever intuitive about using a mouse because it's based on motor ability skills that people must learn. Just watch anyone who has trouble equating the movement of the mouse itself on a horizontal surface, such as a mouse pad, with the movement of the pointer on the vertical surface of the monitor. There is also nothing intuitive about typing, especially when the typing involves the pressing of multiple keys almost simultaneously, as so many computer commands do.

That's why the keyboard and mouse options in the Windows XP Accessibility Wizard are so welcome and why they should not remain so hopelessly buried. They will assist the physically disabled, and they will also assist anyone else who has trouble manipulating these two crucial interface components. You can do yourself a real favor by trying them out and tailoring them to your own needs.

When setting all options in the mouse and keyboard categories, you should work in conjunction with the Accessibility Options dialog box (see Figure 18-4) available on the Control Panel (Winlogo+R, **control access.cpl**). The Accessibility Wizard turns the options on or off, but you can configure them further in Accessibility Options.

Figure 18-4: One of five tabs of the Accessibility Options in Control Panel. This dialog is separate from the Accessibility Wizard, although clearly they overlap in function (the wizard combines settings from numerous separate Control Panels).

Keyboard Accessibility Settings

The keyboard is the primary interface between you and your PC — to the extent that getting anything done in Windows programs very often requires keyboard skills more than anything else. For this reason, Microsoft has developed accessibility options for the keyboard to render it more usable for users with disabilities affecting the use of their hands. In addition, as with all other accessibility options, these features can prove useful to any user under certain circumstances.

Caution

One of the reasons Windows XP lets you turn off the shortcuts to these various keyboard options is that it's too easy for people who need some of these features to toggle them on accidentally. If you have difficulty releasing keys after pressing them, for example, you might turn on ToggleKeys by holding Num Lock down for five seconds without realizing it. On the other hand, the FilterKeys option for ignoring repeated strokes works completely against your ability to use the shortcut for StickyKeys (five consecutive Shift key presses). Be careful, in other words, not to counteract your own choices.

StickyKeys

The first stage along the keyboard and mouse path leads to StickyKeys. Essentially, this feature holds down some important keys for you — specifically, Shift, Ctrl, or Alt. Whenever a command you need requires a key combination, such as Shift+F12 to save a document or Windows' popular Alt+Tab task-switching feature, StickyKeys lets you press the two keys separately rather than together.

StickyKeys takes some getting used to. Here's an example of how to use it in conjunction with the Alt+Tab feature in XP:

1. Enable the StickyKeys feature itself, from either the Accessibility Wizard or the Accessibility Options dialog box. Alternatively, you can press the Shift key five times in a row to activate StickyKeys. With the former option, StickyKeys remains turned on; with the latter, you activate it only when you need it.

2. Press the Alt key twice and release it both times. This key, called the *modifier key*, is the single most important component to understanding how StickyKeys work. You have to press the modifier key twice to make the key "stick." In a word processor, for example, you normally press the Shift key along with a specific letter key to create an uppercase version of that letter. With StickyKeys, you press Shift twice in succession to turn it on. After which, you press the letter. In such a case, Shift is the modifier key.

3. Press the Tab key once, and release it to reveal the task-switching menu. Press it repeatedly until you reach the icon for the task you want to bring to the front of the screen. When you've reached that icon, press and release the Alt tab once again. This action turns off the StickyKeys action and brings the window to the front.

StickyKeys become tricky in cases in which you need to press two modifier keys to perform the action. In the good old Ctrl+Alt+Delete combination, for example, you must press the Ctrl key twice to make it stick, followed by the Alt key twice to make it stick, and then the Delete key to bring up the Windows Task Manager dialog box. You then need to press the Alt key to turn it off and then press the Ctrl key to turn it off.

You can configure StickyKeys to your preference through the Accessibility Options Control Panel applet. Open the Accessibility Options applet in the Control Panel, choose the Keyboard tab, and click the Settings button in the StickyKeys area. Here, you can choose whether to use the shortcut for enabling StickyKeys (pressing Shift five times in succession), and you can also choose *not* to require the double pressing of the modifier key to lock it into place. If you turn the double-pressing off, every time you press a modifier key (including the much used Shift key, as well as Alt or Ctrl), you will lock it. This will take considerable practice to work with effectively. You can also turn off the sounds StickyKeys makes when you press a modifier key.

BounceKeys

Press Next on the Accessibility Wizard to move to the next choice, BounceKeys. If you have difficulty with repeated keystrokes — for example, you tend to hold keys down too long, which creates repeated characters across the screen — you can turn repeated keystrokes off completely.

Tip

For a quick adjustment to key repetition, open the Keyboard applet in the Control Panel (Winlogo+R, **control keyboard**) and decrease the Repeat Rate. That way, the repeat feature is still on, but you have to hold the key longer to activate it.

Filterkeys and SlowKeys

The Accessibility Options Control Panel applet gives you detailed control over BounceKeys. In fact, it's so detailed that it goes by a different name, FilterKeys (I've honestly no idea why). Open the Keyboard tab of the Accessibility Options Control Panel applet, and click the Settings button in the FilterKeys area. You can choose whether to use the FilterKeys shortcut (holding the right Shift key for eight seconds), and you can opt between ignoring repeated keystrokes or ignoring quick key-strokes. Ignoring repeated keystrokes tells Windows not to act if you press a key more than once in a specified period of time. Half a second is the default setting, which is, in fact, quite long. You can change this timing by clicking the Settings button. The Settings button for ignoring quick keystrokes is much more elaborate, letting you set both the time after which the keyboard starts to repeat and the rate of repetition.

Here, you can also set an option called SlowKeys in which you instruct Windows to display a key only after you've held the key down for a specific duration. The default is one second — once again, a good long time.

ToggleKeys

The wizard next takes you to ToggleKeys, an option in which Windows plays a sound when you press one of the three keyboard lock keys — Caps Lock, Num Lock, and Scroll Lock. This option is extremely useful for notebook users. You can turn this feature on by holding down the Num Lock key for five seconds. The Settings button lets you toggle the shortcut off if you wish.

Extra Help

The final keyboard choice is extra keyboard help in programs that support it. This help is designed for users who have difficulty using a mouse (or who don't want to use one) but require extra infor-mation about using the keyboard in those programs. Each program displays this help system in its own way, so you'll have to search for it.

ACCESSIBILITY CHOICES FOR THE MOUSE

The next three screens in the Accessibility Wizard give you added control over your mouse. Actually, the first screen, MouseKeys, lets you eliminate the need for a mouse completely by enabling the numeric keypad to simulate the mouse. Clicking Yes results in the following interface changes with all actions taking place on the numeric keypad:

- You use the arrow keys to move the pointer.

- You press the minus sign (–) key to switch from the left mouse button to the right mouse button and the forward slash key (/) to switch back to the left mouse button. The following keys work regardless of whether you're emulating the right or left mouse button:

  - You press the 5 key to simulate single-clicking the mouse button.

  - You press the plus sign (+) key to simulate double-clicking the mouse button.

  - You press the Ins key to simulate clicking and holding the mouse button.

  - You press the Del key to simulate releasing the mouse button (after using Ins).

You have further options available on the Mouse tab of the Accessibility Options Control Panel applet. You can turn on or off the shortcut for using MouseKeys (press the Alt+left Shift+Num Lock combination; you have to wonder who made that one up), and you can alter the pointer speed. You can also choose to have MouseKeys available when the Num Lock key is off instead of on. This is a useful option if you have your computer configured to leave the Num Lock key off when Windows boots.

The next stage of the wizard lets you choose the cursor you prefer, and the final two stages let you configure your mouse for right-handed or left-handed use and set the pointer speed as well.

I Want to Set Adminstrative Options

The final option on the opening screen of the Accessibility Wizard (that is, after choosing font size) is to configure various administrative settings related to the accessibility features. You have only two options here, but it's a useful start. First, you can choose to leave the accessibility features on at all times or turn them off as a group after the PC has detected no activity for a specified period of time. The default is five minutes, but you can change this to anywhere from 5 to 30 minutes. This setting affects the following accessibility features:

- StickyKeys

- FilterKeys

- ToggleKeys

- High Contrast

Click Next to move to the final screen, which asks if you want to establish the current accessibility options as the default for yourself and other users' accounts, including new ones. If you click No, Windows configures only your account with these options.

Tailoring the Interface with PowerToys

Over the years, Microsoft has established a tradition of releasing for each version of Windows a set of utilities known as PowerToys. These utilities range in function from providing an alternative to the Alt+Tab task-switching feature to a utility called Tweak UI that lets you alter the Windows interface dramatically. This section examines the PowerToys for Windows XP in general, with primary attention on Tweak UI.

Caution

Microsoft makes it perfectly clear on its Web site that it does not officially support PowerToys. It never has, and it apparently never will. This means that you install them at your own risk and, if something goes wrong, you're on your own to figure out what the problem might be. Then again, you've quite likely had precisely the same experience with fully supported software, so you might not notice much difference. At any rate, before installing the PowerToys, set a restore point with the System Restore utility so that you can revert to the pre-installation configuration if you need to. (See Chapter 6 to learn more about setting a restore point.)

Installing the PowerToys

To get the Windows XP PowerToys on your system, you must download and install each component separately. You'll find them all on the Web at the following address microsoft.com/windowsxp/downloads/powertoys/xppowertoys.mspx.

   You have 11 different PowerToys available to you. Each Power Toy has its own .exe file to download. Installing it is a simple matter of clicking the link to the file, choosing Save in the subsequent File Download dialog box, saving it to your hard drive, and launching it from your hard drive. None of the downloads takes more than a couple of minutes.

Digging into the Interface with Tweak UI

Even though all the PowerToys have something to offer, the undisputed prince is Tweak UI. With this utility, you can customize an extremely large array of interface elements, which, when combined with the enhancements covered in this chapter and the previous chapters, enable you to further tailor the interface to your needs and likes. The following sections cover the major features of Tweak UI.

   To open Tweak UI, install it and then use the All Programs menu to navigate to the PowerToys for Windows XP folder. Alternatively, click Start → Run, type **tweakui** into the Open field, and press Enter. Figure 18-5 shows a typical view of Tweak UI. You click the plus signs to expand the menus and then click on the individual element to customize (if you've used early versions of Tweak UI, you'll notice that the tabs have disappeared from the top of the dialog box). Tweak UI displays a separate dialog pane for each element. Notice that every element — not just subitems — has one or more configurable choices. There's a ton of stuff here.

   Ultimately, you should poke through all the screens in TweakUI, even if you don't change anything. In the following sections, I'll point out a few of my favorites; you'll discover your own.

Figure 18-5: The dual-pane look of Tweak UI.

GENERAL CHOICES

Clicking the General item reveals an extensive list of configurable options. Most of these choices — but not all — affect your system's resources. Unchecking them reduces the amount of system memory XP uses. All animation options — window animation, ToolTip animation, menu fading, menu section fading, and so on — fall into this category.

The other choices have different functions. Unchecking Beep On Errors tells Windows not to play a beep sound whenever errors happen. Unchecking Optimize Hard Disk When Idle stops Windows from automatically repositioning the files and folders on your hard drive whenever your PC is on but not in use (you can perform this function manually by using the built-in Defragmentation tool, which is covered in Chapter 22).

Two submenus are available form the General menu, as discussed in the following two sections.

Focus

One of the problems with Windows XP is its tendency for some programs to take over from other programs, even when you're busy working with the original application. This tendency can cause problems, particularly when the second program steals focus as you're in the process of pressing a key that affects the new program. On the Focus submenu you can tell XP to stop doing this as well as how you want to be informed that a program needs attention: You can have it flash the Taskbar button continually or a limited number of times.

Alt+Tab

When you press the Alt+Tab combination while working in Windows, the middle of the screen displays a temporary window that doesn't have an official name but that should be called the Task Switcher. By default, the window is three rows by seven columns in size. You can change those dimensions here.

Tip

You can replace the Alt+Tab Task Window entirely by installing the Alt+Tab replacement PowerToy, which is covered in the "Playing with the Rest of the PowerToys" section later in this chapter.

MOUSE CHOICES

You can adjust mouse behavior in numerous ways. From the primary Mouse menu item, you can set the amount of delay before submenus appear when you hover the pointer over them. At the fastest setting, they appear immediately. At the slowest, they don't appear at all. In which case, you have to click the item to reveal the submenu. From this dialog box, you can also adjust the mouse sensitivity—both the speed at which Windows reads a double-click and the number of pixels you must drag an item (such as an icon) before Windows performs the drag action. Both choices help you avoid accidental actions.

Three submenus are available under the Mouse item:

- **Hover:** You *hover* the mouse when you hold the pointer over an icon or other item. Changing the hover sensitivity alters the size of the area in which the pointer activates the hover effect. Increasing or decreasing the hover time changes the number of milliseconds you must hover the pointer in that defined area before the hover effect kicks in.

- **Wheel:** Here you can set the scrolling options, precisely as you can in the Mouse utility from the Control Panel.

- **X-Mouse:** Unix users have long been accustomed to the X-Mouse feature in which you choose a window by simply moving the pointer onto it without the need to click that window. The X-Mouse option lets you configure Windows XP to work the same way. By checking the Auto-raise option, you tell Windows not only to select that window when you move the pointer over it but to bring it to the front of all the other windows as well.

Caution

Using the X-Mouse option takes extensive practice if you're used to the standard Windows window selection method. It's easy to confuse yourself as you move the mouse around the screen. To minimize the impact, turn on the activation feature first, practice with it for a while, and then choose the Auto-raise option.

EXPLORER CHOICES

By right, the Explorer item in Tweak UI requires a chapter all its own. A huge array of choices appears in the main dialog and the Explorer subdialogs (see Figure 18-6). Many of which significantly affect the user experience.

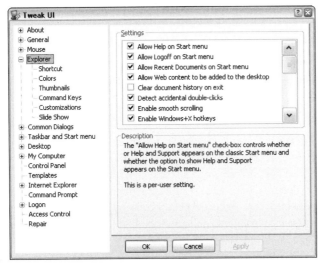

Figure 18-6: The tip of the iceberg of Explorer tweaks.

With this one part of TweakUI, you can do the following:

- Remove several items from the Start menu — Help and Support, Logoff, and Recent Documents.

- Establish whether you allow Web content on the desktop and, if you have such content, if you want to lock the content into place and not allow content to be added or removed.

- Configure Windows to cover your tracks whenever you log off so that nobody else can see your document history, the commands you've typed into the Start → Run feature, or URLs you've typed into the Address bar of Internet Explorer.

- Clear the network history to remove items from My Network Places on exit.

- Get rid of the option to view other computers on the local network.

- Add an Encyrpt command to the context menu of each file or folder.

- Change the interface so that pressing the Tab key in a dialog box menu takes you to the next item on that menu instead of to the next field of the dialog box.

The following sections explain the things you can modify in the subdialog boxes under Explorer.

Shortcut, Colors, Thumbnails, and Slide Show

The Shortcut item lets you change the appearance of the little curving arrow that appears on short-cut icons or get rid of them completely. Under Colors, you set the colors for compressed and encrypted files as well as for items you hover (the feature is called Hot-tracking) over if you've chosen the single-click interface. Hot-tracking provides a visual cue that clicking the item will launch it.

With the Thumbnails option, you choose the image quality of thumbnails that appear in your folders, as well as the size of the thumbnail in pixels. You can pack smaller thumbnails on the screen or make them larger to really see what they contain.

The other major display task in image folders, Slide Show, is also open to customization here. Click the Slide Show item and set the time in milliseconds that each image remains on the screen before switching to the next one.

Command Keys

If your computer has specialized keys for actions such as launching your Web browser or email program, for copying and pasting, for controlling volume, and so on, you can customize the action of each of these buttons through the Command Keys dialog box. From the list of command keys, choose the appropriate one from the list (not all keyboards support all the listed keys), and click the Change button.

You can tell Windows to perform the action displayed on the key's label or to do nothing (thereby disabling the key). You can also reprogram the key to perform a different action entirely. To do so, click the radio button labeled Run a Custom Program When the Key Is Pressed and type the path of the file you want to launch. The dialog box doesn't include a Browse button, so you need to know the full path of the item in order to make it work.

Customizations

When you customize your folders, Windows XP requires considerable resources to store and recall the customized settings as you open the folders. To free up memory, you can restrict the number of folder settings Windows remembers. The default is 400, but, because most people open only a limited number of folders as they work, you can cut this number significantly before noticing any difference. As you work, the folder customization settings drop off the list in the reverse order of how often you've loaded them into memory.

INTERNET EXPLORER CHOICES

If the Internet Options utility doesn't offer you enough ways to customize Internet Explorer (see Chapter 9), Tweak UI offers another wealth of possibilities. From the main link, you have only two options: one for automatically changing the backslash character to the forward slash and one for increasing the range of the automatic search function. However, the subitems make this section worth visiting. These include the following:

- **Toolbar Background:** Tailor the background of the IE toolbar and/or the Windows Explorer toolbar by checking the appropriate box and clicking the Change button to choose the background image you want the toolbar to display.

- **Search:** Develop an easy-to-use search system by creating shortcut names for popular search engines and then typing the shortcut and the search string in the Address bar. This eliminates the need to go to the search engine site before searching.

- **View Source:** Change the program that launches when you choose the Source command in IE's View menu. By default, this program is Notepad, but there are many more capable editors.

- **Small Animation and Large Animation:** Choose a new icon displayed in the top-right corner of each IE window to show that activity is under way. The Windows logo is there by default, but you can choose an Internet Explorer icon or any other image you want. To create an animated icon, you must develop a sequence of images 26 pixels square for the small animation and 38 pixels square for the large.

- **Image Toolbar:** Configure the minimum size of the image that will trigger IE to display the Pictures toolbar when you hover on that image.

LOGON CHOICES

The final major set of configurations rests with the Logon item and its submenus. In the main dialog box, you can choose which account names to display on the desktop's Welcome screen, including the Administrator account, which is hidden by default.

Caution

By default, Windows XP hides the Administrator account from the Welcome screen. This account is built into Windows during installation and provides complete control over the system. Even though you can password-protect the Administrator account, for full security, you should let it remain hidden so that other users don't become curious about its function. You can access this account by using the User Accounts utility in the Control Panel. Here, you can change the way users log on and off by reverting to the Windows 2000 logon screen and typing the account name and password into the older-style logon dialog box.

- **Autologon:** Bypass the Welcome screen entirely by configuring XP to log on to a specific user account automatically. If you have password-protected the account, click the Set Password button to include the password in the Autologon.

Caution

The Autologon option is a really, *really* bad idea from the standpoint of system security. However, it is convenient if you don't have those security concerns.

- **Unread Mail:** Change the way the Welcome screen displays the number of unread email messages waiting for each user. Because this number is substantially useless, you can uncheck the box and eliminate the notice entirely.

- **Settings:** Change the appearance of the Welcome screen by copying your desktop settings — fonts, colors, smoothing effects, wallpaper, and more — to make it look like your desktop.

- **Screen Saver:** Configure the number of seconds the screen saver will allow before prompting you for your password on the Welcome screen when you touch the mouse or keypad.

MY COMPUTER, CONTROL PANEL, TEMPLATES

The My Computer item provides a variety of items related specifically to the My Computer folder. Under the main heading, you establish which of a few items appear in the My Computer folder, whereas the Drives heading lets you check which drives — floppy, fixed, and removable — you want the My Computer folder to display. Special Folders lets you change the location of folders, such as CD Burning, My Documents, Programs, Favorites, and My Pictures, whereas Drive Letters lets you change how the drive letter and the drive's labels display.

The Control Panel item displays a lengthy menu of utilities that display in the Control Panel. Checking an item displays it, and unchecking hides it. By default, most items in the list are displayed so the only reason you would typically use this menu is to reduce the number of Control Panel icons.

In the Templates item, you can choose which file types you want in the submenu that appears when you right-click the desktop or inside a folder and choose New. Many programs add their own file type to this list, so feel free to remove items if you don't typically use them. If you use file types not in this list, click the Create button to add them yourself. Navigate to the document template for the program you wish to add, and click Open to complete the addition.

COMMON DIALOGS, DESKTOP, AND REPAIR

These three items contain relatively few options, and, as a result, they are covered together here.

The Common Dialogs item lets you specify if you want to enable the AutoComplete function in all dialog boxes that let you edit filenames. This item also lets you specify whether you want Open and Save dialog boxes to display the arrow to the right of the File Name field, which allows you to recall recently edited names. You can also edit the Places bar, which lets you select frequently accessed folders easily, or customize it to include the folders you want. You must know the path name if you wish to include folders not included in the drop-down menu.

With the Desktop item, you can determine which icons you want to include or exclude from the desktop. You can also specify which icon appears first — My Documents (the default) or My Computer.

Clicking on the Repair item displays a single menu from which you can command Windows to rebuild the default icons, the font folder, custom icons for the My Pictures, My Music, and My Video folders, Regedit, and the unread mail count. Use this feature when Windows displays incorrect icons or information.

Playing with the Rest of the PowerToys

None of the remaining PowerToys presents anywhere near the complexity of Tweak UI. Each exists for a specific purpose, either as an enhancement to the XP interface or as a replacement for an existing interface element. This list outlines uses for the remaining toys:

- **Alt+Tab Replacement:** The taskswitch.exe file replaces the existing Alt+Tab Task Switcher with a more elaborate version. Figure 18-7 shows the more advanced Task Switcher. The PowerToys version shows a small thumbnail of the open files as you tab through them. In addition, clicking an icon immediately brings that window to the front (clicking the standard Task Switcher causes the utility to disappear).

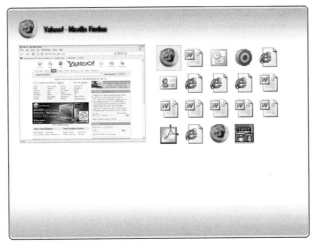

Figure 18-7: The replacement Alt+Tab Task Switcher.

- **CD Slide Show Generator:** The Slideshow.exe file lets you view the images on a CD as a slide show.

- **HTML Slide Show Wizard:** The Htmlgen.exe file creates a wizard with which you can put together slide shows of images for the Web, which is ready for publishing to a site.

- **Image Resizer:** The ImageResizer.exe file gives you a right-click context menu that allows you to resize images on the fly.

- **Open Command Window Here:** The CmdHere.exe file adds an item to a folder's right-click context menu that lets you launch a command window with that folder currently selected.

- **Power Calculator:** The PowerCalc.exe file gives you a more full-featured calculator than the one installed by default in XP.

- **Taskbar Magnifier:** The Magnifier.exe file installs an icon on the Taskbar with which you can magnify a specific portion of the screen.

- **Virtual Desktop Manager:** The Deskman.exe file adds a multiple desktop feature to Windows XP. You can add folders and icons to each desktop, although you cannot format each desktop differently as you can in some third-party programs. The Virtual Desktop Manager is an extremely useful addition to the Windows interface for anyone who works with numerous open windows that need organization for efficient use of space.

- **Webcam Timershot:** The Timershot.exe file adds a utility that lets you take pictures from your Webcam at specific intervals. You can save the pictures to any location you like, including a Web site. This feature is perfect for demonstrating how dull your workday really is.

Summary

With a look at the Tweak UI interface utility, the Accessibility options of Windows XP, and some methods of getting Windows XP to look and feel more like Windows 2000, this chapter concludes the discussion of customizing your Windows interface. By this point, you should have a Windows XP interface that works exactly the way you want it to, as well as the knowledge necessary to continue to make changes as you need them. The idea is to take control of this complex operating system. Chapter 19 extends this idea with a look at installing programs to make your Windows installation even more your very own.

Part V

Utilities

I f working through Part V hasn't caused you to spend way more time than you should customizing your Windows XP desktop, you can find any number of utilities to help you use the rest of your precious hours. Some of the utilities that let you customize your desktop do nothing more than make aesthetic changes, while others let you customize the interface more quickly, easily, and effectively to let you change Windows into whatever you want to make it.

Shells and Interface Customizers

Ever since Windows first appeared, developers of freeware, shareware, and commercial software have been providing software to let you change its look and feel. In fact, Microsoft itself got into this game in 1995 with the release of Microsoft Bob, which attempted to make the desktop look like an actual desktop and the office like an actual office, but despite a certain appeal, it was a little too cutesy at the time, to say nothing of being extremely slow. But it showed that putting a customization layer over Windows was not only possible, but potentially dramatic.

Your first stop in the Windows customization field should be Stardock (www.stardock.com), which offers a fascinating array of products designed specifically to make Windows whatever you want. WindowBlinds is the major offering here, downloadable as a free trial and then available for $20. But in a much better deal, it's also available for $50 as part of Object Desktop, the entire suite of Stardock products. In addition to WindowBlinds, you get IconPackager and IconDeveloper (change and create icons), WindowFX (add visual effects to Windows elements), SkinStudio (create new skins for Windows), Object Bar (replaces the Start bar), Virtual Desktops (create multiple accessible desktops), DesktopX (even greater customizability of the Windows desktop), and more. WindowBlinds itself gives you the tools to change the look and feel of Windows XP in numerous ways, including different layouts of icons and windows, much different looks, and different functions for keystroke combinations and mouse clicks. Get WindowBlinds alone and you can play — uh, create — for hour upon hour. Get it as part of the entire Object Desktop package as a whole, and it's probably impossible to run out of customization ideas.

3DNA Desktop (www.3dna.net) gives Windows a three-dimensional appearance. Actually, it does more than that, providing 3-D "worlds" that take over your Windows desktop. You can download a wealth of worlds and even separate skies for those worlds; the skies can even change as you work. You can even play with 3-D toys. Most important, though (well, for the worker in us), 3DNA is an organizer, letting you organize your folders, files, favorites, and much more. After you get your 3DNA desktop up and running, you really do have a completely different environment to work with.

Talisman Desktop (www.lighttek.com) takes interface customization a step further, enabling you not only to alter the existing Windows desktop as dramatically as you wish but also to replace the Windows desktop completely with Talisman itself. The result is your ability to build fully customized user interfaces for special purposes, such as providing a specifically designed interface for public terminals (for businesses, stores, clubs, schools, and so on). You can also use the program to allow each user to create her/his own interface, or for tailoring the interfaces of the users to your own satisfaction (useful for creating child-friendly interfaces, for example).

A similar program is Aston (www.astonshell.com), which also replaces your existing Windows interface. Sophisticated scrollbars on the Aston interface give you easier access to your documents than Windows does, and it also makes it far easier to determine space available on your drives (hard and removable alike). Another fascinating utility is NextStart (www.winstep.net), which replaces the Start menu and other menus on your system, complete with a HotSpot feature that lets you apply links to specific menus from any other interface element. Combined with WinStep's WorkShelf, which is a full Windows desktop replacement, NextStart gives you a huge range of possibilities for reconfiguration. Both utilities (along with a font browsing utility) are available in the WinStep Full Pack.

Less comprehensive interface tools are also readily available. For example, PaneKiller (www.maddogsw.com) gives you detailed control over the Start menu as well as the options for the My Computer and Control Panel and any other folder you'd like to add to the customization mix. Because it replaces some of the functions of the Internet Explorer toolbars (which adds a Favorites folder to the Windows interface, for instance), PaneKiller is ideal for users who want to remove IE from their systems and work with another browser instead.

Virtual Desktop Managers

Virtual Desktop managers give you several different desktops to work with and switch to. For example, you might want your main desktop to contain folders and program icons for some home office uses, while a second contains all the folders and icons you need for a specific work function (graphics creation, let's say) and a third contains an entertainment/leisure desktop environment. Using a virtual desktop manager, you can create each of these customized desktops and switch among them either by using hotkeys or by clicking among the workspace icons created by the manager and placed (usually) at the bottom of the screen.

Unlike the majority of desktop managers for Linux, which include virtual desktops as part of the package, Windows requires a separate installation if you want to use one. Microsoft has a virtual desktop utility as part of the Windows XP PowerToys package. (Go to microsoft.com and search for Power Toys.) Called the Virtual Desktop Manager (yet another stunningly inventive title), this utility offers four separate desktops and works, generally, quite well. It has crashed my system more often than I'd like, though, so I tend to steer clear of it.

Virtual Desktop Toolbox (www.r2d2-software.com) is one such utility, allowing for as many desktops as you want, although as with any program, desktops get extremely impractical once you're past six or eight. Virtual Desktop Toolbox includes a variety of useful features such as controlling remote desktops (in conjunction with Windows Remote Desktop). GoScreen (www.goscreen.info) works similarly, letting you create up to 40 virtual desktops. An interesting approach to virtual desktops is MaxiVista (www.maxivista.com), which uses the networking features of Windows XP to allow a second, third, and fourth PC (that is entirely separate machines) to function as desktop extensions for the primary PC. You can drag a window from one to the other, and yet (unlike multiple monitor support on graphics cards) the other PCs can still be running their own programs.

In addition to these two types of utilities, you can download a wealth of themes, screensavers, icons, and much, much more, turning your Windows desktop into anything you want it to be. Microsoft itself offers the Plus! SuperPack for Windows, which gives you a good selection of alternative themes as well as software for creating slideshows and CD/DVD labels, and a few high-resolution screensavers. Themes are available for download all over the Web. (Do a quick Google search and you'll unearth hundreds of them.) You can often find backgrounds, themes, and screensavers on entertainment sites as well; most new high-profile movies have them, for example. The trick with all of these utilities is to experiment until you find something that works for you, or until you've satisfied yourself that you can, in fact, boot your PC into pretty much any environment you want.

Part VI

Installing and Removing Software and Hardware

Chapter 19

Installing Software

No matter how many programs you already have for your Windows PC, more await you on store shelves, on download sites, on CDs and DVDs that come with magazines, and as trial software on corporate sites. In fact, if you buy a PC with anything less than an 80–120GB hard drive these days, you stand a very real chance of filling it up with programs alone. This is especially true if you install extremely large programs (computer games are a major culprit here) or programs designed to create files that themselves become very large. Video creation software, although it frequently takes up relatively little room on its own (today, less than 100MB constitutes "relatively little room"), creates files that can quickly overrun a small hard drive. Graphic design programs also produce files that eat up disk space, primarily because designers, especially professionals, create many versions of the same data file as the editing progresses.

This chapter outlines typical practices and methods for installing new software and examines issues such as automatic installation and end-user license agreements.

Planning the Installation

First of all, do something you'll never ever regret. Before installing any program whatsoever, do yourself a favor and take a snapshot of your system with the System Restore utility. That way, if something unwanted occurs during the installation, such as a system crash or a previously installed program not working properly, you can use System Restore again to undo the installation and return Windows to its previous state.

Cross-Reference
Chapter 6 covers the details of System Restore.

The size of the data files is important when planning the installation of a program. First, before even starting the installation, check to see that you have enough disk space, especially if you have only one hard drive with one partition. If you have more than one partition, whether on one hard drive or several, determine on which partition you want the new program to reside. By default, Windows installers place each program in its own subfolder within the Program Files folder of the primary hard drive, usually drive C.

Tip

Many programs detect, during the installation process, whether or not you have sufficient disk space. You can do this yourself by using Windows Explorer (Winlogo+E) and selecting My Computer, then a drive — free space will show in a pop-up menu, the status bar or in View → Details. Some even give you a summary of the space available on all your drives as a means of helping you decide the drive on which you wish to perform the installation. Don't be afraid to install on a different hard drive, and in a different folder, from the default locations offered by the installation program. There's no real reason to have all your programs in the Program Files folder on your main hard drive; decide for yourself how you want to organize your disk space.

To find a program's executable file — the file, almost always with an extension of .exe, loads the program and its associated files and libraries — you can look in that program's folder within Program Files. You can launch the program by double-clicking this executable. But in the majority of cases in Windows, you launch not from the actual program file, but from a desktop or menu shortcut that does nothing more than tell Windows to locate the file at the specified location and launch it for you. Shortcuts simply prevent you from having to find the resource yourself.

But you need not install the program where the Windows installer recommends. When you begin an installation, the program's installer asks where you want the program to reside. You can type a path manually or use the Browse button to locate a preferred folder. If you want to install in a non-default location, before starting the installation you should use Windows Explorer or My Computer to create a folder specifically for the new program's data files. Then you can direct the installation to that folder or, after the installation is complete, use the Properties or Options dialog box in the program to assign data files to your new folder.

Planning to install a program includes two other considerations as well:

- Know that you may have to reboot your system after or during installation, so it's a good idea to save all open documents and close as many open applications as possible. With earlier versions of Windows, installing almost any program resulted in a restart. With Windows XP, programs require a reboot somewhat less often, with even major programs, such as the Microsoft Office System 2003 suite, not forcing a reboot at all.

- Plan what to do if the installation routine asks if you want the new program to serve as the default programs for specific file types. Many programs do precisely this. For example, if you install a graphics program, during installation a dialog box will almost certainly recommend that you make the new program the default for graphics files such as JPG, GIF, TIF, BMP, and more. You should prepare for this question because in many cases the option does not arise until near or at the very end of the installation. At that point, you'll simply want to get the whole thing over with and start clicking Next whenever you see it. It can be extremely frustrating, however, to discover later that double-clicking on a file on your desktop or in a folder launches a different program than the one you want.

Note

In some cases, programs you install seem to ask constantly for permission to be the default owner of a given file type. Web browsers are famous for this, as are media players such as QuickTime and RealPlayer, and email programs such as Outlook Express. In many cases, the only way to get the program to shut up is to go into its preferences and disable the nag feature, although some programs offer a check box on the nag screen itself to let you turn the auto-checking off. During installation, the best bet is usually *not* to let it take over the file types it offers to own; instead, make that decision only once you know that you definitely want this program on your system.

If you grant ownership of a specific file type to a program and you later uninstall that program, ownership does not automatically revert to the original program. Sometimes, in fact, the only way for the original program to retake ownership is to reinstall it. Keep this in mind when making your ownership choices during installation.

What happens when you install a program

If you've installed even a half dozen software packages on your Windows XP system, you've undoubtedly come across at least one, and possibly two, installer environments: InstallShield and Wise. These competing utilities exist for the purpose of helping software developers and manufacturers get their products to you in a form that allows an almost guaranteed hassle-free installation. The fact that practically every Windows user can pop a CD into the drive and carry out the installation proves, beyond the shadow of a doubt, that these utilities are fulfilling their purpose.

Both programs do essentially the same thing: They produce files for use by the Microsoft Installer (MSI). These MSI files act as a script, carrying out the steps that the scriptwriter has programmed into them. Each file contains a database, a directory structure, information about source media and destination folders, and details on modifying the Windows registry, adding shortcuts to the desktop, placing icons and their associated image files, storing files such as dynamic link libraries (DLLs), and more. Microsoft Installer steps through the process one stage at a time, showing you what is transpiring at any given moment and informing you when the installation has finished. The installation utility itself provides a set of features designed to help the programmer organize the information MSI needs.

To see the sheer usefulness of these programs, go to a machine running Linux, even one of the most recent versions, and try to download and install a half-dozen programs. Over the last year or so, software installations on Linux have improved dramatically, but there is virtually no comparison in usability between installing a program on Windows and installing even the same program on Linux. In fact, when you read a published comparison of the two operating systems in which Windows receives higher usability marks than Linux, software installation almost certainly rides at the top of the list of differences. In this regard, Windows still flat out works better.

Performing the Installation

With your planning out of the way, it's time to proceed with the installation. This can take any of the following forms:

- Insert the CD that came with the software package and wait for AutoPlay to start the installation procedure automatically. More often than not, this will start the installation.

- Insert the CD that came with the software package, open My Computer, locate the icon for the relevant CD-ROM drive, and double-click on that icon to start the installation procedure.

- Insert the CD that came with the software package, open My Computer, and locate the icon for the relevant CD-ROM drive. Right-click it, and choose Explore from the context menu. In the main window of the resulting Windows Explorer utility, locate the Setup file (typically called setup.exe but sometimes install.exe), and double-click it.

- Insert the CD that came with the software package, open Control Panel, and double-click the Add or Remove Programs utility (see Figure 19-1). Wait until the list of items appears in the Currently Installed Programs area (the more you have, the longer it takes for the list to appear), and then click the Add New Programs item in the Taskbar on the left. Click the CD or Floppy button; with the CD in the drive, click Next on the Install Program from Floppy Disk or CD-ROM Wizard. Add or Remove Programs searches these devices for the installation file.

Tip

You can use Add or Remove Programs even if you don't have a CD or floppy disk with the installation file. Step through the process until the wizard tells you to insert the CD-ROM or floppy disk; when it fails to find one, click Browse on the Run Installation Program dialog box. Manually locate the installation file, and click Finish to begin installing the program.

- Install the program from a downloaded compressed file, as detailed in the following section, "Installing from Compressed Files."

Installing from Compressed Files

Locate the compressed .exe or compressed (most commonly .zip) file you downloaded to your computer from the download site. Double-click the file. If the file is an uncompressed .exe file, the installation should start, and you need do nothing extra. If the file is compressed, however, the unzip utility will be launched. If this happens, click Unzip to uncompress the files and launch the installation procedure.

If the installation procedure does not begin after double-clicking the executable file, click Unzip again and watch the utility to see where Windows places the unzipped files. Navigate to that folder and double-click the setup.exe file to begin the installation.

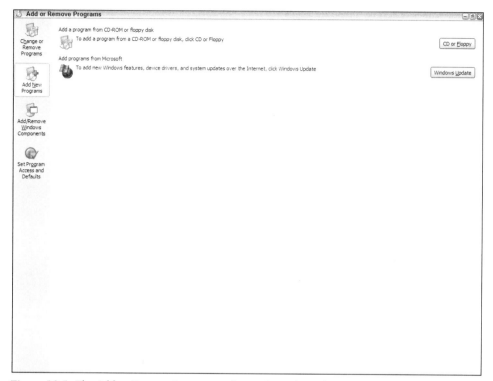

Figure 19-1: The Add or Remove Programs utility in Control Panel.

If the downloaded file is a .zip (compressed files) instead of an executable, you'll need to locate the .zip file you downloaded from the download site. Double-click the file to open it, and locate the setup.exe file. You now have two choices:

- The most sure-fire process is to click the Extract All Files item in the Folder Tasks area on the left of the Zip folder (if you don't see the Task pane on the left, click the Folders button to display it and then highlight the .zip file). Following the Extraction Wizard, choose a folder into which to extract the files, or create a new one expressly for this purpose, then click Next until you reach the Finish button. Click Finish to close the Extraction Wizard and simultaneously open the folder where the extracted files now reside. Double-click the setup.exe file from this folder.

- If you wish, you can perform the installation directly from the compressed folder by double-clicking the setup.exe file, but this method can fail because of the compression, and the process typically takes considerably longer (up to double the amount of time) even if it does work. The better idea is to extract the files and then, once the installation is complete, delete both the compressed folder and the uncompressed files to reclaim your hard disk space.

Removing the highlighting from new programs on the Start menu

When you install a program, Windows XP highlights that program on the Start menu in two ways. First, hovering over the Start button reveals a ToolTip (the New Program notification) stating that new programs exist. Second, the folder for that program and the shortcuts inside that folder bear a yellow background color—that is, the traditional color of a highlighter. When you launch the new program from within the All Programs menu, the highlight disappears.

Well, the highlighting is supposed to disappear, at least. In practice, sometimes the highlight stays around through multiple reboots, becoming increasingly annoying. Furthermore, because the New Program notification pops up when you hover over the Start button, depending on the current screen resolution it can hide the Log Off and Turn Off Computer buttons. Without question, on a crowded system highlighting new installations helps locate them (especially when the folder name does not match the program name), but sometimes you just want to turn the feature off.

To turn off the highlighting, open the Taskbar and Start Menu Properties dialog box by right-clicking the Taskbar and selecting Properties. Click the Start Menu tab, click the Start Menu radio button, and then click the Customize button. Click the Advanced tab of the resulting Customize Start Menu dialog box and, under the Start Menu Settings heading, uncheck the Highlight Newly Installed Programs option. Click OK until the dialog boxes all disappear.

Other Installation Types

The installation methods outlined so far represent, by far, the most common forms of installation. Over the course of your Windows XP travels, however, you might encounter additional installation procedures. These procedures tend to dispense with either the InstallShield or Wise Wizards in favor of a range of other methods that ensure the various files end up in the right place on your hard drive and the registry entries undergo the appropriate changes.

Actually, in one increasingly rare case, no installation process of any kind takes place. In the days of MS-DOS, installing a program frequently consisted of copying the files for that program to a folder (it was called a directory back then) of your choice, including the executable file that runs the program. If you have one of these programs—many users still work with WordPerfect 4.1, for example—you need only ensure that the files end up together and that you can locate the .exe file. You can create a shortcut to run this program or simply navigate to the correct folder and double-click the .exe file. Some early Windows programs, especially simple games and utilities, worked this way, and these are sometimes still available.

You can also install some programs from .inf files, typically used for information about hardware or software settings. The primary source of installable .inf files has been Microsoft, which until recently distributed its popular set of Windows utilities called PowerToys as .inf files. In fact, right-clicking any .inf file yields the Install command in the context menu, so .inf is clearly an option for program distribution. In the majority of cases, however, the .inf file represents only a small portion of the full program. So, not only is there no point in installing it, but you may also cause difficulties with other programs if you do so.

Cross-Reference
To find out more about PowerToys, see Chapter 18.

As the World Wide Web continues to grow, so do the number of ways in which developers, both beneficent and malevolent, exploit the capability of users to make things happen with a simple mouse click. ActiveX installation routines provide one significant example of this trend. Microsoft, Macromedia, and many other major companies make use of ActiveX to simplify installation by popping up a dialog box when the installation is required (see Figure 19-2).When the browser encounters a Macromedia Flash object, for example, but the system does not have the correct version of Flash installed, an ActiveX dialog box asks if you want to install it. At least, you'll get this questioning dialog box if you leave Internet Explorer's security settings in their default locations. You can completely override those settings and allow all ActiveX installations to proceed unchecked, but doing so would allow all sorts of intrusions and malicious code into your machine. So, it's best to leave the settings as they are.

Figure 19-2: This Security Warning dialog box begins
the ActiveX installation process.

Even more installation procedures exist in the Windows XP world. Windows Update provides a primary example. Although I covered Windows Update in full in Chapter 5, it bears mention here because its basis lies in new and updated installations. Windows Update provides a means for Windows XP owners to keep their PCs up to date according to the criteria Microsoft has established. If you go to the Windows Update site and allow your computer to be scanned, you can select any updates from the three areas — Critical Updates and Service Packs, Windows, and Driver Updates — and click the Review and Install Updates link to begin the installation procedure. Figure 19-3 shows the results of clicking this link: the Install Now button leading to the Microsoft Windows Update dialog box in which you accept or reject the license agreement (see the "Inside a license agreement" sidebar). Clicking the Accept button initiates the installation.

Other programs offer similar means of automatic updating. Probably the most common programs of this type are virus checkers, which depend on frequently updated definition files — files that contain the details the program needs to recognize each virus — to do their job. Every antivirus program lets you manually update it either by downloading the virus definition files and applying them to the program or by connecting to the manufacturer's site from within the program itself, an easier process because you don't have to apply the definition files yourself. Other programs that depend on frequent file updates for their usefulness, particular security-related programs such as anti-spam, anti-spyware, anti-malware, and firewall software, all offer similar updating methods. In addition, many programs provide a feature, typically called Check for Updates, that connects to the manufacturer's site and downloads and installs program patches and changes, in some cases replacing the original program completely and installing a new version from scratch.

If you prefer, you can configure Windows Update and other programs to perform the installations automatically (see Chapter 5 for details on doing this with Windows Update). In an automatic installation, a program connects to the Internet and downloads and installs files; all of this activity occurs in the background and without action on your part. Actually, that's not quite true — at one point, either during initial setup or through a separate configuration dialog box, you have to configure the program to perform this sequence of actions periodically. But once automatic installations are in place, only when they have occurred do you know they happened. Microsoft's Windows Update and Symantec's Norton AntiVirus, for example, perform either the download or the installation (you can specify the degree of automation) in the background and inform you, through a small pop-up box, that they have completed the activity. Other programs use similar techniques.

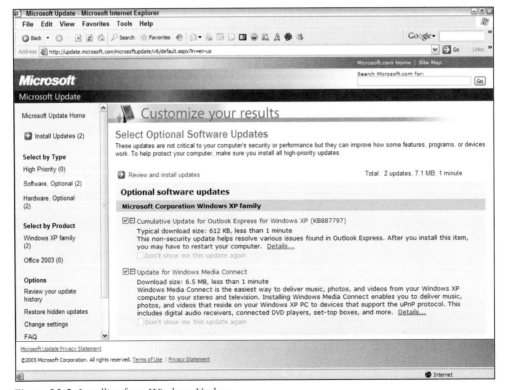

Figure 19-3: Installing from Windows Update.

Inside a License Agreement

Whenever you install a program and in many cases a software update, the installation procedure shows you a license agreement, or at least a link to a license agreement, that you must accept in order to continue with the installation (see the following figure). Sometimes this process takes the form of clicking an Accept button; other times it's a check box. In rare cases, to force you to pay attention to the license, you must manually scroll to the bottom of the agreement before the Accept button becomes active. In most cases, you don't have to read the agreement, but you must acknowledge that you accept it.

License agreements go by several names, with Software License Agreement (SLA) and End-User License Agreement (EULA) being the most common (see the following figure). In the Windows world, EULA seems the most common by far, in part because Microsoft uses that terminology. You don't get anything from Microsoft (not even the tiniest Windows Update file) without a EULA tagging along.

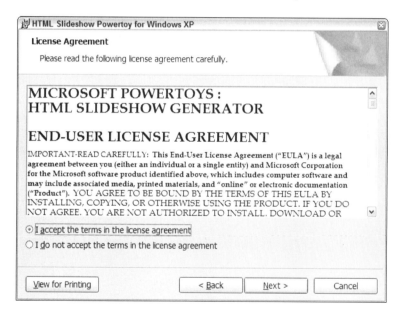

The EULA provides information on some or all of the following:

- Making an archival copy of the software

- Installing your software on more than one computer

- Selling your software to another person

- Using components of the programs (including data files) in commercially available products

- What the manufacturer is responsible for, including situations in which you suffer damage as a result of software failure (the answer is almost always nothing at all)

Continued

Inside a License Agreement *(Continued)*

The important point about the EULA is that it is a legal document. By accepting it, you bind yourself to its conditions and to the possibility that you can be penalized for using the software illegally (such as putting a copy on each of your home machines). You should definitely read the license before proceeding with the installation, but the fact remains that very few people do. The EULA holds the same awe over computer owners as the FBI warning at the beginning of videotapes and DVDs has always held over VCR owners. Obviously, you'll do whatever you want, but don't dismiss the EULA without understanding the possible — though unlikely — legal ramifications.

You should allow automatic installations only if you are completely confident in the company and the process. On the other hand, if you purchase a program that requires frequent updates in order to work effectively, don't go out of your way to deny it the right to update itself. If you get nailed by a new virus because you don't like the idea of your virus checker performing automatic installations, you end up doing the suffering.

Note

One of the problems with automatic updating is precisely its background operation. Some virus checkers, for example, check for new definition files whenever you power on your computer. Often this activity slows down your computer, to the extent that, in the case of Norton Antivirus, you can get frustrated because Windows responds to your mouse actions so slowly, and you end up clicking numerous icons. A few seconds later, up pops the Norton notification window, and then an entire series of frustration-driven program launches. You can stop this behavior only by shutting off the automatic updating feature in Norton AntiVirus, but do so only if you can remember to perform a manual check for definition files regularly.

Summary

By installing software programs, you (hopefully) add more functionality or entertainment to your PC. You can install programs that help you get your work done, that keep your system in good repair, that give you a creative outlet, or that let you fritter away untold numbers of hours in blissful amusement. Most programs install in much the same way, and they all take advantage of the broad range of technologies that underlie Windows XP. They provide the building blocks of a Windows system that works the way you need it to work.

Of course, the counterpart to installing software is removing it, and as you'll see in the next chapter, Windows XP offers a number of methods to accomplish this task as well.

Chapter 20

Removing Software

Y ou'd think that removing software would be easy—nothing more than a few mouse clicks to take care of everything. And, to be sure, often a few clicks *are* all it takes. But, in far too many situations, uninstalling the software on your system causes more headaches than installing it. In this sense, you could argue that software is a little like termites and speeding tickets—much easier to get than to get out of—but software is supposed to be much simpler to deal with. Install, use, uninstall, done. Nobody wants it to be any more involved than that—with the possible exception of the software vendors themselves. But, they're not in charge. You are.

Back in the days of MS-DOS, uninstalling a program typically meant one thing only. Delete the folder in which the program's files resided. Sometimes, but not usually, you had to go to the extreme of deleting a line or two in the system's configuration files. However, with the release of Windows 3.x, system files suddenly took on a new importance. Even though program removal remained relatively easy, the need to delete lines manually from the system files (system.ini and win.ini) grew more important. Installing a program meant adding lines to one or both of these files—sometimes entire sections in fact—and these lines provided instructions for Windows that, once the programs were removed, sometimes resulted in system errors. If the program called for Windows to load a specific file during the boot process, for example, and you deleted the file when you manually deleted that program's folder, Windows could stutter or even hang as it started up.

The release of Windows 95 saw the importance of the system files reduced in favor of a new and more all-encompassing technology: the Windows registry. Less open to manual editing, if only because its contents are obscure to all but the most technically inclined, the registry has given new focus to installation and removal. Both actions modify the registry when initiated by a Windows procedure, and, in some cases, you cannot completely remove a program without editing the registry on your own. After several months of use, with software actively installed and removed, the registry in most Windows systems is cluttered with entries no longer relevant to the PC's operation. Usually these entries can simply remain in the registry without affecting the performance of Windows, but they sometimes make a very real and, unfortunately, negative difference.

This chapter shows you how to delete programs from your computer by outlining a variety of methods and techniques for making sure the job gets done completely.

Note

This chapter refers to getting rid of programs by using the following interchangeable terms: *uninstall*, *remove*, and *delete*.

The Easy Way: Add or Remove Programs, Built-In and Third-Party Uninstallers, and System Restore

The three methods outlined in this section represent the easiest — and usually the most — effective means of removing programs from your PC. However, in difficult cases, they do not perform the uninstallation to the most complete extent; in those cases, you should refer to the section later in this chapter titled "The Harder Way: Mnaual Installs." Most of the time, the easier methods discussed here will do the job just fine.

Caution

See Chapter 4 on backing up your data. If there is any chance you'll change your mind, be sure that you have the original program installer.

Add or Remove Programs

The Add or Remove Programs utility in the Control Panel provides the easiest and most consistent way to remove software from your system. In fact, you can help your chances of keeping your PC in better working order by opening Add or Remove Programs regularly — at least once a month, for example — and carefully examining the list of installed programs. Often, you'll find programs you haven't used for a while. At other times, you'll find programs you've forgotten you'd even installed. You might also see programs in the list you can't identify at all. All three types need your attention.

Figure 20-1 shows the Add or Remove Programs utility. Installed programs appear in the main window and, in this case, one of them has been selected. One or two buttons appear to the right of the program's name. If you installed the program but did not include one or more separately listed components, both the Change and Remove buttons appear. Click Change to remove specific components or to install additional ones. If you have installed a program that cannot be altered but only removed, you see only a Remove button. The majority of programs offer a combined Change/Remove button, which opens to a separate dialog box in which you can typically modify, repair, or remove the program.

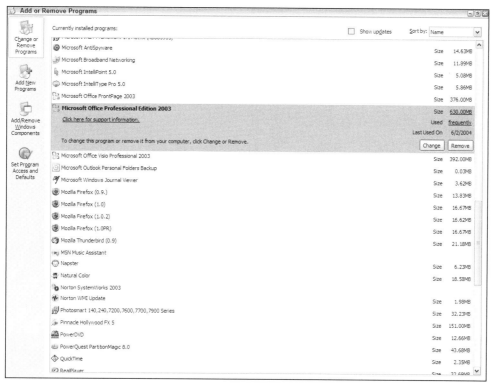

Figure 20-1: The Add or Remove Programs utility.

Figure 20-2 shows this dialog box for a program called Partition Magic 8.0 (from PowerQuest Corporation). If you want to reinstall the program precisely as you installed it initially, choose Repair. This option is especially useful if the program has — for any reason — stopped performing the way it did initially. The Modify option lets you add or remove individual components of this multipart utility. The Remove option, as its name implies, uninstalls the program from your hard drive by deleting the files in the program's folder, associated files in other folders, and registry entries relevant to that program.

Many uninstallations remove the majority of the files from a program's folder but not necessarily all of them. For numerous reasons, among them the use of one of the program's files at the time you attempt removal, files can remain in the folder, and the folder can continue to exist on your hard drive. In some cases, the folder remains in order to hold the data files. The uninstall procedure assumes (usually correctly) that you want to get rid of the program but not its associated data. Leaving the data files in place allows you to reinstall the program later and still use these files. Data files are, after all, the most important files in any program.

Third-Party Uninstallers

You don't need to restrict yourself to the uninstallation procedures already on your machine. You can add third-party utilities to help you keep track of programs and their uninstallation demands, and you can also perform the removals manually.

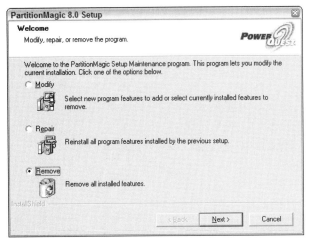

Figure 20-2: The options for Partition Magic's uninstallation process.

If you install a great deal of software, you should consider buying and installing one of several utilities designed expressly for this purpose. These utilities can help you locate and get rid of programs already installed on your system, but they work best when you use them during the installation as well. Essentially, these programs monitor your PC; as you install programs, they create a database of details about what the installation actually does.

For example, the database contains complete information about the files installed and their locations, files replaced and their locations, registry entries created and modified, shortcuts and their locations, and more. When you want to uninstall the program, you launch this utility instead of (or, in some cases, in addition to) the Add or Remove Programs utility in Control Panel. The program reverses all additions and changes originally put in place by that program's installation process and, in some cases, asks if you want to remove associated installations as well.

Figure 20-3 displays one of the better known uninstall utilities: Norton CleanSweep. Part of the Norton SystemWorks suite of utilities, CleanSweep provides a monitoring feature and also lets you search for programs to uninstall. This figure shows the result of a search for programs on all drives with a list appearing in the main window. Clicking any of the programs yields a brief description of the program that helps you decide if you should consider deleting it.

Clicking OK for this file opens the CleanSweep Uninstall Wizard. The first stage of the wizard asks where you want to store the backup. Immediately, the difference between CleanSweep and Add or Remove Programs becomes apparent. In addition to removing the program, CleanSweep backs it up in case you realize you made a mistake and want to reverse the uninstallation.

Furthermore, the rest of the wizard shows the additional power of the program as it asks you if you want to confirm the deletion of each item. Figure 20-4 shows the result of answering Yes and moving past the next step. That step contains a View button to let you see (and possibly modify) the list of items CleanSweep will uninstall along with the main program. The list shows what CleanSweep has determined it should remove, but you can uncheck items you don't want removed for whatever reason. The Links button is an extremely powerful tool. It opens to reveal two lists: one consisting of programs or files that use the program you have slated for removal and the other showing programs or files that the currently selected program uses. These lists let you determine if removing the program might cause a ripple effect by rendering other programs suddenly nonfunctional because they depend on this one. Click OK and then Finish to remove the program.

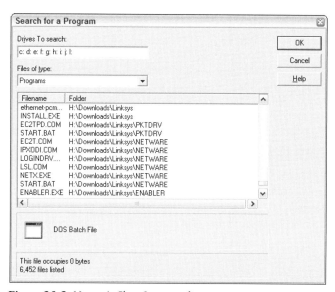

Figure 20-3: Norton's CleanSweep utility.

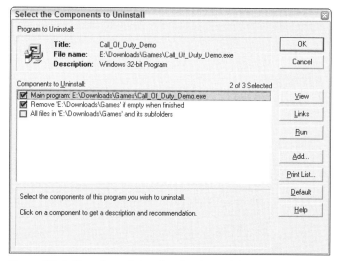

Figure 20-4: CleanSweep's interface for determining program dependencies.

Third-party uninstallation utilities typically do more than just help you remove programs. They also do the following:

- Monitor your system cache, your browser cache, history, cookies, and more

- Provide an endless amount of information about what's going on under the hood of your PC

- Help you decide what to keep and what to remove

As you can see, uninstallation utilities are very useful, and most users would do well to have one. However, for maximum effectiveness, configure their options to have them load automatically with Windows so that if you begin an installation, the utility is sure to track it. Otherwise, you largely defeat the purpose of these programs.

The Desperate Way: System Restore

Although a little bit along the lines of overkill, you can remove a program by using the System Restore utility found in the System Tools subfolder of the Accessories folder. By setting a restore point before installing a program, you ensure that you are able to turn Windows back to the moment immediately before the installation changed your registry, your Windows System folders, and more. Figure 20-5 shows the System Restore utility with several restore points highlighted on the calendar portion of the interface.

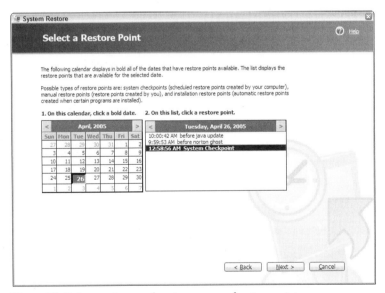

Figure 20-5: System Restore showing a range of restore points.

Chapter 6 covers the use of the System Restore utility in detail. Here, the important thing to keep in mind is to be sure to create a restore point whenever you install *anything* on your PC: hardware and software alike. The only problem comes when you want to turn back the clock more than one installation ago. For example, if you install Program A on September 15 and Program B on October 30 and set a restore point before installing each program, restoring your PC to its state on September 15 wipes out the installation you performed on October 30. Because System Restore leaves all data files entirely intact, as long as you have the installation media or the downloaded file for the software installed in October, you can reinstall that program.

The Harder Way: Manual Uninstalls

When all else fails, do it yourself. Great dictum, of course, but it's not always practical. When it comes to computers, unless you're willing to learn a great deal about the underlying principles and processes that govern your software and its interaction with the Windows XP operating system, you can quickly get yourself into a fair bit of trouble doing everything manually. But, sometimes you have no choice. So, here's a rundown of how to get rid of a program or the pieces an uninstaller leaves behind.

Figure 20-6 shows the Windows registry after the uninstallation of a game. This particular uninstall did not delete all the registry entries; although, in most cases, it will do so. With the vast majority of software, leaving entries in the registry won't cause any problems; but if you find Windows continually searching for files or data that once belonged to a program you have uninstalled, you might consider removing these registry entries. However, there are two major problems with this idea:

- A single misstep while editing the registry can cause irreparable harm to your Windows XP system.

- Some programs place so many entries into the registry that tracking them all down can take hours. To find them, expand all items, and look for the name of the vendor and the name of the program as well as the file type if the program works with a specific data file extension. In addition, perform a search (Edit → Find) on the vendor and program name (or on a specific filename if you know of a file used exclusively by that program).

To remove a program manually, perform the following steps:

1. Use the System Restore utility to set a restore point for your system in case anything with this process goes wrong. See Chapter 6 if you need a refresher on setting a restore point.

2. Ensure that you can't remove the program with Add or Remove Programs by opening the Add or Remove Programs utility and examining the list. Also look in the Add or Remove Windows Components list by clicking that button on the utility.

3. Look in the program's folders for an uninstall utility, such as unwise.exe or an icon with a filename beginning with Uninst or just Un. Again, if you can do the job this way, you'll save yourself time and possible trouble. Assuming that neither step 1 nor 2 gets you anywhere, you can begin the manual removal.

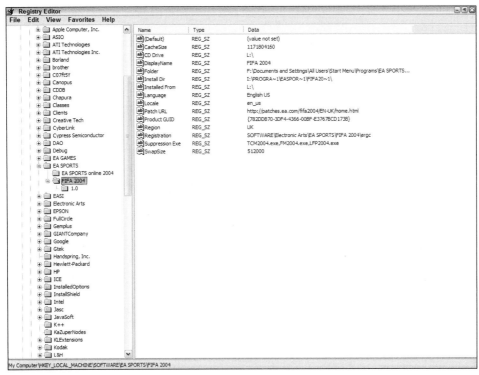

Figure 20-6: The registry after the incomplete uninstallation of a game.

4. Locate the program's folders and files. Typically, these reside inside the Program Files folder on your primary Windows drive (usually your C: drive). If you can't locate the program because the name doesn't appear, right-click the program's icon, and choose Properties to locate the file this way. Alternatively, you can open the program and choose About to see who manufactures it and then look in Program Files to see if Windows has stored it in a folder of that name instead.

5. Examine the folders carefully for data files you created yourself. If you find some files, but you're not sure if they're yours, open the program and use the File Open dialog box to load the files into memory. In any event, if you find data files and want to keep those data files, copy or move them into another folder on your hard drive. Sorting files by date may help.

6. Delete the folders containing the program and its files and subfolders. Be careful not to delete the entire Program Files folder by accident. It's been done before.

7. Reboot your computer and see if anything fails to work. If you run into problems, open System Restore and bring the program back by choosing the restore point you created in step 1.

8. If everything works, edit the registry with the Regedit program. (Click the Start button, choose Run, type **redgedit**, and press Enter.) In the Software section called

HKEY_LOCAL_MACHINE, locate the keys for the software you just removed. Programs are listed by vendor. If you have more than one program from the same manufacturer, drill down through the items to make sure that you delete only the keys for the program you want to remove. Right-click each entry, and choose Delete.

9. Perform the same function for the HKEY_CURRENT_USER section of the Registry Editor.

10. Reboot to ensure that everything works. If it doesn't, use System Restore to turn back the clock.

11. Open the System Configuration utility (click the Start button, choose Run, type **msconfig**, and press Enter), and click the Startup tab. If your program appears in the list, uncheck it, and click OK until the utility closes.

12. Reboot Windows.

Tip

If you manually remove a program from your PC, the name of the program remains in the Add/Remove Programs list. You can remove it in two ways. First, if you try to uninstall it, Windows tells you it cannot do so and asks if you want to remove the name from the list. Click Yes. Second, you can remove the program from the list by installing the TweakUI PowerToy (see Chapter 18 for details on TweakUI) and using its option to remove items from the Add/Remove list.

There is actually a third way to manually remove a program — one that the first two methods accomplish in a friendlier way. Open the registry using the Windows Registry Editor (click Start, choose Run, type **regedit** in the Open box, and press Enter) and navigate to the key at HKEY_LOCAL_MACHINE\Software\Microsoft\ Windows\CurrentVersion\Uninstall. Scrolling down this list reveals the names of the programs on the Add or Remove Programs utility. With the utility open so that you can double-check what you're doing (the registry does not offer a particularly user-friendly appearance), right-click in the registry on the items you wish to remove from the list and choose Delete. The next time you open Add or Remove Programs, you will no longer see the item.

Summary

When everything behaves as it should, removing software is a piece of cake. Unfortunately, and for various reasons, perfect behavior isn't nearly as common as it should be. So, besides the Add or Remove Programs utility of Windows XP, you may need additional techniques to get the job done. With the range of proactive through protective techniques covered in this chapter, you should have very few problems getting rid of programs you don't want — even those that don't seem to want to leave.

Chapter 21

Installing Hardware

Even a heavily discounted computer in today's market contains a decent collection of hardware. You get lots of RAM, a fairly fast processor, a large hard drive, and built-in audio and graphics capabilities at a reasonably high level. You also get a CD-ROM drive at the very least or — more frequently now — a CD-RW drive. Moreover, many machines now ship with combo DVD/CD-RW drives and, increasingly, DVD burners. Most PCs come with several USB 2.0 ports, and many also have FireWire ports. When you buy one of these machines, you plug it in, boot it up, and glory in your newfound power.

For a while, anyway.

This chapter covers hardware installation in your Windows XP machine, including physical installation of the hardware itself and, once you have your new device in place, how to locate and install the necessary drivers.

Why You'll Want to Install Hardware

Sooner or later, you'll want to upgrade your PC. Here are just a few examples:

▓ Your computer has trouble running that new graphics program you bought, so you decide you need more system memory and/or a new video card.

▓ You want a second (or third) monitor to increase workspace (XP supports up to 9).

▓ You start running out of disk space, so you decide one of those new whopping hard drives would solve the problem.

▓ A new printer catches your eye.

▓ You want to start creating video more seriously.

▓ You get a new mobile audio player (such as an iPod) for your birthday.

▓ You want a second mouse, trackball, or pen (XP supports multiples of each).

▦ You need more USB connections for all these other devices (or you're tired of crawling under your desk to plug in a flash drive — get a USB hub).

▦ You wake up one morning with your sights set on buying yourself a new and faster processor and then discover that, in order to use it, you have to install an entirely new motherboard.

All these cases deal with installing hardware, an often intimidating and too often frustrating (even infuriating) process. Adding software to a computer seems much less complex. Adding software is a bit like adding the pictures of your latest vacation to your photograph album — the pictures improve the album, but they don't fundamentally change it. When you add hardware, you alter the machine itself — either by appending another device to it (adding external hardware) or popping the hood and inserting a device inside it. As a result, in addition to the device itself, you need to install a *software driver*, a set of software instructions that tell Windows how to interact with and utilize the device. In addition, you have to concern yourself with plugging the wires in correctly, not an inconsiderable point when it comes to installing hardware inside the box (and sometimes a bit tricky even outside the box).

Nobody really minds plugging in a new printer or scanner and getting it up and running. Adding a new video card, networking card, hard drive, or memory module, however, can make anyone nervous — and for good reason. When you install software, or external hardware, you have little chance of actually damaging something. With hardware, you can actually cause physical problems or even render your computer processor dead.

All of that said, as long as you work even reasonably carefully, don't let the warnings stop you from trying. You can improve your PC noticeably by adding new memory, a new hard drive, or a new video card, and neither one of these tasks takes more than (at most) an hour of your time. In fact, with some PCs, the most significant challenge for all three might very well be getting the case apart. Once inside, a bit of planning, a bit of maneuvering, and a bit of gentle persuasion can get the job done quickly.

Hardware Basics

Computer hardware comes in two basic types: external and internal. Printers, scanners, and digital cameras are always external devices; system memory (RAM), hard drive controllers, and motherboards are always internal. Hard drives themselves, along with CD-RW drives, network cards, and USB or FireWire adapters, can be either. You will always find it easier to install an external device than an internal device — primarily because you don't have to open the computer case.

For this reason, computer vendors have been pushing external devices increasingly over the past few years. They know that very few users feel comfortable opening their computer cases. With notebook computers, doing so sometimes even voids the warranty. However, if you ultimately want to upgrade your computer rather than buy a new one, and if you don't want to pay your local shop to do the work for you, you'll end up getting your hands dirty (figuratively speaking only — computer cases shouldn't have any real dirt in them) and opening the case.

Whichever type of device you choose to install, Windows XP handles all hardware installations according to the same basic principle. You must connect the hardware to the computer, and you must install a hardware driver to allow Windows to communicate with the new hardware. Without the driver, the hardware does not work. From the operating system's perspective, it doesn't even exist. Where do you get drivers? Three sources, mostly:

- **The manufacturer:** When you buy a new hardware device, the manufacturer includes a CD or (rarely today) a floppy disk containing a set of drivers or, more typically, the drivers and other software. A typical scanner package, for example, contains one or more CDs containing the software drivers, scanning software, and often a full, trial, or limited version (often called a *lite* version) of both photo-editing software and optical character recognition (OCR) software — the latter for converting scanned text documents to word processing files. Buying a portable MP3 audio player gets you the necessary drivers, along with software to rip songs from music CDs and copy them to the player.

- **Windows XP:** Windows XP ships with hundreds of hardware drivers on the installation CD and has proven more capable than any other Windows version to date at recognizing hardware and installing drivers automatically. Sometimes, you might not get the most up-to-date driver available, but you'll often be able to use the device minutes after plugging it in. In fact, this feature of Windows XP has proven one of the most important features of all. For the first time, even computer novices can buy a hardware device for their computer and install it with a reasonable degree of confidence, even nonchalance. For users who have worked with earlier versions of Windows with hardware installations that resembled arcane cult rituals combined with advanced automobile repair, adding hardware to Windows XP has proven extremely agreeable. Imagine, you plug it in . . . it works! Oh, brave new world!

- **Internet download areas:** You can acquire and upgrade software and hardware drivers from the Internet, which is applicable with newly acquired hardware when you didn't receive a driver disk or CD with it (as often happens when you buy a hardware device from a friend). However, if this is your situation, you should see if you can find the driver on the Internet. Your first destination should be the manufacturer's Web site, usually the support or download section (you might have to drill through product lists to get to it). Failing that, you can get good results by visiting a paid driver service such as www.drivershq.com or www.windrivers.com. Other sites, such as www.Driverzone.com, provide links to a wide range of manufacturer sites for drivers. Windows Update will offer device drivers if it recognizes them upon scanning your PC, but often these aren't the absolute latest versions. They are, however, usually very safe.

Installing External Devices

When you add external devices to your system, you don't need to open the computer case. For this reason, the process is fairly easy because all you have to do is attach the cables and install the drivers. If you are installing a printer using the parallel port or any device using the serial port (rare) or mouse or keyboard ports, you must turn the computer off before attaching the device. In the case of USB, USB 2.0, FireWire (IEEE 1394), or PC Card (PCMCIA) devices, you don't even need to do that much. Just plug them in and watch Windows do the rest.

Actually, it might not prove quite that easy. Especially in the case of devices that connect through a USB port; read the installation instructions to determine if you should install the driver first or the device first. Most manufacturers specify that the driver comes first so that Windows can load that driver automatically when it recognizes the device. If you do not follow this sequence, it could take you two or three tries to get the hardware device to function.

One other element can come into play with external devices: power supplies. Hardware devices installed inside the PC draw electrical power from the power supply inside the PC itself. External devices, with a very few exceptions, require power from an electrical outlet in your building. The devices come with their own power supplies, and you must plug them into the wall socket or a power bar (which itself plugs into a wall socket). By itself, this isn't a problem because the manufacturers supply the necessary items. Unfortunately, many manufactures use the type of connection in which the connectors for the wall socket emerge from the large transformer itself. This results in gargantuan plugs that can make it nearly impossible to plug in even two devices. In fact, some users have even let the type of connector stand as the final decision point between one piece of hardware or another when considering the two for purchase.

Tip

If you have a computer with multiple devices installed internally and multiple devices attached externally, consider having an electrician install a separate electrical line for your computing use only. Otherwise, once you start using all your hardware devices, you might notice power fluctuations, and fluctuations can damage a PC very quickly. You should also consider using a high-quality surge suppressor (not the $4.95 item that claims to suppress surges), or, better yet, an uninterruptible power supply (UPS). A good surge suppressor costs $30 or more, with a good UPS closer to $100. But if they protect you from even one power surge, you will most definitely not mind having spent the money. UPS hardware goes so far as to keep your computer running when the power goes out completely, which is long enough for you to shut down all your programs and then the PC itself. The better UPSs even perform the shutdown for you in case you're away from the machine.

Installing Internal Devices

Installing an internal hardware device means opening your computer case and rooting around inside. To do so, you usually need to remove a few screws from the back of the machine and slide or jiggle the cover away from the case itself. Often, you remove only one side of the case, but the case sometimes slides off the sides and the top. In some cases, especially with older cases, you must remove the front cover as well by prying it away from the case.

Some general rules apply to installing hardware in a PC:

- **Take your time:** Internal hardware installations seem designed for Murphy's Law, and Murphy seems to sit in wait of people who are in a hurry. When everything goes perfectly, the installation can take as little as five minutes. But you should count on at least an hour for any single piece of hardware you want to install, and entire evenings for more complex jobs.

- **If you have an important deadline approaching, don't open your computer case if you can continue working without doing so:** The installation might fail. Worse, it might render the system unusable or even just wonky. Neither outcome is likely, but you must remember our friend Murphy.

- **Be awake and alert:** It really does help.

- **Always power the machine down before beginning and unplug the power cord.**

- **Touch the metal side of the case to discharge static electricity from your hands before touching anything inside the case:** If you have a plastic case, touch something else that's metal.

- **If anything metal falls into the computer (a loose screw, for instance), don't even consider turning on the machine until you get it out.** If you can't find it, take everything apart until you do. Otherwise, you can short out your entire system.

- **Perform one hardware installation at a time:** Restart your computer each time to make sure that everything works. Then, go through the installation procedure all over again for the next device.

- **Have a screwdriver, preferably a screwdriver set with two or more sizes of Philips (star-shaped) heads at hand.** You might need flat heads as well.

The process itself depends on what hardware device you want to install. However, before you can begin, you need a sense of what you're looking at. The first thing you're likely to see is a disarray of cables with one end attached to a device and the other leading to the rectangular circuit board covering much of the bottom of the case. This board is known as the *motherboard*, or *mainboard*. Ultimately, every hardware device in your PC attaches to this board. Some devices are built into the board, whereas others connect through wires. You connect others by plugging them into slots placed at various locations on the board—the processor and RAM modules attach this way, as do, very often, the video and sound boards, the USB and FireWire ports, and the network cards. However, manufacturers often build one or more of these devices into the motherboard. At which point, they take on the term *integrated*.

RAM modules are long, narrow circuit boards arrayed perpendicularly to the motherboard and attached to the system in slots, which is usually near one edge of the board (often the edge closest to the power supply—the large, cube-shaped item to the side of the motherboard). Each end of the slot has a plastic connector that resembles a clip. To remove the RAM module, you pull the clips away from the module. To install a module, you press the module into the slot until the clips hold it in place. Again, see the instructions that came with your specific PC.

At right angles to the back of the PC, you'll see the peripherals in their slots. Most computers have two kinds of slots: PCI and AGP. Typically, motherboards have one AGP slot and 3–8 PCI slots. In most PCs, the AGP slot, which is usually located close to the RAM modules, already contains the video card. If not, the video system is probably built into the motherboard. You can tell by locating the connector the monitor is plugged into. On older PCs, your video card might plug into a PCI slot instead, but PCI video cards have become rare. Unless you have an integrated video system, you can replace the video board by removing the old one (you must undo the screw holding the card to the case first) and inserting the new one. In the case of integrated video, you can install a video card and either use the two together in a dual-monitor system or enter the BIOS setup program and disable the onboard video. Installing any other peripheral card (sound board, network card, or FireWire card) follows much the same procedure. Find an empty slot or remove an existing board, push the card *firmly* into the slot, and attach it to the computer case via the screw and the notch at the board's top.

To add an internal drive of any kind, you must physically insert the drive into one of the drive *bays* (one of several possible openings designed to hold a 3.5-inch or 5.25-inch drive), screw it into place, and connect at least two cables from the device to the motherboard. The first cable gives the unit power. Take one of the unused female power connectors (most PCs have two or three available), and plug it into the power connector at the back of the device. The second cable handles data transfer and plugs into the back of the drive and onto the controller ports on the motherboard. Use the instructions that came with your hardware for this procedure. Sometimes, you need to set "jumpers" or pins on the board, and each device can be different. The procedure is not difficult, but read all instructions thoroughly and be prepared to redo it if it doesn't work correctly the first time you turn on your PC.

With the hardware installed, ensure that all screws are in place and then close the case. Plug in the power cord and anything else (such as the mouse, keyboard, or monitor) that you might have unplugged, and power the PC on. Watch the boot sequence to see if the PC has any trouble recognizing any of the new hardware. If it does, reopen the case to make sure you've attached everything correctly.

As Windows boots, it attempts to install the drivers for the newly installed hardware. See the following "Installing Drivers" section.

When Windows finishes loading, use Device Manager to ensure that all new components appear as part of the system. Chapter 22 covers all the elements of Device Manager. For now, you should determine if your system displays the correct amount of RAM and the correct hard disk size if you installed one or both of those devices. If not, reboot your PC once or a few times to let the machine's BIOS fully recognize all components and report them correctly. Sometimes, the initial boot doesn't do the trick.

Installing Drivers

In an ideal world, Windows XP would take care of all drivers for all hardware so that you could simply plug the item in, boot your PC, and start working with your new device. Sometimes indeed, given the large number of drivers included with the Windows XP installation, that's precisely what happens. However, brand-new products usually ship with new drivers to allow Windows to use all the features of that device, and you must install this particular driver for the new hardware to work.

Cross-Reference

For details on installing drivers, see Chapter 22, which covers the issue of locating drivers more specifically than the general guidelines examined here.

Unless your hardware manufacturer specifies when to install the driver, you can install the driver for your hardware devices at either of these two times:

- **Before installing the device:** With Windows XP running, place the driver installation CD in the CD drive, and install the driver by launching the Setup file located on the CD. After completing the installation, connect the device and, either by rebooting or simply waiting, let Windows recognize the device and load the driver. If no Setup file exists, you must install or connect the hardware first. You can also use this method if you download the driver from the Internet.

- **After installing the device:** You should use this method for all internal hardware installations to ensure that Windows recognizes the hardware properly. Many non-USB printers also install more easily this way. With the PC powered down, install the device and restart the computer. As it boots, Windows prompts you for the driver. Put the driver CD in the CD-ROM drive and either let Windows XP find it on its own (it automatically attempts to do so) or browse the CD to point Windows to the file it needs to find.

If Windows boots and does not notify you that it has found new hardware, go ahead and try to use your hardware to see if it works. In some cases, such as mass storage devices — a category into which Windows XP places external hard drives, digital cameras, hard disk–based audio players, and more — you might not need the manufacturer's included driver at all. As long as Windows can use it without asking, just go along for the ride.

Summary

Some hardware installations proceed flawlessly. Others result in annoyance and headaches. Windows XP offers the best installation assistance of any Windows version to date, but difficulties remain. The secret, as difficult as this might seem when you can't wait to get started with that new device, is to perform the installation of the device and its driver slowly, methodically, and carefully. This is especially true for internal installations, but it is true as well for the easier task of adding external hardware. After all, the goal isn't just getting hardware that functions but getting hardware that functions properly. This chapter has focused on installing hardware. Chapter 22 examines the process of troubleshooting and updating it once you have it installed.

Chapter 22

Hardware Configuration, Maintenance, and Troubleshooting

Ideally, once you have installed your hardware, you can use it repeatedly and constantly, never needing to dig into the multitude of Windows XP settings and make changes. Unfortunately, all too often this ideal falls somewhat short of what actually happens. Sometimes, you have to reconfigure your hardware. Other times, you must reinstall it in order to get it to work. At still other times, you may simply want to upgrade the software components to take advantage of new or improved features. Windows XP offers a host of wizards and dialog boxes to help you work with your hardware's drivers and settings, but the most important tool, Device Manager, provides the central focus for this chapter.

Windows XP also contains a number of tools for maintaining your system. Because your hard drives constitute the single most important hardware component to maintain, this chapter also covers hard disk maintenance tools. Between Device Manager and the hard drive utilities, you can keep the hardware on your system humming along smoothly.

Working with Device Manager

Without question, Device Manager serves as your best friend in uncovering and solving hardware problems. As Figure 22-1 shows, Device Manager displays a list of all your hardware arranged in categories with each item accessible by locating the correct category and expanding it by clicking the plus sign (+) to its left. This figure displays the list of three hard drives in this particular system, as well as the display adapter (that is, the graphics card), the DVD/CD-ROM drive, the imaging device (that is, the scanner), and the mouse. You can expand the other categories to detail additional specific items.

Device Manager's usefulness comes to the fore when a device malfunctions. Figure 22-2 shows very much the same list as Figure 22-1, but from a different system with a few problems. Here, the icons for three of the devices are flagged to indicate different kinds of problems. The highlighted floppy disk shows an X, actually in red, which denotes a completely malfunctioning device (in this case, it was deliberately disabled). The HID-complaint device (HID stands for Human Interface Device — in this case, a pen tablet) bears a yellow warning icon, indicating that Windows XP detects a problem with the device (in this case, it was abruptly unplugged). Finally, the Unsupported Device shows a yellow question mark, a signal that XP needs additional information in order to have it function properly (in this case, the device needs a driver, which we will discuss later in this chapter).

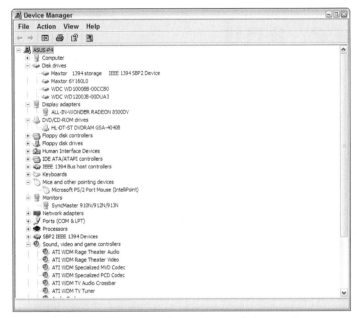

Figure 22-1: Device Manager with several expanded categories.

Even if a device is flagged in one of these ways, it may not be a real problem if, as far as you can tell, the device seems to function. If you agree with XP that there is a problem, you might try disconnecting the device and reconnecting it. If this doesn't fix anything, read on.

To open Device Manager, right-click My Computer and choose Properties (or Winlogo+Break). From the resulting System Properties dialog, click the Hardware tab. In the Device Manager section of the dialog box, click the Device Manager button. After a brief delay, the Device Manager utility opens. Your first survey of hardware status takes place immediately, according to the following views:

- If all categories display as closed, with no individual devices showing, Device Manager does not know of any malfunctioning hardware. The device still might not work, but from the standpoint of Windows XP, it works just fine.

- If Windows XP sees any device as malfunctioning, Device Manager opens with that device's category automatically expanded to reveal the problem hardware. After upgrading to Windows XP or installing it for the first time, you should expect one or more devices to be displayed as nonfunctioning, awaiting drivers.

Figure 22-2: Three devices are flagged for different kinds of problems.

Repairing Hardware Devices

Device Manager gives you two major options for configuring your hardware devices: configuring the resources it uses and changing the drivers associated with it. Of these two, you'll find yourself updating drivers more frequently than configuring resources because Windows XP has proven itself notably adept at managing system resources. Still, if you must, you can adjust system resource conflicts manually. In this way, you can solve virtually all hardware problems from within Device Manager, except those in which the hardware itself does not work because of mechanical malfunction.

Tip

If a hardware device stops working completely and you can't solve the problem in just a few minutes, you might have a mechanical problem instead of an electronic one. Consider removing the hardware device and installing it in another PC if one is available. If the hardware still doesn't work, and you still get no response from it, you can assume that it has bitten the dust and can be discarded. In the case of expensive hardware devices such as printers or monitors, you might consider sending it to a repair shop.

CONFIGURING SYSTEM RESOURCES

To adjust the resources a hardware device uses, open Device Manager, locate the item you want to configure, right-click its icon, and choose Properties. Click the Resources tab and uncheck the Use Automatic Settings option. In many cases, this option has been grayed out, which indicates that you cannot change the resources this item uses. However, if you can make changes, choose an item from the Setting Based On drop-down list, highlight the resource you want to modify, and click the Change Setting button.

Figure 22-3 shows the Edit Interrupt Request dialog box for configuring a specific hardware device (here, a communications/serial port). Initially, the interrupt request (IRQ) setting of 7 resulted in a hardware conflict with the floppy disk controller. If this user never used the floppy drive, the conflict would probably cause no problems, but the function of the Conflict Information window is to help you avoid all conflicts completely. Click the up and down arrow boxes at the right end of the Value field until you see the notice `No devices are conflicting`, check the hardware manual to make sure your device can function with that IRQ, and click OK.

Figure 22-3: Setting the interrupt request.

Several hardware Properties dialog boxes offer tabs containing settings specific to a particular device type. For example, communications and parallel ports, which are typically used by modems and printers, respectively, feature a Port Settings tab leading to a dialog box where you can configure how that port should operate. Figure 22-4 shows the Communications Port Properties dialog box, along with the Advanced Settings dialog box, that results from clicking the Advanced tab on the Port Settings tab. Similarly, opening the Properties sheet for an IDE channel (the motherboard's connection to disk drives, including hard disks, CDs and DVDs) provides you with an Advanced Settings tab in which you can set the DMA mode required by some CD and DVD applications (DMA stands for Direct Memory Access and can speed up disk connections, if the device supports DMA).

Figure 22-4: Configuring a serial port.

INSTALLING AND CHANGING DRIVERS

By far, most of the time you spend in Device Manager will be to install or change device drivers. To access driver information, locate the device in Device Manager, right-click its icon, choose Properties, and then click the Drivers tab on the resulting Properties dialog box. To see the specific details about the driver, including the files this driver uses to do its job, click the Driver Details button.

Figure 22-5 shows the Drivers tab for a video driver, as well as the Driver File Details information screen. Both screens display the version of the driver. This is extremely important information when you are considering performing an upgrade or a rollback. Before doing either, examine the driver version to make sure that the action will provide you with either the newer or the older driver you want. Otherwise, your system might behave differently from what you had in mind.

Figure 22-5: Everything you could possibly want to know about a video driver.

If you experience problems after installing a video driver, or if the driver manufacturer's Web site informs you that the driver contains bugs and should be uninstalled, click the Roll Back Driver button. This highly useful feature offers a one-click method for uninstalling the current driver and reinstalling the most recent one, which is typically an excellent solution for misbehaving hardware. Of course, if the previous driver also caused problems, a complete removal is a better idea. In this latter case, you can click the Uninstall button.

Note

You can also uninstall some drivers via the Add or Remove Programs utility in Control Panel.

To install a new version of a driver, click the Update Driver button. This launches the Hardware Update Wizard. Because you are supplying the driver on your own, choose the Install From a List or a Specific Location (Advanced) option on the Welcome screen and decide whether you want Windows to search for the driver on the subsequent screen. If you do, help Windows by narrowing the search. Click the Browse button to locate the folder to which you downloaded the new driver, and uncheck the option to search removable media.

If you know the driver you want Windows to use for this device, click the Don't Search radio button, and click Next. This yields a list of compatible drivers from which you can make your choice. If you want to search for still more already installed drivers, uncheck the Show Compatible Hardware option and drill through the Manufacturer and Model lists.

Caution

If you decide to choose a driver manually, pay attention if Windows tells you it won't work with your hardware. In the vast majority of cases, Windows is absolutely right; you risk negatively affecting your system performance by going ahead with the installation.

GETTING NEW DRIVERS

Sometimes, the hardest part about installing new drivers is finding them in the first place (see Chapter 21 for a basic list of possible locations). Windows Update offers some drivers after they become available, but only those it has approved by digitally signing them (see the "Settings for Unsigned Drivers" section next). To update your drivers without the help of Windows Update, and, therefore several months before they acquire the official Windows XP stamp, you need to do some digging.

As you probably expect, the digging starts and ends on the Internet. Perhaps in no way has the Internet helped PC owners more directly than in the ready availability of software updates with hardware drivers. Hardware manufacturers routinely place new drivers in the Support or Downloads section of their Web sites, which lets you acquire them easily and keep your hardware up to date.

To locate a driver, do the following:

1. Open your Web browser, and go to the manufacturer's Web site.

2. Look for the Support (Software Support, Technical Support) or Downloads (Software Downloads, Driver Downloads) section of the site, and click the link.

3. Find the product you want to upgrade. Depending on the company, this can be a tricky prospect. For ATI video cards, for example, drivers are listed in a number of ways with some drivers available in a package called Catalyst. You need to work through the hardware identification process to end up at the download site. Numerous manufacturers' sites work the same way even though some offer a more direct route to the goal. Figure 22-6 shows the resulting download location for a particular video card, which was made more difficult by the fact that it was a discontinued product and thus was in a separate place on the site (several mouse clicks were required in total).

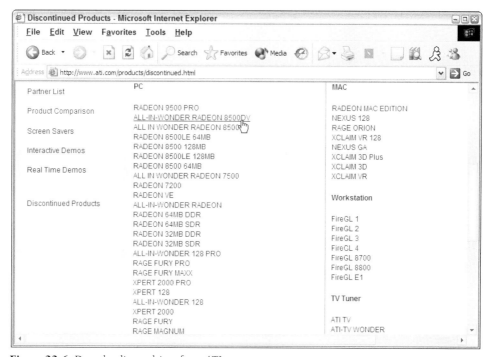

Figure 22-6: Downloading a driver from ATI.

Figure 22-7 shows the location for a different manufacturer. This one required only three mouse clicks.

4. Click the download link and when the Download dialog box appears, click Save to store the driver on your hard drive.

5. Navigate to the folder in which you downloaded the driver and read the instructions, which are often contained in a Readme file. In the case of a zip or .exe file with no other files, launch the file, extract the files, and proceed from there.

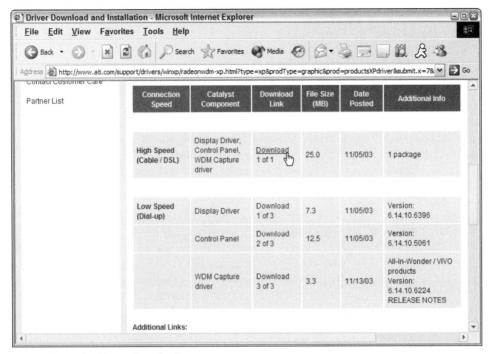

Figure 22-7: The Matrox download page.

Caution

Many manufacturers offer the most recent hardware drivers in an unfinished state. Called *beta* drivers, this software has progressed in the company's estimation to the point where it invites the public to experiment with the drivers on their own systems. Unless you want a specific feature on the latest beta drivers, don't install a beta driver; until they undergo further testing, you risk malfunctions of various kinds. If you decide to install them anyway, make absolutely sure that you create a restore point by using the System Restore utility (described in Chapter 6) so that you can back out of the process if Windows starts misbehaving.

SETTINGS FOR UNSIGNED DRIVERS

Microsoft has strict criteria for deeming whether drivers are fully compatible with Windows XP. To this end, it has created a process called Driver Signing in which the company digitally signs a device driver to provide confirmation that the driver has passed the necessary tests for its inclusion. If you install a driver that bears a Microsoft digital signature, Windows XP installs the driver with no questions asked. If the driver does not bear a digital signature, Windows responds with the Unsigned Driver dialog box that explains the situation and asks if you want to continue with the installation.

If you click the Continue Anyway button, Windows automatically sets a restore point that you can use in conjunction with the System Restore utility if the installation causes problems (see Chapter 6) and then proceeds to install the driver.

Even though Microsoft offers no assurances that unsigned drivers will work, if you download the driver from the Web site of a reputable company, which includes any major hardware manufacturer, you rarely need to worry about unsigned drivers causing problems for your system. Because Windows creates the restore point, the worry decreases even more. Generally speaking, you should feel free to click Continue Anyway if you want the latest driver on your system.

You can change what Windows does when it encounters an unsigned driver during the installation process. On the Hardware tab of the System Properties dialog box, click the Driver Signing button and choose one of the following options:

- **Ignore:** Windows lets you install all the unsigned drivers you want — neither informing you nor warning you. Obviously, you take some chances with this option.

- **Warn:** Windows displays a dialog box each time you begin an unsigned driver installation that asks if you want to continue. This is the default option.

- **Block:** Windows never asks you about the unsigned driver. Instead, it blocks the installation, which completely prevents you from installing unsigned drivers.

If you have an Administrator account, you can specify that the selection option apply to all users on the PC who attempt to install unsigned drivers. To do so, check the Make This Action the System Default option in the bottom section of the Driver Signing Options dialog box.

Establishing Hardware Profiles

Sometimes, you need specific hardware for specific purposes, and you want the capability to load the drivers for that hardware into your system while excluding other drivers when you boot Windows. The Hardware Profiles feature allows you to configure your system in multiple profiles with each profile loading only a portion of the available hardware.

For example, if you use your PC for sound recording, you might discover that your external professional-quality sound card can conflict with the internal sound card when it comes to interacting with your recording software. You might also discover that you need the internal sound card to capture video from your digital camera. One solution is to let Windows load normally and then open Device Manager and disable the unwanted device. However, if you find yourself doing this regularly, you can save time by creating a separate hardware profile for each use.

When you create a second hardware profile (Windows creates a default profile on installation), you add a step to the boot process. Early in the startup, Windows asks which profile you want to use. Highlighting that profile on the list and pressing Enter instructs Windows to continue the boot process and load only the hardware drivers included in the profile. This disables the others and thereby avoids conflicts. You can create as many profiles as you like.

To create a profile, follow these steps:

1. Open the System Properties dialog box by right-clicking My Computer and choosing Properties (or pressing Winlogo+Break).

2. Click the Hardware tab and then the Hardware Profiles button.

3. In the Hardware Profiles dialog box (see Figure 22-8), highlight the current profile (called Profile 1 by default), and click the Copy button. This action creates an identical copy of the default profile for you to change by excluding specific devices.

4. Highlight the new profiles (labeled Profile 2 by default), and click Rename. Give the profile a name you'll remember (renamed to **External sound card profile** in Figure 22-8). Click OK to exit the dialog box.

Figure 22-8: Creating a new hardware profile.

5. Reboot your PC. Watch for the profiles screen, and choose the new profile. Press Enter to continue the reboot.

6. Open System Properties again, and click the Hardware tab. Click the Hardware Profiles button, and check to see that the new profile is indeed the current profile. Assuming that it is, close the dialog box.

7. Click the Device Manager button to open Device Manager.

8. Locate the hardware device you want to exclude from this profile, right-click it, and choose Properties.

9. At the bottom of the resulting Properties dialog box for that device, click the down arrow beside the Device Usage menu. Choose the Do Not Use This Device in the Current Hardware Profile (Disable) option.

10. Click OK to exit this dialog box, and click OK again to exit Device Manager.

11. Reboot your PC, and select this new profile again. This time, Windows boots with that device disabled.

Tip

You can edit a profile as many times as you like and make it increasingly specific to your needs.

If you decide you no longer need a profile, open the Hardware Profiles dialog box, highlight that profile, and click the Delete key.

Maintaining Your Hard Drive

Windows XP provides several tools for keeping your hard drive in good working order. By opening the Properties dialog box for a specific hard drive, you can check the drive for errors, defragment its files for greater efficiency, or back up the data to a separate location. This section covers the first two options; data backup is covered in Chapter 4.

To perform these two important maintenance activities, open My Computer and right-click the hard drive you want to maintain. Choose Properties from the pop-up menu and click the Tools tab to reveal the options. Figure 22-9 shows the result.

Figure 22-9: The hard disk maintenance tools in Windows XP.

All of these tools are perfectly safe to use. Still, many people back up critical files as the first step in this routine maintenance (see Chapter 4).

Using the Error Checking Utility

As its name suggests, the Error-checking option scans your hard drive for errors. (In earlier versions of Windows, the tool bears the name ScanDisk). You should use this tool whenever saving a document or copying files seems to take longer than usual or once every other month or so. This utility ensures that the surface of your hard drives bear no signs of damage.

Clicking the Check Now button opens the Check Disk dialog box for the selected drive. You can choose either or both of the following options:

- **Automatically fix file system errors:** This option instructs Windows to make repairs to the file system if it finds any during the scan. Windows needs to take complete control over the drive in order to start this process. If the drive is currently in use, Windows asks if you want to schedule the disk scan for the next time you start the PC. If you don't say Yes, the disk check won't happen at all, so the choice is really between scheduling the scan or canceling it.

- **Scan for and attempt recovery of bad sectors:** As you use your hard drive, it can develop bad locations known as *bad sectors*. Bad sectors tend to spread as Windows tries to write data to them with the result that your drive eventually slows down and sometimes renders data writing (such as file saving) difficult or even impossible. If you suspect that your hard drive contains errors, check this option to allow Windows to locate the errors and block them off permanently by moving whatever data they contain to a good sector on the disk. Once again, Windows needs complete control over your hard drive to execute this command. If the drive is currently in use, a dialog box asks if you want to schedule the repair for the next time you boot your PC. If you do choose this option, the next time you start the computer, you will have a few seconds to cancel the scan; if you let it proceed (as you will probably want to do), be prepared for a wait while it does its job before Windows loads.

Note that you don't need to select both options. If you choose the second option, Scan For and Attempt Recovery of Bad Sectors, Windows automatically enacts the check for file system errors as well. Consider the bad sector check the complete maintenance package when it comes to repairing errors on the hard drive.

Using the Defragmentation Utility

The second hard disk tool, Defragmentation, speeds up hard disk access by moving all the parts of a file to contiguous sectors. When you save files to a hard drive on a brand new PC, all components of the file stay together in one place. However, when you delete a file, you make additional areas on the hard drive available by, in effect, opening a hole in the middle of other data. When you save the next file to the drive, that file fragments and stores as much as it can in the newly emptied location. The rest is saved on the next available location on the drive. The more you use a hard drive by adding and deleting data, the more fragmented the files become.

The Defragmentation utility (more commonly called *defrag*) rearranges the files to locate all their parts in contiguous areas. To defrag your drive, right-click the drive in My Computer and choose

Properties to open its Properties dialog box. Click the Tools tab and click Defragment Now. In the resulting Disk Defragmenter utility, highlight the drive in question and click Analyze. Figure 22-10 shows the report provided by Windows with the suggestion that Defragmentation isn't necessary. It never hurts to defrag, so you may want to skip Analyze and just go straight to the Defragment button.

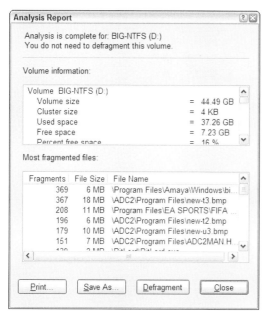

Figure 22-10: The defragmentation analysis report.

Figure 22-11 shows the result of clicking the Defragment button, either on the Report screen or the main Disk Defragment window. The progress bar at the bottom of the window shows the length of time remaining while the Estimated Disk Usage After Defragmentation area changes during the process to reflect the reduced fragmentation visually.

Tip

As with most other types of system utilities, third-party manufacturers such as Symantec and Executive Software offer improvements on the Defragmentation utility found in Windows XP. Symantec's venerable Norton Utilities suite features a fast and fully capable defragmenter called SpeedDisk. Executive Software's Diskkeeper gives you an even faster and more powerful utility for this purpose. Whenever you're dealing with system enhancement software, it's a good idea to check what's available beyond the Windows XP package itself.

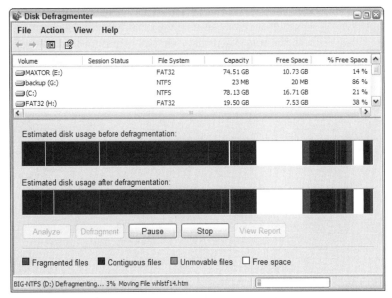

Figure 22-11: Defragmentation in progress.

Summary

Windows XP provides a number of tools for ensuring that your hardware works correctly and efficiently. By far, the most significant such tool for the hardware itself is Device Manager; but when it comes to the proper maintenance of your hard drives, the error-checking and defragmentation tools can help significantly. You can buy third-party tools with additional options for both error correction and defrag purposes, and as you get increasingly serious about your system, you should certainly consider their purchase. But the tools provided in Windows XP itself can help you a great deal. The trick with disk maintenance is not to forget about it until after the damage has been done. The trick with Device Manager is to become comfortable using it to check on your hardware and to update your drivers whenever you install something new or when something old breaks.

Chapter 23

Speeding Up Windows

As operating systems go, Windows XP is neither particularly fast nor particularly slow. If you want pure speed, run good old MS-DOS on that souped-up Pentium IV on your desk; add Windows 3.1 if you need a graphical shell. If you want something truly slow, try Windows NT Server on an old notebook. Windows XP lies somewhere in between, with the speed of your processor and bus systems, hard drive(s), graphics card, and system memory determining how fast it can actually go. Then again, even the fastest system from a technical hardware standpoint is no good if you're clogging your system with unnecessary elements.

This chapter offers nothing fancy, just a set of point-by-point guidelines on how to speed up Windows XP. I figured the last thing you needed was an extensive amount of text accompanying a chapter that was about speed, defeating the entire purpose before you even started. So here we go.

From Zero to Sixty . . .

You install a new program on your Windows XP machine, and the installation program tells you a restart is necessary. You sigh, press the OK button, and prepare yourself to waste yet another five minutes of your life as Windows shuts itself down and then trudges, agonizingly, through the startup sequence. Had you known a restart would be required, you wouldn't have bothered.

Following is a list of considerations for decreasing the time XP takes to go from powering on the PC to displaying a fully functional desktop. I say "fully functional" because far too commonly the desktop is in full view, with everything seemingly accessible, but a quick look at your hard drive's indicator light, along with a click on even something as simple as the Start button, reveals that there's so much happening on your system that you can't really use it yet. More waiting, more sighing, more rolling your eyes and thinking of taking a sledge hammer to the entire shebang—who needs it?

> **Say no to automatic program loads:** Without a doubt, the single most time-consuming part of the startup process, especially for a PC on which you've loaded several software programs since getting the machine in the first place, is the loading of programs configured to launch with Windows itself. The installation sequences of many programs ask if you want to have the program (or a portion of it) load with the operating system. Most users simply say *yes* and let it go at that, thinking it will save time when using the program

if it is already at least partially in memory. And that's true, it will. But this means that these programs will load even if you don't intend to work with them. And in many cases, even if you do plan to use the program, preloading saves no more than a few seconds. It's far better to load them when you need them. In a few cases — but only a very few — preloading is a good idea. This includes a program that schedules your automatic backups (helping you not forget to do so) and, most important, antivirus and anti-malware utilities. Other than that, however, don't let anything load if you can do without it.

- **Get rid of automatic program loads:** Most of us already have programs auto-loading on our systems (indeed, PCs ship this way). To make changes, you have a number of options:

  - Most programs that auto-load place an icon on the System Tray on the bottom right of your screen. You may be able to right-click each of them to access their Options or Preferences areas; if not, look for the program under the Start menu. Through the program's Options or Preferences, specify that the program is not supposed to load with Windows. For example, if you open Windows Messenger and choose Options from the Tools menu, you can prevent WM from auto-loading by clicking the Preferences tab and unchecking the top option, Run Windows Messenger When Windows Starts. To make sure it that it doesn't appear, also uncheck Allow Windows Messenger to Run in the Background. Presto — it's gone.

  - If you know a program auto-loads but an icon for it doesn't appear in the System Tray, locate the program from the All Programs menu (Start button), open it, and disable auto-starting from the Options or Preferences dialog area.

  - Under the Start menu → All Programs, you'll find a submenu called Startup (commonly called the Startup group). These are shortcuts to programs that load automatically at startup. Right click Startup on the menu and choose Open. You can either delete these shortcuts or drag them out of there and onto the Desktop (so you can drag them back if you change your mind).

  - If you still have programs auto-loading, but you can't seem to stop them from doing so, Windows offers a brute force method. Click Start → Run (or Winlogo+R), and type **msconfig** in the Open field. Press Enter and the System Configuration Utility loads. Click the Startup tab, where you can see all the items that load when Windows boots. Figure 23-1 shows this screen, with check marks beside all the displayed items (there are more, as the scrollbar on the right clearly shows). To stop a program from auto-loading, uncheck it in this screen and click OK. Next time Windows starts, a warning message alerts you to the fact that you have made manual changes to startup. If you're not sure if a program should or should not auto-start, examine the Command column to see if you can figure out what the program actually is; if necessary, search the Web for an explanation. Many auto-loading programs simply aren't necessary. Note that msconfig is a troubleshooting tool that can help you determine what you can live without loading. The solution will involve one of these other steps.

  - Stop services from running at startup. Windows XP loads numerous services at startup. Services are components of the operating system that allow specific things to happen: for example, the Windows Security Center (available with Service Pack 2) is an auto-loading service, allowing the Security Center to monitor your system immediately upon loading.

Another one is the Plug and Play service, which allows Windows to recognize devices when you plug them in. But not all services are necessary, including many that are installed with third-party software. To view the services installed on your system, open the Services console by clicking Start → Run (or Winlogo+R), typing **services.msc** in the Open field, and pressing Enter. Figure 23-2 shows the result of clicking on a specific service (Remote Registry in this case) and the explanation that appears in the column on the left.

The Startup Type column shows that it loads automatically. To stop a service from loading automatically, right-click its name and choose Properties. In the Startup Type drop-down list, choose Manual or Disabled (as Figure 23-3 shows) and click OK. The next time Windows starts, this service will not start with it.

Add system memory: Everything in Windows XP can be improved if you up the system RAM to at least 512MB. Most systems today ship with that much; if you don't have that much RAM, consider running out to buy some. Even in older machines with slower processors, system RAM can make a major difference in startup time and the capability to run programs after startup. If you have a newer machine, 1GB of system RAM will improve startup speed slightly, but you won't really notice the difference until you start running graphics-intensive programs (as long as the programs have been written to take efficient advantage of the extra RAM). Go with a gigabyte if you can afford it.

Add hard disk space: Like system memory, adding hard disk space doesn't affect only startup time — indeed, it affects startup even less than more RAM does. However, ensuring that you have plenty of free hard drive space means that Windows can more efficiently swap data in and out of memory and make better use of the system's virtual memory, that is, the paging file. This file (adjustable via the Advanced tab on the System Properties dialog box) operates as system RAM from Windows' perspective, but, in fact, is hard disk space allocated for that purpose. Windows uses it, even during initial startup, to swap data in and out of memory more quickly.

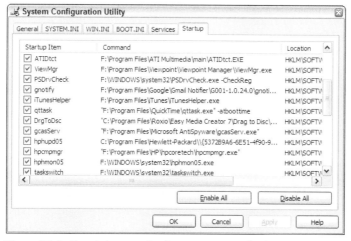

Figure 23-1: Examining auto-loading programs in the System Configuration tool.

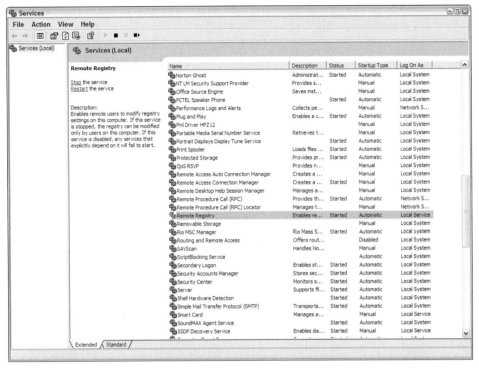

Figure 23-2: The Services configuration screen.

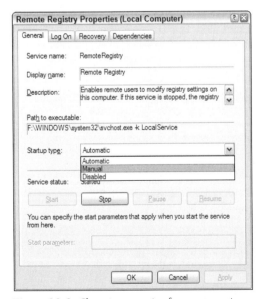

Figure 23-3: Changing a service from automatic start to manual start.

Lowering the Wind Resistance

After it's loaded, Windows tends to coast along fairly well. But once in a while it sputters, stumbles, and seems in need of a pit stop. This is particularly true of some Windows programs and certain actions within those programs. For example, if you copy elements of a Web page and paste them into a Word document, you'll notice a substantial delay if the Web material contains graphics and/or tables. If you work on high-resolution graphics, especially large files (and this is true, it seems, of *every* graphics program out there), you can expect major delays and even crashes when you start manipulating the images in a variety of ways. But even relatively simple activities can cause slow-downs, and you can help the speed overall in the following ways.

- **Increase system memory and hard disk space:** These are covered in the two bullets in the preceding section. The fact is that there is no substitute for increasing memory and disk space; the last thing you want is for Windows to start choking on too little disk space. So, be sure you have several gigabytes (yep, gigabytes) freely available — *especially* on the drive on which Windows itself is installed. If your available disk space ever falls below one 1GB on your Windows drive, you can expect significant delays.

- **Upgrade your graphics card:** Today's computer environments are increasingly graphics-intensive, and you need the hardware to do the job properly. If you bought your PC more than a couple years ago, its graphics subsystem is quite likely inadequate for recent programs. Graphics cards take much of the burden of graphics processing away from your PC's main processor. And the more memory and speed your graphics card has, the faster the graphics processing. Buy the best graphics card you can afford, focusing on the memory available on the card and the purposes for which you intend to use the card. For example, if you need to work with graphics programs, buy a card designed primarily for that purpose. If you want to play games, buy a card designed specifically for games. And so on. Consider a new graphics card that supports two monitors (or leave the old card in for another monitor; XP support up to nine monitors). You might find, however, that the graphics card you buy is actually better than your system can handle. This may be true especially if, for example, it's designed for AGP 4x but you have only an older AGP 2x peripheral slot available.

- **Upgrade your PC's guts:** You don't need to buy a whole new PC to get a major performance boost. Many computer shops offer upgrades; they take your PC and keep what you want (such as the hard drives), replacing the motherboard, processor, and possibly the system RAM with newer and faster components. You can do all of this yourself, but it's tedious, time-consuming, and rather intimidating (it's also fun, in its own way). A trusted shop can do it much more quickly and often nearly as cheaply as you can do it yourself. You come out with a much more capable PC, and you'll notice the speed difference immediately.

- **Shut down unnecessary programs:** It's so easy to switch from program to program, using the Windows Alt+Tab key combination or the Windows Taskbar, that we tend to forget how many programs we have loaded. This is especially true of programs that load multiple

Windows—Microsoft Office programs, for example—and the greatest culprit, Internet Explorer. Pay attention to how many windows you have open, and start closing them when you don't need them. Conversely, if you open and close a particular program such as email or a browser repeatedly throughout the day, consider just minimizing it to save the time opening and closing take. In particular, get rid of Internet Explorer windows that load without your knowledge (usually they're ads, and often they appear last on the Alt+Tab window), and any that have animation or other multimedia displayed, including high-res graphics. All of that stuff takes system memory and clogs Windows with irrelevance. In fact, if you don't need graphics showing at all for the work you're currently doing, toggle them off in the Internet Options dialog box (accessible from Control Panel).

- **Shut down auto-loaded programs:** Even if you don't stop programs from auto-loading with Windows itself (see "From Zero to Sixty" at the beginning of this chapter), you should close any programs that have automatically loaded that you don't currently need. For example, if you don't need Windows Messenger, shut it down. The same goes for items such as the QuickTime quick-start utility, the Microsoft Office quick-start utility, and much more. Check your System Tray to find out what's running.

- **Get rid of eye candy:** This item is somewhat related to doing away with graphics in Internet Explorer. You can help your system's speed by dispensing with other memory-hogging graphics. In particular, some people don't need the system running at 32-bit color (versus 24-bit or 16-bit; you'll never want lower than that) and a high screen resolution (less than 800 width by 600 height in pixels will ruin your Web experience). Open the Display Properties dialog box from Control Panel (or Winlogo+R, **control desk.cpl**, click the Settings tab, and drop Screen resolution or Color quality one step (test these separately); apply the change. While there, click the Appearance tab, click the Effects button, and then uncheck the boxes for the transition effect, showing shadows under menus, and showing window contents while dragging. Your computer is now faster because it's somewhat less visually stunning and demands less of your graphics card (the better your card, the less useful some of these tweaks are).

Slamming on the Brakes

Windows XP takes an often frustratingly long time to shut down. Sometimes, you need to get off your PC quickly, but you also want to make sure the machine does, in fact, turn itself off. You can end up sitting there for several minutes waiting for Windows to gather the information it needs, check all your settings, stop various processes and resources, and finally give up the ghost for that session. Here are some possibilities to help speed up the shutdown process:

- **Shut the PC off manually:** I'm dealing with this first because more and more people tell me it's what they do. They press the Power button on their computer cases, holding it in for six seconds or so if necessary, and stop the PC without letting Windows go through its shutdown procedure. Furthermore, these people never seem to have problems with their systems (or at least they don't call me about them). So yes, this is one way, and unquestionably the fastest way, to power off. But the shutdown process closes services one by one, and allows a specific number of seconds (20 by default) for background applications to close themselves. During a normal shutdown, you'll be prompted to save files you haven't already saved; you'll lose those in an abrupt power off. So, the safest shutdown is one in which you do not go for the brute force power cut off.

Shut down your backgrounds apps more quickly: You can change the time Windows allows background programs to shut themselves down. To do so, you need to edit the registry (as always, back up your registry before doing so, and be *extremely* careful). Click Start → Run, type **regedit** in the Open field, and press Enter. With Regedit open, in the left-hand pane expand the HKEY_CURRENT_USER entry by clicking the plus sign beside it. Then expand the Control Panel entry and, within it, the Desktop entry. In the main panel (see Figure 23-4), locate the key called WaitToKillAppTimeout. Double-click and change the default value (20000) to half or even one-quarter this figure. This changes the time allowed for shutdown of background Windows applications from 20 seconds to 10 seconds or less. Most apps will shutdown in this time period with no difficulty.

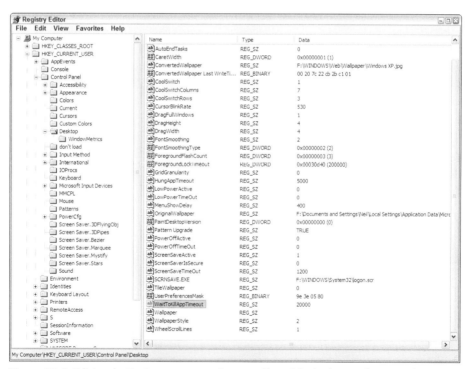

Figure 23-4: Editing the Registry to restrict the time allowed for background apps to shut down.

■ **Hibernate:** In many cases, there's no need to shut down at all. Instead, you can set your PC to enter hibernation state automatically whenever you leave it for any length of time or go into hibernation mode when you press the Power button for only a second or so (instead of the 4–6 seconds it takes to shut down the machine entirely). By default, Hibernation is disabled on older machines but enabled on newer ones. You can check the status and change the setting, if necessary, by opening the Control Panel and double-clicking the Power Options icon (or Winlogo+R, **control powercfg.cpl**). Click the Hibernation tab, and make sure that there is a check mark in the Enable Hibernation box (shown in Figure 23-5). If there is no Hibernation tab, Windows doesn't support Hibernation on your machine. With Hibernation enabled, Windows stores everything that is open in a giant file so that when you next start up, not only will the PC take less time to come to life, but your workspace will also be precisely as you left it — every program, every window. It takes far less time to Hibernate than shut down and far less time to start from Hibernation than normal shutdown. If Hibernation is enabled, you can hibernate several different ways: when you shut down, on the screen that shows Standby, Turn off or Restart, hold the Shift key down and Standby morphs into Hibernate. Or use Ctrl+Alt+Delete to bring up the Task Manager and use the Shutdown menu. Also on the Power Options dialog box, under the Advanced tab, you can specify that the PC is to enter Standby mode rather than shutting itself down when you press the Power button. You can exit Standby mode simply by moving your mouse. Desktop users rarely need Standby (it may save battery power for laptop users). The crucial difference between Standby and Hibernation is that in Standby the machine is still on (and a power failure may cause you to lose data); in Hibernation, the machine is really off.

Figure 23-5: Setting the hibernate option.

■ **Get rid of malfunctioning programs:** If Windows XP can't shut down a background application within the 20-second time limit (or whatever limit you've set manually using HungAppTimeout — see the earlier discussion about WaitToKillAppTimeout for guidance on where to change this), it displays a dialog box asking if you want to Wait, End Task, or Cancel. Keep track of what programs cause this to occur. More often than not, they are proprietary applications such as printer control utilities (which seem to offer numerous problems in general), and you can eliminate the problem by preventing the programs from loading in the first place.

■ **Load multiple operating systems sooner:** If you have more than one operating system available on your PC (including XP and Linux or multiple instances of Windows XP), you can change the amount of time Windows displays the operating systems at bootup so that you can choose which one you want to load. By changing the display time from 30 seconds to, say, 10 seconds or even less, you save yourself that much time whenever you boot or reboot your PC.

Summary

That's it. You now have a faster Windows. So, go use it for a while before coming back to read Chapter 24, where you learn about adding users, groups, and permissions to your Windows environment.

Part VI

Utilities

An enormous variety of utilities fit into the category of tasks outlined in Part VI. Here, I provide a short write-up of some of the more popular, all of which I've used recently to varying degrees of effectiveness. Most of the utilities here assume that there's something about your Windows installation you're not especially happy with and that you have added features that Microsoft has deemed unnecessary or has simply neglected to avoid legal problems.

Uninstallers

Obviously, the Add/Remove Programs utility in Control Panel handles installation and uninstallation of programs, as do uninstallers included with the programs themselves. However, not all uninstallations are complete; files remain behind, program keys remain in the registry, and files such as DLLs (Direct Link Libraries) stay in the Windows folder. Uninstallers attempt to do a better job, removing all traces, not just merely the necessary ones.

Advanced Uninstaller Pro (innovative-sol.com) demonstrates how these programs tend to work. It keeps complete track of the programs you install on your PC, not only the files installed or changed by the software but also the registry settings and any other details caused by the installation. It comes with a database of well over 4000 programs, scans your system to see which of these programs are already installed, and makes them available for uninstallation as well. When you uninstall a program, Advanced Uninstaller cleans out every trace of the installation, including desktop and tray shortcuts. Other very good programs that perform these same functions include Uninstall Plus (www.uninstallplus.com), Ashampoo Uninstaller (www.ashampoo.com), and WUninstaller (www.wuninstaller.com), each of which keeps track of what's been installed and lets you completely delete programs you no longer want. If you want full recovery from installation, consider one of these.

System Repair Utilities

If you've determined that you want to start working directly with the Windows registry, Regedit can certainly do the job. But Regedit is anything but intuitive, and it doesn't help you determine which registry keys work together (and therefore which ones you should manipulate if you're trying to unload a specific program). Nor does it give you any hints about what the registry keys actually do.

Registry Mechanic (www.pctools.com) is basically a registry cleaner. It scans your hard drive and removes registry entries that refer to nothing (and therefore are probably left in the registry from a program you've since uninstalled), and it repairs invalid registry entries to help guard against system problems. It also backs up anything it does change, so that the change can be reversed if the system starts misbehaving as a result of the clean-up. WinASO Registry Optimizer (www.winaso.com) performs many of the same tasks and walks you through a system tune-up to help you see what registry entries are causing problems. Registry Repair Pro (www.pc-test.net) works similarly to both of these programs, offering a strong graphical interface to help you decide what entries you want repaired.

On a somewhat different track, several programs help you repair your system. Norton SystemWorks (www.symantec.com) comes with System Doctor and Norton WinDoctor, which together help you determine where your system is encountering problems and how to tune your system so that the problems disappear. Error Nuker (www.errornuker.com) is designed to locate system errors caused by incorrect registry entries, functioning much like the registry checkers mentioned previously. PC Doc Pro (www.neurosoftcorp.com) includes a free online scanner and then, if you discover numerous errors in the registry, you can download it and correct them. RegRestore PC Tuneup (www.maxionsoftware. com) is another such program and discovers and repairs many of the same errors.

Windows Speed-Up Utilities

Of course, clean registries and efficient use of system resources matter a lot, but when it comes right down to it, what you really want is a faster system. Cleaning and repairing the registry is certainly part of this process, but other tools perform a variety of other tweaks — or let you perform them as you want them — to speed the system as much as possible.

WinXP Manager (www.winxp-manager.com) is one such program, but in fact this is a suite of utilities that lets you perform several useful tweaks. It helps you delete unneeded files from your hard drives, it provides a wealth of system information, and it even optimizes your Internet connection speed through yet another set of registry adjustments. At its core, it optimizes system startup and shutdown, speeding up both significantly, it helps you adjust your hardware settings for peak performance, and it helps you learn about little-known system settings. It also contains security utilities to help you encrypt, shred, and hide files.

Similarly, another utilities suite, SuperUtilities (www.superlogix.net), provides a system cleaner that gets rid of spyware as well as bad registry entries, helps tweak and maintain the Windows system, and offers very useful privacy tools as well. AusLogics BoostSpeed (www.boost-speed.com) contains mechanisms to tweak Windows settings to boost performance, clean out your registry, and maximize your Internet connection speed. Intelli Hyperspeed (www.iobit.com) works primarily at tweaking your system for system performance, analyzing the system for settings that slow it down and offering to reconfigure them accordingly.

If you want an even more comprehensive look at what's going on under the hood, try SiSoftware's Sandra (www.sisoftware.co.uk), a benchmarking and testing utility that helps you understand the problems your system is encountering, although you'll need other utilities to help repair those problems. Useful and informative, it's designed for those who already know a fair bit about what's happening inside their PCs.

Part VII

Who Owns What: Setting Up Users, Permissions, and Policies

Chapter 24

Adding Users and Groups to Your System

by Neil Randall and Michelle MacLean

W indows XP offers a new approach among popular Windows versions for creating and maintaining user accounts. Windows 2000 and Windows NT featured a similar approach, in user properties if not in the user creation interface. But consumer versions of Windows— Windows 9x/Me—all provided a much less professional user creation and management system. In these consumer versions, users can log on to create their own look and feel for the PC, along with a few other niceties, such as a separate inbox for Outlook Express and a separate Favorites folder in Internet Explorer. But these user accounts are not truly distinct from one another from a security perspective. For one thing, you can log on to Windows 9x/Me without using a username at all, by clicking Cancel at the logon screen—obviously an insecure situation and an impossible feat with Windows NT/2000 and Windows XP. The difference nowadays is that Windows XP ships with all PCs, so everybody buying a Windows PC is working with an operating system that provides full separation between users; each user must have an individual user account (whether an individual one or a guest account) in order to log on.

This chapter covers the different types of accounts available in Windows XP and shows you how to add new user accounts by using both the Control Panel and the Computer Management Tool, disable and delete accounts, create and modify passwords, and switch from one account to another. The chapter also covers the creation and management of user groups.

Why Use User Accounts?

User accounts provide privacy, security, and convenience. With passwords protecting their accounts, users know that other people can't read their documents, their email, or other sensitive files. They also know that they have at least some protection from outside intrusion because their accounts, unlike those on some older Windows platforms, aren't simply wide open to anyone. Furthermore, they know that when they configure their PCs to look and work in specific ways, they can leave the PC and be assured that the configurations will not change when they return to it.

Sharing can cause problems, after all. With different people accessing a single machine with a shared user account, files get deleted, documents get overwritten, and folders get rearranged. Even the carefully constructed interface can take a beating because everybody using the PC wants different colors, different icon locations, different toolbars, and different defaults. Password-protected user accounts provide numerous conveniences, including a consistency from day to day that promotes greater productivity.

As with virtually all computer systems, however, one type of account takes precedence over all others: the Computer Administrator account (commonly abbreviated to just Administrator). Anyone with an Administrator-level account on a Windows XP system has complete control over the entire PC, with full access to the resources of all other accounts, including other Administrators. As a user with an individual account, it's important to remember that your files and resources are not *completely* private; the only user with this degree of privacy is the person holding the Administrator account on a single-Administrator system.

Caution

Even when you make an Administrator's folders private (see Chapter 25), other Administrators can gain access either by adjusting the permissions settings using the standard file-sharing method (also described in Chapter 25) or by removing the password from that person's account.

If your PC has limited hard disk space, you might understandably be concerned about the effect of multiple accounts on storage. Each account, when created, occupies only about 5MB of your hard disk. Unless you have been seriously pushing the limit of your storage capacity (in which case Windows XP itself will have problems with day-to-day activity), don't hesitate to add new users for that reason.

Even if your system has only one user, you may find a value in Start → Log Off (or Winlogo+L). Using this to log off will leave your system with the Welcome screen showing. When you return, you won't have to wait the full time a complete system start would take but, if you use a password, you've made it harder for someone else to use your machine.

If your system does have multiple users, you may find a use in Fast User Switching. Using Start → Log Off (or Winlogo+L), Fast User Switching lets you switch between users without first logging off. Perhaps two family members share a machine and your spouse needs access to his or her files *right this minute*. With Fast User Switching, you make the switch and then switch back to find all your stuff still up and running. Be sure to save any open files before you try this.

Adding Users with the Control Panel

You can quickly and easily add users to your Windows XP machine by opening Control Panel and double-clicking the User Accounts icon to open the User Accounts utility (see Figure 24-1). If you are using the new Category view, double-click User Accounts on the Task screen. This utility shows you the accounts currently established on the PC, along with options to create new accounts, change existing accounts, and alter the logon procedure. Another major utility for account creation and management exists in Windows XP: the Computer Management tool. This utility, with its greater complexity, is covered later in the chapter.

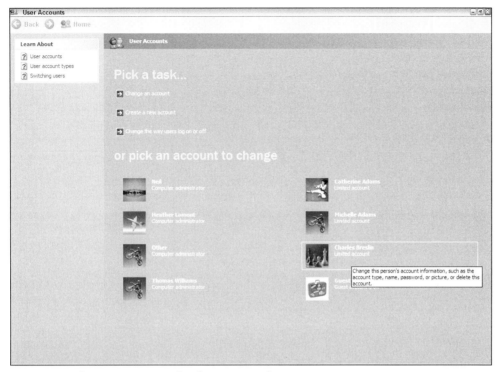

Figure 24-1: The User Accounts utility for creating and managing users.

Follow these steps to add a new user account:

1. Choose Start → Control Panel and open the User Accounts utility (or Winlogo+R, **control userpasswords**).

2. Click the Create a New Account item.

3. Type a name for the account, and click Next.

4. Select the appropriate account type. Figure 24-2 shows the selection screen.

5. Click the Create Account button. Windows creates the new account and adds it to the User Accounts dialog box.

Note
The name that you give to the account appears on both the Welcome screen and the Start menu.

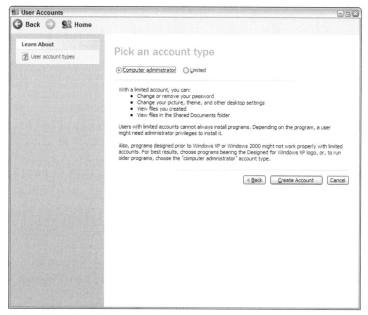

Figure 24-2: Selecting an account type.

Follow these steps to add a password to a specific account:

1. Choose Start → Control Panel and open the User Accounts utility.

2. Click the account for which you would like to add a password.

3. Click the Create a Password option.

4. In the appropriate fields (see Figure 24-3), type the password and then confirm that password by retyping it.

5. If you want to, type a phrase or word to use as a password hint. For example, if you typed **Buffy1Slayer** as your password, you may want to type **best show ever** as your password hint.

6. When you're finished, click the Create Password button.

Note

Password hints are visible to everyone who uses the computer, so try not to make your password hints so obvious that others can guess your password. If you suspect someone has guessed your password, change it immediately! In fact, change it regularly whether or not you suspect that anyone has figured it out.

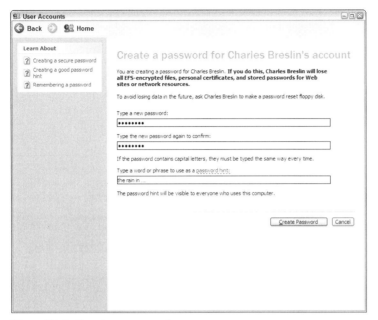

Figure 24-3: Creating a password.

Caution

Figure 24-3 spells out, at the top of the dialog box, the danger of applying passwords to other people's accounts. If that person has already created and stored passwords to use in Web sites or has saved Internet certificates, they will no longer be available after you add a password. The same holds true for user-encrypted files or folders that use the Encrypting File System. To avoid the problem, have the user create the password and simultaneously produce a password reset disk by opening the User Accounts utility and click-ing the Prevent a Forgotten Password item in the Related Tasks area. The password reset disk stores the information necessary to enter the account with full access to encrypted information and other passwords. Be sure to keep all password reset disks safe, however; they allow anyone to access the user's account without knowing the password.

If you want to change a password, open the User Accounts utility and choose the Change My Password option. If you change a password and leave the field blank, Windows does not ask you for a password when logging on.

When you add a user account, some important things happen. Primarily, Windows creates a folder, named identically to the username, inside the Documents and Settings folder on your main Windows drive (C: by default). Inside that user's main folder Windows places the folders outlined in the list that follows. Note again that *each user* has this folder group; this structure allows Windows to keep each user's data separate and, through the creation of passwords and the setting of permissions, private. Windows creates these folders within each user folder:

- **Application Data:** Includes data files belonging to specific programs. On installation, Windows XP creates two subfolders here: Identities and Microsoft. The Identities folder contains subfolders that segregate different profiles in the Outlook Express email program. As you install programs, the Application Data folder expands as the programs create relevant subfolders.

- **Cookies:** Cookies collected from Web sites.

Tip

When you instruct a privacy utility to erase the cookies on your system, it deletes the entries in the Cookies subfolder. You can do so yourself by navigating to this folder and deleting all or some of them manually.

- **Desktop:** Shortcuts on the desktop. Having separate Desktop folders for each user allows all users to have their own customized desktop.

- **Favorites:** Favorites stored in Internet Explorer. Again, all users have their own individual favorites, allowing the Favorites menu to display different Web locations as each user logs on.

- **Local Settings:** More application data, as well as the History file (in Internet Explorer) and Temporary files. Microsoft Outlook stores your email files (PST files) inside Local Settings\Application Data\Microsoft\Outlook.

- **My Documents (or the username may appear instead of My):** The document space for that user, including subfolders My Pictures, My Music, My Videos, and My Received Files. My Received Files is the default folder for the Save As dialog in Microsoft programs and others.

- **My Recent Documents:** Shortcuts for recently opened or saved files (accessible from the Start menu). For quick access to this folder, use Winlogo+R, **recent**. This is much more useful than the Start menu's paltry list. Try sorting these shortcuts by date and using View → Arrange → Show in groups.

- **NetHood:** Shortcuts to network resources as displayed in My Network Places.

- **PrintHood:** Items in printer folders.

- **SendTo:** Items in the SendTo menu accessible by right-clicking inside a folder. SendTo is a way to copy, move, or open a file. You may want to remove shortcuts from this folder for destinations or programs you never use; you may also want to add shortcuts to programs you do frequently use to open more than one type of file (a shortcut to Notepad can be very handy for opening all kinds of files, for example).

- **Start Menu:** Items on the Start menu.

- **Templates:** Shortcuts to program templates. This relates to another context menu item (when you right-click in a folder): New. When you hover over New on the context menu, some of the choices (but not all) correspond to files in this Templates folder. Unfortunately, this isn't as straightforward to alter as SentTo.

In addition to creating individual folders for that user, Windows creates icons for shared programs. For example, if you have Microsoft Word installed on your PC, when you create a user account you also create the capability for that user to use the Word program. Windows places an icon for that program in the All Programs menu.

Windows XP offers four types of user accounts: Computer Administrator, Limited, Standard, and Guest. Most users, however, encounter only the first two of these types, with the Standard account restricted to PCs configured as members of a networked domain and with the Guest account disabled by default during the initial Windows XP installation.

Computer Administrator Accounts

The most powerful account type on a Windows XP machine is the Computer Administrator account. Computer Administrators can perform advanced functions, such as the following:

- Installing programs and hardware

- Making systemwide changes

- Accessing and reading all files, including private files

- Creating and deleting user accounts

- Changing other people's accounts

- Changing their own account names or type

This last item comes with a restriction: Computer Administrators can change their own account types from Administrator to Limited or Standard only if at least one other Computer Administrator account exists. That is, you can't have a Windows XP system without an Administrator. To that end, during installation Windows creates a Computer Administrator account bearing the username Administrator. In fact, when the setup process asks you for a password for the main account, this is the account it is referring to. By default, Windows does not display the primary Administrator account on the Welcome screen, and many users, indeed, don't even know it exists.

In other words, when you install Windows XP, you automatically create two accounts: the hidden Administrator account and the account Windows asks you to create during the installation. Computer manufacturers sometimes rename the automatic Administrator account, but the principle remains the same. You can eliminate all user accounts except the original Administrator account if you like, but in that case you can no longer log in from the Welcome screen unless you use the Tweak UI utility (see Chapter 18) to show the original Administrator account on the Welcome screen.

Limited Accounts

Limited accounts enable users to perform basic functions, such as the following:

- Changing or removing their password

- Changing their account picture

- Creating a password reset disk, setting up a .NET Passport password account (for accessing Microsoft Web services such as Hotmail), or managing network passwords

- Using installed software that supports multiple users

When configuring Windows XP for new users, you should establish Limited accounts unless you have a specific reason to add another Administrator account. The primary reason for giving users Administrator privileges is to allow them to install their own software, which they usually cannot do with Limited account privileges. In a business setting, you will rarely want to do this; in such a case controlling the software on the system becomes critical, and you can establish a policy of, for example, one Administrator account per PC.

On a home system, it can be impractical to disallow software installation because of the tendency of many users to buy or download new software and install it. Unless you want to make yourself available, as the person with the Administrator account, every time someone in the family wants to install a new program (and for antivirus and anti-spyware purposes that's not a bad idea, just inconvenient), you should consider giving at least one other person Administrator status. (Besides, sometimes in a home environment it's much harder to explain to someone why they can't have full access; statements about lack of trust often produce behavior such as pouting.)

What Windows XP needs in a typical household environment, of course, is another account type, one halfway between Administrator and Limited. In fact, that's what the Standard account type provides, but you can establish it only on a networked domain. That said, some programs install just fine with a Limited account. So, by all means try the installation before changing the account type.

Standard Accounts

If you have a networked domain, you can create Standard accounts. These accounts provide precisely the same degree of control as a Limited account, with one primary exception: the capability to install and remove software. They cannot do so in a way that would affect a holder of a Computer Administrator account, so they could not uninstall a program such as Microsoft Word, which ties itself to all user accounts (including Administrators) on installation. They can, however, install programs that do not alter such settings, as is the case with older programs such as shareware versions of graphics software (Paint Shop Pro 4 and earlier, for example) and Internet utilities (such as WS-FTP). In addition, installation wizards designed with Windows XP in mind frequently ask if you want the software available for all users or just the current user; choosing the latter option prevents it from affecting other user accounts.

Guest Account

As you've probably already determined, the Guest account provides access to anyone who does not have a regular account. Guest account holders have no access to settings of any kind or to password-protected files, but they can use multiuser software and—the reason for this account type's existence—the Internet.

By default, the Guest account is turned off when you install Windows XP. To turn it on, open the User Accounts utility in the Control Panel and click the Guest icon in the Or Pick an Account to Change section. You then see the screen shown in Figure 24-4.

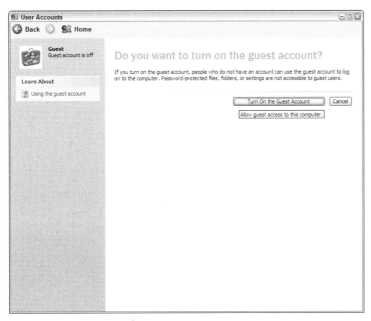

Figure 24-4: Turning on the Guest account.

Tip

Before enabling the Guest account, be sure to establish passwords for all other user accounts on the system. By doing so, you prevent anyone who is using the Guest account from accessing files and folders in password-protected areas such as each user's My Documents folder.

Adding Users with the Computer Management Tool

The Computer Management tool enables you to manage local or remote computers via a console tree. As Figure 24-5 demonstrates, this tool (officially called the Microsoft Management Console, or

MMC), consists of a hierarchical organization of utilities in the leftmost pane, known as the *console tree*. Details about the selected utility appear in the rightmost pane. Because the console tree lists various administrative functions in a single window, the tool makes it faster for you to create or modify user accounts. With this convenience, however, comes a rise in potential confusion and even damage: the former because you have far more choices available to you, the latter because you have access to powerful, system-changing tools from the MMC. For adding and maintaining users and groups, however, and for system management in general, you might quickly find the MMC indispensable.

XP Home Users will be perplexed to find they have MMC and the Computer Management console, but are not allowed to use the User setup snap-in (as Microsoft calls it). The following steps largely apply to XP Professional users. However, both XP Home and Pro users can access some of these features through Winlogo+R, control passwords2 (yes, that's a 2 at the end; control passwords without a 2 bring up the Users Control Panel).

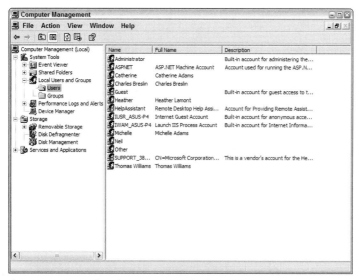

Figure 24-5: Details on user accounts displayed in the MMC.

Follow these steps to add a new user with the Computer Management tool:

1. Open the Control Panel from the Start menu.

2. Click Performance and Maintenance.

3. Double-click the Administrative Tools icon, and choose Computer Management. (Note you can skip all three of the preceding steps by using Winlogo+R, **compmgmt.msc**. XP Home users: you may want to do this to see the other good stuff that is here, but you won't be able to do the next step; you are expected to use Control Panel → Users Groups).

4. In the System Tools tree, click the + symbol to open the Local Users and Groups tree.

5. Right-click the Users folder and choose New User.

6. In the New User dialog box (see Figure 24-6), type the user information in the appropriate fields.

Figure 24-6: The New User dialog from the MMC.

7. Select the appropriate password option.

8. When you're finished, click Create to add the new user.

Password Options

When you create a new user account with the Computer Management tool, you can choose from three different password options:

▪ **User must change password at next logon:** When the user next logs on to the PC, a dialog box appears, requiring the change of password. The user has no choice in the matter; the logon will not continue until the change is made. An administrator might use this to assign you a temporary password that you are required to replace with your own choice.

▪ **User cannot change password:** You set the password and give it to the user, who cannot change it afterward.

▪ **Password never expires:** Using the MMC, you can configure each account in numerous ways, including a password expiration date. To keep your system secure, establish a fairly frequent change of passwords. Checking the Password Never Expires item, however, sets the password for good.

Note

Remember that a good password should be difficult for anyone besides the owner to use. Avoid passwords based on the names of pets, spouses, or any other kind of personal information, and also avoid passwords that spell real words. For the best possible password security, create a password at least eight characters in length, with at least one number, one letter, and one other type of symbol (such as punctuation). Split multi-syllabic passwords at unexpected places with unexpected characters, and do not use easily identifiable number strings such as 4567. It's also a good idea to change your password at least once a month.

Disabling Accounts

If you want to prevent specific users from accessing their accounts, you can disable that account. When you disable an account, you do not delete the information associated with that account; you simply hide the account information. Disabled accounts are not displayed on the Welcome page.

Follow these steps to disable a user account:

1. Open the Control Panel from the Start menu.

2. Click Performance and Maintenance.

3. Double-click the Administrative Tools icon, and choose Computer Management. (Or use Winlogo+R, **compmgmt.msc** to skip these three steps.)

4. In the System Tools tree, click the + symbol to open the Local Users and Groups tree.

5. Open the Users folder by double-clicking on the folder name.

6. In the right pane of the page, double-click the user account that you want to disable.

7. Click the General tab, and then select the Account is Disabled check box.

8. Click OK.

Deleting User Accounts

User accounts no longer being used should be deleted from the computer. When you delete a user account, you have the option of saving the contents of the user's desktop and My Documents folder to a folder on your desktop called *username*. You cannot save a user's email messages, Internet favorites, or other user settings (see Figure 24-7).

To delete a user account, log on as an Administrator and open User Accounts from the Control Panel. Click the account you want to delete, and select the Delete the Account option from the resulting page. Decide whether to retain that user's files, and click either Keep Files or Delete Files. Finally, click the Delete Account button to remove it from the PC.

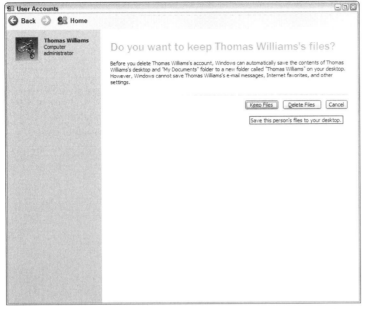

Figure 24-7: Choices to make when deleting an account. The popup for the Keep Files button reminds you these files will be saved to the desktop of the current user (in a folder with the name of the deleted user).

Combining Users into Groups with the Computer Management Tool

You can establish properties for each individual user, but if your system or network contains numerous users, you can create groups of users with all the members of a group sharing the same properties and permissions. You can place each user in multiple groups if you like, or you can carefully segregate them without any overlapping.

Windows XP creates 10 different user groups automatically (see Figure 24-8). You can assign each user to one or more of these groups, depending on your specific needs:

- **Administrators:** Have unrestricted access to the entire domain
- **Backup Operators:** Have the capability to override security restrictions to back up or restore files
- **Guests:** Have basic access to the computer
- **Network Configuration Operators:** Have minimal administrative privileges to manage the configuration of networking features

■ **Power Users:** Have most administrator privileges and can run legacy applications and certified applications

■ **Remote Desktop Users:** Have permissions to remotely log on to the computer

■ **Replicator:** Can replicate files in a specific domain

■ **Users:** Can run certified applications but cannot make systemwide changes or work with most legacy applications

■ **Debugger Users:** Can debug processes on the computer, both locally and remotely

■ **HelpServicesGroup:** Are part of the Microsoft Help and Support Center (Remote Assistance)

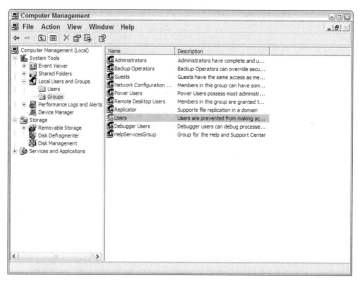

Figure 24-8: Groups and their explanations in the Computer Management console.

Follow these steps to assign a user to a group:

1. Open the Control Panel from the Start menu.

2. Click Performance and Maintenance.

3. Double-click the Administrative Tools icon, and choose Computer Management. (Winlogo+R, **compmgmt.msc**).

4. Click the + symbol to expand the Local Users and Groups tree.

5. Click the Users folder and then right-click on the desired username and choose Properties.

6. Click the Member Of tab to see the current group assignments for that user; then click the Add button to establish the new assignment.

7. Ensure that Group is selected in the object type field and the specific computer or domain is selected in the location field.

8. If you know the name of the group to which you want to add the user, type it in the text field at the bottom of the page and click OK.

9. If you do not know the name of the group to which you want to add the user, click the Advanced button and then click the Find Now button. A list of all the different groups is displayed in the bottom portion of the page (see Figure 24-9). Select a group name, and then click the OK button to add that user to the selected group.

10. Click the OK button when you're finished.

Figure 24-9: The list of available groups.

Tip

To select multiple groups, hold down the Ctrl key on your keyboard and select the various groups to which you want to add the user.

Summary

Creating separate accounts for each user on a single PC solves a great many problems, ranging from privacy and security to the much more mundane issue of unintentional modification or deletion of data files. Even on a single user PC, however, you might well find that an extra account or two comes in handy. For example, if you use your PC to experiment with software, create a separate Computer Administrator account solely for that purpose. If you play games, you can make an addictive game inaccessible from your main account, which can prove a blessing when it comes to productivity. Even though you can gain access simply by switching users, sometimes merely having to do that is enough to keep yourself away from it.

Chapter 25

Controlling User Access with Permissions

by Neil Randall and Michelle MacLean

W indows XP user accounts work effectively as a tool for privacy and security only if you segregate each user's files and folders. In some programs, you can do so with a password generated specifically for that program's data files. For example, you can password-protect your Microsoft Outlook data, forcing users (including yourself) to type a password completely separate from your Windows password in order to view your email messages, calendar, contact information, and everything else you've created in Outlook. To protect your files on a systemwide basis, however, you need a systemwide method of denying access, something that Windows XP provides in its procedures for making files private and for setting file and folder permissions.

This chapter covers the methods for making your Windows XP files and folders inaccessible or only partly accessible to other users of the PC and to those accessing your PC over the local network. In this chapter, you learn how to make folders private, set folder permissions, work with security options, and gain access to protected files and folders.

Note

File-sharing and permissions features on a Windows XP system function only on hard drives formatted with the NTFS file system. Drives formatted in FAT or FAT32, the file systems used by Windows 9x/Me (and by many users of Windows 2000 and Windows XP) do not have these capabilities. For that reason alone, you should seriously consider converting all your drives to NTFS once you've decided to use Windows XP and not go back to earlier versions of Windows.

Simple versus Standard File Sharing

When first installed, Windows XP configures itself to use Simple File Sharing, a method of setting permissions designed to make the process suitable for less technical users. In fact, if you use Windows XP Home Edition as opposed to the more feature-rich Windows XP Professional Edition, you have no choice but to use Simple File Sharing. The OS offers no alternative. With Windows XP Professional, however, you can toggle this feature off in favor of the more advanced Standard File Sharing, with which you can establish much more specific access to resources.

To choose between the two file-sharing methods, follow these steps:

1. Open My Computer or Windows Explorer.

2. From the Tools menu, choose Folder Options.

3. Click the View tab.

4. Scroll to the bottom of the Advanced Settings listing (see Figure 25-1). Check or uncheck the Use Simple File Sharing (Recommended) item, depending on whether you want it on or off.

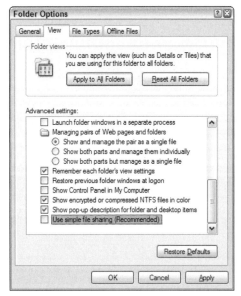

Figure 25-1: Enabling and disabling Simple File Sharing.

5. Click OK or Apply to make the change. The process can take a few minutes if you have a system with many hundreds of files.

Tip

To launch Windows Explorer quickly, you can press and hold down the Windows Logo key and press the letter *E*. The Windows Logo key is the one with an image of the Microsoft "Windows "flag" and is usually located in the lower left-hand corner of the keyboard, between the Ctrl and Alt keys (on North American keyboards).

The difference between the Simple and Standard File Sharing becomes apparent when you examine the Properties dialog box for any folder. Figures 25-2 and 25-3 show the Properties dialog box for the same folder. In Figure 25-2, Simple File Sharing is on, while in Figure 25-3 it is off. Turning off Simple File Sharing adds the Security tab to the dialog box and provides a significantly changed Shared tab. Between these two tabs, you have extensive control over file and folder permissions. If you run Windows XP Professional in a network setting with several users, this is the method you should use to restrict access to resources; in fact, Windows disables the Simple File Sharing feature entirely on computers networked through a domain.

Figure 25-2: A folder's Properties dialog box with Simple File Sharing enabled.

Figure 25-3: The same folder's Properties
dialog box with Simple File Sharing disabled.

Working with Simple File Sharing

How simple is Simple File Sharing? Any type of file sharing has its complexities, but Simple File Sharing succeeds by putting a much less intimidating interface on the process of establishing precisely who gets access to what. At its simplest, the feature lets you set the items in your own My Documents folder to private status so that only you and the primary Administrator can work with them. You have other options as well with Simple File Sharing turned on, including the capability to share files and folders with other users on the local network.

The Windows XP Privacy Levels

Simple File Sharing provides three levels of access to local users and two levels of access to users on the local network:

  ▪ **Level 1:** If you make either My Documents or one of its subfolders private, you prevent access to all other users, including those with Computer Administrator account types. Anyone trying to access the folder receives the dialog box shown in Figure 25-4.

Caution

Even though no other user can directly access the private folder, your files and folders still aren't safe from other users' eyes. Anyone with a Computer Administrator account can change the password of any other accounts on the system (including those of other Computer Administrators) and gain access to those files. Somewhat astonishingly, Computer Administrators can even change the password of the initial Administrator account and gain access to files and settings. Once again, be careful to whom you give Administrator privileges.

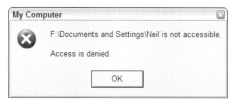

Figure 25-4: Windows XP denies access to private folders.

Level 2: When you create an account of any type, that account's My Documents folder and all its subfolders assume a Level 2 privacy setting. Only the owner of the account, along with all Computer Administrator account holders, can access the folders. Holders of Limited accounts cannot access them at all. This is a primary reason for giving all users (except a single Administrator) Limited accounts; they automatically cannot look at each other's My Documents folders.

Level 3: The third level really has nothing to do with setting folder permissions or making them private. It pertains, instead, to the Shared Documents folder on the PC, which Windows automatically restricts to users of that PC. Administrators have full control over the files in Shared Documents, while holders of Limited accounts can read the documents but not write to or delete them. Shared Documents serves precisely the purpose its name suggests: it lets everybody on a multiuser PC share files.

Level 4: The bottom half of Figure 25-2 shows the Network Sharing and Security area of the Properties dialog box for the selected folder (that is, not just the Shared Documents folder from Level 3). If you check the Share This Folder on the Network option, you establish Level 4 privacy. This setting allows users on the network to read the files but not modify them.

Level 5: If you check both the Share This Folder on the Network and Allow Network Users to Change My Files options, you establish the weakest privacy, Level 5. This level functions essentially as an open invitation to anyone to read and change your files, so use it carefully if at all.

Making Folders Private

You can increase the security and privacy of your Windows XP user account by using the Simple File Sharing interface to make your folders and files private. Private, according to Windows XP, means that only the current user and a Computer Administrator can access these files to read, change, or delete them.

Follow these steps to make your My Documents folder or other folders private:

1. Open My Computer or Windows Explorer (Winlogo+E).

2. Right-click the folder you want to make private, and choose Properties (or Sharing and Security).

3. Click the Sharing tab.

4. Select the Make This Folder Private check box, as shown in Figure 25-2.

5. Click OK.

In addition, the first time you create a password for your account (from within the User Accounts utility in Control Panel), you can set your entire My Documents folder to Private status. After adding a password, the User Accounts Wizard offers a button with the option to make the folders private (see Figure 25-5). Click the button and then OK to render everything in My Documents private.

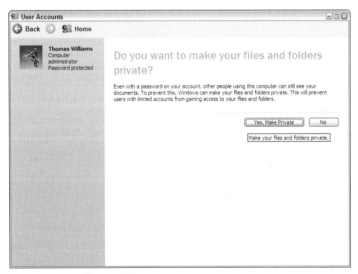

Figure 25-5: Making a folder private.

If, at any time, you want to remove the privacy on your files, open the Properties dialog box for that folder and uncheck the Make This Folder Private option.

Caution

You should consider unchecking the privacy option for your own folders if you decide to reinstall Windows XP but keep the files from the initial installation available. On a new installation, you will not have access to private folders because you are not actually a user on that system. Nor can you access the User Accounts dialog boxes in order to change passwords. See the "Gaining Access to Protected Files and Folders" section later in this chapter for information on gaining access to restricted folders.

6. Click the Add button to apply permissions to a group or user that does not appear in the Group or usernames list, and then type the name of the group or user that you want to apply permissions to. Alternatively, you can select the name of the user or group in the Group or usernames list.

7. Select the appropriate check boxes to grant that user or group the capability to perform the actions described, or clear the check boxes to prevent the selected user or group from performing the actions described.

8. Click OK when you're finished.

Working with Standard File Sharing

The Standard File Sharing option gives you far more precise control over file and folder access on your PC. For most users, this level of control is likely unnecessary, but if you share your PC in a larger office setting or on a larger network, you should use this option to set restrictions. If your computer is part of a network, you have no choice; in that case, Simple File Sharing is not a selectable option.

Standard File Sharing offers a number of advanced options. For one, you can control the number of users who can access the folder at any one time. For another, you can establish precisely what each user group, or each individual user for that matter, can do with the files in the selected folder. In the case of your Shared Documents folder, for example, which by default does not allow holders of Limited accounts to change files, you can manually configure the permissions so that a specific Limited account can change files while still retaining Limited account status. Also, if as an Administrator you deem it necessary, you can take ownership of a folder so that you can access it but the original owner no longer can. The options are numerous.

The items covered here assume that you have turned on Standard File Sharing. If not, and if you want to follow along, open the Folder Options dialog box and choose Standard File Sharing now.

Sharing versus Security

As you already know, enabling the Standard File Sharing feature changes the Properties dialog box of the selected folder to include two tabs: Sharing and Security. The Sharing tab applies only to network use. Unlike the Sharing tab of the Simple File Sharing dialog box, it does not allow you to restrict access to users on the same PC as the shared folders themselves. To perform those functions, click the Security tab. A blizzard of initially confusing options allows you to control precisely which user on your PC, as well as users logging in to your PC locally or remotely via technologies that simulate local use (such as Virtual Private Networking and Remote Desktop), can access which resources.

If you're just getting started working with these concepts, you can make life relatively easy by configuring your PC with Simple File Sharing and then switching to Standard File Sharing when you're ready to make more precise distinctions in user access. When you make the switch, Windows retains the permissions established with Simple File Sharing, and you need only fine-tune from there.

To see this switch in action, examine Figures 25-6 and 25-7. Figure 25-6 shows the Security tab for a folder in the My Documents folder of an Administrator's account. Only two users have access: the user and the default System account (System has access to all accounts). As the Permissions list demonstrates, the user has Allow permissions for everything in the account and Deny permissions for nothing. This means that the user can do anything allowed to the files in those folders, including read, write, list contents, and execute programs. You can tell that this folder belongs to a user with a Computer Administrator account because users in the Administrators group, which is made up of other Administrators, do not have permission to do anything in the folder.

Figure 25-6: Administrator account Security tab.

By comparison, Figure 25-7 shows a folder in the My Documents folder of a Limited account. Here, three users are listed: the user, the System, and the Administrators group. By definition, as discussed earlier in this chapter, Limited accounts are controlled by the user, but all Computer Administrators have access. This screen shot clearly demonstrates that principle.

Figure 25-7: Limited account Security tab.

Limiting the Number of Users

For any number of reasons, you have the option of restricting the number of users who can access a particular resource at the same time. For example, in the case of shared folders with extremely large files, you might want to limit user access considerably to avoid bottlenecks and bandwidth loss caused by too many users opening, working with, and downloading too many files. You might also want to restrict users as a means of more easily monitoring file use in order to determine patterns among users and the files they choose. Whatever the reasons you need this feature, Windows makes it easy to configure.

Follow these steps to set a specific number of users who can access the shared folder:

1. In My Computer, navigate to the folder you want to restrict.

2. Right-click on the folder, and then choose Sharing and Security.

3. If the folder is not already being shared, select the Share This Folder radio button.

4. Select the Allow This Number of Users radio button, and then select a number using the arrows.

5. Click OK when you're finished.

SETTING SHARE PERMISSIONS

You can set specific Share permissions on a shared folder for users who access the files over the network. For example, you can grant a specific user Full Control to the folder, enabling that user to modify the folder and even delete it. You can also grant Change permissions to a specific user, enabling that user to modify the folder; or Read permissions, allowing the user to read the contents of that folder. Generally, network administrators grant Read permissions to large groups of users and Change permissions only to those authorized to make changes to the folder or its documents. Only network administrators get Full Control of the resource, and only selected administrators at that. Allowing Full Control to large numbers of people can cause a wide range of obvious problems.

Caution

If you grant a specific user or group Full Control permissions to a folder, that user or group can delete any files in that folder regardless of the permissions protecting the files.

Follow these steps to set Share permissions on a folder accessed over the network:

1. Navigate to the shared folder.

2. Right-click on the folder, and choose Sharing and Security.

3. If the folder is not already being shared, select the Share This Folder radio button.

4. Click the Permissions button. By default, the group called Everyone has permission to read this folder. For better control, remove the Everyone account and replace it with specific users or groups. But keep in mind that doing so prevents blanket access and, therefore, could result in even more work for yourself in assigning large numbers of specific permissions.

5. To set Share permissions for a specific user, click the Add button.

6. In the text field, type the name of the user to whom you want to give permissions and then click OK. Alternatively, click the Advanced button, followed by the Find Now button, to display the users and groups already established on your system (see Figure 25-8).

7. In the Permissions for <*user*> section, grant the permissions that you want to apply to the selected user.

8. Click OK when you're finished.

Note

Deny permissions take precedence over Allow permissions. When you set Deny permissions for a specific user who belongs to two groups — one that is allowed a permission and another that is denied the same permission — then the user is denied that permission.

Figure 25-8: Finding specific users.

Caching Files

Enabling the features in Windows XP that allow users to work with offline files provides a means for users to create and change files in a folder as if they were online, with the same file and folder permissions in place, and then have Windows synchronize any changes with the network versions of the files when the users go back online. This might be useful to a laptop user who connects to the network for only a limited time but needs to work on files stored on the network.

The Windows XP Offline Files feature creates a data cache on each user's hard drive. In this cache, Windows stores any files shared over the network that have been configured as offline files. The Caching button gives you control over the behavior of these cached files, with the three cache settings shown in Figure 25-9:

- **Manual caching of documents:** Users can specify which files from a network folder they want to be able to work with when offline. The manual setting, the default for shared folders, instructs Windows to cache only those specific documents.

- **Automatic caching of documents:** This setting caches all documents in the shared folder whether or not the user specified them for this purpose. If the shared folder contains a more recent copy of the document, the cached version is automatically deleted and replaced by the newer version. Only files the user has opened online can become available offline using this setting.

■ **Automatic caching of programs and documents:** This setting is similar to automatic caching of documents, except that other types of files are also available for caching. Possibilities include program files and items with read-only data. Again, the user does not make the choice of what resources to cache.

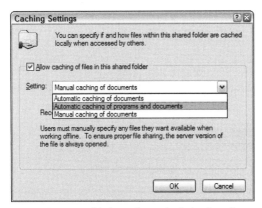

Figure 25-9: Establishing the cache for a shared offline folder.

Follow these steps to enable caching of files in a shared folder:

1. Navigate to the shared folder for which you would like to enable caching.

2. Right-click on the folder, and then choose Sharing and Security.

3. Select the Sharing tab.

4. If the folder is not already being shared, select the Share This Folder radio button.

5. Click the Caching button.

6. Check the Allow Caching of Files in This Shared Folder check box.

7. Select the type of cache setting you want to apply to the shared folder from the Setting drop-down list, and click OK.

Setting Folder Permissions from My Computer

If your computer is connected to a network domain, which by definition requires Standard, not Simple, File Sharing, you can prevent others from accessing your folders and the files they contain by setting permissions on those folders.

Follow these steps to set permissions on a folder:

1. Open Windows Explorer.

2. Navigate to the folder for which you would like to apply permissions.

3. Right-click the folder and choose Properties.

4. Select the Security tab.

Gaining Access to Protected Files and Folders

With a Computer Administrator account, you can gain access to almost any file or folder on the PC, no matter which users have been granted permissions to it and even if the Windows XP installation to which it originally belonged no longer functions. As an example, suppose that your system experiences a crippling crash and you can no longer boot into Windows XP, but you have important files in private folders on the now dead system. You can install a fresh instance of Windows XP and take control of the folders anyway. The process is tedious, to be sure, but if the files matter, it's worth it.

Follow these steps to perform this task most effectively, which means to take ownership of the inaccessible items:

1. Log on to your Administrator account, and use My Computer or Windows Explorer to locate the folder in question.

2. Right-click the folder, choose Sharing and Security, and select the Security tab.

3. Click the Advanced button to reveal the Permissions tab of the Advanced Security Settings dialog box (see Figure 25-10).

4. Grant your new account permission to access the resource by clicking Add and then selecting the Advanced tab on the resulting dialog box.

5. Click Find Now and locate your username in the list; then click OK twice to add yourself to the list. The result is the Permission Entry dialog box shown in Figure 25-11, in which you specify precisely what permissions you will hold.

6. Choose Full Control. Clicking this check box automatically fills in the rest of the boxes in the Allow column.

7. Click OK to return to the Advanced Security Settings box, where your username now appears.

8. Check the Replace Permission Entries on All Child Objects check box to gain access not just to the folder but to all subfolders as well.

9. Click Apply to set everything in motion.

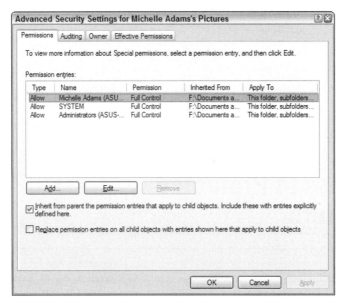

Figure 25-10: Setting permissions in Advanced Security Settings.

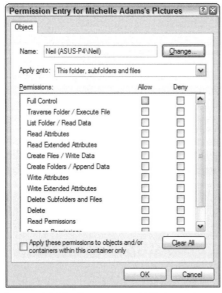

Figure 25-11: Giving a user Full Control over a resource.

10. Select the Owner tab (see Figure 25-12), and click your username in the Change Owner To window.

Figure 25-12: Taking ownership of the folder and subfolders.

11. Check the Replace Owner on Subcontainers and Objects check box immediately below the window to apply the changes to the folder and subfolders; then click Apply to take ownership.

   You should now be able to access the folder. Open My Computer or Windows Explorer, locate the folder, and copy the files you need from it.

Summary

Setting permissions enables you to establish who has access to which resources on your PC. For privacy, security, and even legal reasons, it might well be the most important Windows XP configuration you perform. Unlimited access can quickly lead to abuse or innocent, but nevertheless destructive, carelessness. Fortunately, Windows XP provides you with a variety of means to control access, and this chapter has covered several important ones. For further details on controlling your system, turn to Chapter 27 to explore Group Policies. For details on locating, migrating, and accessing user data, see Chapter 26.

Chapter 26

Locating and Migrating User Data

by Neil Randall and Michelle MacLean

Consider the following two scenarios.

Scenario #1: You've purchased a new PC with all the latest bells and whistles. Windows XP Professional hums along nicely; you've spent numerous hours performing mandatory testing on the subwoofers, the digital camcorder, the DVD burner, and all those other essential items. You've updated the virus definition files and added everything that Windows Update has to offer. Everything seems ready to go. Only one problem: your documents, work files, and email are still sitting on the old machine.

Scenario #2: You've finally committed the time necessary to perform that long-awaited backup — the one you should have been doing regularly but somehow never managed to get around to. You fire up your backup software, step through its wizard, and suddenly realize that backing up your nearly full 80GB hard drive will require more than 100 CDs and roughly a gazillion hours. Backing up to a DVD burner would improve the picture, but you'd still need 15–20 discs. So, you decide to back up only your most important files: word processing documents, spreadsheet files, scanned photos, edited videos, and, of course, your email. Your backup software lets you choose this kind of limited backup, but you quickly discover that these files are scattered all over your PC. You can find some, but not all. And you don't want to complete the whole thing only to launch Internet Explorer and realize that all your favorites have disappeared because you've forgotten to back up the appropriate folder.

In both scenarios, you need to know where your user data resides. In the case of user-created documents, you probably won't have to look far for the answer because users tend to save files in three major locations:

In the Event of System Failure

Sometimes a Windows XP installation can fail to the point where you can do nothing to save it. Maybe you can't get as far as the Welcome screen, and maybe you can't even get into Safe Mode. For whatever reason, your Windows installation is toast.

You have a number of options, such as attempting to repair the installation or, at the other extreme, reformatting all your hard drives and starting over (see Appendix B). Often, the easiest approach is to install a fresh instance of Windows XP on a new hard disk partition (see Appendix A) and then work from the new installation to recover data from the old installation.

The trick here is the separate partition. When you install Windows XP, you install a number of folders along with it — all on the same partition as Windows itself. If you perform a fresh installation on the same partition, you overwrite these folders. By contrast, installing to a separate partition keeps those folders in place (Windows creates new ones on the new partition), letting you access that separate partition later and reclaim your files. (See Appendix B for details on reinstalling Windows XP to a separate partition.)

If your system currently has only one partition, the nonfunctioning Windows XP is on that partition. You can't use the old DOS-oriented FDISK to create the new partition in this case because FDISK knows how to make and delete partitions, not split existing partitions into two or more. To divide your partition, you need a third-party disk-partitioning package such as Symantec's Partition Magic or V Communications' Partition Commander. These programs work superbly, but they require an operating system to function. Because you can't get into Windows in the first place, you can't use these programs.

In such a situation, your only real choice is to install a second hard drive. You don't need a large drive — in fact, an old 20GB drive will do the job — but because this drive will hold your operating system, you might as well get the fastest and largest drive you can afford. Install it in your PC — much less difficult than it might seem — and install Windows XP on it. When you've finished, you can begin retrieving your data files from the Documents and Settings folder (and other relevant folders) on the old drive.

Yes, this method costs a bit of money. And yes, it takes a great deal of time. But if you need your data files, you're probably willing to invest the time and money. If only you had made a thorough backup (see Chapter 4).

- My Documents folders and subfolders

- The Desktop and subfolders

- Inside the folders containing the programs used to create the files

- A separate folder (or folders) created by the user to hold only data files

By default, most Microsoft software and increasing numbers of third-party software use My Documents for this purpose, with the software frequently creating a subfolder to segregate the files belonging to that specific program. For several reasons, though, some of them having to do with old habits dying hard, many users create separate folders in which they store all — or at least the majority — of the data files they produce.

For other user data, however, you often need to look harder. Simply put, it could be almost anywhere. This chapter examines the most likely places to find folders, files, and other items you want to make sure you save when it comes to moving data from one Windows XP installation to another.

Copying from Documents and Settings

The Documents and Settings folder contains data files and personal settings for each user who has an account on the computer. Windows XP checks this folder to determine things like which programs show up on a specific user's Start menu, the list of favorites to show when the user launches Internet Explorer, the various documents that are accessible by that user, and so on. Think of your account subfolder inside the main Documents and Settings folder as your personal identity on the computer. You have some choice over its contents, such as whether to store your word processing files in My Documents or somewhere else and the photographs from your digital camera in My Pictures or a different folder entirely, but Windows and other programs store many files in your Documents and Settings area without asking your permission.

Note

This chapter discusses some files and folders that Windows hides by default. To navigate to the folders, you must first make them accessible. To unhide hidden files and folders, open My Computer and choose Folder Options from the Tools menu. Click the View tab in the Folder Options dialog box, and scroll to find the Hidden Files and Folders item. Click to check the Show Hidden Files and Folders radio button, and click OK. When you return to the folder you were viewing, all files and folders — including hidden ones — now appear. If you don't enable this feature, you could easily miss a folder that the user, for whatever reason, has designated as hidden.

The first step in migrating user data from one Windows XP system to another is to copy the files from that user's Documents and Settings subfolder from the old Windows XP installation to the new. If the new installation resides on a different partition of the same computer as the old one, your job is quite easy. As long as you have access to the user's folder (see Chapter 25 if you do not), simply use Windows Explorer to display your old and new user folders and copy the files from the former to the latter.

Caution

To avoid all possible problems, refrain from copying subfolders created by Windows in case the folder has been tied to your user account by the system-created Security Identifier (SID). The SID controls the full working of your main folder inside Documents and Settings to the extent that copying the old Documents and Settings\ *UserName* folder from the old machine to the new might result in an inability to work with the Windows XP privacy and security settings in that folder. Leave the original folder where it was, and copy the files instead.

If the new installation resides on a different machine, the task doesn't change but the time needed to complete it increases. Copying data between machines always takes longer than copying it from hard drive to hard drive inside the same machine. An external USB hard drive or a network connection can make this much easier.

Copying Other User-Specific Files

After transferring the Documents and Settings subfolder for your user account, the rest is a matter of remembering where you put all your files or, if you're performing the migration for other users, working with those people to locate all the files they want to preserve. This process can take, quite literally, days — especially when migrating from a PC with one or more large hard drives filled with programs and data. For some programs, finding these files can prove exceptionally difficult, even to the extent that different versions of the same program might very well save the data files in different locations. If possible, erase absolutely nothing from the old installation until you (and any other users affected by the change) have had time to work with the system and discover missing elements. In particular, look for the following:

- Data files for productivity programs such as word processors, spreadsheets, graphics software, presentation software, database — anything not saved to the user's My Documents folder but rather in a separate data folder.

- Back up data files, copies of other data files, with the backup folders possibly containing additional documents.

- Data files saved in the same folder as the program that created them or to a subfolder of that program — which means searching the Program Files folder on the old Windows installation as well as any other folder to which programs are installed.

- Documents of any kind bearing CD keys, registration codes, and anything else required to reinstall programs.

- Downloads of programs no longer available, at least in the version the user prefers — older shareware programs, for example, or software for which the user has a registration key and does not wish to upgrade.

- Address books (and email) from email programs or any other type of program.

- Documents containing personal information including insurance policy numbers, student numbers, logon information for other sites, and so on.

- Files to which other documents make reference, in the form of a hyperlink or a Direct Data Exchange (DDE) object. If an important Word document contains an embedded Excel spreadsheet object, for example, and the actual spreadsheet resides in another folder, you must find both to keep the document complete.

- Web site files, in the case of software, such as Macromedia Dreamweaver or Microsoft FrontPage, that synchronizes files between the remote server and the local machine — otherwise the synchronization process must be recreated, an often lengthy procedure.

░ Temp files for software that creates these files as a means of recovering the main files. Word is a classic example: It saves the main file, with the most recent changes you've made, plus a Temp file that contains the changes immediately following the Save action. You often have to search for these files, but you should do so for the best possible backup.

░ Files that track progress in games — hey, if the person has spent 200 hours getting to a certain point in the game, you don't want her spending another 200 getting back to the same point.

Migrating Your Email

No matter which email program you use on your PC, the program stores your email messages on your hard drive. Unfortunately, it's not always easy to determine where. In fact, Microsoft's two email clients, Outlook and Outlook Express, store email in different locations and in different formats, with neither of them easy to locate. Other email clients — Eudora, Netscape Mail, Mozilla Mail, Pegasus Mail, and all the others — store their associated data files in still other locations and in still different formats. While the protocols used for sending and receiving mail reflect a great deal of standardization, the files that make up your inbox, address book, and other mail folders show anything but. In fact, the only thing consistent about email inboxes today is their willingness to collect spam.

To locate your email files, follow this procedure.

1. Open your email program and locate the option that allows you to configure preferences or data files. In Microsoft Outlook, choose Tools → Options, and click the Mail Setup tab. Click the Data Files button, and then double-click the Personal Folders item in the resulting Outlook Data Files dialog box. This action reveals the properties dialog box for that data file (see Figure 26-1), with the path name for the data file displayed in the Filename field.

Tip

To see the full filename in the Outlook properties dialog box, click inside the Filename field and use the arrows to move right and left.

2. Using My Computer or Windows Explorer, navigate to the folder and examine the way in which your email program stores your mail. Figure 26-2 shows a folder containing Outlook Express mail files, each in DBX format. As you add folders, Outlook Express adds DBX files for each of those folders. Some email programs store messages as running text files; others, such as Outlook Express, as small databases.

3. Copy the files and folders containing the email to the new Windows installation. Be sure to copy subfolders as well, in case they also contain relevant files.

Figure 26-1: The Data Files properties dialog box in Outlook.

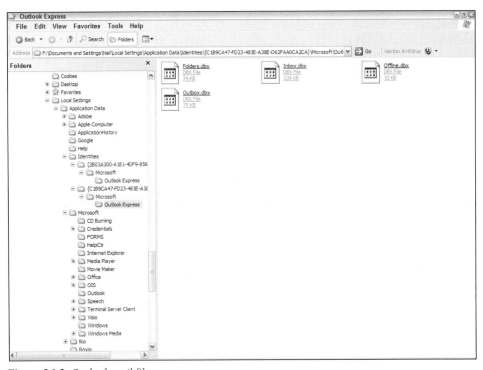

Figure 26-2: Outlook mail files.

4. In the new Windows installation, open the email program and determine how to import files from other locations. Perform these actions, keeping in mind where you stored the copied files and folders from the old installation. For example, Figure 26-3 shows the Import Personal Folders dialog box in Outlook. Migrating from one Outlook-enabled PC to another requires this kind of importing in order to rebuild the user's previous mailboxes and folders.

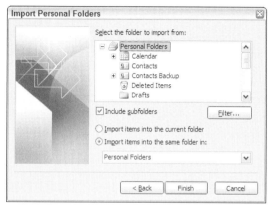

Figure 26-3: The Import Wizard in Outlook.

Note

Outlook Express stores its email data in the following folder within Windows XP:

C:\Documents and Settings*username*\Local Settings\Application Data\Identities\IdentityNumber.

Outlook stores its email data in the following folder:

C:\Documents and Settings*username*\Local Settings\Microsoft\Outlook.

Migrating Favorites and Cookies

Each user account on a Windows XP installation has a folder called Favorites inside that user's main folder in Documents and Settings. Typically, the Favorites folder houses URLs collected during Web travels and bookmarked with the Add to Favorites command in Internet Explorer. Because Favorites is merely another folder, you can house anything from links to music to documents in your Favorites folder and organize your data accordingly. For the most part, though, Favorites functions as a Web bookmarking tool, and Internet Explorer uses this folder to let you navigate to stored Web addresses quickly.

Also inside each user's main Documents and Settings folder is the Cookies folder. Here, Windows stores the cookies Internet Explorer has accepted while the user navigated the Web. When you visit a Web site, information is saved on your hard disk so that the Web site remembers your information the next time you visit that Web site. Because each request for a Web page is independent of all other requests, the Web page server has no memory of what pages it has previously sent to your computer. *Cookies*, the term for small files used by Internet sites to keep track of user preferences and information, have developed a reputation as being dangerous from a security standpoint. In fact, they're quite harmless. Still, you can prevent users from using their stored cookies by not migrating them to the new PC, keeping in mind that they will begin to collect cookies again as soon as they launch Internet Explorer (unless you've configured Internet Explorer not to allow cookies).

Even a Cookies folder that's only a few months old is likely to have hundreds or even thousands of cookie files in it (see Figure 26-4). Quite simply, these things proliferate. If you open a cookie file, however (which you can do in the Windows built-in text editor, Notepad), don't expect to make much sense of it. They contain code for the server to use, and typically the only detail you'll get by reading the file is the name of the organization that generated the cookie in the first place. Because cookies tend to store such information directly in their name, however, opening the file serves no real purpose.

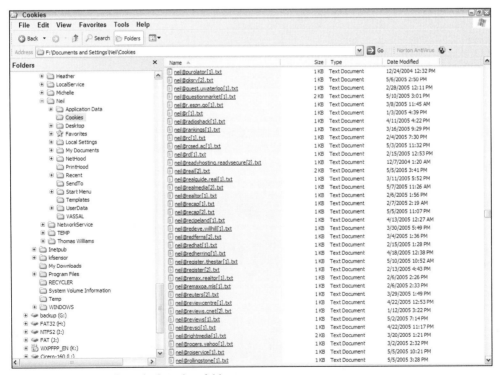

Figure 26-4: A typically packed Cookies folder.

Tip

If you don't want other users who access the computer to see a trail of the Web sites you have visited, it's not a bad idea to clean out your list of cookies on a fairly regular basis. You can do so using the Internet Options dialog box available in Internet Explorer and in Control Panel or by opening your Cookies folder and getting rid of cookies whose names provide too much information about your Web navigation habits.

In the cases of both favorites and cookies, migrating data is considered optional by many; that is, you don't *need* them even if you may *want* them. Certainly that's true of the Cookies folder, but some users want to keep their cookies for a variety of reasons, many of them legitimate. Favorites are a different story, however. If you've spent numerous hours — weeks and months, in fact — building up a list of favorites that let you work more effectively and locate the information you need, you should, by all means, migrate the Favorites folder. Actually, you don't need to migrate the entire folder at all. As long as you store the Favorites files somewhere, you merely have to copy them to the Favorites folder of the new installation to make full use of them again.

The Files and Settings Transfer Wizard

To help make the transition from one machine to another as painless as possible, Windows XP comes with a feature called the Files and Settings Transfer Wizard. When you use the Files and Settings Transfer Wizard to move data files and personal settings from one computer to the next, you eliminate the need to configure a wide range of options on the new computer. Furthermore, this wizard gives you the option of transferring many items discussed during this chapter; for example, you can move entire folders — such as Favorites — or specific files to your new computer. You access this wizard by choosing Start → All Programs → Accessories → System Tools → Files and Settings Transfer Wizard.

Microsoft strongly recommends connecting your new and old computers via a serial cable (Direct Cable Connection) or by using home networking to make the most out of the Files and Settings Transfer Wizard. You can also transfer via floppy disks, but you need several of them to carry out the transition. This method can be painful if you have a lot of files. If you choose to transfer only settings instead of files, however, the wizard transfers primarily small files. So neither floppy disks, with their extremely limited capacity, nor Direct Cable Connection, with its extremely limited speed, actually presents any major difficulty.

Note

The major problem with Direct Cable Connection is the fact that very few people have an appropriate serial cable. You can get one at your local electronics store (and some computer stores), but unless you're a computer veteran with many years' service (in olden times, collecting a variety of cables simply came with the computing territory), you are unlikely to have one sitting around.

Figure 26-5 shows the first stage of the Files and Settings Transfer Wizard. The Old computer represents the PC that currently holds the desired files and settings, whereas the New computer represents the PC to which you want to transfer these files and settings. You begin by running the wizard on the Old computer to gather the files and settings you want. Any PC running Windows 95 or later can act as the Old computer. But in order to perform this step with anything other than a Windows XP machine, you need to use the Windows XP installation CD (which contains the program for older Windows versions to use) or run the wizard first as the New computer and create a floppy disk with the Transfer Wizard for the Old computer.

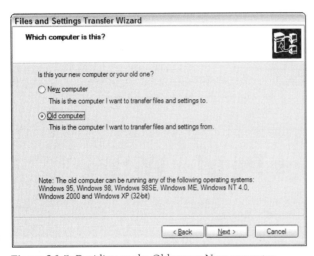

Figure 26-5: Deciding on the Old versus New computer.

Next, decide among the four transfer methods: Direct Cable, Home or Small Office network, Floppy Drive or Other Removable Drive, or Other (removable drive or network drive). Using Other, you can store files and settings on any location on your PC, making them ready for transfer to the new machine. With this choice made, the wizard asks what items you want to transfer. As Figure 26-6 shows, you can transfer only settings or only files, or you can combine them. To be precise about your choices, check the Let Me Select a Custom List of Files and Settings box, or simply let the wizard decide for itself.

The wizard divides the possible transfer items into three main sections:

- **Settings:** The settings of your existing programs and configurations, ranging from Windows accessibility settings and the settings in the Display Properties dialog box to settings for Outlook Express, Windows Media Player, and your networks.

- **Specific folders:** The folders that contain your preferences, such as Desktop, Favorites, My Pictures, and more. Keep in mind that transferring My Pictures and My Documents could result in a very large amount of data, given the size of some graphics and document files.

- **File types:** A huge array of file types, everything from PDF to JPG. Again, because of the size of many of these file types, the transfer might be huge.

Figure 26-6: Deciding what to transfer.

With your choices made, the wizard compiles information about the settings and files you've selected. Depending on those choices, this process could take several minutes or longer, even on a fast computer. Figure 26-7 shows the last stage of the wizard on the Old computer, instructing you to move to the new one and perform the transfer.

Figure 26-7: The initial collection stage completed.

On the New computer, run the wizard again, instructing it where to find the stored files and settings, and watch as it applies the data to the new PC. Your migration is complete.

Summary

All users change computers at some point. When they do, they sometimes experience the problems of setting everything up anew. Careful migration of user data, however, can help speed the transition, and in some cases only migration makes the transition possible at all. Ultimately, to migrate user data you must copy files and folders, and to copy them you must locate them; both processes can take a great deal of time. You can help yourself by performing regular backups of your important files and by investing in data-imaging software (also called ghosting software), designed specifically to let you back up your installation completely and restore it on the new PC exactly as it was. Most likely, you'll find yourself using several migration methods as you move from PC to PC, and getting used to all of them can only be a good idea.

Chapter 27

Configuring Group Policies

by Neil Randall and Michelle MacLean

O ut of the box, Windows XP provides wide-ranging flexibility in how users can configure the operating system's many options, in effect allowing them to build their own personalized interfaces. Sometimes, however, this much flexibility hinders rather than helps usability and productivity. If you are in charge of an office full of 10 PCs or more (and certainly once that number rises to 50 or more), standardizing the PCs starts to make a great deal of sense. For one thing, training becomes easier because everyone sees the same desktop and works with the same interface. Also, helping users with day-to-day PC-based activities and problems becomes easier because the people designated to give this help (whether or not you have an official help desk) don't have to spend the first 15–30 minutes figuring out how each user has configured the various elements of the interface.

Windows XP Professional (*not* the Home edition) contains precisely the tool you need to standardize the interface and other elements of the user experience: the Group Policy Editor. This tool enables you to assign specific properties to specific users and specific PCs, configuring them the way you want them to look and function. This chapter takes you through the process of installing the Group Policy Editor and working with it to achieve the standardization results you want.

Installing the Group Policy Editor

Before you can use the Group Policy Editor, you must install it in the Microsoft Management Console (MMC). To do so, follow these steps:

1. Click the Start button, and choose Run.

2. Type **mmc** in the Open box and press Enter to launch the Management Console.

3. Choose File → Add/Remove Snap-in.

4. On the Standalone tab of the Add/Remove Snap-in dialog box, click the Add button.

5. Scroll down the list of snap-ins until you see Group Policy (see Figure 27-1). Select it, and click the Add button.

Figure 27-1: Installing the Group Policy Editor.

6. The resulting Group Policy Wizard shows the Local Computer as the object of the Group Policy. If you want to set a Group Policy on a different computer, click the Browse button and locate the other computer on the network. This chapter assumes you want to work with the local PC, so simply click Finish.

7. With Local Computer Policy now displayed under the Standalone tab of the Add/Remove Snap-in dialog box, click OK. The Console Root window now shows the policy (or policies) you've added.

If you need to set Group Policy for more than one computer, add them at the same time by repeating the procedure starting with step 5 in this list, locating the networked PC, and clicking Add. Figure 27-2 shows the result of adding two computers to the Group Policy Editor.

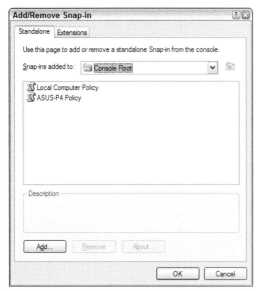

Figure 27-2: The Add/Remove Snap-in dialog box with two Group Policy objects (GPOs) added.

Configuring Policies

You can establish and revise your Group Policies either directly from the Management Console or from a separately loaded Group Policy Editor application. To open the separate editor, choose Start → Run and type **gpedit.msc** in the Open field. Press the Enter key to launch the program. The two show the same information, so we work with it in this chapter primarily because the separate editor is dedicated to Group Policy configuration only. Feel free, however, to edit Group Policies whichever way you want.

As Figure 27-3 shows, the editor is divided into three main areas: the Folders pane on the left, the Details pane on the right, and, between the two of them, the Help pane. You can get rid of the Help pane by clicking the Standard tab at the bottom of the window, but for the first set of users you'll undoubtedly find the Help pane worth leaving visible. Whenever you click on an item in the Details pane, the Help pane offers either a brief description only — when you click on a folder — or a much lengthier description — when you click on a nonfolder item. The nonfolder items are called *policies* and are phrased in a way that reflects that terminology.

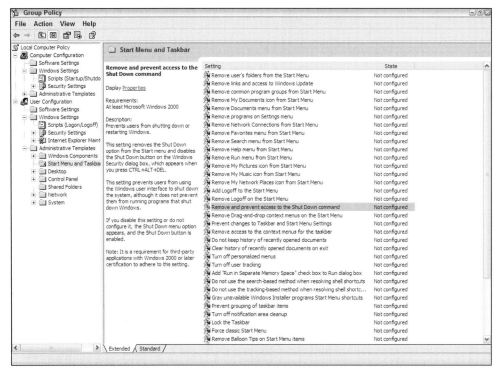

Figure 27-3: The Group Policy Editor.

Look at the example in Figure 27-3. The Remove and Prevent Access to the Shut Down Command policy located in the User Configuration\Administrative Templates\Start Menu and Taskbar folder lets you alter the Windows user interface so that clicking on the Start button no longer reveals the Turn Off Computer icon (see Figure 27-4), thereby preventing users from shutting Windows down. As the Help pane explains, setting this policy also disables the Shut Down button on the Windows Task Manager, the dialog box that appears when you press Ctrl+Alt+Delete (or select Task Manager from the menu by right-clicking the Taskbar). The full text of the Help pane shows the usefulness of the explanations, hence the suggestion to keep the pane open. Even without it being open, you can access the Help text (and in somewhat more readable form) by double-clicking on the policy and clicking the Explain button. But the Help pane works well when moving through the list policy by policy, trying to determine which one does what you want.

When you find a policy you want to configure, double-click it (or right-click and choose Properties) to open its Properties dialog box. As Figure 27-5 demonstrates, this dialog box shows the name of the policy at the top (and in the title bar) and offers the options Not Configured, Enabled, and Disabled. The bottom of the dialog box displays a field labeled Support On, which briefly outlines the Windows versions (or client software within Windows) that support this policy setting. For example, the majority of the Start menu and Taskbar policies require At least Windows 2000 while the policies in the Terminal Services folder state At least Microsoft Windows XP Terminal Services.

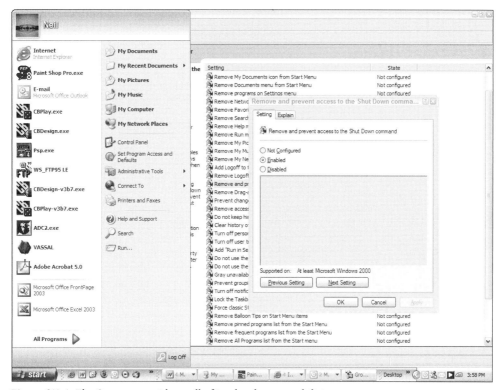

Figure 27-4: The Start menu without all of its shutdown capabilities.

Figure 27-5: A Group Policy Properties dialog box.

Configuring a policy means making changes to the Windows registry. These three options change the registry as follows:

- **Not Configured:** No changes to the registry. The option retains the default behavior as established with the initial Windows installation.

- **Enabled:** The registry changes to show that the policy has been toggled on.

- **Disabled:** The registry changes to show that the policy has been toggled off.

For many policies, those are the only possibilities. However, in numerous other cases, the Properties dialog allows additional settings, depending on the function of the feature to which it refers. In fact, you can look at the Group Policy Editor as a graphical interface that lets you dig into the registry without actually opening it and trying to figure out what goes where (the Registry Editor — regedit — can be brutally user hostile).

Figure 27-6 shows a more elaborate Properties dialog box that's designed to control the behavior of the user's PC when it disconnects, for whatever reason, from the network server on which it depends. Clicking the Enabled button gives you access to the drop-down menu in the middle window with an explanation of each choice. Other customized Properties dialog boxes in the Network window let you specify options for activity logging, determine which files and folders are always available offline, and set the number of seconds between each appearance of the balloon that reminds users about the status of offline files and folders. Again, each of these changes alters an entry in the registry.

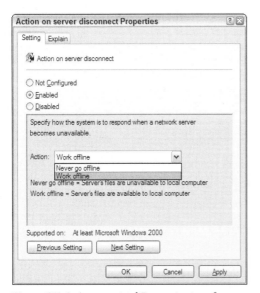

Figure 27-6: A customized Properties interface.

Still other Properties dialog boxes offer an entirely different kind of interface. Instead of the Not Configured, Enabled, and Disabled radio buttons, these interfaces give you a range of options specifically relevant to the object you want to change. To cite two typical examples, you can use the Important URLs Properties dialog box to configure the Web pages your employees will open when they click the Home button, the Search button, and the Help → Online Support menu item in their browsers (see Figure 27-7). Similarly, a customized interface appears when you open the Properties dialog box for Browser Toolbar Customizations. Here, you can customize the background image for the Internet Explorer toolbar and even add custom toolbar buttons. When you choose to add a button, a secondary dialog box appears in which you set the caption for the button as well as the script or program file defining the button's action (so that the button actually does something). You must also specify the color and grayscale icons for that button so that Internet Explorer can display the button properly.

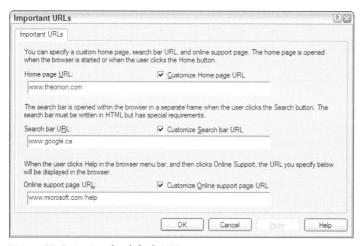

Figure 27-7: Setting the default URLs.

Understanding the Policy Hierarchy

As long as you have the administrative permissions to do so, you can configure Group Policies at any level of the network, — from the local computer all the way up to the network domain and beyond. If you have Administrator privileges for your particular machine or local network, but the machine is part of a larger network or the local network part of a domain, you will quickly find that the policy modifications you make seem to have no effect. That's not the case, in fact, but it's very true that your changes might well be temporary. Group Policy works under a specific hierarchy, and it's important to understand how this hierarchy works.

From top to bottom, the Group Policy hierarchy looks like this:

1. Organizational unit policy
2. Domain policy

3. Site policy

4. Local PC policy

In other words, the higher up the chain you set the policy, the greater the chance it has of taking effect. If you modify a policy at the domain level, every PC on that domain adheres to it, even if a conflicting policy is set on a local PC. If you set the Internet Explorer home page to one URL for all users on the local machine, for instance, and Joe in the corporate office changes that policy for the entire organizational unit, Joe's URL wins. If you change the home page after that, your changes take effect temporarily, but only until the next time the Group Policy settings are refreshed. By default, refreshes occur every 5 minutes on a domain controller and every 90 minutes on a server or work-station. In practical terms, therefore, and assuming that you have nothing better to do with your day, you can keep changing the Group Policy settings immediately after each refresh and enjoy a few minutes of boundless freedom.

This hierarchy means, quite simply, that if you want to apply a policy, you should determine the level at which you want to configure it. Practically, of course, you might not have any choice; your level of IT permission in the organization dictates what you can actually accomplish with policy modifications. Yet even if you have charge over only a small office network, you need to consider the effect of configuring a policy. Do you want a policy setting to apply to a specific machine, for example, or to all the machines on the network?

Tip

If you modify the Group Policy settings for an office network, be sure to explain to employees what they'll find different from before and how to work with the changes. Many people find any changes to their PCs discon-certing and possibly even stress-inducing; you can lessen this reaction by letting them know exactly what to expect when they log on. You might very well still get complaints (because that's what people do about com-puters), but complaints are much easier to deal with if you've already addressed those complaints in a proactive way.

Examples of Policy Configuration

Because configuring Group Policies can seem rather obscure, the remainder of this chapter consists of examples to demonstrate how policies work. Outlined in the following sections are two groups of policy changes that could fairly easily reflect viable possibilities on a PC shared by multiple users or on a small network.

Example 1: Setting Password Policies

One of the easiest and most effective forms of control you can take over the security of a PC or net-work lies in password requirements. Under the Windows Settings\Password Policy folder of the Group Policy Editor, you can configure the following settings:

■ **Enforce password history:** Sets the number of passwords that Windows remembers for each user. When changing passwords, the user cannot reuse a password before creating this number of unique passwords. This setting prevents the time-honored and security-destroying method advanced by users over the decades of switching between two passwords when the system forces a password change. The default setting is 0.

■ **Maximum password age:** Sets the maximum number of days that each new password remains in effect before it must be changed. The default setting is 42. (Honest, that's what it says! One wonders if the Microsoft programmers had the fabled computer Deep Thought in mind when designing this option.)

■ **Minimum password age:** Sets the minimum number of days that each new password remains in effect before the user can change it. This setting represents another way of defeating time-honored and security-destroying user practices, this time changing a password and then changing it right back again. The default setting is 0 (see Figure 27-8).

Figure 27-8: Setting the number of days a password may remain unchanged.

■ **Minimum password length:** Sets the minimum number of characters in each password. The number can be anything between 0 and 14, with 0 meaning that users require no password at all — obviously not a good idea. The default setting is 0.

■ **Password must meet complexity requirements:** The greatest bugaboo of computer security is still, after all the ink that's been spent on it, bad passwords. Many people use their street name, a family member's name, a pet's name, or even just their own first name because they want to make the password easy to remember. But if a password is easy for a user to remember, it's also easy for an intruder to crack. So, the Group Policy system includes a built-in password complexity feature that you can enable if you want better passwords. This policy forces users to create passwords with the following requirements. Combined with the minimum password age policy, these requirements result is passwords that are substantially more difficult to crack:

- At least six characters long

- Containing three different types of characters, chosen from four categories: numeral from 0 to 9, uppercase alphabetic character, lowercase alphabetic character, and a symbol (such as punctuation)

- Doesn't replicate all or part of the user's account name

- **Store password using reversible encryption for all users in the domain:** Reversible encryption means, in practice, no encryption at all. Unless you absolutely need plaintext passwords, avoid this policy completely.

Clearly, a password policy that includes complexity, history, and minimum and maximum aging results in a consistent use of passwords that should do their job well. Furthermore, while these policies might seem restrictive, most users fully recognize the need for strong password protection. Indeed, most also realize that they should change their passwords regularly, just as they know they should back up their data files regularly. Sometimes, it's a good idea to have computers enforcing good ideas.

Example 2: Setting Windows Explorer Policies

Through the Windows Explorer item in Group Policy Editor, users control a great deal of what goes on in their systems. It lets you configure a full range of options, and in configuring these policies you substantially alter the Windows XP interface. Policies include the following:

- **Removes the Folder Options menu item from the Tools menu:** The Folder Options dialog box offers control over many options, including displaying hidden files, turning on Simple File Sharing, and associating file types with specific programs. This policy removes the item from the Tools menu in Windows Explorer and My Computer (and indeed from any folder), and it also removes it from Control Panel window.

- **Remove the Search Button from Windows Explorer:** Deletes the Search button from the toolbar of all folders. Enabling this policy has no effect on the Search button in Internet Explorer or the Search item on the Start Menu. You can remove the latter, however, by enabling one of the policies in the Start menu and Taskbar area of the Group Policy Editor.

- **Remove Windows Explorer's default context menu:** Eliminates the menu that appears when you right-click on an object.

- **Hide these specified drives in My Computer:** Causes the icons for the specified drive combination to disappear from My Computer, Windows Explorer, and the Open and Save dialog boxes. You can still access these drives via methods such as typing the path in the Address field of an open folder. Figure 27-9 shows the dialog box for this policy.

- **Remove Security tab:** Gets rid of the Security tab from the Properties menu of an object (such as a folder or drive) in Windows Explorer or My Computer. Enabling this policy prevents users from changing security settings for that object and also from seeing the list of users with access to that object. Because the Security tab does not appear on these dialog boxes when Simple File Sharing has been toggled on, the policy has no effect in that instance.

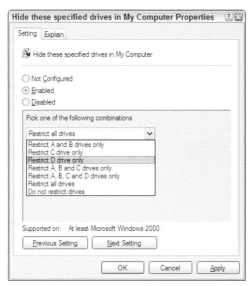

Figure 27-9: Hiding specific drive icons.

- **Remove CD burning features:** Disables the built-in CD-burning capabilities of Windows XP. However, third-party CD-burning software still works. So, if as an administrator you're trying to prevent CD burning, remember to search for additional programs as well.

- **Do not move deleted files to the Recycle Bin:** Results in the permanent removal of files instead of having them placed in the Recycle Bin when you delete them using the Delete command. As a result, delete means delete, with no way to bring them back (except for some fairly esoteric command-line utilities). You can still manually drag files to the Recycle Bin, however.

- **Items displayed in Places Bar:** Located inside the Common Open File Dialog folder, this policy lets you add items to the Places Bar in the Open and Save dialog boxes. The Places bar, located along the left side of these dialog boxes, contains shortcuts to specific resources. You can add icons pointing to folders on your local PC, to computers on the network, and to the numerous items called Common Shell Folders: for example, My Documents, My Pictures, and Program Files. Figure 27-10 shows the formlike interface for configuring these places.

Making any one of these changes alters the way in which users of your PC or network interact with Windows. Change them all, and you create significant differences. But if your company policies require specific methods of interaction, by all means make the necessary changes.

Figure 27-10: Adding to the Places bar under the Common Open File dialog.

Caution

Before making any changes to the Windows Explorer policies, run some usability tests to ensure that you don't lose in productivity what you hope to gain in security. You can run formal tests in a usability testing lab, but you can also design your own tests quite easily. A good method of testing is to determine several tasks your users typically perform and observe them on a modified PC (without assisting them) while they perform these tasks. Listen to what they have to say, and assess the policy changes accordingly. And remember that you're testing the interface, not the users; if they have trouble performing a task because their computer functions differently, don't make the common testing mistake of placing blame on the user, especially if more than one person encounters the same difficulties.

Summary

The Group Policy Editor gives you an enormous degree of control over how each user's PC functions, looks, and behaves. When combined with all other aspects of user restrictions and permissions, policies help you ensure that nobody has access to resources they shouldn't and that the resources they can access are the resources deemed appropriate by the organization. With consistent interfaces and consistent interactions, training becomes more streamlined and assistance more immediate. Of course, if you get carried away with configuring policies you also run the risk of becoming restrictive to the point of limiting the users' ability to actually get anything accomplished, so be sure to test your changes thoroughly.

Part VII

Utilities

I n this section, you take a look at some of the utilities available for working with user accounts and for increasing your account security even more than Windows does. These utilities are useful primarily for business users, but there's certainly no reason you can't use some of them on a home system if you need that additional security. However, if you're using Windows XP Home Edition, by far the most valuable single step you can take, before trying anything else, is to upgrade to XP Professional.

Password and Password Recovery Utilities

There's nothing better than having a great password, and there's nothing worse than not remembering what it was. One class of utilities helps you establish, keep track of, and transport your passwords, whereas another class gives you help in recovering passwords for your documents and email message stores.

Password Office Deluxe (www.compelson.com) is an example of a password manager program. The program helps you generate passwords that others will be highly unlikely to guess and then stores them so that you don't have to. It works with login passwords for your system, for Web forms, and for other programs as well. If offers strong encryption and Trojan protection for what it calls "secure notes," a system whereby you can store anything that requires secrecy and assign protection to it (credit card numbers are a prime example of this). You can store your passwords on a smart card or flash drive, both secured, for when you need to take them with you.

Network Password Manager (www.sowsoft.com) is another feature-rich password manager. Designed for business use, this product keeps a multiuser database of all the users on your network, helps you (and them) create effective passwords, manages the passwords for whatever network functions you choose, and offers a centralized backup feature to let you keep track of all passwords and fill-in fields for your network users. Billeo Password Manager (www.billeo.com) also keeps track of passwords, including login passwords and Web site passwords (such as banking and credit card details), protecting the data using strong encryption.

For examples of the password recovery category, you can start with Intelore (www.intelore. com). Here, you'll find a series of programs under the general name Password Recovery, one each for Word, Excel, Access, Outlook, Project, Outlook Express, and the compression utility RAR. If you've password-protected any documents in any of these programs, or email data files in the case of the two Outlooks, these utilities can recover those passwords for you. They're extremely handy for gaining access to documents you might have forgotten about, but obviously they make the password protection for these programs rather suspect. In fact, numerous password recovery programs are available for Microsoft Office products, so you can rest assured that Microsoft hasn't provided a particularly secure password environment.

Account Utilities and Biometric Solutions

Windows XP Professional has its own user and domain administration features, but once again, except for the standard user configurations, the tools lack user-friendliness. Ideal Administrator (www.pointdev.com) gathers all the Windows account and domain functions together into one interface, allowing you to add, delete, or change any configurations more easily than with XP itself. User Account Manager (www.it-direct.co.nz) lets you quickly create user accounts with specified drive shares, group membership, and more, and includes the ability to move accounts between Windows XP, NT, and 2000 servers.

One solution for controlling users and their accounts is to purchase biometric access products. These products usually work with fingerprints, although some use Webcams to take facial images and unlock Windows from there. Fingerprint solutions include a fingerprint reader of some kind, either a standalone unit on which users place their fingertips or a mouse whose button includes a fingerprint reader. As an example of the latter type of solution, American Power Conversion (APC at www.apc.com), best known for its uninterrupted power supply (UPS) solutions for business and home users, has announced the production of a biometric mouse that will determine which user is attempting to access the PC and whether to allow it. The user does not type a password (usually) but instead relies on the biometric reading to determine access validity instead.

Another fingerprint access product is Kanguru's Biometrics USB 2.0 Flash Drive (www.kanguru. com), a 256MB thumb drive that contains a fingerprint scanner with storage space for five fingerprint images. The idea is to use as much of the drive as you want (all of it, half of it, whatever) as a secure data storage device, unlocking the secure area by letting it scan and recognize your fingerprint. Microsoft offers a standalone fingerprint reader for use with all versions of Windows XP (www.windowsmarketplace.com). DigitalPersona (www.digitalpersona.com) sells a variety of biometric products for consumer and business users. Each of them works with fingerprint analysis as a means of accessing Windows user accounts.

Part VIII

Networking Your Home or Business

Chapter 28

Planning Your Network

Your Windows XP machine works very well as a standalone PC, but it begins to show its true potential when you make it part of a network. Whether that network consists of the two PCs you use at home or dozens of machines in an office, the network expands the computing experience, with shared resources providing a main focal point of computing activity from the moment the network exists.

With each successive version of Windows, connecting PCs to a network has become easier. Even so, Windows XP raises the standard considerably, to the degree that, after setting up the necessary hardware, developing a network typically takes only a few mouse clicks. Furthermore, sharing an Internet connection with Windows XP is not only easy to implement, it's also expected. This is an operating system built for networks. Even so, you can't just plug one computer into another (well, you can with an unusual cross-over cable); networks involve more than that.

This chapter outlines the major considerations in planning a small network. Chapter 29 covers the various methods of establishing that network. By the time you've finished both chapters, you'll have a good grasp of what a network entails, what to do with one, and how to set one up.

Why Plan?

Many Windows networks, especially in small offices and many homes, undergo almost no planning at all. People buy new computers as needed, using them as independent workstations until the realities of sharing files, printers, and the Internet kick in. Then someone figures out that everyone could work more efficiently if they combined their computers into a network, to share printers, an Internet connection, and files such as those for photos and music. So the hookups begin. Within a short while, the network is in place, with everybody more or less trained on at least a few of the functions networking provides.

Even a small network can benefit from planning, however. By determining in advance the elements you need, you also figure out what you might not need. For example, perhaps you have decided that you do not need wireless network access. But in observing your employees, you discover that they frequently hold impromptu design sessions with their laptop computers in the lunchroom. So, you might want to reconsider your decision, providing wireless access as a way to encourage this type of productive impromptu meeting. Similarly, perhaps you currently have small printers for each employee. But in observing them, you find that only two or three people use their printers extensively. So, you might consider setting up a single networked printer for the others to share.

Peer-to-Peer versus Client-Server Networks

When planning a network, you must first decide which basic type of network you want: peer-to-peer or client-server. The difference, as the names suggest, lies in the relationships among the network's machines.

On a *client-server network*, at least one of the computers acts as a central resource, making programs and data available to the other machines on the network. These machines are called *servers*, with the connected workstations called *clients*. Clients have the power and capabilities necessary to provide their users with their many computing needs, while the server stores and delivers data and other resources, such as programs themselves, to the client machines. A client requests information from a server, and if the client possesses the proper authorization to receive that information, the server fulfills it. A client-server network requires a network operating system (NOS) to provide *services* such as file sharing, email, and telecommunications. Windows XP Professional has certain server capabilities, but businesses and organizations typically use Windows 2000 Server or the more recently introduced Windows Server 2003 as the Windows server OS. Many organizations, indeed, go outside the Windows family entirely for their server needs, preferring Linux or Unix. The Internet is the biggest client-server network, largely founded on Unix.

A *peer-to-peer network* considers all machines as equals — that is, *peers* — with no central computer operating as a server. Workstations (no longer called clients) connect directly to other workstations, at varying levels of security, to exchange information. Windows XP offers extensive built-in peer-to-peer networking features, and this chapter assumes that you want to create a peer-to-peer network.

A peer-to-peer network works well in homes, in small offices, and as a subnetwork in larger settings. It functions primarily as a means of sharing specific resources, particularly Internet connections, files, and printers. People can collaborate on documents by storing them in a single location on the network rather than on their own local hard drives, and they can all use a printer connected either to one of the peers or, in the case of Ethernet-equipped printers, directly to the network itself (making the printer yet another peer despite its limited capabilities). In addition, all peers on the network can share a single Internet connection, preferably by using a router in order to track which machines initiate requests for data and route the data to the correct PC. Whether you only have dial-up access in a home network, or an ultra-high-speed dedicated Internet connection in a larger office network, you share the connection in much the same way.

Furthermore, although a peer-to-peer network has no server, you can improve the security, manageability, and efficiency of resource sharing by casting one of the peers in a serverlike role. If you have a little-used machine, perhaps one less powerful than the others but that still supports a Windows XP installation (even a 500 MHz Celeron processor will do so in a pinch), why not put it in an out-of-the-way location (preferably a locked room), clean off its hard drives, and configure it to store files to be shared among the other peers? You can connect the primary printer to it and share it as well. You might even consider buying a large hard drive for it (160MB or so) and using it as the networked backup store. Technically, the machine remains a peer, rather than a server, but for all intents and purposes it functions as a server. (See Chapter 29 for details on setting up a peer-to-peer local area network — LAN).

Next, you look at different technologies for connecting machine to a network. As you read on, keep in mind that much of the discussion applies to either client-server or peer-to-peer networks.

Ethernet Networks

Most wired LANS (still the most common network type) use the tried-and-true technology known as *Ethernet*. Now approaching its 33-year anniversary, Ethernet has developed into a high-speed, ubiquitous network architecture that provides endless flexibility and easy connectivity. Part of the reason for its success has been its inclusion as a primary network type in all operating systems, with even consumer level OSs such as Windows 95 and low-end Macintoshes supporting Ethernet right out of the box. Today, virtually all PCs ship with built-in Ethernet ports, ready for connection to an Ethernet LAN.

A number of speeds of Ethernet connectivity (measured in megabits per second — Mbps) are available today. The following are the most common. Over three decades, Ethernet has gotten markedly faster. Three speeds are common today. Many devices support more than one of these speeds:

- **10 Mbps (10Base-T):** The original Ethernet, and still the maximum speed for Internet connections except for the most expensive high-speed variety. If you have a 10-Mbps Ethernet card in your PC and you upgrade to a 100-Mbps version, you will notice no difference in the speed of data transfer over the Internet.

- **100 Mbps (100Base-T):** The most popular speed for office LANs. It is often combined on a single card with 10Base-T, resulting in the designation 10/100.

- **1000 Mbps (Gigabit Ethernet):** The most recent, widely available enhancement to Ethernet, providing 1GB per second transfer speeds. With prices for Gigabit Ethernet cards coming down, you might even consider building your network such that all PCs have one, although for most networks 100-Mbps Ethernet remains more than sufficient. At this speed, however, the PC itself becomes a bottleneck because the card can take data faster than the PC can provide it.

Chapter 30 provides details on setting up an Ethernet-based network.

Wired versus Wireless Networks

While wired networks remain the most common type of network, particularly within organizations, wireless networks have grown rapidly and show no signs of slowing down. With two protocols in widespread use — 802.11b and 802.11g — and another out there making itself known — 802.11a — wireless networking, or Wi-Fi as it's commonly called, promises in the near future to change the way we all do our Internet work. Having no wires means having mobility, and for the computer industry at this stage in its history, mobility is one of the biggest buzzwords of all.

Following are a few facts about wired versus wireless networks:

- Wired network connections represent the fastest possible means of transferring data from one computer to another. At some point in the future, after physical connections reach their theoretical limits for performing data transfer functions, wireless connections might catch up, but for now, the difference in speed remains profound.

- On a small peer-to-peer network, and even on many larger ones, few activities actually require the speeds available with even a 100-Mbps network card, let alone the capabilities of today's Gigabit Ethernet speeds. Except when transferring extremely large files, few users will notice the difference between a wired and wireless network.

- Wireless networks offer the convenience of mobility, untethering employees and home users from their desks and enabling them to take their notebook PCs into any room for any purpose. Furthermore, with a wireless network, you eliminate the aggravation of stringing, hiding, and replacing wires, a special convenience in a home office or an office in an older building.

- Wired networks offer much greater reliability than wireless networks because wires connect more consistently and lose connections less frequently than wireless systems. Furthermore, wireless appliances do not interfere with a wired signal. Wires can be fairly easily located above a false ceiling, which also provides benefits in soundproofing in an open concept office.

- Wireless networks pose a greater security concern because information is being broadcast over the air. It is far easier to tap into a wireless network undetected than into a wired one; people often do this just to use someone else's Internet connection. Unfortunately, to make wireless devices easier to connect, default settings are often the least secure.

Unquestionably, wireless networks have gained glory recently, with coffee shops and burger joints (okay, restaurants) offering Wi-Fi access to customers who want to eat, drink, and get on the Internet all at the same time. Many university campuses have installed an array of wireless networks to let students access the Internet while doing research in an empty classroom or the library (and apparently for engaging in instant messaging sessions with their friends during lectures). Corporations have begun to espouse wireless networks as a means of providing always-on, always-available Internet access to employees in any office or conference room and even to clients waiting in the foyer. And wireless networks have become popular in home networks as well, getting rid of that unsightly cable hanging out the back of the laptop computer in the family room and allowing, finally, even the deck and the bathroom to become places of work.

Windows XP offers built-in support for wireless networking. Most wireless network adapters released today automatically interact with the operating system, allowing Windows to search the airwaves for available networks using the IEEE 802.11b or 802.11g protocols. If it finds the necessary signal, it connects to the network immediately, establishing itself as a client in an infrastructure network or a peer in an ad-hoc network.

Ad-Hoc Networks (Peer-to-Peer)

If you want a simple, effective, and quickly assembled wireless network, an *ad-hoc network* should do the trick. To build one, you need a minimum of two computers, each with a wireless network adapter in the form of a PC card for your notebook, a PCI card for your desktop machine, or a USB device that works with either (USB is probably the easiest option).

Note

Some network adapter Properties dialogs term ad-hoc networks *peer-to-peer*. Technically correct, the term nevertheless suffers from being indistinguishable from the prevailing uses of the term *peer-to-peer* in traditionally describing non-server–based wired networking, and more recently to describe non-server–based Internet connectivity.

Ad-hoc wireless networks appeal for two main reasons: they cost less than a network with an access point, and they can be set up quickly and easily. By contrast, they have two significant disadvantages: the inability to connect to a larger wired network and a greater difficulty in sharing an Internet connection. This latter difficulty is a function of the Internet Connection Sharing features built into Windows XP. Although ad-hoc networks are not overly challenging to set up, they don't come close to the ease of setting up a cable/DSL router or an access point (the details of which are covered in the next chapter), nor do they have the later convenience that comes with such a setup.

As with all wireless networking connections, getting an ad-hoc network functioning depends on how you configure the settings. Follow these steps to configure the network successfully:

1. Open Network Connections from the Start menu or from My Computer.

2. Click the link on the left of the window to view your network connections.

3. Right-click the icon for the wireless network adapter, and select Properties.

4. In the resulting Wireless Network Connections Properties dialog box, click the Advanced tab.

5. If it is selected, clear the Automatically Connect to Non-Preferred Networks check box to tell Windows to connect only to the ad-hoc network instead of any available infrastructure networks.

6. Click the Wireless Networks tab, and click the Add button.

7. In the resulting Wireless Network Properties box, type a name for your network in the Network Name (SSID, for Service Set IDentifier) field. Click OK.

8. The new network (labeled with your chosen SSID) now appears in the Available Networks window.

9. Install a wireless adapter in the second PC, and open the same Wireless Network Connection Properties dialog box.

10. In the Available Networks window, click the icon for the newly created network, and click OK. The two PCs are now connected to one another.

Note

Different wireless adapters have different properties and settings dialog boxes. If you have trouble connecting, make sure the SSID names are identical, and also look in the configuration dialogs for a channel number setting. Set the channels on all connecting PCs to the same number to allow them to connect.

Infrastructure Networks (Access Point)

Infrastructure networks differ from ad-hoc networks in one crucial respect: the inclusion of an access point. *Access points* do what the name says: they provide a point of access for all PCs connecting to the wireless network. As long as you have a wireless adapter installed in your PC, you need only configure it to see the access point and then you can connect to that network. Windows XP configures some wireless adapters automatically to find access points. But if you have a wireless adapter that does not use these automatic configuration features, you just need to set the SSID and channel numbers to match the access point and you can connect immediately.

Access points provide numerous benefits:

- Access points can communicate with other access points, so you can daisy-chain them together for greater wireless range.

- Access points can bridge with wired networks to provide you with access to both (see the next section).

- Access points can remain powered on at all times, allowing you to connect whenever you want. By comparison, if you turn off the host machine in an ad-hoc network, the network ceases to exist until you turn it back on.

- Access points are frequently built into Ethernet routers to provide both a multi-PC wired connector and a wireless station.

- Access points can share an Internet connection with all wireless adapters attached to it without requiring the setup of the Internet Connection Sharing feature of Windows XP.

- Access points give you built-in encryption technology, helping you make your wireless network as secure as possible.

The only disadvantages of access points are the cost — they add at least an extra $100 or more to even a small network's cost — and, in some cases, the difficulty in configuration and management. Typically, you configure an access point through a browser-based utility such as the one shown in Figure 28-1. At times it becomes difficult to access the settings, at which point you might need to reset the access point and start the setup all over again. As access points develop, though, these inconveniences become increasingly rare. Even more importantly, if you have any concerns about security (which you should) and expandability (which you will), then by all means go for a network based on access points.

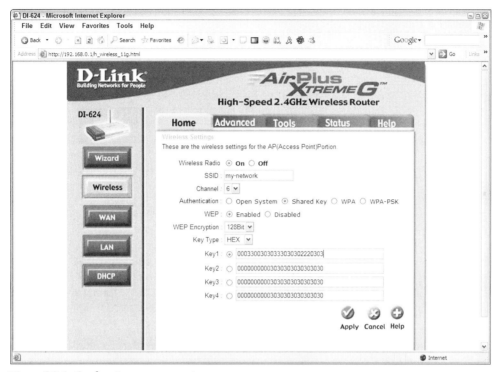

Figure 28-1: Configuring an access point.

Dealing with interference

One problem confronting wireless networking is the possibility of radio interference. Because 802.11b and 802.11g operate in the 2.4 GHz frequency range, the same range as microwave ovens, many cordless phones, and other wireless devices (such as remote video transmitters), interference can and does happen. To minimize interference, however, Wi-Fi uses a technology known as Direct Sequence Spread Spectrum (DSSS), which spreads the signal across 30 MHz of the 2.4-GHz range. In practical terms, this means you have 11 channels to work with, and by carefully setting your channels you can cut the vast majority of interference. If you set two or more access points near one another, however, you should try to spread out their channels, setting them at least five channels apart to avoid interference. For example, you could set one access point to channel 11 and the second to channel 3.

You can further avoid interference by using 802.11a, which operates in the 5-GHz frequency. But this protocol is rapidly losing ground to 802.11g.

When you have your wireless network up and running, the crucial element becomes the strength of the signal. The properties or settings dialog boxes of all wireless adapters show the quality of the setting; even at low setting, the network tends to work at least close to the same speed as at high setting. You can lose the setting completely, though, if something blocks the signal, and these blockages can come from items ranging from walls and ceilings to books, coffee mugs, and even people. As you set up your network, experiment with both the placement of the access points and the settings of the antennae for the best possible signals you can achieve. And try to minimize the number of floors between the access points and the network adapters. You'll also have to work the signal around concrete walls, office partitions, and other similar blockages.

Hybrid Wired/Wireless Networks

Despite the growth of wireless networking in small offices, large offices, and homes alike, the movement is toward hybrid networks, with both wired and wireless doing their parts. As a rule , you should wire the desktop PCs, while providing both wired and wireless options for notebook PCs. You'll find many router/access point combination units on the market today that provide a bridged hybrid network with very little hassle, and for most users such devices are definitely the way to go.

You have two ways to create a hybrid wired/wireless network. Most commonly, you begin with the wired LAN and connect a wireless component to it. Alternatively, you can begin with a wireless LAN and connect Ethernet-enabled devices to it. From the standpoint of Windows XP, the only thing that matters is the existence of the LAN itself. A Windows XP machine makes no distinction between the types of network adapter (except, of course, for the technology it uses to make each one work); it sees only that it is part of a network and can take advantage of the networking features built into the operating system. The advantages one network type has over another network type have nothing to do with how Windows XP uses the network, nor can Windows XP compensate, in any great part, for whatever disadvantages either network type brings with it. For example, 802.11x networks are famous for suffering from security problems, but Windows XP does not compensate for those problems specifically. You can create complex passwords and develop access restrictions, and you can load the Internet Connection Firewall on each Windows XP machine, but those features can apply to any network and, indeed, to standalone Windows PCs as well. To Windows XP, a network is a network is a network.

Whether you begin with a wired or a wireless network (and again purely apart from Windows XP itself), you need a mechanism that allows the two network types to communicate with one another. Specifically, you need a network bridge. If you're setting up a small office network or a home network, you're in luck: Practically all available cable or DSL routers that you'll likely use to share your Internet connection contain bridging software. If you plan to build a larger network, you might need a separate hardware bridge to go with a hardware switch, but the principle is the same. The bridging software recognizes the existence of the two network types and bridges them together so that data from one network can travel along the other, all without the user being aware of any of it. Windows XP displays the network bridge in the Network Connections window, as shown in Figure 28-2.

You can also manually bridge two network adapters together in Windows XP by highlighting the two connections in the Network Connections window, right-clicking, and choosing Bridge Connections. Once these connections are in place, you can add still more adapters by right-clicking on their icons and choosing Add to Bridge. The Windows XP network bridge ties all networks together in a single logical network, allowing them all to talk to one another. Typically, however, connecting a wireless and wired network through a router creates the bridge for you, so you need to use the manual bridging feature only if you want to connect two networks that do not automatically see each other.

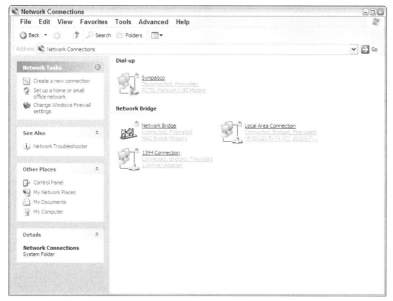

Figure 28-2: The network bridge appears at the bottom of the window.

Summary

With the network planned and the hardware in place, you need only to connect the PCs to make it work. Chapter 29 looks at the details of getting the PCs working together to share information and resources.

Even with your network up and running, however, you'll probably find it necessary to continue planning. If you need to add PCs to the network, for example, use that occasion as a reason to reconsider the entire network, adding routers and access points to accommodate even further growth. Think about upgrading network printers, fax devices, and other shared equipment as new technologies emerge that suit your particular needs. As your need for shared resources grows, so will your network.

Chapter 29

Connecting Your PCs in a Small Workgroup

C hapter 28 covered network basics and the planning of networks. This chapter steps you through the process of connecting PCs through a small workgroup. The process begins with a single Windows XP desktop PC and a direct Internet connection and ends with two Windows XP machines sharing a broadband Internet connection, a shared documents folder, and a printer — all across a hybrid wired/wireless network with the capacity for extensive expansion. The wonderful thing about networks, after all, is that once you've established them, you can just keep adding to them; and Windows XP makes it remarkably easy to do so.

Beginnings: A PC and an Internet Connection

This chapter takes you through a scenario. In it, you're the owner of a one-person business, which (because it's you, of course) begins to succeed to the point where you have to add one employee, then another, and so on. This discussion is just as relevant to a home with different machines in various rooms.

You start out with a single computer that connects to the Internet through a DSL or Cable broadband connection. As the sole employee of the business, you need nothing besides your PC and Internet connection. You conduct business primarily from your two-room office and meet your clients at their locations rather than your own. But then your business picks up, and you hire your first employee. This person, too, requires a PC with an Internet connection. You decide to buy a notebook, to save room and to provide the greatest possible flexibility.

The desktop PC has an internal Ethernet card (sometimes called a NIC, network interface card), with a category-5 Ethernet cable running from the Ethernet port on the network adapter to the Ethernet port on the DSL modem. The notebook sports a built-in Ethernet adapter, and your first idea is to share the Internet connection between the two PCs using the Internet Connection Sharing system built into Windows XP. You do your homework, however, and realize that you will achieve better expandability and numerous other conveniences by purchasing a four-port cable/DSL router that will let you connect the two PCs in a LAN and share the Internet connection seamlessly. The greatest single benefit of the router at this stage in the growth of the network is that you don't have to leave your PC turned on for your employee to have access to the Internet. With the Internet Connection Sharing feature and without the router, this is precisely what you would have to do.

Expansion 1: The Broadband Router with Access Point

Broadband routers, also called cable/DSL routers, come in several shapes and sizes. Among the most popular configurations are:

- Four 10-Mbps Ethernet ports

- Four 10/100-Mbps Ethernet ports

- Four Gigabit Ethernet ports

- One 10-Mbps Ethernet port and an 802.11b access point

- One 10/100-Mbps Ethernet port and an 802.11b access point

- One 10/100-Mbps Ethernet port and an 802.11g access point

- Four 10/100 Ethernet ports and an 802.11b access point

- Four 10/100 Ethernet ports and an 802.11g access point

Other configurations exist as well. As Ethernet has gotten faster, Gigabit Ethernet capabilities have become more popular. And as wireless technology has improved, the venerable 802.11b has begun to fade away. The point here, for your business, is that you need to make a choice between a cable/DSL router with an access point or without. If you can afford the few extra dollars for the access point, by all means get it. You don't lose any wired capabilities (unless you choose an access point with only one port), and you gain the capability, either now or in the future, to add wireless devices to your network. These devices can include notebook PCs, PDAs, 802.11x-enabled telephones, and even game consoles.

Even with some exceptionally good bargains on four-port routers without access points, you decide to plan for expansion and spring for a router with four 10/100-Mbps Ethernet ports and an 802.11g access point. Even if you could find an 802.11b version, there's no point bothering with it. 802.11g has become the standard (besides, g supports older b devices, if any turn up).

For various reasons, you decide to go with the well-known LinkSys brand name, purchasing their AirPlus Xtreme High-Speed DI-624 wireless router. Like numerous other products from other reputable companies, the DI-624 gives you the Ethernet and Wi-Fi connectivity you need for the network. Then, because you got a good deal, you purchase a Microsoft MN-720 Wireless Notebook Adapter. This card gives you 802.11g wireless connections at a good price.

With new products in hand for under a couple of hundred dollars, you're ready to give the connections a go.

Connecting the Router to the PC

The DI-624 comes with a series of cables. Your first step is to plug the power cord into the unit and into the wall receptacle. Next, plug one end of the included Ethernet cable into the Ethernet port on the DI-624 and the other end into the Ethernet card of the PC. The cable from the DSL modem already occupies that port, however, so unplug it first. With the router/access point now connected to the Ethernet card, plug the original cable from the DSL modem into the port on the router marked WAN (short for wide area network).

Tip

The port into which you plug the Ethernet cable from the broadband modem goes by several different names, depending on the router manufacturer's preference. Typical examples include Cable/DSL, Broadband, and To Modem.

With the router powered on and connected to the PC, it's time to test the connection by opening the configuration utility. Doing so requires a Web browser and the IP address of the router itself. The router's manual includes the IP address needed to access the utility, but to make sure that you have access to this information whenever you need it, write it down elsewhere (on paper) and also store it in a text file on your PC. Once past the first two components of the IP number, always 192.168 to designate locally reserved IPs, the remainder of the four-part number differs from manufacturer to manufacturer. Some routers use the address 192.168.1.1, others 192.168.2.1. Some insist on a significantly more esoteric number altogether. D-Link uses 192.168.0.1 for its broadband routers, and this is the one you type now (the http:// prefix can be omitted, but even today browsers sometimes respond with it more quickly if you include it).

Figure 29-1 shows the opening screen of the DI-624 configuration interface. As with all such tools, the first task is to type a username and password. A router always has a default password (Linksys routers sensibly use **admin** for their default), but for the sake of security you should always create one for yourself. These things can be hacked.

The router installation has passed the first test. Because the configuration pages appeared, the PC and the router have established communication. On to the Internet.

Connecting to the Internet

Connecting to the Internet through a broadband router might require no additional actions. By default, manufacturers set their routers to obtain an IP address automatically from the Internet service provider (ISP), by far the most common configuration with commercial ISPs today. If you connect through a cable modem, in fact, you have a very good chance of already being on the Internet because cable ISPs typically forgo any special configuration, including a username and password. DSL providers, however, use a protocol called Point-to-Point Protocol over Ethernet (PPPoE), which almost always requires authentication.

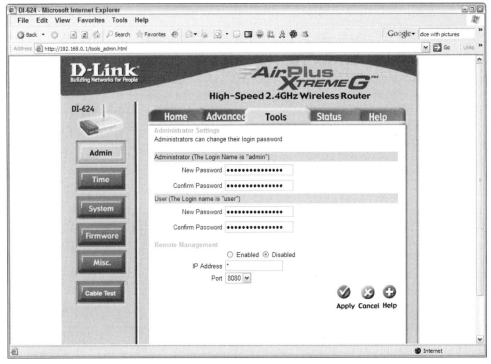

Figure 29-1: The password screen of the configuration screen.

To connect to the Internet, configure your router as follows:

1. Locate the Internet connection settings section or page on your router's configuration pages.

2. For cable modems, choose the Dynamic IP option to receive an IP address from the ISP. For DSL modems, choose the PPPoE option because you need to connect to the ISP servers using a username and password.

3. If your ISP requires a Host or Service name, enter that name in the appropriate location on the configuration screen. If you're not sure, leave this blank.

4. If you connect via DSL, fill in the username and password in the appropriate fields. You can also typically set the number of seconds of idle time allowed before automatic disconnection and whether or not you want the router to connect on demand — that is, as soon as it sees a request for the Internet.

5. If you connect via DSL, locate the Connect button and click it to make sure that it will perform the connection.

6. With the configuration utility still open, launch another browser window and navigate the Web. In addition, check your email. If everything works, close the configuration utility, saving the settings.

Tip

Despite the recent proliferation of broadband routers, many cable and DSL service providers refuse to provide technical assistance for their users when they connect through one of these devices. If you have trouble with your Internet connection, you should disconnect the router and plug the broadband modem directly into the PC as it was before and attempt a connection before calling the ISP.

Figure 29-2 shows the completed configuration screen for the Wide Area Networking settings of the DI-624 configuration interface, complete with the necessary PPPoE settings.

After you've connected to the Internet, go back to the information page and examine your Internet settings. You'll notice two things. First, the router has acquired an IP number from the ISP. Second, your PC has a local IP address provided by the router's built-in DHCP server (see Figure 29-3). The Dynamic Host Configuration Protocol takes a single IP number from an ISP and shares this number among all the devices connected to the router. DHCP provides the basis of Internet Connection Sharing built into Windows XP, and the same technology allows you to share a single Internet connection among several computers from a router as well. The magic of Internet Connection Sharing lies in the ability of the DHCP server to keep track of which machine made each request so that the response can find its way to the originating PC.

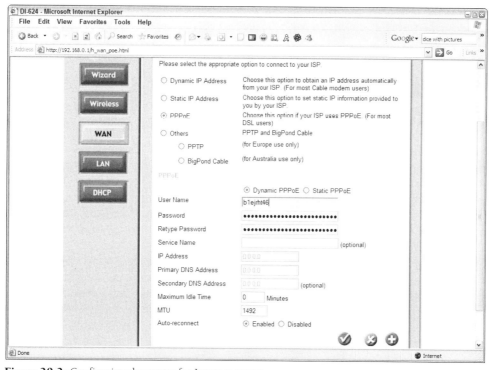

Figure 29-2: Configuring the router for Internet access.

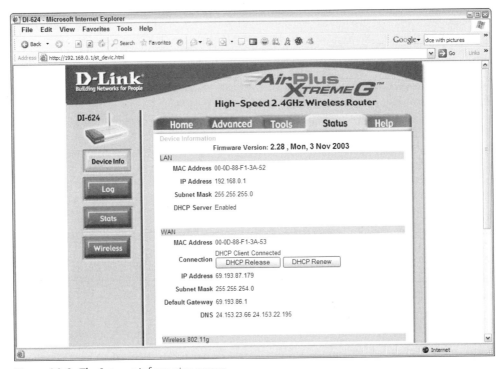

Figure 29-3: The Internet information screen.

Expansion 2: The Notebook PC with Wireless Adapter

Now that you have successfully connected to the Internet, it's time to turn your attention to the wireless portion of your network. You slide the Microsoft adapter into the PC Card slot on the side of the notebook PC and install the software driver as instructed. You now need to configure the wireless adapter so that it communicates with the DI-624 access point. Opening the configuration utility again, click the Wireless menu item and notice that the access point uses a default channel of 6. Give your wireless network the name (SSID) **unwired** (any name will suffice), as shown in Figure 29-4, and click Apply to set this configuration in place.

After you establish the wireless settings on the router, you must configure all wireless network adapters to show the same SSID and channel number. Windows XP takes control of an increasing number of wireless adapters and can, therefore, see access points automatically. But some cards, including brand-new ones and several older models, contain their own configuration utility. Referring to the product manual, change your card's settings to match your access point, restarting Windows if necessary to get the data communication flowing.

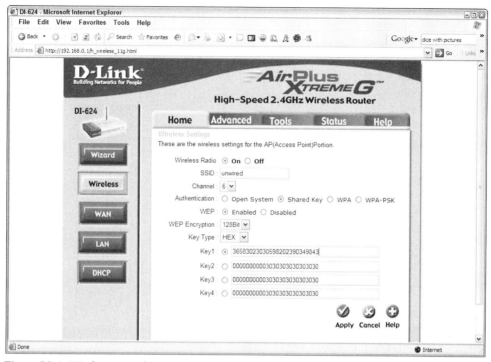

Figure 29-4: Wireless network settings.

Tip

You can tell in two different ways when you've successfully established communication between the wireless adapter and the access point. First, you should be able to access the Internet from the PC on which you've installed the wireless adapter. Second, you should be able to call up the router's configuration screens. If you can do the latter but not the former, recheck your Internet connections.

Creating the LAN

You now have two PCs sharing an Internet connection, but so far they can't see each other. To create the local area network itself, you need to open the My Network Places folder and click the link to set up a home or small office network.

The resulting Network Setup Wizard takes much of the traditional pain out of establishing a small LAN. You need to make several decisions as you work through this LAN, but by the time you finish, the PCs can see each other, and mutually shared folders are in place and ready for use.

Click Next on the wizard until you reach the third screen, where you decide whether to share the Internet connection. Check the default radio button (Yes), and click Next again. The next screen asks if you want Windows to determine the appropriate network connections. Here, too, the answer should be Yes unless you have a reason to disallow specific network bridging processes from occurring. Typically, you want all available connections bridged on a small LAN. On the subsequent screen, type a description for your PC and verify the computer name; then click Next and choose a name for the workgroup. HOME or OFFICE are the names that Microsoft suggests here, but like the computer description on the previous screen, this name can be whatever you want.

Figure 29-5 shows the final stage of the wizard, a summation of all the choices. Click Next to begin the process of creating the network. When you've finished, open My Network Places to see if you can see the other PCs on the LAN. Then open My Network Places on each PC and determine if they can see your PC as well. If not, run the Network Setup Wizard on each PC until all computers can see each other.

Figure 29-5: The Network Setup Wizard is ready to initiate the LAN.

Tip

After creating the network, the wizard asks if you want to create a network diskette. If you plan to include any Windows 95, Windows 98, or Windows Millennium Edition PCs on your network, create the diskette and run the setup wizard as instructed on those PCs. Earlier versions of Windows need this help to partake in a Windows XP network.

Sharing Resources on the Network

When you establish a network using Windows XP, Windows automatically creates a shared resource for each connected machine. The Shared Documents folder becomes available to each computer on the LAN, with each renamed SharedDocs with a reference to the PC on which it resides. The easiest and safest way to share files is to copy them into this folder so that everyone else can get at them.

To take advantage of this LAN, you'll want to share folders, even printers, for other LAN members to use. You can even share entire hard drives, but Windows XP warns you against it when you open the Sharing tab of the Properties dialog box for that drive. A successful network shares a limited number of resources from PC to PC. As the network grows, it further restricts certain resources to specific users. See Chapter 25 for details on granting access permissions.

Caution

Sharing files and folders can cause problems if those resources contain sensitive data. Part of planning your network consists of deciding precisely what you can safely share and, for each resource, which users can safely share it. Some folders can safely be shared among all network users, while you might grant access for another folder to only two people. For details on sharing resources on both a single PC and over the network, see Chapter 25.

The final task for this small network lies in sharing a printer among the PCs. Open the Printers and Faxes folder on the PC to which the printer is attached. Right-click the printer's icon and choose Sharing. A Properties dialog box opens with a Sharing tab. Click the radio button labeled Share This Printer, and give the printer a recognizable name (or use the name Windows supplies). Click OK to share the printer across the LAN. Before doing so, if your network contains PCs running other versions of Windows besides Windows XP, click the Additional Drivers button and select the operating system for which you want to install drivers (see Figure 29-6).

Figure 29-6: Adding drivers to a shared printer.

You can wait for your shared printer to be discovered by the network (it takes awhile) or you can go to other computers on the network and use Add a Printer. Use the network printer option. Finally, print a document or a test page from each of the PCs sharing the printer to make sure that the printer works from each one.

Summary

Peer-to-peer networks form the backbone of many small businesses and also add valuable convenience and enhanced productivity for home users. Although not especially difficult to set up, creating a peer-to-peer network may require both patience and careful attention to details. You want to ensure that you share folders and so forth properly, maintaining security while aiding the activities of users working with the various resources on the network. A peer-to-peer network can save you money by letting you share hardware such as printers, backup drives, and Internet connections, and it can save you aggravation by letting users gain access to a document or other resource without having to sit down at another PC and work from there. Using the Internet-sharing capabilities of a router, the wireless capabilities of an access point in conjunction with Windows XP, and the ease of LAN creation provided by the Network Setup Wizard, you can have a fully functioning hybrid wired/wireless LAN up and running in only a short time.

Chapter 30

Using Windows XP as an Internet Server

Windows XP contains several built-in Internet server functions. Although you won't want to bet your company's future on using Windows XP as your primary server environment, you can most certainly configure this OS as a decent low-level server for specific purposes, including one major function: hosting Web sites. To build a full Internet server environment, you should look to Windows Server 2003 or the Small Business Server 2003. But for small office and home office use, as well as for developmental and experimental purposes, Windows XP works well.

Windows XP includes two server types of particular interest for these purposes: File Transfer services (FTP) and Web services (HTTP, HyperText Transfer Protocol). These FTP and HTTP services (known to some as daemons, from Unix) provide the highly useful services of hosting downloading (and uploading) sites and Web sites. This chapter focuses on installing and configuring these two server types.

What is a Server?

In the computing world, two major types of networking dominate: peer-to-peer and client-server. You can tell the difference between the two by their names. In a peer-to-peer network, each computer has equal status; each computer makes requests of other computers and has requests made of it. The much-discussed MP3 file-sharing systems, such as Kazaa and Morpheus, as well as fascinating projects such as the extraterrestrial life-seeking SETI home initiative, work with peer-to-peer architectures. By contrast, the World Wide Web, like the vast majority of Internet technologies, operates as a client-server architecture. In a client-server arrangement, one computer contains data that it makes available to computers that connect to it and request that data. The computer with the data is the *server*; the computers connecting to it are the *clients*.

A simple restaurant analogy might help make this point. When you take your family to a restaurant, you are the clients. The person who comes to your table to take your order and then brings you your food is the server (waiters and waitresses in traditional terminology). The clients make requests of the server who processes the request, and, a few minutes or a couple hours later (depending on how posh the restaurant is), delivers the food. Each server serves a relatively defined number of clients. In a large restaurant, several servers are at work, each serving a certain number of clients.

Continued

What is a Server? *(Continued)*

The PC from which you connect to the Internet is called a *client*. The programs you use to do most of your useful tasks on the Internet are called *client software*, or just *clients*. Clients on your PC include your Web browser (Internet Explorer, Netscape Navigator, Opera, and so on), your email program (Outlook, Outlook Express, Netscape Mail, Eudora), your newsreader (Agent, Outlook Express, Netscape Mail,), and your FTP program (WS-FTP, AbsoluteFTP, CuteFTP), among others.

The salient feature about a client is that, to be functional, it must connect to a *server*. In the case of client PCs, they connect, along with other client PCs, to a server computer. Similarly, your software clients need software servers. Every time you use your client software to interact with the Internet, you send a request to the corresponding server software and wait for the server to respond. Clicking on a hyperlink in your browser sends a request to a computer running *Web server* software — more precisely, software that can read and respond to requests with the HTTP protocol). Pressing the Send/Receive button in Outlook and Outlook Express sends two types of requests to a computer running *mail server* software — or, more precisely again, software that can respond to requests issued through the POP3 (Post Office Protocol 3) (or IMAP [Internet Message Access Protocol]) and SMTP (Simple Mail Transfer Protocol) protocols. FTP clients use the FTP protocol, news readers use the NNTP (Network News Transfer Protocol) protocol, and so on, to accomplish data transactions in much the same fundamental way: The client requests, the server responds, ad infinitum.

P2P has drawn attention precisely because it doesn't work this way: It eliminates the *server* from the data transfer process. On first consideration, you might conclude that, because P2P gets rid of the server portion of the client-server-client relationship, it could have been called client-to-client, or C2C. But in computer networking lingo you can't have a client without a server, so the equally traditional peer-to-peer terminology kicked in. Peer-to-peer networking has been part of the personal computer since pretty well its beginnings, with the term meaning, in essence, two or more computers linked together for the purpose of sharing data. Your home network is probably a peer-to-peer network, with no server needed to send information between them.

Note

To use Windows XP as a server with Microsoft's own server software, you need Windows XP Professional, not Windows XP Home Edition. You can purchase server software for other Windows environments (as well as for Windows XP) from third-party vendors.

Installing and Starting FTP and Web Services

To use Windows XP as a server, you must install the server software. Microsoft calls its Web server software Internet Information Services (IIS), and it includes both HTTP and FTP servers. For this procedure, you need your Windows XP installation CD (or access to the installation files, if you copied them to your hard drive).

1. Place the Windows XP installation CD in your CD-ROM drive.

2. When the Welcome screen appears, click the Install Optional Windows Components link. If the Welcome screen does not automatically appear, open My Computer or Windows Explorer, navigate to the CD-ROM drive, and double-click the Setup icon.

3. In the Windows components dialog box (shown in Figure 30-1), click the check box beside Internet Information Services.

4. With Internet Information Services highlighted, click the Details button. In the resulting Internet Information Services dialog box (also shown in Figure 30-1), check the box beside File Transfer Protocol (FTP) Services. World Wide Web Service (HTTP) should be checked. You can probably uncheck SMTP (used for mail services; this will not affect your email program). Leave all other boxes as they are by default. Click OK to exit this dialog box.

5. Click Next to begin the installation. By checking the FTP box, you install both the FTP and Web server software at the same time.

Figure 30-1: The Windows components dialog box and the IIS dialog box.

Starting and Stopping the Services

A service must be started in order to work. By default, IIS and the FTP service start as soon as you install them, but you have full control over this process if you want from that point on. To configure your services, open the Services utility, accessible via the Administrative Tools folder in the Start menu (which is visible only if you have configured the Start menu settings to display it) or via the Control Panel. To open the utility via the Control Panel, open the Control Panel, double-click the Performance and Maintenance icon, and then double-click Administrative Tools. Launch the Services utility from the resulting window (Winlogo+R, **compmgmt.msc**).

Figure 30-2 shows the Services utility, with the World Wide Web Publishing service (that is, IIS) highlighted at the bottom. In a somewhat intimidating display, you have access to all the services displayed in this window. As you can tell by the length of the scrollbar, numerous other services await your perusal above the part of the list you can see. This chapter covers only two — World Wide Web Publishing and FTP Publishing — but you can see the range of possibilities for Windows XP services (along with the potential complexity) simply by reading the entries in the Description column beside each service name.

The Services window has a column labeled Status, in which it displays Started or, if stopped, nothing at all. Besides the Status column, the window also displays the startup type.

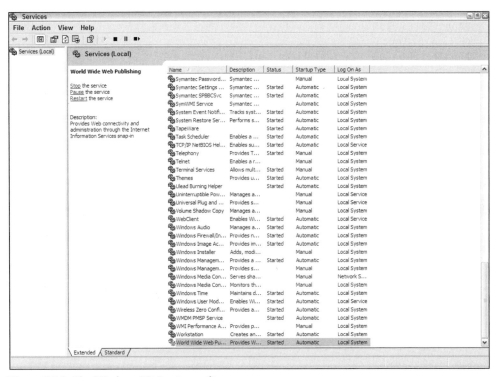

Figure 30-2: The Windows XP Services utility.

To configure any of these services, right-click on the item and choose Properties. As Figure 30-3 demonstrates, the Properties dialog box provides information that includes the name of the service, its description, the path to its program file, and the service's status. The status area contains one of two notifications: Started or Stopped.

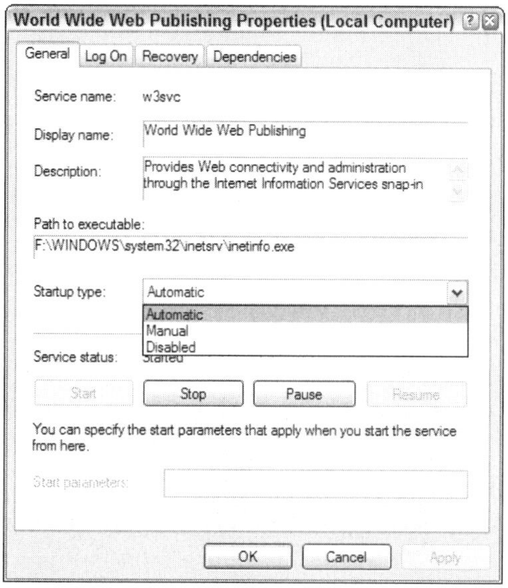

Figure 30-3: The Web Services Properties sheet.

You control the status in the following ways:

- If the service is currently Stopped, you can start it by clicking the Start button.
- If the service is currently Started, you can stop it with the Stop button.

In both cases, however, you change the status only until you reboot Windows XP. When you do so, the service reverts to its default Startup mode.

To change the Startup mode, use the drop-down list beside the Startup Type label. You have three options:

- **Automatic:** This option starts the service automatically whenever you start your computer. If you plan to use the service frequently, and if you do not have access to the server machine at all times (if it's in a remote location, for example), choose Automatic to ensure the service is running when you need it.

- **Manual:** A user or another service — one that depends on this service — can start the service when required. The service remains Stopped until that time, however, including when Windows boots.

▪ **Disabled:** This option disables the service entirely. If another service requires this service in order to start, it will not start. To start the service, an Administrator must first change the mode to Manual or Automatic.

Be careful about changing the Startup type. If a service is disabled, a dependent service or program cannot start (see the Dependencies tab under Properties for more guidance). Remember what you change here in case you have to change it back.

To configure the remainder of the items available in the Service Properties dialog box, see the specific sections on Web services and FTP services later in this chapter.

Caution

Stop your services, and even disable them, if you do not intend to use them. Your services invite traffic from the Internet, and if you leave them on, you will almost certainly get traffic you don't want. Intruders have long targeted unused but open server software, and you *will* become a target if you leave this situation unattended. It really is that bad.

Allowing Server Traffic through the Firewall

Before going any further in configuring your servers, make sure that your users can access them. If you run a firewall — and you should — you need to configure the firewall to admit traffic for those servers into the PC itself. The procedure here applies to the Windows XP Firewall. But if you run a different firewall, you must perform similar procedures in order to open the ports necessary to let the traffic flow.

Follow these steps to configure your firewall to admit traffic:

1. From the Control Panel, choose Windows Firewall (or Winlogo+R, **control firewall.cpl**).

2. Click the Advanced tab.

3. Under Network Connection Settings, click the Settings button.

4. In the Services tab of the Advanced Settings dialog box, check the services whose traffic you want to allow. In the case of this chapter, check Web Server (HTTP) and FTP Server.

5. As you make each selection, Windows displays the Service Settings dialog box for that service. Figure 30-4 shows the Service Settings dialog box for the FTP service, with the name of the host PC the only possible modification.

   Do not randomly choose a name; the name or IP address must match the name or IP of the computer on which the server software resides along with the files you want it to serve. In most cases, simply accept the default and press OK. When you've finished, the Advanced Settings dialog box will contained two checked services, as shown in Figure 30-5.

Figure 30-4: Identifying the serving computer.

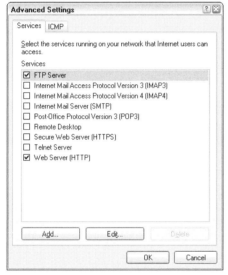

Figure 30-5: The Advanced Settings dialog configured to allow HTTP and FTP traffic.

In the case of third-party firewalls, such as those included in broadband routers, open your router's configuration utility (usually a Web-based utility — see your product manual) and navigate to the area in which you can allow specific types of traffic or open specific ports. In the case of Web traffic, you must open port 80; for FTP traffic, port 21.

Serving Up a Web

With all the preliminaries out of the way, you can begin setting up your Web. First, start the Web server — if it's not already started — by opening the Services utility, double-clicking on the World Wide Web Services item, and clicking the Start button. You now have a Web server running.

Note

This chapter discusses setting up a Web server on a local machine only. For that reason, it will use the Web address http://localhost and the FTP address ftp://localhost. *Localhost* refers to the machine at which you are currently logged on; if you prefer, you can use the localhost numeric IP, 127.0.0.1. The procedures for setting up a Web site on a public server are the same as those used here, but the varieties of public and private IP addresses are too broad for this book to cover. Moreover, establishing a localhost server is a common practice for testing purposes. One other note here: If your computer already has its own dedicated IP address (you can check by opening a command box and entering **ipconfig** at the prompt), your localhost server and your public server are one and the same. In other words, whatever you put on your site and can access via http://localhost or http://127.0.0.1 (or, indeed, http://*computername*), anyone on the Web who knows your IP address can also see.

To see the server, open your Web browser, and enter one of the following in the address bar:

- http://localhost

- http://127.0.0.1

- http://*computername* (replace *computername* with the network name of your PC)

Any of these addresses leads to the same place: the Web site on your local PC. When you first view it, your browser loads the default home page, as shown in Figure 30-6. Until you alter the contents of the home page, this page is displayed whenever you access your site.

From this point on, you can create whatever content you like in your Web site. This book does not cover the creation of Web content because for even reasonably decent coverage the topic requires a book of at least the same size. The following steps, however, will get you started with basic Web site creation:

1. Using Notepad, Microsoft Word, Microsoft FrontPage, Macromedia Dreamweaver, or any combination of dozens of Web design packages, create your pages. If you use Notepad and you want to get started quickly, search the Web for tutorials on writing HTML (HyperText Markup Language) files.

2. When you've created a single Web page or a basic set of files linked together via hyperlinks (that is, when you've created a Web site), store the files in the following folder: C:\Inetpub\wwwroot. This is the folder Windows XP creates as the root folder for your Web site. This folder contains the default Web site you saw when you first accessed http://localhost.

3. Using your Web browser, open your home page—typically default.htm or index.htm, but you can configure this as well—and examine your files. Edit them to make changes, resaving them in the same location. If you include graphics or other files on your site, copy them into a subfolder of Inetpub\wwwroot so that you can always access them easily. You can

change the default location by configuring Internet Information Services (covered immediately following this list). The Read permissions extended to the Inetpub folder do not extend to the rest of the PC.

Note

For more information on Web design, a couple of good books are *Web Design For Dummies* by Lisa Lopuck or the *HTML 4 Bible*, 2nd Edition, by Bryan Pfaffenberger and Bill Karow (both published by Wiley).

You can set the specifics of your Web site, and create additional sites, by using the Computer Management utility in Administrative Tools. Open Control Panel, click Performance and Maintenance, and open Administrative Tools. Open the Computer Management tool (or Winlogo+R, **compmgmt.msc**) and expand the Services and Applications item in the leftmost pane, and then expand Internet Information Services, Web Sites, and Default Web Site in that order. As Figure 30-7 shows, you can now see the files and folders that constitute the default site. Note that you can get just the Internet Information Services tools by using Winlogo+R, **inetmgr**.

Figure 30-6: The default home page for your new Web site.

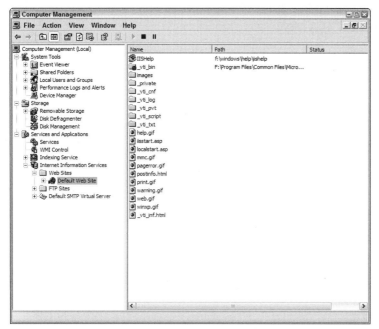

Figure 30-7: The default Web site in Computer Management.

You can edit the properties of the Web site by right-clicking on the Default Web Site folder in the leftmost pane and choosing Properties. Figure 30-8 shows the first screen of the multitabbed Properties dialog box. You can change the Description and assign a new IP Address from here, and you can alter the port if you want to do so. You can also set the number of seconds after which any idle connections automatically disconnect and whether you want to enable the technology known as HTTP Keep-Alive (whereby the Web browser can signal the server to keep the connection open). Finally, you can decide whether to create a log file for your server. A log file is always a good idea because you can track usage and errors. Clicking the Properties button in the Enable Logging area lets you schedule the log and configure it in numerous ways, including the specific server activities you wish to capture.

Tip

Assigning a nonstandard port number to your Web site renders it inaccessible to anyone who does not know the port number. For this reason, you can use this technique effectively in creating an internal or private site, giving the URL with the port number to those you want to visit it. If you do so, the port number appears after the base URL, in the form http://www.mycompany.com:*pn* (replace *pn* with the port number).

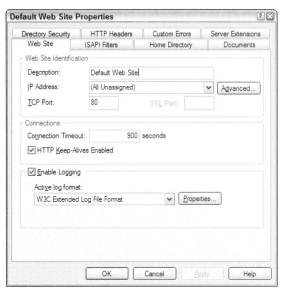

Figure 30-8: The Web Site tab of the site's Properties dialog box.

Each of the other tabs in the Properties dialog box offers its own selection of configurable elements. On the Home Directory tab, for example, you can choose if the content for the site should come from a specific directory on the local PC, from a network share, or from a remote Web server to which this site connects through a redirection command. In other words, you can configure the Web site to take material from another folder or machine entirely, an excellent technique for the sake of managing the site and developing security. Remember that C:\Inetpub\wwwroot automatically handles access privileges. If you change the Home Directory, you will need permissions for that folder (and you may be prompted to login), this is why most users are best served by leaving the default and putting their Web site files in that default folder.

Under the Documents tab, you can establish which document serves as the default document, listing a number of them in the order you choose (the Web server can serve the document according to the characteristics of the connecting browser). While most of you won't need this, someone working with PHP (P HyperText Preprocessor, a Web development scripting language), might add the PHP extension to the list (as well as PHP services, a topic beyond this coverage). Each file within the Web site has its own similar but smaller Properties dialog box, complete with a supplementary dialog box to set security issues such as whether the page requires a password for access.

Obviously, configuring a Web site can become extremely technical, and as the scope and purpose of the site grow, so must your attention to these details. The good news, though, is that the default Web site works perfectly well without configuring it at all. Add the content you want and make it available to others; or just test it for yourself, and you needn't go any further unless you are a professional Web developer.

Note

If you want to establish a Web server for access from outside your network, you should acquire a dedicated IP number. To get one, contact your ISP and explain your needs. Most ISPs offer business services and can set you up with a dedicated, unique number, along with the full control necessary to set up your own range of servers. You'll probably pay an additional monthly fee for the dedicated address.

Uploads and Downloads via FTP Services

The File Transfer Protocol is one of the oldest on the Internet, with FTP clients predating Web browsers by roughly two decades. FTP sites offer a convenient way for people to upload and download files, with the FTP server storing the files and allowing access from the outside. If you want an easy way to set up a file-sharing service for a small group of users or simply a way to access your files on a remote machine, an FTP site works well.

Before starting the FTP service, however, keep one extremely important point in mind. By default, Windows XP configures the FTP server for anonymous access; in other words, anybody can get into it. You need anonymous access if you set up a download site for public use on the Internet, but unless you have this specific need, you should disable anonymous access immediately. To do so, follow the steps outlined here:

1. Open the Computer Management tool from the Administrative Options utility in Control Panel.

2. Expand the Services and Applications item in the leftmost pane by clicking on the plus (+) sign.

3. Expand the FTP Sites folder.

4. Right-click on the Default FTP Site item and choose Properties.

5. In the resulting Properties dialog box, click the Security Accounts tab (see Figure 30-9).

6. Uncheck the Allow Anonymous Connections item at the top of the dialog and click the Yes button on the Internet Service Manager warning box that appears. You have now turned off the anonymous access feature.

When a user logs in to your FTP site, the FTP service automatically grants him or her access to a specific folder and to *only* that folder and its subfolders. Click the Home Directory tab on the FTP Sites Properties dialog box to configure that folder. For maximum control and maximum security, you should create a new folder (using My Computer or Windows Explorer), copy any shareable files into that folder, and then establish that folder as your FTP default using this Properties sheet. Click the Browse button and search for the folder to establish it as the site directory (ideally, the folder is on a partition or hard drive different from Windows XP and your most important data folders). Now, when anyone connects to the site via FTP, he or she has access to that folder for uploading and downloading but to no other folder on your system.

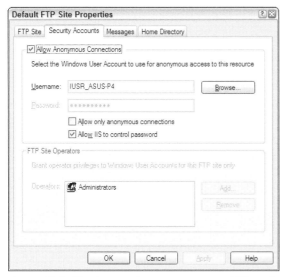

Figure 30-9: The Security Accounts options in FTP configuration.

Tip

With anonymous access disabled, only people with user accounts on your Windows XP machine can access the FTP site. If you want to grant access to more users, you can create a separate user account for FTP purposes only, giving that account name and password to anyone you want. Add this account using the User Accounts utility in Control Panel.

To access your FTP site, use a dedicated FTP client program (you can find many that can be downloaded from the Internet). If you don't have such a program, use your Web browser. You can access your default FTP site by opening your Web browser and typing the following in the address bar: **ftp://*username*@localhost** or **ftp://*username*@127-0.0.1** — replacing *username* with the name of your Windows XP user account for that computer. Windows responds with a Password box. After successfully logging in with your password, you can copy files to and from the browser window.

Summary

In addition to using your Windows XP Professional installation as a Web server and FTP server, you can purchase or download software to make it into a mail server, file server, application server, and more. All these possibilities require additional configuration, and few functions with as little effort on your part as Web and FTP servers. With HTTP services to host a Web site, publicly or locally, and FTP services to transfer files to and from another Windows XP machine quickly and easily, you've already made good use of the operating system's server features.

Part VIII

Utilities

Here, you look at software available to make your Windows XP machine into an Internet server. Chapter 30 covers a few of the tools available in Windows XP itself, but you'll find a far wider range of choices if you move into third-party offerings instead.

Web and FTP Server Software

Yes, Internet Information Services has everything you need to set up Windows XP as a Web and FTP server, but to make it a server with the power to serve a large audience, you need to upgrade to Windows 2003 Server (or its Small Business Server edition) or look elsewhere.

Abyss Web Server (www.aprelium.com) is an example of a small Web server that runs on versions of Windows other than Windows XP and Windows 2000. The free Personal edition offers almost all the features of the inexpensive Professional edition, so by all means give it a try to decide if you want to work with it. The server supports Perl, Python, ASP scripts, and more and offers strong access control, so it's certainly not something to dismiss without a look. On the other side of the coin, Xeneo Web Server (www.northernsolutions.com) supports multiple domains, all popular Internet scripts and technologies, unlimited virtual hosts, and the latest version of Secure Sockets Layer (SSL) security, and you then use Windows XP's full multithreading capabilities.

Two of the most interesting Web servers available are also open source projects and, therefore, free. The World Wide Web Consortium (www.w3.org), the organization created by the originator of the Web, Tim Berners-Lee, offers Jigsaw, a server implemented in the Java programming language designed not only to serve Web sites but also to demonstrate upcoming new features available to the Web community. But the primary Web server out there anywhere, and the one you should certainly try as soon as you want to establish a serious server, is Apache (www.apache.org). Well over half of all Web servers on the Internet use Apache, primarily because it's the software of choice for Linux servers but more recently popular with Windows servers as well (despite the ubiquity of Microsoft's IIS). Mind you, there's nothing particularly easy about using Apache, and everything from its download page to its configuration screens practically screams "Geek!" but it's powerful, full-featured, highly reliable, and free. You can't ask much more than that.

A number of easy-to-use FTP servers are available, perhaps the easiest being, well, Quick & Easy FTP Server (www.pablosoftwaresolutions.com). You set up your FTP server using the built-in wizard, and you can add users and folders anytime you want through the graphical interface environment. Each user is assigned a home folder and permissions in that folder and other folders to download, upload, delete, create directories, and so on. Each user can also have a disk quota for storage and for data transfers. GlobalScape (www.cuteftp.com), the maker of the well-known FTP client CuteFTP, has a server of its own — Secure FTP Server — with a somewhat less user-friendly graphical interface, but with a wide range of administrative options for its virtual disk system and a direct linkage to Windows XP user accounts (optional but useful) to help you create your FTP accounts.

If you want a tiny FTP server, in the sense that is uses as little system memory as you're likely to find anywhere, give Xlight FTP Server (www.xlightftpd.com) a try. This server offers a clearly designed graphical interface and incorporates features such as SSL (Secure Sockets Layer) and remote database connectivity. TurboSoft's Turbo FTP (www.turboftp.com) also features these protocols, provides firewall and proxy server support, and in an interesting feature, allows automatic updates of any files copied or saved to the user's home folder, obviating the need to connect to the FTP site for uploading purposes.

Mail Servers

Windows XP does not include mail server software. If you want an email server, you have to install a Linux box and activate one of its built-in servers, or use a third-party product designed for Windows.

Ability Mail Server (www.code-crafters.com) provides support for all major Internet mail protocols, including SMTP (Simple Mail Transport Protocol), POP3 (Post Office Protocol version 3), IMAP4 (Internet Message Access Protocol), and LDAP (Lightweight Directory Access Protocol). It also offers strong 128-bit security, built-in virus protection, built-in spam protection, filtering of mail content, and the use of mailing lists. MailMax (www.smartmax.com) offers similar features along with extensive user mailbox configurations for full control over your mail system's users. Ipswitch's well-known iMail Server (www.ipswitch.com), highly regarded over the last several years, has now been packaged with a number of other server programs in the Ipswitch Collaboration Suite. In addition to its established email server, the suite offers email collaboration services, instant messaging services with built-in security, workgroup collaboration features such as shared calendars and contacts, and spam and virus protection.

Part IX

Appendixes

Appendix A

Installing Windows XP

If you've never installed an operating system before, you can rest assured that no matter how complex the process seems with Windows XP, it doesn't hold a candle to the confusion and the sheer number of possible problems engendered by Windows installations of the past. Installing Windows 95 meant figuring out a way to get the CD-ROM drive working with the setup procedure using a start-up floppy disk, or, for the truly patient, installing the OS from roughly 20 floppy disks, one of which (usually in the #15–#17 range) would almost certainly malfunction and stop the installation cold. Windows 98 solved some of the CD-ROM problems, but as with Windows 95, finding and installing hardware drivers tended to bog things down. Windows 2000 proved itself the most stable Microsoft OS release until (and some still argue including) Windows XP. But for desktop users, it suffered from compatibility problems with both hardware and software. Windows Millennium Edition took the first real step toward recognizing hardware during the installation, but mysteriously it still often failed to make that hardware function until you found the drivers.

Windows XP, from its initial release, pointed to the future of OS installation, recognizing a wide range of hardware and configuring itself to take advantage of each individual PC. It's not perfect, but it has demonstrated that pain-free Windows installations might actually occur one day.

No two PCs are identical (well, few that you'll likely deal with as a home user anyway), so the number of possible installation scenarios is high. This chapter outlines a range of scenarios and steps you through the process of installing Windows XP. The next appendix is about reinstalling Windows XP.

Notes on Dual Booting

If you're installing Windows on a system that includes Linux, be very careful how you perform the installation. If you have installed Linux onto your PC in a dual-boot configuration with Windows XP and you boot from one of the Linux boot managers — LILO or GRUB — installing Windows XP will delete that boot manager in favor of Microsoft's bare-bones boot manager that (naturally) recognizes only Windows XP. Before installing Windows XP, boot into Linux and create a boot disk using the appropriate utility in your Linux system. After installing the new instance of Windows XP, boot into Linux from your boot floppy and reestablish LILO or GRUB as your bootloader.

Continued

Notes on Dual Booting *(Continued)*

Note, however, that you should perform multiple installations in a specific order. If you install Windows 95, 98, or Me (collectively know as Windows *9x*), do that installation before installing Windows XP. Otherwise, installing Windows *9x* will render Windows XP inaccessible. If you plan to run Linux, have all your Windows versions installed, including Windows XP, before installing Linux. Also notice that when you install Linux, which you do on separate Linux partitions, you must make absolutely sure that you don't wipe out a Windows partition in the process. Many users have installed Linux only to discover they had destroyed the boot partition for Windows or even erased Windows altogether.

Setting the CD-ROM as the Primary Boot Device before You Install

In order to boot directly from the Windows XP installation CD, you must configure your CD-ROM as the primary boot device. On many systems today, this configuration already exists, so before starting the configuration process put the installation CD in the CD-ROM drive and reboot the PC. If you get the message `Press any key to boot from CD-ROM`, you don't need to change the configuration.

If you don't get this message, you have to do a bit of digging inside your system's more esoteric software, specifically the BIOS settings. Also sometimes called Setup, the means of entering the basic input/output system (BIOS) settings area appears when you turn on your PC (just restarting may not give you this option; turn your computer off and on again). Look for a notice similar to `Press Delete to enter Settings` or `Press F10 for Configuration`. On most PCs today, you enter the BIOS menus by pressing the Delete key while that notice is on the screen, but other methods (such as pressing a function key) still occur. Whatever the case, as long as you time it correctly (don't wait too long), you will find yourself looking at a list of configuration possibilities related to your hard drives, system memory, PCI and USB settings, and much more.

You can ignore everything on the Setup list of configuration possibilities except one: boot order. Each BIOS manufacturer places this setting in a different place, so navigate around the menus (usually with the keyboard) to find it. With this setting, you instruct your PC which drives to look for, and in which order, when you boot or reboot your PC. Often, PCs are configured to look for the floppy drive first, then the primary hard drive, and then the CD-ROM, in order to find a bootable operating system. You need to use the BIOS interface to change the boot order so that your system looks for the CD-ROM before it looks for the hard drives. While not strictly necessary, you should also put the CD-ROM ahead of the floppy disk, in case you leave a floppy disk in the drive accidentally.

With the configuration changed, save the settings, put the installation CD in the CD-ROM drive, and reboot the computer. You will now boot from the CD-ROM. After you've completed the installation, you can change the boot order back if you wish, instructing the PC to boot from the hard drive first, to make booting faster.

Installation Scenarios

The *one size fits all* mantra does not apply to operating system installation, although manufacturers have started doing everything in their power to try to force it to fit. The fact remains, however, that different users have different needs, and a successful installation depends on whether the outcome satisfies those needs. Here are some installation scenarios reflecting several possible situations.

Scenario 1: Installing Windows XP on a New Computer or New Hard Drive (PC with One Drive)

The process for putting Windows XP on a brand new computer and on a new hard drive in a one-drive system is precisely the same. Known as a clean install, this process requires only the Windows XP installation CD and, possibly, your CD-ROM drive set up as the primary boot device (see the preceding section). Possibly, that is, because if you have no other operating systems on your hard drives, and no boot disk in the floppy drive, your PC automatically looks to the CD-ROM as the next possible location from which it can start. It needs an operating system, and it searches your drives until it finds one.

Before you begin, make sure that you have the CD Product Key (it's a long mix of letters and numbers on the back of the case); without it, you won't be able to install Windows.

To start Windows Setup, place the installation CD in the CD-ROM drive and start (or reboot) your PC. Watch the screen for the notification Press any key to boot from the CD-ROM and, as it says, press a key (anything on the keyboard will do). Setup begins:

1. On the first blue screen, choose the To Set Up Windows XP Now, Press ENTER option and press the Enter key.

2. On the next screen, press the F8 key on your keyboard to accept the Windows XP Licensing Agreement.

3. Work begins on the third blue screen. Setup lists your PC's hard drives and the partitions on each of them. Because this scenario assumes a single-drive system, only one hard drive appears. Because the hard drive is new, it has either one partition only or nothing but unpartitioned space. Either way, because the scenario assumes that you have no data on the drive you want to save, you should start from scratch. If you have an existing partition, proceed to step 4; if you have only unpartitioned space, proceed to step 5.

Note

You have probably heard the phrase *formatting the hard drive,* sometimes in a negative way because formatting a drive wipes out existing data. In fact, however, formatting works on partitions, not drives. For a hard drive to be useful, it needs partitioning first and formatting next.

4. Delete the existing partition by highlighting it and pressing the D key on your keyboard. Windows responds by asking if you want to proceed with the deletion. Confirm the deletion by pressing the L key. The partition is now gone, replaced by unpartitioned space.

5. Highlight the unpartitioned space, and press either Enter or the C key. Pressing the Enter key instructs Windows to use the entire hard drive for the installation, with your entire hard drive serving as a single partition. Pressing C tells Windows that you want to divide your hard drive into more than one partition. If you have a large hard drive (over 60GB), you should consider creating more than one partition. This gives you a partition to use in case your Windows installation stops working, as a backup partition away from the main partition, or for future installation of a second instance of Windows XP or a different operating system entirely (such as Linux) in a dual-boot system. If you press the Enter key, proceed to step 7. If you press the C key, go to step 6.

6. By default, Windows configures itself to use the entire hard drive for a single partition, exactly as if you had pressed the Enter key in step 5 instead of C. To give yourself the versatility partitions offer, you may want to divide the hard drive into two or more partitions. At this stage, however, you need define only one partition and leave enough unformatted space to use later (including immediately after Windows has finished installing). Jot down the number currently displayed in the partition size area (so that you remember the default), and chop that number in half, one-third, or two-thirds — any size you like. For example, on a 60GB hard drive, you could create a 30GB partition for Windows and leave the other 30GB as unformatted space. Create the partition now by entering the size you want for the first partition in the space provided. This first partition is called the primary partition (C:); others are known as extended partitions (D:, and so on.). You don't have to use more than one single full-sized partition.

Note

The partitioning screen uses megabytes rather than gigabytes as its measure. When specifying the size of the partitions, create a 30GB drive by typing the number **30000** because 1GB equals (roughly) 1000MB. Actually, 1GB equals 1024MB, so the numbers never work out quite evenly; but at this level, working in 1000s is fine. For a 40GB drive, type **40000**.

7. When you have finished creating your partitions, Windows returns you to the partition selection screen. Highlight the partition you have just created (it shows up first in the list), and press Enter to instruct Windows to install itself on that partition.

8. You now arrive at the formatting screen. Here, Windows asks you how you want to format your partition. To take full advantage of the advanced file-sharing and user permissions features of Windows XP and to have a far more secure PC, choose the Format The Partition Using the NTFS File System option. To speed up the process, select the Quick option, which takes much less time but (in theory at least) can run into difficulties. Reports of such difficulties are few and far between, so save yourself some time and use the Quick format.

9. On the next three screens, wait while Setup formats the partition, copies the setup files from the installation CD to your hard drive, and reboots your computer.

10. After the reboot, the graphical Setup program appears. Stay by your computer for the first part of the graphical installation because Setup requires your interaction in the following stages of installation:

   a. After approximately five minutes, the Regional and Language Options dialog box appears. You can keep the defaults, which depend on where you bought the software (U.S. English and a U.S. English keyboard layout for U.S. purchases), or click Customize for the standards and formats or Details for the keyboard and change the defaults. Assuming that you want to keep them as they are, click Next.

   b. Shortly afterward, the Personalize Your Software dialog box appears. Type in your name and organization. Windows specifies no formats for either, so type in whatever you want here, and click Next.

   c. Immediately afterward, the dialog box titled Your Product Key appears. You can find the product key on the back of the CD case. Type it in carefully and click Next; if Setup says you've made a mistake (as it does with stunning regularity), compare the original with what you've typed and make the necessary changes. If you don't have a product key, you cannot continue the installation. Once Setup accepts it, click Next.

Tip

You don't have to use uppercase letters when entering the product key; the letters on the product key printed on the CD case are uppercase for clarity only.

   d. Shortly afterward you enter the product key, the Computer Name and Administrator Password dialog box appears. You can name your computer whatever you want: DELL SYSTEM, WORK MACHINE, THE OSBOURNES' PC, SUPERBEAST, or just plain JOHNNY. It's your choice. Next, type in a password for the primary Administrator account, the one named, in fact, Administrator. Write this password down for safe-keeping, but keep it safe from prying eyes. With the Administrator account, you have virtually full control over the PC. Make the password something that only you could possibly know, and include numbers and punctuation characters if you feel that you can remember them. When you've finished, click Next.

   e. Immediately after you enter your password, the Date and Time Settings dialog box appears. Set the date and time here, and specify which time zone you are in. If you live in an area with daylight-saving time, click the appropriate check box. Then click Next.

   f. At this point, Setup seems to be doing well on its own, and the temptation to go have lunch often becomes irresistible. Resist it, however. After four or five minutes Setup displays the Network Settings dialog box, asking if you want typical settings or custom settings. Unless you have a local area network that you now want to configure, always stick with the default typical settings, and click Next. Why Microsoft did not design this dialog box to accept the typical settings after a specified time, five minutes perhaps, is mystifying. Many users have left their PCs after configuring the Date and Time Settings dialog box. When they return an hour or so later, assuming that Setup has been completed, they discover the Network Settings dialog box waiting stupidly for them to click Next and proceed with the remaining 30–50 minutes of the installation.

g. From this point on, Setup takes whatever time it needs to complete the installation. At the end of the process, Setup reboots your PC and Windows is launched for the first time. Setup's final task is to ask your permission to adjust your screen resolution (click OK), after which the desktop appears with its bright photograph and the Start menu open for action. You have to wade through Windows asking if you want a tour of the operating system (just say Yes, or it will never go away) and if you want to set up a .NET Passport account (for use with Hotmail, Windows Messenger, and an increasing number of Microsoft-based services). This is your choice entirely.

Scenario 2: Installing Windows XP on a Multiple-Drive PC with a New Primary Drive

Things start to get a bit more complex when you have more than one hard drive in your system. As in Scenario 1, when you reach the partition screen you have to instruct Setup as to which partition you want to use for the installation. But here you have more choices because you can divide each of your drives into multiple partitions. Scenario 2 has become common in recent years as people buy inexpensive new hard drives and add them to their systems, installing Windows on the new drive after it is in place. In all cases, the new drive contains neither data nor partitions, but in many cases important data remains on the original drive.

If one or more of your drives contain data that you want to keep, you must either back up the data before installing the operating system or avoid installing the OS on the partition where the data resides. To do so, make sure that you know which drive and which partition contain that data, and configure Setup to use a different drive or partition. Once you have chosen the drive that will house the installation, follow steps 3 through 10 in Scenario 1's numbered list to partition and format the drive and install the OS. With the installation completed, load My Computer or Windows Explorer and navigate to your other drives and partitions.

Caution

Windows starts numbering hard drives with 0 (zero), not 1. The primary hard drive is Disk 0, the second Disk 1, and so forth. The partition containing C:\, therefore, is almost always located on Disk 0. Keep this in mind when determining the partition on which to install Windows.

Scenario 3: Upgrading a Previous Windows Version

You can upgrade to Windows XP from an earlier Windows version under a variety of different circumstances. Table A-1 covers the various upgrade possibilities. Keep in mind, though, that many users have a great deal more trouble after an upgrade than after a clean install. So, use the upgrade installation only if you have no real choice — for example, if you no longer have the CDs for the programs currently installed.

Table A-1   Upgrading to Windows XP

Existing Version	*Possible Windows XP Edition*
Windows 3.1 or Windows 95	None
Windows 98, Windows 98/SE, or Windows Millennium Edition	Windows XP Home and Professional
Windows NT Workstation 4.0, Windows 2000 Professional	Windows XP Professional
Windows XP Home Edition	Windows XP Professional

To upgrade from your existing Windows version, assuming that you have the correct Windows XP edition according to the table, follow these steps:

1. With your current version of Windows running, place the Windows XP installation CD in the CD-ROM drive.

2. When the Welcome screen appears, click the Install Windows XP option. If the Welcome screen does not appear on its own, use My Computer or Windows Explorer to navigate to your CD drive and double-click the Setup program.

3. In a few seconds, the Welcome to Windows Setup screen appears. In the Installation Type menu, make sure the Upgrade (Recommended) option is selected. Click Next to continue.

4. On the resulting License Agreement screen, click the I Accept This Agreement radio button and click Next.

5. Follow steps 10(c) through 10(g) in the numbered list under Scenario 1 earlier in this chapter.

When this process has finished, you have a new version of Windows. Try it out to ensure that everything works: your programs, especially non-Microsoft programs and older programs, and your hardware, especially very old or extremely new hardware. In either case, if the items do not function properly, head for the Web sites of the product manufacturers and download and install patches and drivers as required.

If you've upgraded from Windows 98 or Windows Me, you can upgrade further by changing the file system from the current FAT or FAT32 to NTFS, the native file system of Windows XP. NTFS gives you several security advantages over FAT32. You will be able to convert to NTFS anytime after the installation. Search Windows Help (Winlogo+F1) for "convert FAT to NTFS."

Scenario 4: Dual-Booting Windows XP on a System with Another Windows Installation

One of the more fascinating possibilities with Windows XP is a dual-boot setup. When you install Windows XP on a PC that currently contains a Microsoft operating system (anything from MS-DOS and Windows 3.1 up through Windows XP itself), by performing a new installation (called a *clean install*) instead of an upgrade, you end up with both Windows versions available for use. You must, however, install each version on a separate hard disk partition; this is one of the reasons I suggest in step 6 under Scenario 1 that you leave unpartitioned space available for other uses. When you boot your PC, Microsoft's boot manager presents you with a list of operating systems to choose from. You simply move the cursor to the one you want and press Enter to launch it.

Why would anybody want two operating systems or more? First of all, if you enjoy computers, having two OSs can be just plain fun. More important, if all the software and hardware on your current operating system works flawlessly, you can leave that OS in place while you install Windows XP and get everything up and running equally well on it (anyone with numerous games installed will be particularly grateful for this because some games work better on older Windows versions). You can also move to other operating systems if one of them fails to load. Finally, Windows XP creates a new installation faster than an upgrade installation — in fact, frequently over twice as fast. If you have the disk space, why not?

As long as you have room on your hard disk for a second partition, creating a dual-boot system is remarkably easy. Just follow steps 1–6 in the numbered list in Scenario 1. In step 6, choose the unformatted space item and create a new partition here. Format it as an NTFS partition, and instruct Setup to install Windows on it. Continue the process until Setup has been completed, and then reboot to see the Microsoft boot manager screen. Choose the operating system you want to run, presumably Windows XP, and press Enter to load it.

If you're reading closely, you'll note that in the previous upgrade scenario, I said you can convert from FAT to NTFS anytime. That's true, and it is appropriate in an upgrade without formatting. In this case, you're formatting the partition and might as well use NTFS from the start.

If you have only one partition on your drive, you need to create another. Unfortunately, Windows Setup will not let you do so, and neither will Windows itself. You can either install a second hard drive and create the partition on it, or purchase disk-partitioning software such as PowerQuest's Partition Magic or V Communications' Partition Commander. These utilities let you resize a partition (as long as it's not completely full of data) in a manner known as *nondestructive*, meaning that you lose no data. With your current partition decreased in size, you now have unformatted space to work with, and you can continue your Windows XP installation at that point.

Note

PCs on which you can boot to two or more operating system installations are typically called *dual-boot systems*, but by all rights they should be known as *multiboot systems*. There's nothing whatsoever stopping you from building a PC that allows you to boot into Windows 98, Windows 2000, two installations of Windows XP Home, three installations of Windows XP Professional, and at least one version of Linux. As long as you have enough hard disk space, and as long as you've created enough partitions, go to it. In fact, having more than one installation of an OS offers an excellent way to test new hardware and software, especially prerelease software (beta versions).

What to Do About SP2

Let's say that you have your original Windows XP CD, along with the CD installation key and everything else you need to install the OS. You also know that Windows XP Service Pack 2 upgrades the OS to a significantly more secure version, so you want to be sure to end up with an SP2 installation. The question is: do you install the original XP and upgrade over the Internet using Windows Update, or do you get yourself either a CD that contains SP2 only or one that includes XP with SP2 built in.

Obviously, if you have no intention of replacing your CD, you simply do the former. Install Windows and, as soon as you get it running, use Internet Explorer to access the Microsoft site and let Windows Update do all the upgrading for you. For the vast majority of home users, this is a perfectly valid process.

For security-conscious businesses and home users with permanent Internet connections, however, the better answer is to install from a CD that contains SP2. Why? SP2 offers enhanced security, to be sure, but only once you have it installed. Between installing and running Windows XP the first time and downloading SP2 and performing the upgrade, your PC can be hacked to the extent that you end up with a compromised system even with SP2 installed.

Here are the possible methods for obtaining SP2 *before* installing XP:

- **Order the SP2 CD:** Microsoft will ship you (free) a CD with Service Pack 2 on it. In this case, disconnect your PC from the Internet and install Windows XP; then install SP2 from the new CD. Only then should you connect to the Internet in order to register and validate your copy of XP. You can order the CD by going to Microsoft's Windows page (www.microsoft.com/windows) and following the links to the security page and the Service Pack downloads. At the time of this writing, the order page was http://www.microsoft.com/windowsxp/downloads/updates/sp2/cdorder/en_us/default.mspx.

- **Download SP2 and burn a CD:** If you have access to a second PC, preferably one that already has SP2 installed (or one that runs an OS other than Windows), this method can work. You can download the SP2 file from the Windows Update site without actually installing it. Do so, and then burn this 266MB file to a CD. Take the CD to the PC on which you want to install SP2, perform a virus check on the file, and then launch it by double-clicking it in My Computer.

- **Buy a new copy of Windows XP:** If you're financially flush, you might want to purchase a recently manufactured copy of Windows XP that already contains SP2. Check on the box to ensure that it does; otherwise, you're right back where you started. Actually, this method is a very good one if you plan to upgrade from Windows XP Home to Windows XP Professional because it gives you everything you need in one package.

Summary

The installation process for Windows XP offers one of the best ways to get to know your way around computers. If you can put a second partition on your system (ask for two partitions when you order the system from your vendor), you can repeat the installation as often as you want on the second partition without affecting the original installation. By doing so, you become experienced at installing your OS, to the degree that working with the secondary partitions becomes second nature and performing installations for friends and colleagues becomes possible. You also get used to the process of searching for and installing software patches and hardware drivers, something that, again, gives you a way of helping others with their system problems.

Do you need to do all this work? No, of course not. Windows XP runs just fine, as you already know. But enhancing your knowledge of how your system works gives you a set of skills that are not only helpful to others but also valuable in the employment marketplace. Keep upgrading this knowledge, and you might find yourself taking over IT duties at very small offices (where people routinely wear multiple hats) or doing training sessions for other employees. Of course, you also end up getting phone calls from friends and neighbors who have managed to mangle their Windows systems to the point of nonfunctionality, but this, too, can have its rewards. You might, for instance, get the snow shoveled out of your driveway come winter. It certainly worked for this author.

Appendix B

Reinstalling Windows XP

Sometimes, the fastest and most effective way to deal with problems in Windows XP is to reinstall the operating system. But reinstalling it requires preparation. Performing the actual reinstallation isn't difficult at all—just pop in the CD, let Setup begin, and walk your way through the steps. But you can save yourself a great deal of time and prevent possible disaster by performing a number of additional tasks before you begin.

One point here, however. This chapter assumes that you want to reinstall Windows XP and preserve your existing data. If you want to start over with a completely clean slate and you have no need to save any current data, your life gets much easier: just pop in the Windows XP installation CD, tell it to reformat your hard drives, and let it do its thing (see Appendix A for details, including what to do about Service Pack 2). When the purpose of the reinstallation is to come away with a functioning operating system in which you can make use of your existing data, the task becomes significantly more arduous.

You can perform the reinstallation in one of two ways, depending entirely on your needs and your intended result:

- **In-Place Reinstallation:** Also called a *repair install*, this method installs Windows XP on the same partition and in the same folder as the original, in effect functioning as an upgrade. In the process, it overwrites numerous folders and files and overwrites the original installation. Although it does not necessarily overwrite the Documents and Settings folder, it creates a new one and can render the old one inaccessible. Have a backup of at least your data, if not the entire system (see Chapter 4).

- **Clean Reinstallation:** Doing this to a system with a single partition involves wiping that partition clean; be certain you have a working backup of all your latest data (an external hard drive is very handy here). An alternative method involves preserving the existing data on one drive partition and installing Windows XP to a separate partition, but if you don't already have these partitions set up, you risk losing any data you haven't backed up. In effect, this counts as a reinstallation only because you're using the same installation CD and product activation code. Functionally, the method results in a completely new installation to which you can restore the data stored on the original partition.

For the best performance results, choose a clean reinstallation by formatting the hard drive. You will lose everything on that drive (that's what makes it "clean"). Before you begin, see Chapter 4 on backups and make certain you have tested restoring data from that backup; this is a case where a full backup of the entire computer may make sense.

Caution

If you have installed Windows XP service packs, you might have difficulties with compatibility if you perform an in-place reinstallation with the original (pre-service pack) CD. If you purchased Windows XP recently, the installation CD likely already contains the most recent service pack(s).

However, if you don't have Service Pack 2 on CD, you may want to order it before you proceed with this chapter (see Chapter 1 about SP 2). Having the SP2 CD (or a copy of XP so new that it has SP2 included) will save you a lot of time you will otherwise spend at the Windows Update Web site.

Performing an In-Place Reinstallation

Without a doubt, the in-place reinstallation takes less time, effort, and sheer work than the clean reinstallation. Unfortunately, you have less control over the results. If all goes well, after the in-place reinstall you have access to all your files, folders, and programs. Sometimes, however, things go wrong, with loss of data, programs, and more. Still, in-place installations can work miracles; so if you have backup files of your most important documents stored on another hard drive or on removable media, go ahead and give it a try.

Caution

Do not reinstall Windows XP to correct problems with third-party programs, Documents and Settings folders, or other data locations. In the case of programs, uninstall them and reinstall them, using the Add or Remove Programs utility in the Control Panel. In the case of problems with a user's folders in Documents and Settings, create a new account with a similar name (acceptable to the user), copy the old files and folders to the new account's folders, and see if the problems continue. If not, you can then delete the original account, reboot, create a new account with the original name, and copy the files and folders into that account.

In-place reinstalls come in two forms: Update and Repair. Of these two, Update is the most straightforward because it installs from inside Windows (that is, Windows must be working at least well enough to allow you to perform tasks in it). But in both, the principle is the same.

Note

You cannot perform a reinstallation from Safe Mode.

To perform an Update in-place reinstallation, follow these steps:

1. If you can access your folders, back up all important files and folders to another hard drive, another partition on your main Windows hard drive, a network drive, or removable media such as CD, DVD, tape, or floppy disks.

2. If you can access Add or Remove Programs, for maximum compatibility consider removing any Windows XP service packs you have installed. You can find these service packs in the Add or Remove Programs utility in the Control Panel. Scroll toward the bottom of the list until you see Windows XP Hotfixes with an SP1 or SP3 in parentheses. Uninstalling the service pack elements can help but doing so takes a long time.

3. Place your Windows XP installation CD in your CD or DVD drive and wait for the opening screen. Choose the Install Windows XP option.

Caution

If you have installed the Linux operating system on your computer in a dual-boot or multiboot arrangement, and you use one of the two Linux bootloader programs — LILO or GRUB — to select your operating system when your PC boots, you have an additional consideration. Installing Windows XP deletes the Linux bootloader and renders Linux inaccessible unless you've made a boot floppy for your Linux installation. If you do not have such a disk, stop the installation, boot into Linux, use its utilities to create a boot floppy, and then continue reinstalling Windows. After installing Windows, you'll have to restore the Linux bootloader using the boot floppy.

4. Wait for the second installation screen to appear (it can take several seconds), and choose the Upgrade option in the Installation Type drop-down menu. Click Next to continue, and follow the Setup Wizard from here. Within 30–60 minutes, you have replaced Windows.

5. Spend some time with your PC to ensure that everything works: Documents and Settings files, programs, and so on. One thing you do lose with any such upgrade is the capability to use the restore points you established with the System Restore utility. You can, however, start creating new restore points immediately (indeed, Windows already has).

6. Before performing any other functions, install your antivirus software, and then to ensure maximum security, install SP2 from the CD. Once you have SP2 safely installed, you can launch Windows Update (see Chapter 5) to install all other critical and optional updates.

Caution

Remember, you run a considerable security risk if you go online with your newly reinstalled Windows XP before you have installed SP2. And your safest bet for installing SP2 is to order the free CD from Microsoft and install from the CD. In the time it takes to install and run Windows XP the first time, download SP2, and perform the upgrade, your PC can be hacked to the extent that you end up with a compromised system even with SP2 installed.

To perform a Repair install, do the following:

1. Turn on your computer and immediately insert the Windows XP Installation CD into the CD or DVD drive. Wait for the Welcome to Setup screen to appear in all its white-text-on-blue-background, old-style glory.

2. Select the To Set Up Windows XP Now, Press ENTER option by pressing the Enter key.

Caution

Even though you're performing a Repair Install, do not select the To Repair a Windows XP Installation using Recovery Console, press R option. The Recovery Console offers specialized tools for various types of repair, and it won't help you here.

3. At the subsequent screen (the End-User License Agreement), press the F8 key.

4. At this stage, Setup searches for existing installations of Windows XP. When it locates your installation (the one that no longer works properly), it identifies it by the hard drive letter and primary folder (usually C:\WINDOWS). If you have more than one installation on a dual-boot or multiboot drive, choose the one you want to repair by using the arrow keys to scroll the list. If Windows does *not* find an existing version, continuing the installation will destroy all the files on the selected hard disk. Be careful.

5. When you've selected the installation you want to fix, press R. Windows begins copying files, and you can sit back and watch the reinstallation take place, entering the CD key when required, along with other interactions.

6. When Windows completes its tasks, and before performing any other functions, install SP2, then install your antivirus software and then launch Windows Update (see Chapter 5) to install the latest service packs and all other critical and optional updates.

7. Test your reinstalled Windows.

Performing a Clean Reinstallation

A clean reinstallation of Windows XP lets you start all over with a clean slate, that is, a blank hard drive or partition. This method works particularly well for systems that have bogged down over the course of months or years of use, with programs installed and removed, utilities launching when Windows launches, and slowdowns and strange behavior you can't trace or don't want to bother trying to deal with. Many users make a point of reinstalling Windows in this way once a year or so, precisely to flush it out and give it a chance to work without encumbrances.

One thing you'll notice immediately when you reinstall: Windows runs more smoothly, snaps to attention, and loads far more quickly. The trick then is to avoid installing everything you put on the last version, leaving yourself with a less cluttered system in general.

Tip

Reinstallation is useful in a related way. If you have two good-sized hard drive partitions (20–30GB each), why not install Windows XP twice, once on each partition (Appendix A covers the details surrounding dual-booting or multibooting)? This way, you can establish one installation as a work version and the other as more of an entertainment version. Not only do you keep some tempting entertainment programs away from yourself when you're working, but you also have a place to test programs without committing them to the primary version.

Preparing for the Clean Reinstallation

Again, this chapter assumes that you want to reinstall Windows without losing your previous data. To do so requires preparation, including all or some of the following steps. Begin with a current backup of at least your data, if not the entire system (see Chapter 4).

Sorting Out Your Disk Partitions

If you are going to try to reinstall Windows without having to reinstall your data from a backup, you need a separate hard disk partition (and you still need a good backup). To see your partitions, open the Computer Management console (click Start and choose All Programs → Administrative Tools to find it, or use Winlogo+R, **compmgmt.msc**), and click on the Disk Management item on the left. The drive letters appear with each partition, as does the partition type: NTFS, FAT32, FAT, or other (Windows XP does not identify the Linux partitions on the far right of Disk 1). Examine your partitions and write down the names, sizes, and file system types of all the partitions.

Note

Like all good computers, Windows starts numbering at 0 (zero), not 1. The primary partition, C:, is located on Disk 0, not Disk 1. If you've traveled to England and used their elevators — uh, *lifts* — you'll feel quite at home with this numbering system.

Ideally, you'll have enough free space (roughly 15–20GB minimum, although you actually need less) for a fresh XP installation. If you own a disk-partitioning package such as PowerQuest's Partition Magic or V Communications' Partition Commander, you can resize the current partitions to create this space. Otherwise, you'll have to delete — or at least reformat — a current partition to create the necessary room. If you have only one partition, you cannot use the clean reinstallation method without also wiping out data, which you can restore from a backup after the clean installation. The best arrangement is to buy and install a second hard drive (external USB will work great). A second hard drive automatically gives you another.

Preparations for Reinstalling Programs and Drivers

Reinstalling Windows XP means reinstalling your programs and hardware drivers as well. This isn't a problem if you have your installation CDs available, but in many cases these days, installations proceed from downloads rather than from external media. Locate your downloaded programs and have them accessible when you reinstall the OS. In all cases, be sure to have the program keys (CD keys, unlock keys, activation keys) available as well. If you have your keys stored in email files, Word documents, or downloaded Web pages, save them to a floppy or CD, or print them out.

With Windows XP, hardware drivers are less of a concern than with older versions of Windows. The operating system ships with many, many drivers, and it recognizes your hardware extremely well. On the chance XP won't recognize one of your devices (especially the oldest), locate driver disks if you can, or, if you can access the Internet, go to the manufacturers' Web sites and download the latest versions.

Saving Email Stores and Other User Data

Windows XP creates a separate set of data folders for each user, collecting them all under the umbrella folder called Documents and Settings, located under the root folder on XP's partition (usually C:\Documents and Settings). In addition, every email program stores your messages in data files. If you have access to the existing Windows installation, even if it works only a fraction as well as it should, you can save yourself time with the reinstallation process by locating all these files and copying them to external media or a second partition or hard drive. In the case of Microsoft Outlook, you'll find the program's data file, outlook.pst, in the Documents and Settings folder. But keep in mind that Outlook creates a separate outlook.pst file for *each user*. To see the file, use the Folder Options dialog box (View tab) to show hidden files and folders; then use My Computer to navigate to the following folder inside each user's folder within Documents and Settings: Local Settings\Application Data\Microsoft\Outlook. Copy each outlook.pst file to a separate folder on a different partition or disk, or rename them all to reflect their content (but be sure to keep the .pst extension). Files for Outlook Express are also located in each user's folder beneath Documents and Settings, but this time in the Local Setting\Identities folder.

You'll find at least two other useful folders in each user's folder under Documents and Settings: Favorites and Cookies. Copy both to the second partition or drive, renaming the folders to reflect what they are — for example, Old-Favorites and Stale-Cookies. If you want to start over with either or both, don't bother copying them.

Resetting User Permissions

One of the most powerful features of the Windows XP file system (NTFS) is its capability to assign permissions to specific users. As an example, when a user creates a password for his or her account, Windows asks if the user wants to make the My Documents folder (and subfolders) private. From a privacy standpoint, doing so is an excellent idea, but it can make reinstallations more difficult. Before beginning the reinstallation, open the Documents and Settings folder, click on the folder for your username, and uncheck the Make This Folder Private option under the View tab. Otherwise, you'll have to manually — and laboriously — reset all the ownership attributes once you've completed the reinstallation. See Chapter 25 for details on user permissions.

Completing the Reinstallation

With a second partition or hard drive in place, and with as many folders, files, email data, and user permissions looked after as you can possibly manage (or a full system backup you've tested restoring files from), it's time to perform the reinstallation. To do so, follow these steps:

1. Turn on your computer, and immediately insert the Windows XP Installation CD into the CD or DVD drive. Wait for the Welcome to Setup screen to appear.

2. Select the To Set Up Windows XP Now, Press ENTER option by pressing the Enter key.

3. At the subsequent screen (the End-User License Agreement), press the F8 key.

4. At this stage, Setup searches for existing installations of Windows XP. When it locates your installation (the one that no longer works properly), it identifies it by the hard drive letter and primary folder (usually C:\WINDOWS). Because you want a clean reinstallation, however, ignore the first bullet point, which refers to repairing the selected installation, and choose the To Continue Installing a Fresh Copy of Windows XP Without Repairing, Press ESC option. After pressing the Escape key, Windows proceeds with the installation, as covered in Appendix A. Your primary step is to ensure that you choose the correct partition on which to locate the installation. Again, see Appendix A for details.

5. When Windows completes its tasks, before performing any other functions, install SP2 from CD, then install your antivirus software, and then launch Windows Update (see Chapter 5) to install the latest service packs and all other critical and optional updates.

6. Test your reinstalled Windows program.

Product Activation

When you install Windows XP, you must activate it using Microsoft's anti-piracy technology: Product Activation. If you reformat the hard drive and reinstall Windows, you must activate it again. If you reinstall it on a drive you have not formatted, you need to reactivate it only if you have changed numerous other hardware components of your system.

Windows examines 10 different hardware components, ranging from the CPU to hard drives to network and video cards, and creates a unique identifier for your machine upon activation. If you change the hardware components significantly and reinstall Windows, you will need to reactivate it. The term *significantly* means changing 6 of the 10 hardware items, although even this isn't strictly adhered to. Furthermore, you can change any single component as often as you want, and it still counts as only one change.

On reinstallation, if you require reactivation, try to do so over the Internet. If your request is confused, the Product Activation Wizard provides a telephone number along with a lengthy numeric code. Call the number, and punch in the code when so instructed by the automated attendant. In the vast majority of cases, the activation will proceed without incident. If not, and if you do, in fact, have a pirated version of Windows XP, you will probably have to buy a legal copy.

Tip

Windows XP stores its activation database file, wpa.dbl, as well as its counterpart, wpa.bak, in the folder c:\windows\system32. You can avoid reactivation when reinstalling Windows on the same PC by copying these two files to a disk, performing the reinstallation, navigating to c:\windows\system32, copying the copied files over the new files, and then rebooting.

Summary

Reinstalling Windows is sometimes necessary, sometimes just a good idea, and always time-consuming. But as long as you plan your reinstallation, you should experience a minimum of difficulties. Moreover, once you've completed the task once, the next time you'll find it considerably easier and almost completely stress-free (or as much as anything computer-related can be). In subsequent reinstallations, simply keep in mind that your two purposes are a Windows installation that works the way it should and full access to all the programs and data files you had on your system before.

Index

A

B

continued

continued

continued

continued

continued